Books by Eric Berne, M.D.

A Layman's Guide to PSYCHIATRY and PSYCHOANALYSIS

The third edition,
extensively revised and enlarged
from the original work,

THE MIND IN ACTION

by Eric Berne, M.D.

With contributions by Hilma Dickson, R.N.,
John Dusay, M.D., Mary Edwards, M.S.W.,
Muriel James, Ed.D., Ray Poindexter, M.D.,
and Claude Steiner, Ph.D.

SIMON AND SCHUSTER   New York

To my mother Sara Gordon Berne

CONTENTS

Part One   NORMAL DEVELOPMENT

Chapter One   WHAT PEOPLE HAVE TO WORK WITH

Chapter Two   WHAT PEOPLE ARE TRYING TO DO

Chapter Three   THE GROWTH OF THE INDIVIDUAL

Part Two   ABNORMAL DEVELOPMENT

Chapter   NEUROSES
Five

Chapter   PSYCHOSES
Six

Chapter   ALCOHOL, DRUGS, AND SOME
Seven   BEHAVIOR DISORDERS

Part Three METHODS OF TREATMENT

Chapter Eight PSYCHOTHERAPY

Chapter Nine TRANSACTIONAL ANALYSIS

by John M. Dusay, M.D.

Chapter Ten ALLIED PROFESSIONS

A. Psychiatric Social Work, by Mary Edwards, M.S.W.

PREFACE TO THE FIRST EDITION BY DR. A. A. BRILL (1947)

This book is unique in more than one way. The author is a well-trained psychoanalytic psychiatrist, an avowed Freudian, and yet it took a number of chapters before I was actually convinced of it. For, unlike those who espouse certain theories and plunge right into the midst of them, Dr. Berne maintains such an objective and unbiased attitude that he at first gives the impression of a keen prober rather than an ardent adherent of Freud. The Mind in Action starts with a sort of biological survey of the general aspect of mental development. It is a lucid exposition, unencumbered by technical expressions, which explains the normal functions of the brain, in terms of feeling and action; the most powerful urges and their control in childhood and adult life and the reaction of the whole organism to the environment. Dr. Berne has the happy faculty of documenting and presenting abstruse mental processes in such a simple and alluring way that he can hold the interest of even a jaded psychoanalytic reader. But following him for a few chapters one realizes that Dr. Berne endeavors to embody Freud into everything that touches on and appertains to the functions of the mind.

In my efforts to explain the author's mode of operation it occurred to me that psychoanalytically Dr. Berne is just about 40 years younger than the present writer. In other words he belongs to the post bellum *period of psychoanalytic recognition, and hence can evaluate Freud's contribution as part and parcel of the whole progressive development of psychiatry. In other words Dr. Berne is a young Freudian who like the new generation of Egyptians "did not know Joseph" and hence could follow a new path and expound the new psychology without the affectivity of the older Freudians. The psychoanalytic theories were well established when Dr. Berne mastered them; that is why he could complacently survey the whole field of psychoanalysis, the* fons et origo *as well as all the deviations from it, and then easily separate the kernel from the sheaf. Having read everything written on Freud and psychoanalysis since I first introduced him here, I feel that Dr. Berne has succeeded in presenting "the mind in action" in a manner that will interest and instruct not only the intelligent layman but also the psychoanalyst and physician.*

FOREWORD TO THE THIRD EDITION

It is gratifying to realize that there has been a steady demand for this book during the past twenty years. It was written while I was a medical officer in the Army during World War II and had the choice every evening of listening to the clack-clack of my typewriter or the click of the slot machines at the Officers' Club, and for the most part I chose the former. It was originally published in a hard cover as *The Mind in Action.* In that form it received satisfactory and even enthusiastic reviews in the literary, psychiatric, and psychoanalytic press, and was subsequently published in Great Britain and translated into Swedish, Italian, and Spanish. In 1957 the second edition appeared as a "quality paperback" with the title *A Layman's Guide to Psychiatry and Psychoanalysis,* under the imprint of Simon and Schuster; and a few years later Grove Press put out a low-priced paperback edition with the same title, so that two competing editions were on the market at the same time. In these various forms the book has sold well over 250,000 copies.

Radical changes in the practice of out-patient, hospital and community psychiatry have resulted from the rapid advances in drug therapy and group therapy during the last ten years. In addition, transactional analysis and other new approaches to psychotherapy have gradually been taking over in areas where psychoanalysis has not proven satisfactory. In fairness to the public, therefore, since interest in the book promises to be sustained, the present extensive revision was undertaken.

After careful deliberation, I decided to retain the section on physical types, as an indication that the body is here to stay—something which is too often overlooked by nonmedical therapists, particularly those trained in the social sciences. Part I and most of Part II treat the human being as an energy system, and for this point of view Freudian theory is the best approach. I have followed the "strict" version of Freud, which separates the sex instinct from the death instinct, and have given equal weight to Eros and Thanatos. That makes everything much easier to explain, and certainly fits in better with the historical events of the last thirty years, which are not easy to understand from libido theory alone, but become much clearer by introducing Paul Federn's concept of mortido.

I have included contributions from several of my colleagues. Dr. Claude Steiner, who specializes in the treatment of alcoholism, drug addiction, and other forms of what he calls "tragic" behavior, has contributed to the rewriting of Chapter Seven, which deals with those topics. Dr. John Dusay has written a chapter on transactional analysis, and Mrs. Hilma Dickson, Mrs. Mary Edwards, Dr. Muriel James, and Dr. Ray Poindexter, have each contributed a section on their respective specialties. They know more about their fields than I do, and Dr. Dusay has treated transactional analysis much more objectively than I could, and I am grateful to all of them.

E. B.

Carmel, California
September 1967

FOREWORD TO THE SECOND EDITION

Few relationships in my experience are as consistently gratifying as that between a contented author and a contented publisher. Each communication which the author receives brings material as well as spiritual nourishment. If the critics and the public are also contented, then the satisfaction is complete. The reception accorded the first edition of this book in America, Great Britain, Sweden and Italy has been with few exceptions a source of pleasure during the past ten years. This has been in considerable measure the result of the friendly editorial advice of Mr. Henry W. Simon.

Rereading the book after a decade, I found it rather appealing, and at times had the well-known Wilde reaction: "I wish I'd said that!" It was agreeable, after a moment's reflection, to remember that I had. My only regret was that the war seemed, in minor instances, to have distracted me from broader scientific points of view. I am glad now to have an opportunity to reconsider.

As to the changes in the present edition, the section on "Man As a Political Animal" has been deleted, and this topic will be treated in a separate volume.* In its place, a section on the new "wonder drugs" of psychiatry has been inserted. The section on group therapy has been rewritten, and the section on shock treatment has been brought up to date. The Footnotes for Philosophers have been revised and the bibliographies have been brought up to date where this seemed advisable. In some instances, however, the old books still seem better than the new. And here and there a paragraph has been altered to accord with new approaches. It is hoped that any nonspecialist who desires information about contemporary psychiatry or psychoanalysis will in most cases find it here; the footnotes are designed to give reputable sources from which further details can be obtained.   E. B.

Carmel, California
March 1957

* *The Structure and Dynamics of Organizations and Groups,* Philadelphia: J. B. Lippincott Company, 1963; New York: Grove Press, 1966.

14

AUTHOR'S FOREWORD

The object of this book is to make the dynamics of the human mind intelligible to those who are more interested in understanding nature than in using big words or memorizing definitions. I have attempted to put ideas on a practical level which will give as clear and simple a picture as possible of complicated happenings. Long words have been avoided wherever this could be done without sounding clumsy. The object is to give the reader a better understanding of himself and others, and not to make a tearoom psychiatrist out of him. For those who want more details, the bibliographies should be an ample guide, and for those who want a technical vocabulary, a short glossary is appended.

Every psychiatrist has his own way of looking at people, derived from his own clinical experience. The ideas set down here are based on what I learned from my teachers, principally Dr. Eugen Kahn, formerly Professor of Psychiatry at the Yale School of Medicine, and the late Dr. Paul Federn, of the New York Psychoanalytic Institute, modified by my own thoughts, observations, and interpretations of the psychiatric and psychoanalytic literature. My teachers did the best they could for me while I was in their hands, but otherwise they are in no way responsible for what I say. It is taken for granted that most of the ideas, like the ideas of every dynamic psychiatrist, are based on the work of Sigmund Freud, but the emphases and the manner of formulation are my sole responsibility, and no group of psychiatrists or psychoanalysts has authorized me to be their spokesman.

In order to help in preventing misunderstanding on the part of professional readers of what I am trying to say, notes are added at the end of each chapter, in which qualifications and reservations are made, and the more technical aspects of the matters dealt with are discussed. Should any of the books referred to in these notes be unobtainable through ordinary channels, the yellow pages of your telephone directory may give you the name of a local psychiatric bookseller, or you may write directly to the publishers of the books mentioned.

For the sake of clearer understanding, a short semantic glossary is desirable in addition to the technical glossary at the end of the book. *He* refers to human beings in general of either sex. Where *she* is used, according to the context it may imply that a phenomenon occurs more frequently among women than among men. *We* in an appropriate context refers to "the majority of those psychiatrists for whom I have the most respect." *Is* in a sentence referring to technical matters means "seems to be, in the opinion of most thoughtful psychiatrists and from my own experience with the problem." *Seems to be* means "appears to me, from many observations, but not enough to make me certain in my mind, though corroborated by the opinion of one or more psychiatrists for whom I have a high respect." *Philosopher* is used to mean anyone who likes to think about what he reads. Tensions are spoken of as being *relieved, satisfied,* and *gratified.* The latter two are incorrectly used in this connection, but their use prevents repetition and serves to emphasize the idea that "tension" and "wish" are almost synonymous. After careful thought, I have retained the term *mental illness.* Although it is not necessary in a speaking vocabulary, it is difficult to think of any other term to use in writing. I have also reluctantly stayed with the word *neurotic* (noun and adjective), as it is difficult to find a substitute which will still fit into the Freudian framework.

The pseudonyms of the patients described in the case histories are not arbitrarily chosen, but are nearly all derived and "Americanized" from historical and mythological sources related to the case in question. This may intrigue some readers, but it need not complicate matters for those who are not interested in names. The case histories represent types and not individuals, and any resemblance to any living individual in external circumstances or characteristics is accidental and unintentional.

While many of the case histories exemplify commonplace occurrences, some of them are meant to illustrate clear-cut types of mental illnesses and emotional abnormalities; that is, they describe pathological personality types. In such instances the situations and reactions dealt with may occasionally strike the reader as unusual. This is more a matter of degree than of quality. If the reader will consider carefully, he will find that while the intensity of the reactions of our subjects may sometimes be startling, their modes of reaction are far from unique. The histories serve to emphasize by exaggeration things which everyone may find to some extent within himself and those around him. If this is not apparent at first thought, it may become clearer with the lapse of time. This means that the "mentally ill" do not have different instincts, but only express differently those which are universal among human beings.

Thanks are due to the various audiences of soldiers and civilians in California, Utah, and Washington who helped me clarify my formulations by their questions, comments, and objections. I especially appreciate the personal assistance given to me by the following individuals:

The publisher's staff, and especially Henry Simon, were of major assistance in preparing the manuscript and offering constructive suggestions. Dr. Paul Federn gave me much advice which he left it my option to follow or disregard. He has no other responsibility for the contents. Robert Peel, of Denton, Texas, and Frances Ordway, of Carmel, California, gave me invaluable time-saving assistance with the typing. Major, now Dr., Samuel Cohen, of Philadelphia, and Major, now Dr., Paul Kramer, of Chicago, helped me by their consideration while it was necessary to work on the manuscript under the difficult conditions of Army life. Colonel and Kippy Stuart, Doris Drake, Louise Masters, and Captain, now Dr., George Ambrose were also of help during this period. To those who read the manuscript, or who listened while I read it at the Short home in order that they might make suggestions, I offer a toast of Carmel wine in memory of much help and many pleasant evenings. These include Marie Short, Jake Kenny, Mr. and Mrs. John Geisen, Muriel Rukeyser, Dr. and Mrs. Russell Williams, Mr. and Mrs. Frank Lloyd, Sam Colburn, Gretchen Gray, Katie Martin, and a score of other Carmelites.

E. B.

Carmel, California
January 1947

INTRODUCTION

A psychiatrist is a doctor who specializes in helping, advising, and treating people who suffer from emotional difficulties, disturbed personal relationships, self-destructive behavior, and, in severe cases, abnormal feelings, beliefs, and sensations. The objects of his study are the motives of human beings, and the question he asks is: "Why does this individual have a need to feel, think, or act the way he does?" Since the workings of the body affect the emotions and the emotions express themselves through the body, the psychiatrist, like other doctors, must start with a sound knowledge of anatomy and physiology; he must know what the stomach, the blood vessels, the glands, and the brain look like and how they work. He must also know how certain chemicals such as alcohol affect the mind, and how the mind can affect certain chemicals of the body, especially those which are manufactured by the sex glands, the adrenal glands, the thyroid gland, and the pituitary gland.

While he is building up his knowledge of the way the human body works, the student psychiatrist must also be observing how human beings from various kinds of families behave in different situations in the country where they are living. In listening to the unlettered and the well-educated, the poor and the rich, talking about their children's report cards, he notices the differences and similarities in their attitudes, and wonders how these things affect their children's progress at school.

After he has become familiar with the different ways in which healthy people react in mind and body, the student begins to observe sick people. He studies individuals with stomach ulcers, for example, and tries to see what they have in common in their stomachs and their feelings, and whether there is any connection between their emotions and what the X rays show. He talks to people with abnormal fears and observes the reactions of both their minds and their bodies to see if he can find in what way each has gone wrong.

Besides helping to prevent future difficulties by talking with young couples who are about to be married, and to mothers who are having problems with their children, and taking care of people who are abnormally sad or excited, or who have abnormal feelings and impulses, it is the psychiatrist's province to deal with certain conditions which involve special organs of the body as well as the emotions, or which result from taking excessive quantities of certain drugs. For this reason, he has to have a sound knowledge of the working of the body. To treat serious mental illnesses, he must also understand the effects of electricity and of various powerful medications on the human body.

In addition, the psychiatrist is often called upon to decide the part played by the emotions in cases of stomach ulcer, high blood pressure, thyroid disease, heart disease, backache, paralysis, asthma, skin diseases, and other conditions which are often difficult to cure by ordinary medical methods. In such cases, he must have a sound knowledge of the workings of the affected organs.

Before trying to help anyone, the psychiatrist likes to know what kind of egg his patient came from—that is, what his forefathers were like in body and mind, and under what influences the egg developed into the adult human being. After he has found out these things, the psychiatrist can judge better what the individual started with and what he went through to arrive at his present condition. He tries to discover what assets and liabilities his subject came into the world with or acquired in early childhood, and then how he has been handling his life with whatever he has.

Many features of the personality are based to some degree on inheritance. Heredity determines the upper limits of abilities and when they are normally going to increase or decrease. For example, it determines whether a man could possibly be a great musician or mathematician (and chess playing should be included here as well), and at what age he will be able to have complete sexual relations. Environment, however, determines what he actually does. In other words, heredity determines possibilities, and environment determines how closely these are approached. But to spend too much time asking which is more important in real life is as misplaced as asking: "Which is more important for strawberries and cream, the strawberries or the cream? Do the berries float in the cream, or does the cream surround the berries?"

There is no proof that environment cannot change some of the so-called inherited qualities of the mind. Nearly every human ability can be improved by proper training, and the opinion that a disability is "inherited" does not mean that the sufferer should give up. The study of the glands in years to come is going to be very important for changing those things we now regard as inherited, just as psychiatry is now becoming more and more important for changing those qualities we regard as being due to environment. Therefore, instead of asking what is due to heredity and what is due to environment, we should ask rather, "Which qualities can be changed with our present knowledge, and which cannot?"

This book talks about the human being as an energy system among all the other energy systems in the universe, because that is one of the easier ways to understand people. This is the approach developed by Sigmund Freud. There are other approaches as well, some of which are described later on. We shall begin by studying what different people have to work with and what they are trying to do with what they have, and then go on to see how they grow and develop, what can go wrong in the course of development, and what can be done about it if things turn out unhappily. After that we shall consider some of the mysterious happenings in the mind which baffle us in our present state of knowledge.

EPIGRAPH

Remember one thing, and it will stand you in good stead—whatever you may think of him as a person, and whatever his followers have or have not done, Freud was right. *This is a cantrap which you should carry always in your purse, and use whenever common sense fails.*

—CYPRIAN ST. CYR, *Letters to My Wife's Maid*

Part One

NORMAL DEVELOPMENT

1

WHAT PEOPLE HAVE TO WORK WITH

1

Can people be judged by their appearance?

Everyone knows that a human being, like a chicken, comes from an egg. At a very early stage, the human embryo forms a three-layered tube, the inside layer of which grows into the stomach and lungs, the middle layer into bones, muscles, joints, and blood vessels, and the outside layer into the skin and nervous system.

Usually these three grow about equally, so that the average human being is a fair mixture of brains, muscles, and inward organs. In some eggs, however, one layer grows more than the others, and when the angels have finished putting the child together, he may have more gut than brain, or more brain than muscle. When this happens, the individual's activities will often be mostly concerned with the overgrown layer.

We can thus say that while the average human being is a mixture, some people are mainly "digestion-minded," some "muscle-minded," and some "brain-minded," and correspondingly digestion-bodied, muscle-bodied, or brain-bodied. The digestion-bodied people look thick; the muscle-bodied people look wide; and the brain-bodied people look long. This does not mean that the taller a man is the brainier he will be. It means that if a man, even a short man, looks long rather than wide or thick, he will often be more concerned about what goes on in his mind than about what he does or what he eats; but the key factor is slenderness and not height. On the other hand, a man who gives the impression of being thick rather than long or wide will often be more interested in a good steak than in a good idea or a good long walk.

Scientists use Greek words to describe these types of body-build. For the man whose body shape mostly depends on the inside layer of the egg, they use the word *endomorph*. If it depends mostly upon the middle layer, they call him a *mesomorph*. If it depends upon the outside layer, they call him an *ectomorph*. We can see the same roots in our English words "enter," "medium," and "exit," which might just as easily have been spelled "ender," "mesium," and "ectit."

Since the inside skin of the human egg, or endoderm, forms the inner organs of the belly, the viscera, the endomorph is usually belly-minded; since the middle skin forms the body tissues, or soma, the mesomorph is usually muscle-minded; and since the outside skin forms the brain, or cerebrum, the ectomorph is usually brain-minded. Translating this into Latin and Greek, we have the *viscerotonic endomorph,* the *somatotonic mesomorph,* and the *cerebrotonic ectomorph.*

Words are beautiful things to a cerebrotonic, but a viscerotonic knows you cannot eat a menu no matter what language it is printed in, and a somatotonic knows you cannot increase your chest expansion by reading a dictionary. So it is advisable to leave these words and see what kinds of people they actually apply to, remembering again that most individuals are fairly equal mixtures and that what we have to say concerns only the extremes. It is easier to study these types in men than in women.

Viscerotonic endomorph. If a man is definitely a thick type rather than a broad or long type, he is likely to be round and soft, with a big chest but a bigger belly. He would rather eat than breathe comfortably. He is likely to have a wide face, short, thick neck, big thighs and upper arms, and small hands and feet. He has overdeveloped breasts and looks as though he were blown up a little like a balloon. His skin is soft and smooth, and when he gets bald, as he does usually quite early, he loses the hair in the middle of his head first.

The short, jolly, thickset, red-faced delegate with a cigar in his mouth, who always looks as though he were about to have a stroke, is the best example of this type. The reason he makes a good delegate is that he likes people, banquets, baths, and conventions; he is easygoing, soothing, and his feelings are easy to understand.

His abdomen is big because he has lots of intestines. He likes to take in things. He likes to take in food, and affection and approval as well. Going to a banquet with people who like him is his idea of a fine time. It is important to understand the natures of such men. One mistake to avoid is taking them at face value. They often make jokes about themselves when they are feeling good. In such cases, it is a good idea to smile politely, but refrain from laughing, because later, when they are feeling bad, they may feel angry at someone who laughed, even though they themselves invited it by making a joke.

Somatotonic mesomorph. If a man is definitely a broad type rather than a thick or long type, he is likely to be rugged and have lots of muscle. He is apt to have big forearms and legs, and his chest and belly are well formed and firm, with the chest bigger than the belly. He would rather breathe than eat. He has a bony head, big shoulders, and a square jaw. His skin is thick, coarse, and elastic, and tans easily. If he gets bald, it usually starts on the front of the head.

Li'l Abner, and other men of action belong to this type. Such people make good lifeguards and construction workers. They like to put out energy. They have lots of muscles and they like to use them. They go in for adventure, exercise, fighting, and getting the upper hand. They are bold and unrestrained, and love to master the people and things around them. Knowing the things which give such people satisfaction, one can understand why they may be unhappy in certain situations.

Cerebrotonic ectomorph. The man who is definitely a long type is likely to have thin bones and muscles. His shoulders are apt to sag and he has a flat belly with a dropped stomach, and long legs. His neck and fingers are long, and his face is shaped like a long egg. His skin is thin, dry, and pale, and he rarely gets bald. He looks like an absent-minded professor and often is one.

Though such people are jumpy, they like to keep their energy and don't fancy moving around much. They would rather sit quietly by themselves and keep out of difficulties. Trouble upsets them, and they run away from it. Their friends don't understand them very well. They move jerkily and feel jerkily. The person who understands how easily they become anxious is often able to help them get along better in the sociable and aggressive world of endomorphs and mesomorphs.

In the special cases where people definitely belong to one type or another, then, one can tell something about their personalities from their appearance. When the human mind is engaged in one of its struggles with itself or with the world outside, the individual's way of handling the struggle will be determined partly by his type. If he is a viscerotonic he will often want to go to a party where he can eat and drink and be in good company at a time when he might be better off attending to business; the somatotonic may want to go out and do something about it, master the situation, even if what he does is foolish and not properly figured out; while the cerebrotonic may go off by himself and think it over, when perhaps he would be better off doing something about it or seeking good company to try to forget it.

Since these personality characteristics depend on the growth of the layers of the little egg from which the person developed, they are difficult to change. Nevertheless, it is worthwhile for a person to know about these types, so that he can have at least an inkling of what to expect from those around him, and can make allowances for the different kinds of human nature, and so that he can become aware of and learn to control his own natural tendencies, which may sometimes guide him into making the same mistakes over and over again in handling his difficulties. The "egg layer" system is the best one known at present for judging people by general appearance.

2

Where does human energy come from?

In order to understand anything in this world, we have to ask first, what parts does it consist of and how are they put together, and secondly, where does its energy come from and how is that energy conducted into the proper channels. To understand an automobile, we must first describe the various parts and where they are, and then see how the energy of the gasoline is changed into rolling motion through the workings of the mechanism. To understand a frozen water pump, a broken television set, an inspiring comet, a fair waterfall, a growing tree, or an angry man, we must follow the same course. The construction is called *structure* and the working is called *function*. To understand the universe we study its structure and function. To understand an atom we study its structure and function. Then we can navigate a ship, and build an atomic engine.

We have seen that in structure the human being consists of three kinds of tissue and that the way these are put together will partly determine how he acts and reacts. If we now study the glands and the brain, we shall have the beginnings of an idea as to how the energy of a human being is controlled as he functions.

The energy of man comes from food and oxygen, as far as we know. The amount of food he eats, together with the amount he has stored in his body, determine the amount of energy he can release by means of oxygen. The result of digestion is to change the food into fairly simple substances which can be stored and used as required, to release energy by changing chemically. Vinegar and baking soda fizzing in a glass produce heat, which is energy. In a more complicated way, body chemicals and oxygen fizzing in the body produce heat, so that a certain amount of food produces a certain number of calories of energy for the body to use. How this heat is changed into the kind of energy needed by the body is not yet clearly explained.

We can recognize human energy in two forms: bodily energy and mental energy—just as we can recognize that the energy used in going for an automobile ride comes partly from the car and partly from the driver.

The glands have much influence in determining how fast bodily energy is used and for what general purpose it is employed. The thyroid gland acts like an accelerator and keeps the individual running at high speed or low speed. It may keep him running faster than his food provides for, so that he uses up all kinds of reserve chemicals, such as fat, to supply the energy needed, and thus a person whose thyroid is overactive tends to lose weight. On the other hand it may slow him down so much that he takes in more food than he can use, and the excess is stored as fat and other substances, so that the person whose thyroid is underactive may put on weight.

If we compare the thyroid to an engine accelerator, we may say that the adrenal glands, which are found attached to the kidneys, are like rocket fuses. When we need an extra push, the adrenals release a sudden huge supply of energy. This happens usually when we have to fight or run; the adrenals are the glands which gird us for action when we are angry or afraid. Sometimes we are angry or afraid without being able to do anything about it, so that we are unable to use up the extra energy. Something has to happen to this energy and since the normal path of expression is blocked, it may exert itself on the muscles of the heart or other inner organs, causing pounding and other disagreeable sensations. In any case, the extra energy does not simply vanish; if it is not used up at the time by fighting or running away, or by palpitations of the heart or contractions of the other internal organs, it is stored up until it finds a chance to express itself directly or indirectly, as we shall see farther on.

Both the thyroid and the adrenals are set differently in different people. Because of their thyroids, some people are always on the go and some are always sluggish. There are other reasons for such differences in energy output besides the thyroid, but one always has to think of this gland in trying to account for restlessness or sluggishness. In the same way we have to think of the adrenals when the question of differences in excitability arises. Some people's adrenals are set on a hair trigger, so that their bodies are frequently in a state of turmoil, while others never feel the surge of animal strength that comes with profound anger or panic.

The thyroid affects the total amount of the individual's activity, regardless of what he uses the energy for. The adrenals release additional energy to aid the individual in separating himself from things which threaten him or stand in his way, whether he accomplishes the separation by running, or by destroying the threatening force, or by causing it to leave in a hurry.

The sex glands also affect the output of energy, and like the adrenals the energy they release has the quality of supplying vigor for certain special purposes. We may say that the adrenals assist the instinct of self-preservation by releasing added strength for separation or destruction. The testicles and ovaries assist the sexual instinct by giving added interest to certain constructive activities. Their earthy purpose is concerned with sexual union, but part of the energy they release can be usefully applied in any romantic or sublime activity which has the feeling of approach, affection, or creating.

In thinking about these glands, it should be understood that we have no right to say that they are the source of the energy and desire for creating and destroying; but they do serve in some way to give added zest to such desires, and to release *extra* energy to accomplish them. Older people whose glands are quieting down can still create and destroy, but they usually do not have the same passionate excitement and concentrated energy that younger people do.

Furthermore, the glands have nothing to do with the special way the released energy is applied. For instance, the adrenals make the muscles of the arms and legs stronger and quicker, but they do not determine whether the limbs will be used for fighting or for running away. The sex glands make the individual feel strong and restless and increase the attractiveness of outside objects, especially other human beings, usually of the opposite sex, but they do not determine how he goes about getting closer to people, nor whom he chooses. With glands alone and no brain, a human being would show little more initiative than a bottle of fermenting wine. This can be shown by removing the outside parts of the brain from a cat. Under the influence of the adrenals, the cat will then go into rages with almost no provocation at all, and be prepared for violent action, but he neither knows the true object of his rage nor can he deal effectively with anything that really threatens him. He becomes steamed up but does not know how or against whom to act. The brain is necessary for effective action in accomplishing a definite purpose.

An interesting link between the glands and the brain is provided by the pituitary, the "master gland" that controls the others. It lies just beneath the brain and is closely connected to it, so that under the direction of the lower, more primitive part of the brain, it can send chemical messengers to the other glands.

The energy of thinking and feeling is harder to understand than the energy of moving, and hardly anything can be said about its origin. It is known that energy is used whenever the mind is active, and it can be shown that the brain gives off electric waves and uses up oxygen. This may mean that the energy used by the mind is not completely different in kind from that used by the body; it may well be the same energy used in a different way. It can be shown experimentally that there is a difference in electrical pressure between the brain and the body, and between the different parts of the brain, and that these differences change when the mind is active. This shows that mental activity is accompanied by electrical changes.

A good deal of mind energy is used in doing nothing, or rather in keeping from doing things. One of the main functions of the brain is to keep the individual's activities toned down, and prevent the rest of the nervous system from running wild, as it does in the cat without a full brain. Keeping a firm grip on the lower nervous system requires energy, just as keeping in hand a team of restless horses does.

Mental energy is also required to keep certain ideas and feelings apart in order for the mind to remain tidy. If all sorts of ideas and impressions were allowed to run together without hindrance, the human mind would be as disorderly as a haystack. If ordinarily separated ideas or feelings are allowed to come together, as in jokes or embarrassing situations, the energy formerly used to keep them apart is released, and can then be used for other purposes; for example, it may play a part in starting an explosion of laughter, tears, or blushing.

In situations involving social prestige, for example, the feeling of respect which "inferiors" may have is usually kept separate, by the use of mental energy, from the feeling of resentment which such situations arouse. Sometimes the pent-up resentment is allowed to express itself openly in rebellion. In other cases, some of it is expressed in disguised form as a joke; then the energy which was formerly used to keep it in check is released in the listeners, and this, in addition to the energy of the freed resentments, gives them a charge which appears as a smile or a laugh.

This is illustrated by the joke about the woman who got on a bus and refused to pay her fare. When the driver insisted that she would have to pay or leave the bus, she said haughtily:

"You can't force *me* to pay. I'm one of the directors' wives."

The driver was not impressed.

"I don't care if you're the director's *only* wife, you'll still have to pay," he replied, to the delight of the other passengers.

In this case the listeners sympathetically went through in their minds the same process of defiance and freeing of resentment as the driver did in actuality. He used the energy thus freed for talking; they used theirs for smiling. Added to this in both cases was the energy released by bringing openly together the ideas of "wealth" and "polygamy." The laying open of these and other hidden connections freed blocks of energy which were used by the various parties concerned for laughing, smiling, talking, or expressing irritation.

We see, then, that our energy comes from the food we eat and the air we breathe, and that the glands play an important part in determining the rate at which it is released in quiet times and in times of excitement, while the mind, in the end, determines the exact purpose for which it is used. If it is desired to change the amount or direction of a person's energy output, therefore, there are three points of attack. Changing the production of energy from food and air belongs to the field of internal medicine and is a problem which arises in cases of liver, lung, and muscle diseases, anemia, and so on. Changing the release of energy by glands is a complicated matter on which internists and psychiatrists can work together. The control of energy output by the mind is the problem of psychiatry and that is what we shall deal with in the rest of this book.

3

What is the brain for?

The brain was formerly not too accurately compared to a telephone exchange, because it is concerned with making connections between ideas, and between things that happen and what we do about them. Even in this respect, the brain is more complicated than anything man could manufacture. There are more possible connections in one brain than there would be in a world switchboard if every living human being had a telephone. In addition, one part of the brain seems to be able to substitute for another in an emergency with more ease than would be possible with any man-made switchboard. Nowadays we can compare it to a computer. Certain parts of the brain probably do work like a computer, and there again it is the most compact, advanced, efficient, self-correcting computer so far known in the universe.

The brain is enclosed in the top part of the skull. It is split part way down the middle and is about the size of a large coconut. The spinal cord is shaped like a thin cane with a knob on top of it. The brain surrounds this knob and is connected with it by a million little nerve cords.

People often wonder how much of the brain is really used, and how much of it one could do without. Sometimes the brain is injured before, during or after birth, and then we can answer these questions, for the injured part may liquefy after a while so that the brain substance disappears and a collection of watery fluid replaces it. It is amazing in such cases to see how much of the brain can be destroyed without the individual or his friends knowing that there is anything wrong. One man had several of these large pools of fluid inside his brain, so that from birth only about half of the tissue was left, yet he apparently went through high school normally, and was doing a good job as an auto mechanic at the time he came to see the doctor. The only reason he wanted medical attention was that he suddenly began to have epileptic convulsions. Until these began, neither he nor his family had suspected that there was anything wrong with him. It was only when he went to see a specialist that anything extraordinary was noticed. Because of certain small irregularities in his vision and muscle development, which had never interfered with his work enough for him to notice them, the neurologist took special X rays, which showed up the holes in his brain.

Some parts of the brain have special uses, but other parts are capable of gradually replacing one another. If one of the special parts liquefies, the individual will not be able to carry on whatever function that part of the brain is concerned with. If one half of the rear end disappears, the individual will be unable to see one half of what is in front of him, and will be blind on one side (not in the right eye, for example, but in the right half of each eye). If both sides of the rear end liquefy, he will be almost completely blind. In some cases, the duties of even these special parts can be taken over by other sections of the brain. An apoplectic stroke, or shock, as it is sometimes called, is due to destruction of a part of the brain which controls certain muscles. When this portion is destroyed, the muscles stiffen and the individual is unable to control them normally. With long practice, however, other parts of the brain often can be taught to take over, so that some apoplectics regain control of themselves after a stroke. In the case of the mechanic mentioned above, it happened that most of the destroyed brain tissue did not have any special function, so he was able to carry on normally.

The reason so much brain tissue can be dispensed with is that the brain usually acts as a whole. In this, as in many other ways, it works differently from a telephone exchange or a computer. If some of the telephone exchanges in France were destroyed, there would be less telephone service in that country. Similarly if some of the "memory drums" of a French translating computer were destroyed, the computer would lose that much translating ability. But if a man learns the French language, that knowledge cannot be partly destroyed by destroying any special part of the brain, because he knows French with his whole brain and not with any part of it. There is no "bump of languages."* One might almost say that the absence of some parts of the brain no more interferes with knowledge, thinking, and other aspects of the mind than the absence of one leg does. Indeed, in real life, a missing leg often causes more mental symptoms than missing brain tissue.

The brain should be regarded as part of the energy system which is a human being. If we look at it in this way, we may allow ourselves to suppose that the brain has another function just as important as being a telephone exchange or computer, and that is, to store energy. There is some evidence that this is actually what the brain does. We may remember in the case of the cat with the top part of its brain removed, that the animal seemed to be unable to store any of its feelings, and gave way immediately to rage on the slightest provocation. It was also unable to store any memories of what had happened, or to delay other reactions, such as moving its limbs when they were stimulated. In the case of human beings who have whole brains, the ability to store mental energy is highly developed. Normal grownups can store their feelings until it is more convenient to express them at some later time, instead of flying into frequent rages without restraint; they can store memories and recall them later; they can store the desire to move their limbs in response to stimuli, as they must do in the dentist's chair. There are cases in human beings where the front part of the brain has been sliced through as a treatment for certain types of illness,

---

* There is an apparent exception to these statements in the complicated condition called "aphasia," which we need not go into here.

and then we see things which lead us to believe that the individual is unable to store his feelings and impulses as well as he could when the brain was all in one piece. After such an operation, the person will act more impulsively and show many of his feelings more quickly than he did before.

Many otherwise mysterious things can be explained if we suppose that it is a function of the brain to store energy. From this point of view, the brain is the organ of waiting.

One of the most important things in family and social behavior and the relationships between human beings is the ability to store energy without distress when the individual's judgment tells him that it is advisable to wait before acting. If our supposition is correct, it is the brain which stores the energy released by the glands and other sources until the proper moment arrives, and in this way the storage capacity of the brain would play a part in preventing people from doing foolish things just because their tensions encouraged them to. We may even imagine the brain in everyday life being charged and discharged like a living storage battery, as illustrated in The Case of the Ten Dollar Slap.

Midas King, the owner of the Olympic Cannery, was a plump, fidgety, somewhat irritable viscerotonic. Things were not going smoothly in the cannery during the busy season. Everyone was working at top speed, there was a high staff turnover, and mistakes, sometimes serious ones, were frequently made. The days were a continual series of annoyances to Mr. King, but he always tried to control himself at the office. He came to Dr. Treece for psychiatric treatment for high blood pressure.

Mrs. King, who accompanied him, told the doctor of an incident of the previous evening. Upon coming home from the office, Mr. King had seemed peaceful enough until their little three-year-old boy had done something bad; whereupon Mr. King had suddenly given him a terrible slap on the head. Mr. King had felt that he was justified, but his wife had told him he had gone too far, and had taken the boy in her arms and soothed him. The cause of Mr. King's burst of anger was that the child had torn a dollar bill into pieces. Mr. King now felt sorry for what he had done.

"I think I see what happened," said Dr. Treece. "The boy tore up a dollar bill, but instead of slapping him one dollar's worth, you slapped him ten dollars' worth, is that it?"

Mr. King and his wife agreed that that was a good description of what had happened.

"The problem is," said the doctor, "where did the other nine dollars' worth of annoyance come from?"

"Of course he brought it home from the office, poor dear," replied Mrs. King.

"His feelings got charged up at the office and discharged at home," said the doctor. "And now, after some years of this kind of thing his blood pressure doesn't come down after a restful weekend as easily as it used to. So we'd better find out how he can keep from becoming so easily irritated during the day." Meanwhile he was thinking: Something wrong here. Even after he hits the boy on the head, she still calls him "Poor dear." The first thing I've got to do is stop him from hitting the boy on the head. Restful weekend?

We might remark here in passing that the child, like the criminal, learns what punishment to expect for any given misdeed. This amount of punishment he is often prepared to accept without holding a grudge. But if he is punished ten dollars' worth for a one-dollar crime, he feels nine dollars' worth of resentment, since, inexperienced though he is, he nevertheless realizes somehow that he is being made a scapegoat for someone else's sins and resents this unfairness.

This example shows how the storage of energy and its manner of release are all-important in keeping the body running smoothly, and in relationships with other people both at work and in the home. Besides feelings, knowledge and experience are also stored, in the form of memories. In mentally retarded individuals there is less ability for this latter kind of storage, so that they have trouble remembering certain things. The two kinds of storage are distinct. A man's ability to store knowledge has nothing to do directly with his ability to store feelings. That is why some "intelligent" people behave badly in their relations with others, and is also partly the reason that being slow of understanding does not prevent a person from getting along with others. We admire people for their intelligence, but we like them for the way they handle their feelings. Those who wish to develop their personalities, therefore, must decide whether they want to develop one side or the other, or both. If they develop only their storage of memory images, they may be admired, but not necessarily liked. If they want affection as well as admiration, it might be of help to develop their ability to store their feelings and express them in an acceptable way.

While these are both things of the mind, the brain is probably the organ of the body most directly concerned. It is the organ of learning and waiting, which stores memory images and feelings; it is as well the central organ which deals with the connections between ideas, and with what goes on outside ourselves and what we do about it.

4

Why people act and feel the way they do

A person acts and feels, not according to what things are really like, but according to his mental image of what they are like. Everyone has images of himself, the world, and those around him, and behaves as though those images, rather than the objects they represent, were the "truth."

Some images have the same pattern in almost every normal individual. The Mother is virtuous and kind, the Father stern but just, the body strong and whole. If there is reason to think anything to the contrary, deep down in their minds people hate to believe it. They like to continue to feel according to these universal images, regardless of whether they correspond to what is really there. If they are forced to change them, they become sad and anxious, and even mentally ill.

People's images of their own bodies, for example, are very difficult to change. A man who has lost a leg finds it hard to settle down until he has gone through a period of sadness or "mourning" during which he succeeds in changing his body image to correspond to his new situation. Even then, deep down in his mind, he keeps his old image of himself. For years after he has lost his leg, he may see himself as a whole man in some of his dreams, and sometimes he stumbles because for a moment he forgets. These things show that his mourning has not been completely successful.

People's images of their parents are also difficult to change. In some dreams, the weak father may be strong, the drunken mother pure, and the dead still living. It is hard work to change an image when it has to be done, which is one reason that people hate to do it. If a loved one dies, the effort of changing one's mental image of the world to correspond to the new situation, which we call "mourning," is quite exhausting, and leads to tiredness and loss of weight. Oftentimes mourners, when they get up in the morning, are more tired than when they went to bed and feel as though they had done a hard night's work. The reason is that they *have* done a hard night's work, altering their mental images.

There are other images which belong only to certain individuals because of special circumstances, and these also are hard to change. "The phantom in the bedroom," the mental image of a man's first wife, may spoil his relationship with his second wife; "the mother with her hand on the doorknob" is a mental image which may keep a woman from being emotionally free even when she is far away from home; she always feels as though everything she did were being criticized by her absent or dead mother as if the latter were listening outside the room. Actually, she is carrying her mother's image around in her head, and in that sense her mother *is* listening.

The story of Nana Curtsan illustrates another type of individual image which may persist and influence conduct after the reality has changed. Up to the time of her father's tragic death, Nana had been quite plump. Because she had no mother, and her father was a drunkard, she was starved for affection, and was willing to do anything to get it. As a result she got a very bad reputation, which distressed her; but she felt quite helpless to control her craving for male company, and because of her poor figure she had to go to extremes to obtain it.

After her father died, she lost a good deal of weight and her true figure emerged from its cushion of fat like a slender, graceful sculpture from a block of stone. Two of her old friends, Ralph Metis, the banker's son, and Josiah Tally, the cashier at the bank, were so dazzled by her new-found beauty that they began to think of marrying her, in spite of her reputation.

Unfortunately, Nana was unable to change her image of herself. In spite of what her mirror and her comrades told her, she continued to think of herself as a physically unattractive girl who had to go to extremes in order to gather affectionate garlands. She persisted in her previous conduct and the result was that with the assistance of the horrified parents of Ralph and Josiah, she lost her chance for a good marriage.

The story of Nana, who did not give up thinking of herself as "the homely Dryad," is just the reverse of that of many a middle-aged or elderly woman, who continues to believe that she is "the enchanting Sylph" of her youth, and acts accordingly, sometimes with pathetic results, and sometimes, by good fortune, with charming success.

Such mental images, which guide our behavior, are charged with feeling. When we say that we love someone, we mean that the image of that person in our minds is highly charged with constructive, affectionate, and generous feelings. When we say that we hate someone, we mean that that person's image is charged with destructive, angry, and ungenerous feelings. What the person is actually like, or how he appears to other people and how they feel about him, does not come into the picture except indirectly. We don't fall out of love with Pangyne and in love with Galatea, but out of love with our image of Pangyne and in love with our image of Galatea. All that Galatea does is make it easy for us to form a lovable image of her. If we are particularly anxious at the moment to fall in love, we help her along by picking out the lovable things to emphasize in our image, denying or neglecting the undesirable qualities. Thus it is easier for a person to fall in love "on the rebound" than it was in the first place, because when the image of his first love breaks down, it leaves an empty space in his mind with a large charge of feeling which is urgently looking for a replacement. Driven by the anxiety of the vacuum, he romanticizes the image of the next woman who comes along so that she can fill the niche quickly.

Though we like to cling to our images and are loath to alter them, over a period of time we do have a tendency to make them more romantic than the vanished reality. Old people think of the dubious past as "the good old days," and some people long for home when they are away from it and are often disappointed in it when they return. Most people are glad to see old friends and old enemies after a forgotten interval, since they have softened the bad and emphasized the good in their images of them during their absence.

Hector Meads and his family were good examples of how

people tend to make their images of absent things and people more romantic as time passes. Hector was the only child of Archie Meads, who owned the Olympia Garage. Through no desire of his own, Hector became an employee of the United States government, and after a couple of years in Europe, he was sent to a small country in Asia. When he returned after twelve months there, he was restless, fidgety, irritable, and dissatisfied at home. He grumbled so much and seemed so strange that his mother, a nervous woman at best, became quite agitated from worrying about how to please him.

After six weeks of restless roaming around the house, listening to the radio, and drinking wine, he went to work for his father. He quit that because he was unable to get along with the customers and with Philly Porenza, the mechanic with holes in his brain. He and Philly had been good friends before Hector went away, but now Hector complained that Philly was a loafer and didn't understand what life was really about. Hector also quarreled with his former girl friend, Ann Kayo, the police chief's daughter, and took to dropping over to Foamborne Street to see Nana Curtsan occasionally. He tried working at the Hotel Olympia, McTavish's Dry Goods, and the Depot Meat Market, but it was six months before he finally settled down to a job, in King's Lumber Yard. He was always finding fault with his boss or with working conditions. He was certainly not the easygoing boy who had left Olympia more than two years before.

What had happened was this: when Hector and his family had said goodbye on his departure, they had each kept an image of what the other looked like. While he was away from home and lonely, Hector had often thought about his family, Ann, Philly, the garage, and various places around Olympia. He thought about the good things and the bad things too. As conditions grew worse and he became more lonely and uncomfortable far away from home, Olympia and its people had come to seem increasingly desirable to him. There were so many worse things where he finally landed that he gradually forgot all the bad things about Olympia. Home as he now remembered it seemed more and more romantic to him. He expressed these feelings in his letters.

The people at home went through the same sort of change. They all missed Hector and would often think how amusing and cheerful he was. They gradually forgot all the bad things about him, his thoughtlessness, untidiness, and carelessness about his work. They were touched by his letters, and their feelings became more and more romantic as the months slipped by.

By the time he was due to come home, Hector had a very exaggerated idea of how wonderful Olympia was, and Olympia had an exaggerated image of how wonderful Hector was. In both cases, the images were based on the way things were the day Hector left, with a lot of romance added.

In the meantime, of course, both the real Hector and the real Olympia were changing. Hector saw a lot of trouble over there in that little country, and he was no longer just a trying but lovable boy who liked women to fuss over him. He was thoughtful and self-reliant, and a man among men. Olympia too had changed and was no longer just a growing village, but a town among towns. Ann was grown-up and sophisticated, though still kind and beautiful; his parents were a little older and a little more set in their ways. Philly Porenza had turned a little sour on the world after he had started having convulsions.

When Hector returned, both he and the townspeople were shocked. Both thought they were prepared for changes, but their images of each other hadn't changed the way the realities had; in fact they had changed in the opposite direction, if anything. Their new images were so far from the new realities that even with the best will in the world they couldn't get used to each other at all for about six weeks.

In many people it seems to take about six weeks for a mental image to change to correspond to a new reality. People don't really feel at home in a new house until they have been there about six weeks. By that time their image of "home" has had a chance to change to resemble the reality of the new house. After six months or so, the altered image has become solid enough so that the individual can settle down permanently without further anxiety from that source.

Though the individual himself may change his images gradually as time passes, he does not like to have others try to change them for him before he is ready. That is why people shout and become anxious during an argument. The better the logic of the opponents, the more anxious they make the individual for the safety of his cherished images, and the louder he shouts to defend them; and the more anxious his opponents make him, the more he dislikes them. We have an understandable but unreasonable tendency to dislike people who "beat us" in an argument, who tell us that our loved ones are not all that they are cracked up to be, or who try to make us like people of whom we have a hateful image. In the old days, would-be conquerors often executed messengers who brought them bad news. It was not the messengers' fault that they had to disturb the emperor's image of himself as a world conqueror, but unfortunately they did, and they suffered the consequences of the anxiety they aroused. It is still worth a man's neck to disturb an emperor's image. Nowadays the ax falls more subtly and the execution may be postponed, but sooner or later it comes. It is always wise to be tactful in undertaking the pleasant or unpleasant task of bringing a superior, a friend, a husband, or a wife face to face with the fact that their images and reality do not correspond, or in other words, that they have made a mistake in judgment.

What is called "adjustment" depends on the ability to change one's images to correspond to a new reality. Most people can change some images but not others. A religious person may be willing and able to adjust to any change but a change in religious outlook. A good business executive may be able to change his image of a business situation in a few minutes on the basis of new information brought from the market, but be unable to change his image of how children should be raised on the basis of information brought from the nursery school. A poor businessman may not be able to change his image of a business situation as rapidly as the market changes, but be able to change his image of his wife from time to time as she changes in reality, so that his marriage is a continued happy success. (It may be judged from this that flexibility is often more important than intelligence for success in any field.)

Images are made of stuffs of different flexibility. Some people have brittle images, which stand up against the assaults of reality with no change up to a certain point, and then suddenly crack wide open, causing great anxiety to the individual. These are the rigid personalities. Others have waxy images, which melt before the eloquent words of a salesman or critic. These are the suggestible personalities.

It is most clearly in matters of love that people show the quality of their mental images and how they handle the problem of trying to make reality and images correspond. Some men, for example, have such rigid images of the ideal woman they must marry that they will have no compromise. They never meet anyone who fits perfectly into the pattern they have in mind, so either they never marry or else they marry again and again, hoping that eventually they will find a woman of low melting point who will pour herself into the long prepared mold. (Incidentally, this is an excellent example of how the same basic psychological characteristic can lead two people by different routes into exactly opposite courses of conduct, which is one claim of psychiatrists that outsiders have difficulty in understanding.)

The successful man is the one whose images correspond most closely to reality, because then his actions will lead to the results which he imagines. A man's failures depend upon the fact that his images do not correspond to reality, whether he is dealing with marriage, politics, business, or the horse races. A few lucky ones can make their successes by simply describing their mental images, which may correspond to what a lot of people would *like* theirs to be. These are the poets, artists, and writers, whose images, therefore, need not match reality in order for them to get along. A surgeon, on the other hand, must have images in absolute accordance with reality. A surgeon whose mental image of the appendix was different from the reality in any respect would not be a good surgeon. The whole training of surgeons and engineers is a meticulous attempt to make their images correspond with reality. A scientist is a professional image-sharpener. A man who buys a lottery ticket is an example of how anxious people are to make the world match their images with as little effort as possible.

The idea of images is useful in thinking about mental illnesses as well as in studying character. A man with the condition known as hysterical paralysis, for example, may be thought of as a man with an altered image of his own body. He is paralyzed because he has a highly charged image of himself as paralyzed. He is paralyzed "in his mind," and because his mind has control of his body, it makes the real body correspond to the mind image as much as possible. In order to cure the hysterical paralysis, the psychiatrist has to offer some other image for the patient to charge with feeling. If the patient removes the charge of the feelings from the false body image to a new image formed with the assistance of the psychiatrist, the paralysis will vanish. Since this process is not entirely under the conscious control of the patient, it cannot be brought about by ordinary methods.

The case of Horace Volk, which we shall hear more about in a later chapter, illustrates this. Fear of his father and other strong emotions altered Horace's image of himself so that in his mind his voice was paralyzed, and hence in reality he could not talk above a whisper. Dr. Treece, the psychiatrist, with careful handling, succeeded in diminishing the intensity of Horace's warping emotional tensions by making the boy weep; and then by suggestion he helped him to form again a normal body image. During this process, Horace formed a strongly charged image of the doctor, which absorbed some of his abnormally strong tensions and helped to relieve the pressure which was distorting his image of himself. When the pressure was thus relieved, Horace's body image returned by "natural elasticity," as it were, to its normal state, and he was then able to talk as usual. None of this could have been done by conscious willing on Horace's part. Even the simpler part of the procedure, the weeping, was beyond his conscious control. It is very difficult for even a talented actress to make herself shed real tears by willing them.

A great man is one who either helps to find out what the world is really like, or else tries to change the world to match his image. In both cases he is trying to bring images and reality closer together by changing one or the other. Einstein's work caused nearly all physicists and mathematicians to change their world images to correspond with the "reality" he had discovered. Shakespeare helps people to have clearer images of what the world is like. The messiahs of various religions were good men who would have liked the world to correspond to their images of what it should be like.

Some evil men try to change the world by force to match their images of what they want it to be. Hitler had an image of the world as a place where he had supreme power, and used force to try to make the world correspond to his image.

In the mental illness called "schizophrenia," the patient imagines that the world does correspond to his image of it, and does not bother to check. He differs from the aggressive reformer or conqueror in that he is unable or unwilling to do the work of changing "I want" into "is." Sometimes he starts out as a reformer, and finding that this change is too difficult to bring about in reality, he changes it in his own mind and rests content with that.

One of the most important things in life is to understand reality and to keep changing our images to correspond to it, for it is our images which determine our actions and feelings, and the more accurate they are the easier it will be for us to attain happiness and stay happy in an ever-changing world where happiness depends in large part on other people.

5

How emotions change experience

The mental images we have been talking about cannot be thrown upon a screen, nor even clearly explained to ourselves, but this does not mean that we must doubt their existence. No one has ever seen an atom or electricity, but we must not for this reason doubt the existence of the forces of nature or we shall be quite unable to understand the physical world. Nature proceeds *as if* what we speak of as atoms and electricity existed, and so we suppose that they do exist. Similarly, human beings proceed *as if* the kind of mental images we have been talking about existed, and so we suppose that they too exist. Each person knows, or can check with a little effort, that he has images in his own head, but no one can ever be certain that other people have such images in their heads. Nevertheless, we shall speak from now on as if dynamic mental images were as real as electrons and gravity.

These dynamic mental images consist of two things: a representation, and a charge of feeling. The charge may be "positive" or "negative," love or hate, and often is both. The representation gives the image a shape, and the charge gives it energy.

It must be clearly understood what is meant when we talk about a representation, shape, or idea. Shape, as far as a dynamic mental image is concerned, includes function as well as structure, and so shape in our minds means more than physical shape. Everyone knows the physical shape of an airplane. The mental shape, representation, or idea of an airplane includes not only its appearance, but also some idea of what it does and how it works. It is easy to see, therefore, that one must have intelligence as well as eyes to form good representations, and that other things being equal, the more intelligent a person is, the more complicated and accurate his representations of the things around him will be. Furthermore, the accuracy of his representations has nothing to do with how he *feels* about airplanes. Some people who understand airplanes very well dislike and fear them, and some who have no idea how they manage to fly love them. Thus the representation of an airplane may be a "positively" charged image or a "negatively" charged image, regardless of whether the shape of the image is simple or complicated, accurate or inaccurate.

The distinction between feeling and representation is frequently seen in social relationships. People can often remember exactly how they feel about an individual without being able to remember his name, or they may remember a name without being able to recall what its bearer means to them. Mr. and Mrs. King were once planning a party, and Mrs. King asked, "Shall we invite Mr. Castor, that interesting horseman from Hawaii?"

"I remember the name well," replied Mr. King. "He is a tall fellow with hearts and flowers tattooed on his arms, but I can't remember how I feel about him, nor whether I like him or not."

In this case it is apparent that Mr. King had a good representation of Mr. Castor, and remembered his shape well. His image was clearly formed, but he could not bring up the attached emotional charge, so he did not remember just how he felt about him. Mrs. King then suggested: "Shall we invite that marvelous fellow What's-his-name, that that hateful Mrs. Metis hates?" It was plain that she didn't remember much about the shape of Mr. What's-his-name, not even his name, but she did remember the strong and pleasant feeling charge of his image; she didn't recall who he was exactly, but did feel that she liked him, mainly because her enemy Mrs. Metis hated him.

What this means is that an image can be broken up, and the feeling and representation separated from each other, so that the feeling remains conscious and the representation becomes unconscious, or vice versa. In such cases, the feeling separated from its representation "floats" in consciousness, and may "support itself" by becoming attached to another representation which has something in common with its own. This helps to account for slips of the tongue and other mistakes which are made in everyday life. If it is the representation which floats, it supports itself on another image charged with a related feeling.

Different people have different abilities to store charges and representations. A mind which cannot store ideas with clear-cut shapes cannot learn properly. Individuals who have this difficulty are said to be mentally retarded. (They used to be called "mental defectives.") Only after repeated and prolonged attempts to form well-shaped representations do they understand the things around them. At the same time, they have to express their feelings like anyone else, but not having clear-cut images, they may make mistakes and get into trouble.

Sometimes the problem is different. A mind which was once able to understand things and form good representations becomes twisted so that distorted feelings and distorted representations result. An aeronautical expert, for example, may come to feel that airplanes have a personal enmity toward him and follow him around in an attempt to injure him. The result of this distorted mental image of airplanes is that he cannot be understood by those around him and is unable to get along normally in the world. Many such abnormalities are found among the schizophrenics we have already spoken about, and since they act in accordance with their distorted and abnormally charged images instead of in accordance with normal ones, their behavior is difficult for healthy people to understand.

This should help to make it clear why a "nervous breakdown" has little to do directly with intelligence, and why people with "nervous breakdowns" may be able to remember and to think about certain problems as well as or better than the average person. A "nervous breakdown" of any kind is a disturbance in the way feeling charges are distributed on the individual's images of his own body, his own thoughts, and the things and people around him, so that some of the images are distorted; while mental retardation is a subnormal ability to construct and store shapes or representations. Mental illnesses have to do with emotions; mental retardation has to do with understanding. Sometimes, it is true, people suffer from "nervous breakdown" and mental retardation at the same time, but this is just an extra misfortune, because the two conditions are separate.

Human beings would be much simpler if they just learned automatically from experience and formed images to match what actually happened to them. In this case they would resemble adding machines, which form absolutely correct and rigid conclusions from the keys which are punched by the outside world; or pieces of clay, which bear a true and unvarying imprint of everything which touches them. The reason we are not like these dull objects is that our inner spirits give new and individual meaning to everything which happens to us, so that the same event is experienced differently by every person, and each one forms his view of what happened to suit his own emotional make-up. If an adding machine does not like the look of a 9 in a column of figures, it cannot change it to a 6 for the sake of beauty, but a human being can. If clay feels that an imprint is too sharp, it cannot round the corners, but a human being can round the corners of his experiences to suit himself.

The inner forces which change the individual's way of experiencing are the forces of love and hate in various forms, which we shall hear more about. All his images are molded out of their true form by these two feelings, and since he acts in accordance with his images and not in accordance with reality, every one of his acts is or can be influenced by love and hate. The individual's images are molded also by three ideas or beliefs which are fixed deep in the unconscious mind of each person and can rarely be completely eliminated. These beliefs maintain the immortality of his being, the irresistibility of his charms, the omnipotence of his thoughts and feelings. Complementing these ideas are their conscious opposites, which develop later—the threat of the eternal presence of death, the sense of being flawed, and of impotence in relation to the world and to the people around him.

Even if a person likes to think that he has shaken himself free from one or all of these, they remain hidden in the depths of his mind and are most likely to influence his behavior whenever he feels uneasy or unsure of himself. The most easily observed of the three is the "omnipotence of thought," since many superstitions are based on the idea that thoughts and feelings are all-powerful. This concealed belief becomes especially active in certain emotional disturbances.

Wendell Meleager dreamed frequently that he killed his mother's brother. After he heard that his uncle was killed in an automobile accident, Mr. Meleager began to suffer from palpitation and insomnia. He took to reading books on superstition, so that he could avoid doing anything which they said might bring him harm. Whenever he saw a policeman, he became shaky and felt faint. In short, he behaved exactly as though he himself had murdered his uncle; he finally had to give up his law practice temporarily because of his anxieties.

Although actually he had no connection with his uncle's death, and consciously his feeling was one of affection for him, his unconscious image of his uncle was charged with murderous thoughts. He certainly unconsciously overestimated the power of these thoughts, since when the event took place he behaved as though he had been the direct and malicious cause of his relative's death. His way of experiencing the announcement was warped because he had a warped image of his uncle in his unconscious mind and unconsciously believed in the omnipotence of his destructive thoughts.

The individual's belief in the irresistibility of his charms shows itself most clearly in dreams, where the dreamer may experience without surprise the joys of winning effortlessly the affection of the most desirable men and women. A reflection of this is seen in people who are almost irresistible in real life; sometimes they are more interested in the one person who can resist them than in all the others who cannot. Almost is not enough. Everyone secretly would like to prove that he is absolutely irresistible, but some people give up too easily, while others do not give up when they should.

The belief in immortality is recognized by most religions, and in spite of all conscious attempts at resistance it seems to persist in the minds of even the most atheistic heretics. Hardly anyone can imagine his own death without finding himself surviving as a spectator at the funeral. If he tries to eliminate the funeral by picturing a bomb explosion, he may see himself being blown to bits, but he will discover himself watching as the smoke clears away. Furthermore, this web of infinity extends to the past as well as to the future. Although for some people nothing existed before they were born, others imagine their essence extending back to the beginning of time. It is difficult to imagine one's own children springing from nothingness by a mere act of will. This is expressed by the frank or disguised ideas of reincarnation which are found in some religious systems.

It is the forces of love and hate, and of these three wishes or beliefs and their opposites, which lend color and individuality to human life, and keep people from becoming machines or clods. It is these same forces which make trouble when they get out of control. It is noble for them to tint our images under the eyes of our intelligence; but when they color them completely and take over control from the rational mind, steps should be taken to restore the balance.

We should try to become aware of how much our feelings affect our behavior, our experiences, and our ideas of the people and things around us, so that we can try to avoid unreasonable actions, excessive worry, and mistakes in judgment. From psychiatric experience the suggestion comes that when in doubt, it is more comfortable in the long run to act, feel, and think from love than from hate.

6

How people differ from one another

We are now able to understand some of the differences between human beings.

As we have seen, their bodies are often unequally developed in various directions; in some people the digestive organs, in others the muscles and bones, and in still others the skin and brain predominate. When one system is out of proportion to the others, more thought, feeling, and action often seem to be devoted to that system. So we have viscerotonic, somatotonic, and cerebrotonic

minds, each with its own way of reacting, which we may summarize as soothing the environment, mastering the environment,
and getting away from the environment, respectively. Thus constitution determines in the beginning something of how a man handles
his surroundings.

His glands influence greatly the strength of his urges and the
amount of energy he can put into satisfying them, as well as the
speed at which he uses his energy. There is another important
factor which the glands undoubtedly influence but which we know
little about, and that is mood. Some lucky people are always gay,
and some unlucky ones are always sad. Most people swing between mild sadness and mild happiness. Of course people's moods
are affected by what happens to them and how well things go, but
there is more to it than that. It is sometimes surprising to see how
much misfortune a person in a good mood can suffer without
getting downhearted, and it is equally surprising to observe how
many "nice things" can happen to one in a sad mood without
cheering him up. Another very important factor here is the person's earliest cradle experiences with his mother and his father too.
Also, people differ in the speed with which they change from happiness to sadness, and vice versa.

The efficiency of the brain, we may suppose, affects the ability
of the individual to store his feelings and postpone satisfactions
until the best possible moment. Some people are prudent and.some
are impulsive. Some can stand waiting and some cannot. While it
is not always wise to wait, it is always desirable to have the ability
to wait if it should become advisable. This is something people can
usually cultivate.

There are different kinds of impulsiveness. Some people have a
quick, impulsive, and proper reaction to each situation; others go
along showing very little reaction to a number of situations, and
then suddenly and impulsively release a burst of stored-up energy.
The first kind is understandable and others sympathize with it;
they know why the man got affectionate or angry and he doesn't
have to explain it to them. The second kind is difficult to understand
and makes others feel uneasy; they feel that maybe the man had a
right to get affectionate or angry, but he shouldn't have got *that*
personal about it. This latter type of reaction occurs unexpectedly,
and since it uses energy released not only by the situation of the
moment, but also that that is pent up from other situations, the re-

action seems to go too far, and the onlooker questions it in his mind.

Another feature useful to think about is the relationship between imagination and action. Some people are too much given to daydreaming. Since they cannot by any means carry out all the dreamy desires they become conscious of, they may go through life feeling perpetually disappointed. Thus they imagine things they would like to do, mull things over, and carry out few of their plans. Other people have few conscious desires which cannot be handled in a practical way, so that they do not indulge much in fantasies they cannot carry into action.

The first group may in this connection be regarded as having a weak "barrier" between the unconscious and conscious parts of the mind, and a brittle "barrier" between the conscious mind and deliberate action; they daydream freely but do little about it. The other group have a strong "barrier" between the unconscious and conscious minds, and a flexible "barrier" between the conscious mind and action; they daydream little, but act freely. The "inhibiting" first group usually go no farther than thinking about their images; the "repressing" second group try to make the outside world correspond to them.

In this section we might also consider what is generally called "intelligence," as measured by "intelligence tests." It is said that there are three kinds of "intelligence": intelligence with abstract ideas, mechanical intelligence, and intelligence in getting along with people. The possible intelligence of an individual depends on the constitutional ability of his mind to form and retain accurate representations and relate them to each other. The amount of intelligence that he actually shows and uses depends on this ability minus the effect his emotions have in blinding him to facts and distorting his images. This means that by straightening out a person's emotional life, we may be able to increase his usable intelligence to its highest possible level. In one experiment, some mentally retarded children from an institution were paired off with foster mothers chosen from a nearby home for delinquent girls. Each child then received motherly love and attention which had previously been lacking in its life. Under this emotional influence, there was an increase in the intelligence which the children showed. Furthermore, the intelligence which the "mothers" showed also increased, since they too had filled a gap in their emotional lives: each one of them now had a child to love. Loving and being loved increased well-being and intelligence in both parties as any lovers might anticipate.

The differences between people and their ways of handling their inner energy depend upon many things. So far we have discussed mainly factors which are already influenced at birth, that is, "constitutional" factors: physical build and the corresponding mixtures of reaction patterns; the activities of various glands; the ability to store energy and the manner in which it is released; and, also, the plasticity of images and the ability to form and retain clear-cut representations and keep them from being too much distorted by emotions. These are among the basic things that people have to work with in forming their personalities as they grow and develop in their surroundings.

Footnotes for Philosophers, Chapter One

1. *Physique*

The ideas used in this section are modified from Sheldon.

The Varieties of Human Physique, by W. H. Sheldon, and others. New York: Harper & Brothers, 1940.

The Varieties of Temperament, by W. H. Sheldon and S. S. Stevens. New York: Harper & Brothers, 1944.

While these ideas seem to be useful in dealing with normal people, their superiority over Kretschmer's classification remains to be demonstrated in regard to psychotics.

2. *Endocrines*

The discussion in the text refers to the adrenal medulla, which has not been distinguished from the cortex. Other generalizations and omissions have been made for the sake of clarity and simplicity. The powerful effects of chemicals extracted from the adrenal cortex, the corticosteroids, are now well known. Their story can be found in:

The Stress of Life, by Hans Selye. New York: McGraw-Hill Book Company, 1956.

Two of the most interesting books containing reliable information about the endocrine glands are:

The Nature of the Beast, by Ruth Crosby Noble. New York: Doubleday, Doran, 1945.

Sex and Behavior, edited by F. A. Beach. New York: John Wiley & Sons, 1965.

See also the article on "Hormones and Behavior" in *The Encyclopedia of Mental Health,* edited by Albert Deutsch, Vol. 3. New York: Franklin Watts, 1963.

3. *Brain*

The concept of the brain as the organ of waiting is a useful one for didactic purposes. The mode of "storage" of "energy" is a legitimate subject of inquiry. For a discussion of the function of the brain consult:

Man on His Nature, by Charles S. Sherrington. New York: Cambridge University Press, 1963.

Design for a Brain, by W. R. Ashby. New York: John Wiley & Sons, 1960.

4. *Images*

The idea of images presented here is modified from Freud, Jung, Schilder, and Burrow. Compare:

Psychological Types, by C. G. Jung. New York: Pantheon Books, 1959.

5. *Presentations*

This discussion of images, charges, and representations has as its foundation the Freudian concepts of presentation and cathexis. Freud's ideas about these subjects are scattered through his collected papers. For an interesting discussion, with some remarks about the omnipotence of thought, see "Totem and Taboo," which can be found in:

The Basic Writings of Sigmund Freud, edited by A. A. Brill. New York: The Modern Library, 1938, pp. 865–77.

A development of these concepts suggests a graphic method of representing metapsychological ideas, similar to the method of analytic geometry. An image might be represented by the curve of the intensity of the cathexes at its various points, rather than in its objective form. In a sense, this is what is represented in the drawings of children.

Hans Vaihinger is the expounder of the "Philosophy of As If." See his book of that name. New York: Barnes & Noble, 1935.

6. *Individual Differences*

The hypothesis that mood is partly dependent upon endocrine influences, reasonable though it sounds, still remains to be proved. The recent work with lithium in the treatment of manic-depressive psychoses is interesting in this regard. The idea of strongly "inhibiting" types versus strongly "repressing" types is a clinically and didactically useful restatement of the concepts of introversion and extroversion (in the Freudian rather than the Jungian sense). The subdivision of intelligence into three spheres can be found in Thorndike.

Adult Learning, by E. L. Thorndike and others. New York: Macmillan Company, 1928.

For a general discussion of intelligence, see:

The Measurement and Appraisal of Adult Intelligence, by David Wechsler. Baltimore: Williams & Wilkins Company, 1958.

The factors mentioned in this section can be tabulated into a useful structural classification of personality. Eugen Kahn's classification, upon which this one is partly based, is discussed in:

The Anatomy of Personality, by H. W. Haggard and C. C. Fry. New York: Harper & Brothers, 1936.

Many people are skeptical about the relationship between constitution and personality, but it works surprisingly well for people who are not skeptical. Polysyllabic adjectives are of dubious value anyway, and constitutional adjectives are no more dubious than psychodynamic ones. *Viscerotonic* is probably of more predictive value than *passive dependent personality,* and is not much more discouraging therapeutically. Certainly the former represents a much more objective evaluation than the latter, which automatically puts the observer one up.

2

WHAT PEOPLE ARE TRYING TO DO

1

What is a human being?

A human being is a colorful energy system, full of dynamic strivings. Like any energy system, he is continually trying to reach a state of tranquillity. He "has to." That's what energy "is for"; its mysterious function is to restore its own balance.

When the powerful mixture of air and gasoline is exploded in the cylinder of an automobile by the spark, it "has to" expand in order to regain its equilibrium, which is upset by compression and by the electric flash. When it expands, it pushes forcefully against the piston, which "has to" move, just as a man has to move if his equilibrium is upset by a heavy thrust. When the piston shoots downward, it upsets the equilibrium of the whole engine, which "has to" turn in order to regain its balance. If everything is in order and the car is in gear when the engine turns, the car "has to" move. That's the way it was made.

Men are also made so that when certain things happen inside or outside, certain other things have to happen sooner or later in an attempt to restore the balance.

In a human being, energy off balance, or tension, shows itself physically and mentally. Mentally it shows itself in the form of a feeling of restlessness and anxiety. This feeling arises from an urge to seek something which is able to restore the balance and relieve the tension. Such urges are called wishes. Only living things can wish, and living things live by wishing. Sexual desire, ambition, and the desire for approval are some of the more complicated human wishes to which we have given names. There are many others, conscious and unconscious, to some of which we have given names and to some of which we have not. One of the most interesting jobs of psychology today is to recognize wishes and study their connections with one another.

The tensions in a good automobile do not have any trouble finding relief, because the insides are arranged on purpose so that the tensions can act in only one direction at a time. But the human being has different wishes pushing him in different directions at the same time, and this may make him quite uncomfortable. A simple example of this is a girl with the hives at her first college dance. She has a wish to scratch and a wish not to scratch; and even a very well brought-up young lady will feel fidgety while she is waltzing, because of such a conflict between her wish to keep her good manners and her desire to scratch herself.

The problem with human beings is that it is necessary to postpone the relief of some tensions in order to avoid setting up new and even more painful tensions, such as embarrassment. This has a lot to do with why some people get splitting headaches and burning pains in the stomach, while some do not. We shall see later that the necessity for the human energy system to postpone the relief of tension is the cause of many interesting things.

A human being is a living energy system whose tensions give rise to wishes which it is his task to gratify without getting into trouble with himself, with other people, or with the world around him.

2

What human beings are looking for

A human being, if nothing interfered, would tend to act in such a way at every moment as to try to relieve his strongest tension by gratifying his dearest wish. Every wish that is gratified brings him closer to his goal, which is a feeling of peace and security, or freedom from anxiety. Anxiety is a sign of tension, and is reduced as the energy balance is restored. No one ever quite attains the goal, because new wishes are springing up all the time, and there are too many wishes trying for satisfaction at once, so that the mere possibility of gratifying one often increases the tension of the others. Even in sleep there is no peace, and the clattering snorer stirs uneasily at regular intervals through the night.

Life is full of irritations like sour cigars and bitter women who left the tickets in their other purse, as well as less humorous inner and outer frustrations which threaten to keep people from being able to gratify their wishes, and thereby increase their tensions and anxiety. It is not events themselves which are important, but their effect on the possible fulfillment of desires. The same thing can happen to two people at the same time and make one of them anxious and not bother the other, depending on their wishes concerning the future. The anxiety may seem to be due to the event itself, but it really arises only because the event affects the possibilities for gratifying wishes. Two automobiles might get flat tires at the same moment on the same stretch of road, but the amount of anxiety which this accident would arouse in each driver would depend entirely upon his wishes concerning the immediate and distant future; how much of a hurry he was in, his financial state, who was with him, and so on; and perhaps in some cases, to take a forceful example, upon the state of his bladder. Some playful high-school boys, far from feeling any anxiety, might regard the event as a lark. Anxiety about losing a job may seem to be caused by the employment situation itself, but it only arises because of the threat to the individual's wishes to be able to fill his stomach, impress his neighbors, and make his children happy. A man who has no family cares and no wish to eat regularly or impress his neighbors with his stainless-steel possessions may never be subject to this type of anxiety and may be perfectly content to be a hippie or a philosopher living in a barrel. What makes anxiety possible is the wishes inside and not what goes on outside. No wishes, no anxiety. A corpse never gets stage fright, no matter how large his audience.

People think they are looking for security, but what they are really looking for is a *feeling* of security; for actual security, of course, does not exist. The feeling of security is increased by having means available for the relief of tensions and anxieties, and the gratification of wishes; this helps to secure balance in the energy system which is a human being. When we see how conflicting our chief wish tensions are, we shall understand why "seeking freedom from anxiety" does not always correspond to what we commonly think of as "seeking a safe situation."

Lavinia Eris offers an example of how feelings of security and insecurity depend more upon what goes on in the mind than upon what goes on outside. During her college days, Lavinia's hobby was collecting specimens of insects and snakes, some of them poisonous, for the zoology museum. At first she was terrified when she had to approach a rattlesnake, but after the novelty wore off and she learned how to handle the beasts, she felt competent and secure. A few years later, however, she began to have frequent nightmares about rattlesnakes, and in this case the novelty never did wear off; each night was as terrifying as the one before. The nightmares, which were caused by powerful conflicting tensions, remained fearsome to her, and she could never feel secure during these dreams even in the absence of outside danger. With the real snakes, however, she had soon begun to feel secure even though the outside danger remained the same. The anxiety caused by the conflicting wishes which were at the bottom of her nightmares was greater and more enduring than the fear caused by actually handling the dangerous reptiles.

Human beings seek to attain a feeling of security by looking for promising ways to gratify their most urgent wishes, but unfortunately other wishes and outside forces interfere. While the fear of outside forces will wear off if it becomes clear that they can be managed or that they are no threat to the attainment of desires, the anxiety linked with wishes does not vanish until means for the relief of tensions is in sight.

3

Which urges are the most powerful?

The two most powerful urges of human beings are the creative urge and the destructive urge. The creative urge gives rise to generous love and giving, ardent procreation, and joyful building up. The tension which drives man toward these constructive goals may be called *libido,* and its most important function for the human race is to ensure that procreation will continue. It therefore finds its most concentrated expression in sexual desire. The destructive urge activates hostility and hate, blind anger, and the uncanny pleasures of cruelty and decay. The tension which lends force to such feelings may be called *mortido.* It finds its most concentrated expression while fighting for survival, so that when properly applied, it aids in saving the individual from inside and outside dangers. In familiar language, libido is the energy of the life-wish which preserves the race, and mortido is the energy of a death-wish which, when turned against a real antagonist, helps to preserve the individual.

Naturally these two drives, which may urge the individual to opposite courses of conduct toward the people and things around him, often come into conflict with each other. Such disagreeable conflicts can be handled in several ways. Usually they are dealt with by pushing one of the wishes out of consciousness and pretending that it does not exist. In peacetime people have a tendency to pretend that mortido does not exist, and in wartime they try to pretend that libido does not exist toward the enemy. Always, however, the drive they are trying to ignore interferes with their conduct in spite of themselves so that neither loving nor hateful behavior is pure for most people. They are only too apt, without always consciously willing it, to bite the kind hand that feeds them and feed the hateful mouth that bites them.

Another way of handling the conflict is to allow one feeling to hold sway one moment and the other feeling to govern the next. The man who alternately loves and hates is often as puzzling to the onlooker as a man who alternately takes bites of ice cream and cheese; the observer may not stop to think how significant it is that both foods could come from the same udder.

Creative and destructive drives, which find their culmination in sexual relations and killing, are the raw material which man and civilization have to work with. In order to preserve himself, society, and the human race, man must apply destructively directed energy to certain goals, such as stamping out cruelty, killing, and disease, and constructively directed energy toward spiritual as well as material progress. The mental development of the individual depends upon his struggle to apply these forces within him to the most productive ends.

There is a difference between wishing and trying to gratify wishes, between feeling love and hate and expressing them. The strength with which the individual expresses his love and hatred for others and for himself, and tries to gratify his libido and mortido, may be called aggressiveness. A man with strong feelings may fool himself and others by expressing them weakly, and a man with weak feelings may do likewise by expressing them freely.

Besides aggressiveness of expression, we should consider the direction of love and hate. Some people direct their love mostly toward others, and others direct it mainly toward themselves. The direction of various quantities may change from time to time. Similarly, one can be very hateful toward others, the most aggressive act in this case being murder; or one can be very hateful toward oneself, the most aggressive act then being suicide. Both murder and suicide are expressions of aggressiveness; the only difference as far as mental energy is concerned is in its direction.

In most people's lives, such extremes are not found. Libido and mortido are well controlled and hidden by each other and possibly by other forces, so that many people go through life without realizing how powerful these two urges are and how much they influence motives and conduct. In fact, we are now ready to say that human behavior is determined largely by the tensions of libido and mortido, which upset the mental equilibrium of the human being and drive him to act in such a way that he has a chance to restore his energy balance. By setting up possibilities for gratifying his creative and destructive urges he can diminish his feelings of anxiety and approach the feeling of security which is his goal. As we go along, we shall see how complicated it is for him to express these urges, how many things can go wrong while he is making the necessary adjustments and compromises, and what happens if he fails to handle his wishes and tensions in a practical way.

The chemicals in the blood must play a considerable part in determining the strengths of libido and mortido. Though one might suggest that the sexual chemicals from the ovaries or testicles influence libido, and that the "fear and anger" chemical from the adrenal glands influences mortido, it is not proved that injecting any of the chemicals we know about so far will make people more loving or more hateful. The results with animals are far more striking than with human beings. Rats which are injected with the "maternal" hormone of the pituitary gland, for example, will show a definite increase in loving motherly behavior. But in spite of the fact that nothing is proved in regard to human beings, we must nevertheless keep the various glands in mind when we discuss these powerful urges.

Many people question the origin of destructive urges, but few deny their existence. Because they do not show themselves plainly at all times does not mean that they are not present. The desire to procreate does not show itself plainly at all times either, but no one denies its existence. Anyone who has children in the house will have to admit that they are destructive and hostile at times, and the evidence is not that they grow out of these tendencies, but rather that they decide it is wiser to express them more cautiously and subtly in later years, as is the case with their affectionate urges. Destructive urges are also manifested in dreams. A person's dreams are his own productions and he can form them into any shape he pleases. That people so often dream about destruction must mean that it pleases some part of them. The chief argument among psychiatrists is whether destructive urges are inborn or develop as a result of thwarting the creative urge. We need not enter into this argument for our purposes, since people behave as though they had always had destructive tendencies and whether they develop during the first few months of life or are present at birth, does not alter what we have to say about their later development.

A human being is one who causes things to happen, and what he causes to happen, and how, and when, depends a great deal upon his two most powerful urges, the aggressiveness with which he expresses them, and the way he solves the conflict between them.

4

The problem of a human being

The problem of a human being is the same as the problem of any energy system, namely, to "find" the path of least resistance for the discharge of tension. An electric battery, which also is an energy system, finds the path of least resistance in a circuit instantly, in a small fraction of a second. A flooding river or a tornado, which are other energy systems, finds the path of least resistance in a matter of hours. The human energy system may take years to find such a path, and can delay indefinitely because it is able to store energy.

The psychic tensions within a human being manifest themselves mainly, if not entirely, as libido and mortido, and these two forces strive for immediate expression. This means that man has a tendency to try to take what he wants when he wants it, and to destroy immediately anything that gets in his way, annoys him, or crosses him up. We can see this direct action often enough in a young infant who has not yet learned from sad experience to restrain himself. Unfortunately, if an adult attempts to do such things, there is interference from two sources: other human beings who also want what they want when they want it and wish to eliminate whoever or whatever gets in their way; and nature, which won't always supply what he wants when he wants it, and won't change in order to make his life easier.

Not only do nature and other people cross him up and keep him from carrying out his wishes on the spot, but they are also continually threatening to destroy him. Every energy system around him, including thundering seas, roaring columns of air which we call winds, earthshaking volcanoes, pouncing animals, and other struggling human beings, is also seeking ways to reduce its tensions directly as they arise. He not only may be upset because these other dynamic things interfere with him, but he also has to watch out that he does not interfere too much or in the wrong way with them. His problem is therefore to find out the best way to handle other energy systems in order to gratify his wishes speedily with the least danger.

In some parts of the world, magic is used for this purpose. For a small fee, such as ten dog's teeth or a swinging record for his phonograph, a New Guinea witch doctor will put a hex on his customer's love rival by sticking thorns into a grass image of him. People who live where there are hurricanes may think that the wind likes raw meat, and may sacrifice animals to the wind god to protect themselves from future frustrations. In some parts of the world, people like to pretend that death is a waiter who likes big tips, so they feel good about giving a lot of money to charity. In our country, of course, people don't believe in any of these things, and feel that the best method is to try to find out how people and nature are likely to act under various conditions, and how to get what is wanted from both of them with a reasonable hope of success. It appears that the more accurately we judge our surroundings, the more likely we are to get what we want.

We can see that in order to gratify their wishes without getting into trouble people have to learn to control their libido and mortido; that is, they have to learn to wait. They also have to learn how to handle and judge their surroundings so as to reduce the danger of being thwarted or destroyed when they finally do act.

This is a problem of control. Man has to learn to control three groups of forces: himself, other people, and nature. This is called the Reality Principle, for the more realistic he is—that is, the more accurate he is in his observations of these three things—the more rapidly and fully will he be able to satisfy his libido and mortido in safety. The Reality Principle requires him to form clear-cut images.

Most people have pretty good images of some of their surroundings. A good farmer understands the workings of nature. A successful businessman understands what people are apt to do under certain conditions. But only a rare individual has an accurate idea of what his own libido and mortido can make him do without even being recognized. It is in this last respect that the greatest and most frequent errors are made.

Fortunately we have within us a way of handling this threefold reality that has to be kept in such nice balance. This system is called the Ego, and is supposed to work in accordance with the Reality Principle. It is supposed to make accurate observations and judgments of the individual's inner tensions and of the tensions of the energy systems around him, and is then supposed to guide his behavior accordingly, to his best advantage. It has to help him postpone his satisfactions when advisable, and try to arrange the world around him so that he can attain them later.

To do all this it has to have some kind of mastery of his psychic energy, and some kind of mastery of people and things. Thus the Ego is the "organ of mastery." The energy for this function is obtained from part of the libido and mortido energy which is gradually split off in infancy and becomes separated from, and actually in many ways an opponent of, the primitive libido and mortido energy. The Ego energy is used in controlling the primitive energy in accordance with the Reality Principle as the person learns about reality. People get great pleasure from mastering their own bodies in swimming and diving, from mastering a rubber ball that flies around a golf course, from mastering little paper dolls that are called playing cards, and from mastering the mechanics of an airplane engine. There is a double satisfaction in all these things; they satisfy not only the primitive libido and mortido, but also those portions of libido and mortido which are split off and obtain their satisfaction by mastering things through the Ego.

Psychiatrists, for good psychological reasons, have come to think of the enormous amount of primitive libido and mortido, left after splitting off the relatively small portions required to form the Ego, as "those things," or simply "It." The libido and mortido of the Ego, and the libido and mortido left in "It" are often opposed to each other rather than working together, because one of the tasks of the Ego is to master and control "It," which always fights back. "It" wants immediate expression and satisfaction, and the Ego often wants "It" to wait.

Because psychiatrists in different countries speak different languages, they have found it convenient, like other scientists, to use for scientific terms Greek and Latin words which have been known throughout the world since ancient times. They therefore usually speak of "It" in the old Roman tongue, as "Id," or "the Id." The libido and mortido left in the Id are then spoken of as the "Id instincts."

We should make sure that we understand at this point that just as what pushes the piston of an automobile is a force, and not a little man, so the Ego energies and the Id instincts are forces, and not little men sitting in the mind with their hands on their holsters, ready to fight each other at the drop of a temptation. (There are little men, and big men, and women too, sitting in the mind ever ready to speak, but they will be discussed later, in the chapter on transactional analysis.)

The reason life is so difficult is that the Ego is in such a complicated situation. It has three forces to contend with, control, and finally pull together for the satisfaction and safety of the individual: the Id instincts, the forces of nature, and other people. Most individuals are aware of the reality of nature and other people, but they do not realize clearly that the Id is also a reality, and an important and troublesome one to be reckoned with. One reason for this lack of appreciation is that the Id is in concealment and finds all sorts of ways of fooling the Ego.

No matter how clever a man is with other people and with the

things around him, he will not find contentment unless he can deal
with his own Id as well. In the end it is not the ability to charm
women or to make money that leads to happiness, but the ability
to make peace in one's own mind. The problem of the human Ego
in a difficult world is to find the path of least inner and outer
resistance for the safe satisfaction of the creative and destructive
urges. The problem of society is to nurture the creative urges and
put down the destructive ones.

5

How do human beings express their urges?

As long as the individual postpones relief of any Id tension, the
energy which is tied up in the "repressed" wish is wasted. In
addition, it is hard work for the Ego to keep the lid on the Id, and
a good deal of energy is wasted in just keeping that part of the Id
hidden. It is much like having a secret police force to keep part of
a nation from freedom of speech. The nation is weakened not only
because a lot of its citizens are discontented and are not allowed to
help in the national tasks, but also because many of them have to
spend their time watching the discontented ones. If the latter could
be satisfied, not only would they work for the nation instead of
against it, but the secret policemen would be unnecessary and they
too could be put to some useful task. Anyone who has seen officers
guarding prisoners can understand what a double loss this is to
society; and in the same way repression is a loss of energy for the
individual human being.

If the Id can be safely satisfied, the Ego can relax, and both Ego
and Id can then devote additional energy to doing something
useful for the individual and for society.

Nature has provided methods for getting around this double
waste of energy, so that Id wishes which are not allowed to express
themselves directly and completely can express themselves indirectly. This means that some, at least, of their energy may go to
useful purposes, and it also means that the Ego can at least partly
relax as the Id tension is reduced.

For a short time it may do no harm simply to press the Id

wishes out of the conscious mind and assume that they don't exist. We should never forget, however, that to assume they don't exist does not abolish them. Eventually they will find their way out somehow in spite of all we can do. If an individual doesn't understand this, he may end up doing peculiar things. He may grant that everybody else has unconscious creative and destructive urges, but deny that he has them himself. In this way, he may be taken by surprise by his own behavior. The more we know about our Id wishes, the easier it is to cut down on sexual "mistakes" and "justified" spitefulness.

One way in which the Id wishes express themselves indirectly after a while, when they have been kept pressed out of consciousness, or "repressed," by the Ego, is to wait until the Ego is asleep at night, and then show themselves in disguised form in dreams.

This does not afford a great deal of relief, however, and if the tensions are powerful and there is no other way out, the repressed Id energy may affect the individual's body and behavior to such an extent that the Ego loses control of a part of the body or a part of the mind. This loss of control expresses itself as a neurosis. A neurosis, or psychoneurosis, which for our purpose is the same thing, is therefore a disguised expression of an Id wish. We shall hear more about this later.

We are mostly interested at the moment in how the Id affects our normal everyday behavior, and how people manage to let off steam without their adult lives becoming a series of violent adventures. This is mostly done by substituting some other object or some other activity for the original goals of their wishes, something close enough to the real gratification to calm the Id down temporarily and distant enough not to give rise to threatening consequences.

The primitive need of the libido is to approach another human being as closely as possible, most of the time one of the opposite sex. Obviously the actual method of satisfaction will depend partly upon age. The closest an infant can get to another person is to suck at his mother's breast, and this is the beneficial goal of the libido in young infants of both sexes. If the child is bottle-fed, he may need extra cuddling to make up for the nursing pleasure he is deprived of. After puberty, the closest approach that can be made is the sexual embrace. In old age,* holding hands and talking may be the best available method of satisfaction of this primitive need.

While bodily contact provides the most direct satisfaction of libido, anything which gives the feeling of "approach," whether it be physical, mental, or emotional approach, may help to relieve libido tension. Thus, moving closer, talking more intimately about common interests, or feeling an emotion together are of value in this respect. Even doing the same things at the same time, though far apart, may help. Some couples who are separated make an agreement to think of each other every day at supper, write letters to each other at the same hour every day, and do other things which "draw them together though they are apart." In some situations, however, such "forepleasures," instead of relieving libido tension, build it up further or mobilize it in larger quantities. In many cases the more of these mental and emotional foreplea-sures that precede the sexual act, if one is to take place, the more pleasurable and complete will be the final satisfaction. Women tend to believe more firmly and at an earlier age than men that the more love between a normal couple and the more things they have in common, the more satisfaction they will get from the sexual relationship.

If sexual relationship with the opposite sex is delayed too long because of outside circumstances or the demands of conscience, there are other possibilities. First, some satisfaction can be obtained from courtship and social meetings. Secondly, some people can obtain almost complete satisfaction without any partner or with a partner of the same sex: that is, by masturbation or homo-sexuality. In the first case they have the proper sexual object, a person of the opposite sex, but don't accomplish the sexual aim, which is intercourse. In the second case, they don't have the proper object, but do accomplish the sexual goal of orgasm. In both cases something is out of place, so we speak of libido dis-placed from its proper aim, and libido displaced from its proper object.

---

* By "old age" I mean eighty-five and over. There is no "natural decline" of sexual powers in middle age, although there is an *artificial* decline. Any lion which has been caged for forty years or more is likely to become dispirited.

Some of the most interesting and socially useful displacements of libido occur when both the aim and the object are partial substitutes for the biological aim and object. This occurs in what is called sublimation, that is, an activity which helps bring other people as well as its creator closer to the sublime or "higher" things of life. Many mental functions are organized to bring such refined forms of pleasure to people. A good example is painting. Here the artist substitutes as object the model for a love partner (and this model need not be a person, but may be some inanimate object, such as a landscape or a bowl of fruit), and as aim the thrill of artistic creation for the thrill of love-making.

The life of Dante Alighieri is a good example of how a great poet expresses himself through his writing when the direct expression of love is impossible. The poet substitutes imaginary, or at least imagined, people and things for the real woman he cannot find or have, and again the ardor of creation for the passion of love. Dante exemplified all these things in the relationship between his poetry and his Beatrice. But it is not necessary to be a genius in order to sublimate. Many people get a creative thrill from carpentry, from adding to their collections of seashells or postage stamps, or from showing or driving the cars and boats they have lovingly put together with their own hands.

There are other satisfactions in sublimation besides the ones we have mentioned; here we are trying only to point out how the pent-up libido uses these activities as an indirect way of relieving the mental tensions that result from ungratified primitive wishes.

The energy of mortido finds similar indirect methods of expression. One primitive need of mortido is to eliminate another human being, usually one of the same sex. Among birds, fishes, and nonhuman mammals, this sexual distinction between the objects of libido and those of mortido can also be seen. Flickers, jewel fish, elephants, and dogs are usually loving and "approaching" with members of the opposite sex, while they readily become enraged and try to "eliminate" members of the same sex. Among human beings, when the restraining veneer of politeness wears off, the same is usually observed, as anyone can verify by visiting a saloon.

Since in our country in peacetime mortido can usually obtain total satisfaction only once, whether by murder or by suicide, it is much more mysterious to us than libido. In wartime psychiatrists learn more about mortido, since they are given the task of studying its effects in the raw. Totalitarian and autocratic governments know far more about it than we do. In our democracy, where violence and torment are regarded as criminal and unnatural rather than as legitimate police methods, we know less about some aspects of mortido. In everyday life libido gets a chance to drain off in various activities, but mortido has fewer such opportunities. Rages are less frequent than orgasms in the lives of reasonably happy individuals.

It may be worth while to consider the influence of unconscious mortido on political decisions. Sometimes the psychological background is overlooked by focusing attention too strongly on external problems and situations. Trying to eliminate war by changing social conditions seems much like trying to eliminate babies by regulating women's clothes. Changing the conditions of the external objects will do little to change the strength of the primitive drives, which in the end may have their way.

Just as anything which gives the feeling of "approach" will help to satisfy libido, so anything which gives the feeling of "separation" will help in the case of mortido. Leaving town, quarreling, sarcasm, and doing everything differently "just to be stubborn," are indirect ways of gratifying mortido. Strangely enough, we know from experience that withholding belongs here also, though on first thought it may appear to be the reverse of "separation."

In their direct satisfaction, both mortido and libido show two faces. Just as libido can be satisfied to different degrees in different people by either approaching or being approached, so mortido can be gratified by either running away or being run away from. The man's passive libido wants the woman to come to him, while his active libido urges him to go after the woman. In the same way, his passive mortido urge is to run away, while his active mortido urge is to chase the other fellow away by fighting. Thus, when mortido is awakened by danger, some people run away and some fight it out. This force has two emotions to deal with, fear and anger, and whichever one is stronger in any situation will determine the individual's behavior. In either case, the task of separating the individual from the outside threatening energy system is accomplished.

Mortido has the same possibilities for varied expression as libido. Instead of eliminating an opponent of the same sex, it can attack him without eliminating him, as in business competition, athletic competition, or making sarcastic remarks. Or, it can eliminate an individual of the opposite sex, as in the case of a man who murders his wife from jealousy, where the usual object of mortido is a person of the same sex; or it can eliminate the individual himself, as in suicide; or it can eliminate an animal instead of a person, as in hunting. In the first case, we have the proper object but the final aim is not accomplished, and we see mortido displaced from its aim; in the other cases we have a different object, but the aim of elimination is accomplished, and we see mortido displaced from its object. Mortido can also be sublimated, as in stonecutting, carpentry, and mining, which create beautiful or useful things by attacking inanimate objects. Surgery involves one of the most useful sublimations of mortido.

The reader is now acquainted with several psychological pairs of great importance in understanding people, which may be listed as follows:

1. Creative urges and destructive urges
2. Libido and mortido
3. Inwardly directed energy and outwardly directed energy
4. Approach and separation
5. Aim displacement and object displacement
6. Active and passive

Let us now go back to the orphan girl Nana, and see some of these pairs in action. We shall also see how unreasonable and undiscriminating the Id is, and how libido tension and mortido tension both try to find expression at the same time whenever possible.

We already know some of the reasons for Nana's early promiscuity. Her mother's early death, her father's dissolute habits, and lack of family life left a deep hunger for affection or anything that looked like affection. When she was nineteen, her father was killed in a daylight attempt to hold up an armored car in front of the First National Bank of Olympia. From the reckless way in which this attempt was made, it was obvious that he had little wish to live and therefore little fear of the threat of death. As he often said, "A fellow that don't care to gamble any more don't care which way the dice fall." The scandal made it difficult for Nana to earn an honest living, and after a while she was forced, in spite of her repugnance for such sordid relationships, to take money from her numerous boy friends. It became the custom among various men of the town to go down to Foamborne Street and visit Nana when they were drunk. The fact that Mrs. Fayton, the town prostitute, screamed jealous vituperation at her on the street added to Nana's distaste for her profession.

In order to better her circumstances in the only way she could, she consented to live with Mr. Krone, a tall, thin, sad old miser who became attached to her. She thought she hated Mr. Krone, who often beat her viciously just as her father had done, but much to her own surprise, when he died a short time later she mourned him bitterly, in spite of the fact that he willed his hoard of money to the Anti-Vivisection Society after he had promised it to her. She was thus forced to return to her old way of life.

It was only a matter of time before Nana caught a venereal infection, which she contracted from Mr. Meleager, a dignified-looking but nervous lawyer who frequently went to Chicago on business. She was shocked and incredulous when Dr. Pell told her what the condition was, but she improved rapidly under regular treatment. When it seemed to her that she was cured, she neglected the doctor's cautions and secretly saw two of her favorite visitors again. The result was that Ralph Metis and Josiah Tally both caught the disease from her.

The chief emotional tensions in Nana were, first, a hunger for the affection she had never received in childhood; secondly, a hunger for beautiful things, exaggerated by the drab surroundings she had lived in all her life (what money she earned beyond her living expenses she spent on reproductions of well-known paintings and books on art, which she kept hidden in her closet and never mentioned to any of her male friends); thirdly, resentment against her father for never having given her the kind and amount of affection she desired; fourthly, resentment against society in general, which she blamed for killing him and for having made her life miserable.

The springs of her conduct were her unsatisfied Id tensions, mostly dating from early childhood. Their expression was now made easy by her "independence" and increased loneliness since her father's death.

It was unreasonable, of course, for her to place the blame for her father's death on the bank which hired the armored car, but that is just what happened. The Id often shifts or displaces blame.

Her way of living enabled her to gratify her starved outwardly directed libido in more ways than one. It did not supply a normal emotional "approach" to another human being, but it did give her a poor substitute. It also supplied her with money to gratify her sublimated creative urge, which showed itself in the secret interest in art which she was ashamed to acknowledge, because of a conflict between her inner delicacy and her self-reproaches. By enabling her to dress expensively, it also gratified her inwardly directed libido, or vanity.

It relieved her inwardly directed mortido because to a woman of her sensitiveness such a life brought much suffering. Mr. Krone gave this aspect a more direct relief by beating her. It gratified her outwardly directed mortido to take some of his precious money from the old miser, and to give her disease to her two friends, resulting in a permanent "separation" from them which satisfied her destructive urge.

If we disregard her explanations of why things happened and look only at what did happen (a procedure which psychiatrists commonly employ), we can see at least two examples of object displacement. Mr. Krone took the place of her father in many ways, and the similarity added to her unconscious pleasure in punishing him financially as well as in being nice to him. That she wasn't completely aware of this displacement of mixed feelings from her father to Mr. Krone was shown by the fact that she herself was surprised when she wept at the old man's death. Ralph and Josiah, the two men connected with the bank, to whom she gave her disease, were scapegoats for "the bank," which she unreasonably wanted to punish for her father's death.

Both activity and passivity played a part in her punishment of the three men. Mr. Krone she actively punished, going out of her way to spend money extravagantly and to make him jealous. The other two men she punished by her passivity. She did not go out of her way to infect them, she simply yielded passively to their persuasions and omitted to tell them of her condition, all in good faith apparently, since she convinced herself that she was cured.

One of the most important things to notice is that in nearly everything she did, she gratified both libido and mortido at the same time. This was most clearly shown on the night of the catastrophe, when she obtained sexual pleasure from the two men and at the same time gave them the disease. It also showed in her mixed feelings toward Mr. Krone. In fact, without being clearly aware of it, she had the same sort of ambidexterous, double-edged attitude toward all concerned, including herself. Such double-valued attitudes, involving love and hate at the same time, are called "ambivalent," and both feelings strive to obtain gratification simultaneously in everything the individual does.

Some people might object that since she "didn't know" that she still had the disease, it isn't fair to talk this way about what happened. It is true that her Ego may not have known that she had it for sure, but some doubts still remained, as she found out later when she came to the psychiatrist for treatment. By "forgetting" and by the sins of omission, the Id makes itself known.

6

How do people handle their surroundings?

People usually handle their surroundings in such a way that either libido or mortido, or preferably both, obtain some satisfaction from almost everything they do. These satisfactions are gained through the feeling of "approach," or creation, and "separation," or destruction. The Id, however, has little if any ability to learn or to put things in what we usually think of as their proper order.

The Ego, which normally controls the faculties by which people handle things, such as their limbs and their thinking, is different. The Id can only wish, while the Ego can arrange and learn. The Id is like a petulant Roman Emperor, and the Ego is like a faithful servant trying to carry out his unreasonable demands. The Emperor says: "I want to have *truffes au champagne* for dinner!" The servant has learned where and how to get what the Emperor wants, and how to arrange for his food to be cooked to his taste. The Emperor could never gather a single black truffle by himself. When he wants anything, he has to get it through a servant, who is his means of communication with the world outside the palace. In the same way, the Id says: "I want to have a wife and some children!" The Ego then has to arrange the individual's life for the next few years so that the wish of the Id will be gratified. The Ego handles the environment in two ways: by arranging and by learning. Just as the work of the Id can be picked out in everything the individual does by noting which wishes are *actually* gratified by the end result (without consideration of how they are gratified or what protests the individual makes); so the work of the Ego is demonstrated by the amount of arranging of ideas and actions which has taken place, and what the individual *thinks* he has done. In dreams, the work of the Id can be detected in the wishes which are gratified by the dream; and the work of the Ego is harder to see unless much arranging has taken place. That is why a dream frequently seems strange or silly to the Ego when it awakens in the morning. In studying mathematics, the work of the Ego is easy to see in all the arranging and learning that has to take place, while the work of the Id is hidden and it is not always easy to see what unconscious wishes are gratified by noticing that two plus two equal four.

In a way, the Id is more "natural" than the Ego, just as a cow is more "natural" than a steak. A steak is a cow which has been arranged by a human Ego. Nature is ordered, not arranged. Trees grow naturally in forests. Only when the human Ego enters the picture do they grow in regularly arranged patterns in orchards. Weeds grow where they find the best nourishment, or where the wind drops their seeds. Only the Ego can make flowers grow in neat rows. It is the Ego which cages animals, cuts canals in straight lines, sees patterns in the stars in the sky, and makes "opposites which exclude each other." In nature and in the Id, there are no "opposites which exclude each other." Everyone is now familiar with electrons and atoms. Is an atom hard or soft, dark or light, good or bad? We cannot even say whether it is matter or energy, time or space. It is both and neither. In psychiatry, as in physics, we have to drop not only the idea of "opposites which exclude each other," but also the idea of "cause and effect" as we are commonly accustomed to think of it. In nature, things are not "caused," or "explained." They simply occur at "different" times. Our Egos invented the ideas of "cause" and "explanation." They are not a part of nature. Such ideas are just another evidence that our Egos like to put things in order. Things don't happen "because." They happen "when," or "as if," and we shall have to be content with that.

In the Id, then, love does not exclude hate. Love and hate may exist side by side at the same time toward the same person and may be interwoven in all our feelings toward that person. But people tend to think of them as opposites which exclude each other, and so the Ego may experience "surprise" on finding that in some cases the extremes of affection and destruction are expressed almost simultaneously. Extreme affection is often closely linked with total destruction. That's why frequently a violent man murders a woman with whom he is passionately in love. The police, who have to deal with realities and not with arranged ideas, realize this, and in such cases the first person they question (and not the last person, as our "logical" Egos might want us to think) is the lover. This idea is so familiar that it sounds "logical," but it is also "illogical," and comes from practical experience and knowledge of the way the Id instincts fly in the face of logic.

The second important faculty of the Ego is learning. People learn about reality by keeping in mind things that will enable them to make general statements, which are a kind of prophecy. A man who does not pay attention to his surroundings may get caught in the rain again and again. But if he lives in one place long enough he comes to learn that a certain kind of cloud brings rain. He generalizes—that is, prophesies—that low black clouds bring rain. From many observations of the sky his Ego extracts or abstracts the ideas of lowness and blackness, in order to make this generalization. The Id is unreliable in this respect because it makes too many unrealistic generalizations which do not work. The child's Ego may learn, if his brothers are born at home, that the visit of the doctor with his black bag means a new baby. The Id makes false generalizations because it does not abstract the proper meanings from all that happens: in dreams, which are the best material for studying the Id, a doctor may mean a baby no matter what he is carrying, or a black bag may mean a baby even if it is not carried by a doctor. If the Ego figured things out that way, it would get nowhere.

The Id is more like nature in the raw than the Ego, but it is not competent to handle reality, because it does not arrange things or generalize in a practical way. People can best handle their surroundings efficiently by observing, learning, generalizing, and arranging, with the aid of the Reality Principle, and by controlling their Id instincts accordingly. Strangely enough, however, in spite of all this, the Id often shows more wisdom than the Ego, an apparent contradiction which we shall hear more about in the section on Intuition.

7

How does a human being grow and change?

It is easy to understand that one "purpose" of libido is to keep the adult human being forever wishing to reproduce. If the libido expresses itself in undisguised form, as it may in many young people, we have an individual who is "continually chasing after the promise of an orgasm," as St. Cyr has aptly said. It is evident also that mortido helps the individual to survive, by giving him the wish to eliminate anything which threatens him. When the individual is living among civilized people, however, he has to disguise these primitive urges. Because life is so complicated, and Id drives are filtered through the Ego, only on special occasions do we see either libido or mortido in the raw.

The Id can only wish. It cannot learn or think or grow, although its strength changes at special periods of life such as puberty, and its direction also changes from time to time, as in parenthood. It is governed by tensions striving for release. There are only two things which can happen to the Id wishes: they can be gratified partly or completely, or they can be thwarted. When they are gratified, there is a relief of tension, as can be seen in anyone who has just had normal sexual satisfaction, or who has just injured himself in an unsuccessful attempt at suicide. When they are thwarted, tension piles up, and further attempts to relieve it result.

Since the primitive creative and destructive urges themselves cannot be basically changed, growth or change in the human personality takes place by changing the manner in which these tensions are relieved.

The Id can only express itself in ways which the body and the surroundings make available. In the newborn infant, many things are undeveloped. The Id of a nursing child cannot express itself in any way which requires walking, because the nerves and organs of walking are not yet fully developed. Many pleasures are denied to the infant because his control of his own body has to await the ripening of the nerves to the various organs and muscles. He makes the best of what he can use. At birth, the most important movements he has at his command are sucking and making sounds. Any gratification of libido or mortido has to be gained through these mechanisms, with some contributions from others which are less well developed. Since the Id instincts usually gain more satisfaction when another person is involved, it can be observed that the infant's greatest contentment comes from sucking at the breast.

As the child grows, his nervous system acquires control of more and more actions—allowing new ways of gratifying his Id—until the age of strength and puberty when adult sexual activity and aggression, the final goals, become possible. His possibilities for getting satisfaction increase, and so does the variety of his activities, since human beings like to branch out when they can. After the period of sucking pleasure, he learns to control his bowels and bladder, and then he is able to get more pleasure from them. As he learns to use his hands and legs, he has even more ways of getting satisfaction. Later in life when his sexual organs mature, he uses them for his greatest emotional and physical gratifications. As each new stage is reached he more or less outgrows the pleasures he obtained at the preceding stage, and uses in a more matter-of-fact way the organs which have been abandoned as pleasure givers. He thus goes through stages of mouth pleasure, bowel and bladder pleasure, body pleasure, and sexual organ pleasure.

Many times, however, the human being will hang on to an old way of getting satisfaction if he is not very successful with a new way, or if circumstances make it difficult for him to experiment with it, as in the case of an orphan child who is deprived of many opportunities for development and therefore continues to suck his thumb after infancy, remaining fixed at one of the early stages. Or, he may develop normally but return to an earlier stage in times of stress, giving up on occasion some of his most recently acquired methods of releasing tension, like an older child who sucks his thumb when his mother is away on her vacation and stops when she returns.

Besides going through the various organ stages in a natural way by keeping pace with the growth of his nervous system, his body, and his glands, the normal human being may change the speed, the manner, the frequency, or the object of his gratifications as he grows up. These changes are greatly influenced by the Ego, usually in accordance with the Reality Principle. He learns that certain ways of getting satisfaction often lead to greater dissatisfaction in the long run, so he tries to be more sensible about it. He profits from experience. The Id seems to be "lazy" and set in its habits, and tries again and again to obtain gratification in the same old unprofitable ways unless the Ego takes a very firm hand. If the Ego doesn't have a watchful eye, the Id compels the individual to repeat the same imprudent or ignoble mistakes over and over.

Not only does the Id have a tendency never to learn, using again and again the same unsatisfactory methods in attempting to obtain gratification, but it may content itself at times with false realities, such as imagination, dreaming, and the visions brought on by drugs. It may even convince the Ego that its imaginations are real, which is what we call "hallucinating." Thus, in an alcoholic delirium, released mortido may seek satisfaction through visions of sinister snakes and monsters, instead of by actual killing or suicide. These visual hallucinations seem real to the individual because the Ego's "reality test" is crippled. Sometimes a young man seeks to satisfy his libido by imagining that some beautiful woman is in love with him, when actually she may not even know that he exists. If he really comes to believe his fabrications, these false convictions are called "delusions." Women may suffer from similar delusions.

As people grow up, they tend to become more dignified in their behavior and more careful to restrain themselves from doing anything which might lose them the good opinion of themselves and their neighbors, so that mortido tensions tend to turn more and more frequently back on the individual himself. A child may vent his mortido in a temper outburst without being too embarrassed, but a grown man who is angered and irritated by his fellow workers usually tries to control himself, with the result that the mortido may take it out on his own body.

Two of the commonest ways it does this are by elevating the blood pressure and by changing the caliber of the blood vessels of the stomach. If such a conversion of a feeling into a bodily reaction takes place too frequently, more or less permanent changes may result. The blood pressure may stay up instead of coming down after a restful weekend, as we saw in the case of Mr. King; or the continual disturbance in the circulation of the stomach may eventually result in a small area being digested away from the wall of that organ, causing a "gastric ulcer." The prevention does not lie in slapping one's stenographer or kicking the foreman in the fundament, but in learning to give up being irritated by little things, including financial losses. After all, you can take your stomach with you, but not your money. Too often a man elects to keep his name on the door and let the surgeons have his stomach.

As the individual grows, the Ego becomes more efficient in accomplishing its three tasks: relieving libido, relieving mortido, and reducing the threat of the outside world. Farming is a good example of this, where mortido gives the energy to attack the earth, and libido gives the energy to nurse the growing crop; while the sale of the crop reduces the threat of starvation and at the same time increases the chance of getting further libido and mortido satisfaction by making it easier to find a wife. With all this, there is still room for the luxuries of "divine discontent" and esthetic experiences.

The personality of the normal human being grows and changes as he learns new methods of gratifying libido and mortido, using new organs and faculties as control of them is learned, and abandoning earlier, less effective ways. The Reality Principle assists in this growth by helping to fight the compulsion to repeat over and over the old and now less efficient and even dangerous methods of attempting to gain satisfaction.

8

Why do human beings control themselves?

A playful child makes no effort to control himself until he learns that direct expression of libido and mortido does not pay. When a sturdy infant wants to break something, he smashes it. When he wants to put his arms around somebody, he hugs her. As he grows up, he learns that similar conduct may in the end lead to more pain than pleasure, that immediate relief of one tension may lead to damming up of a greater tension. It is then up to the Ego to judge, if it is capable, which line of conduct will give the greatest relief of tension in the long run.

If the infant breaks his father's musical saw, he gets spanked or scolded. This is painful and leads to mental tension. Next time he feels destructive, he may stop to think as follows: "Will smashing this fifteenth-century Ming vase relieve more tension than the resulting spanking will create?" If his father has a firm and callused hand, the answer will be: "No!" So the vase remains on its pedestal behind the rubber plant.

Later on in life, the same person may have to answer the question: "Will stealing the judo instructor's girl relieve more tension than being thrown around by a judo instructor will create?" Again the answer is: "No!" so the judo instructor's girl remains on her pedestal down by the rubber plant.

Punishment results in increased tension in several ways. Let us consider here only the increased libido tension due to loss of opportunity to love and the increased mortido tension due to the inability to retaliate. The spanked child is forbidden to hug his father for a while, nor can he gratify his resentment by taking his father over his knee. Even if he is only scolded rather than spanked, the result is the same.

In some cases, punishment brings thrills and relief. If it arouses libido as well as mortido, a spanking becomes sexual. Many adults as well as children get peculiar satisfactions from being punished. That is one reason why certain people are always getting into scrapes. For them, being hurt, rather than acting as a deterrent, is one of the attractions of a dangerous life.

Most people, however, like to avoid what is commonly thought of as "punishment," and find ways of handling their Id instincts so that satisfaction may be postponed if there is any danger of suffering. In this way they hope finally to obtain complete or partial gratification without tears.

Since actual physical pain is rarely used as a form of punishment for adults in this country, people control themselves mainly to avoid the mental pain which results from other forms of punishment. Most people refrain from crime, for example, because for them it would lead to severe libido frustration—loss of self-regard, and the regard and company of friends, families, and mates. The types of sexual activity and outbursts of violence which occur in prisons demonstrate the increase of Id tensions in those who are cut off from ordinary social life. The mortido tension of self-hate is also disagreeable to most people.

We have made no direct mention here of conscience, which after all is what we generally think of as keeping most people well behaved. We have, however, already hinted at its existence when we used such terms as "loss of love," "loss of opportunity to love," and when we spoke of self-hate and loss of self-regard. In the next section we shall see how these things are related to conscience, and whence the latter develops. People are not born "good" or "bad," but they learn their standards of conduct at a very early age from those around them. When a child is "bad," the parents sometimes ask themselves: "How much are *we* at fault? Have we given the child a good example to imitate?"

9

How does a human being make a decision?

People have two ways of making a decision. The first is by thinking. We consider the possibilities on both sides, weigh them, and decide more or less in accordance with the Reality Principle. The second is without conscious thinking. We should be in a continual turmoil of indecision of we had to think about every little thing we did during the day. If we had to decide, each time we buttoned a button, which finger went over the button and which finger went under it, we should take as long as tiny children to get dressed. So the mind has ways of making decisions for us without conscious thought on our part.

One of the ways in which we make decisions without being aware of it is the automatic thought-saving way called habit, which saves us effort in handling simple everyday situations that do not involve any strain on the Id. There are people who do have to think and elaborate about every unimportant thing which would be done from habit by most; these people then have so much to worry about, as we shall see later in the case of Ann Kayo, that they use up time and concentrate energy on worrying, with the result that they have little time left to carry on their normal occupations effectively. Investigation shows that ordinary actions such as buttoning a button or washing the hands, which have little emotional meaning to the average person, have taken on a special significance for such people. Their libido and mortido are too heavily displaced onto trivial objects, and have made too many images uncertain. Since habit can be used only in handling lightly charged situations involving clear-cut images, such "obsessed" individuals have trouble doing things from habit. Parts of the world around them have become too "libidinized" and "mortidinized."

The Id itself supplies an unconscious force for making decisions in more emotional situations. This force is based on emotional attitudes which we gather in early childhood from our parents and others whose love we value and are at pains not to lose. After early childhood, people are able to make certain decisions without conscious thought in accordance with what they imagine the desires of these loved ones would be. They behave as if they said to themselves, for example:

"That is the way I have to do, because that is the way my father would have me do if he were here by my side. If I don't do it that way he might frown on me, as I learned when I was very small."

The important thing to notice is that they do *not* have to say this to themselves, but the result is the same *as if* they did say it. In this way time and energy are saved in making decisions.

Naturally, children whose fathers were not there to bring them up, or whose parents did their parts badly, will have a disturbance in this aspect of their development, which may cause them increasing grief and trouble as they go on in life.

These parental influences, then, incorporate the lessons learned in childhood about how to keep people's affection. The individual learns in infancy how he "ought" to behave, because his parents disapprove when he does not behave as they think he "ought" to, and his feeling of "oughtness" gets so deeply ingrained that it becomes a part of his mental equipment. There is also some "oughtness" acquired later in life (that is, after the age of five or six), which remains conscious in the form of what is called "conscience," and this also plays a part in making decisions. The earlier "unconscious conscience," however, is more important than the "conscious conscience," because it is formed earlier, is more deeply rooted, more powerful, harder to change and control, and affects people's conduct without their clearly realizing it and often in spite of themselves.

When the individual grows up, his parents are not usually standing beside him to punish him if he does not do as they think he ought, but their powerful and heavily charged images are there in his mind, which is just as good, since, we remember, he will act in accordance with his images anyway rather than according to what is really there. The fact that the images of "oughtness" may be twenty or forty years old may make no difference, since they are unconscious, and we know that the unconscious does not age and that its images are imbued with a feeling of immortality which keeps them fresh and young. As for punishing him if he does transgress, his parents do not have to be there for that either. His own Id takes care of it.

Just as a part of his libido is normally turned inward upon himself, so that he respects and admires and protects himself, so a part of his mortido is turned inward to help supply the energy for punishing himself. When he does something which he learned very early he ought not to do, this part of the mortido kindles the disapproving images of his absent parents. The reaction we get when we do something we feel we ought not to do is called "guilt." Even if the individual is not aware of feeling guilty, the unsatisfied tension of inwardly directed mortido resulting from "wickedness" shows itself as a "need for punishment." Guilt and the need for punishment mean that the individual's parent images have become active and are threatening to punish him much as his real parents used to do. Until this need for punishment is satisfied, it will continue to exist, and quantities of this tension may pile up for years, eventually driving the individual into scrape after scrape in an effort to obtain relief. For this reason, inwardly directed destructive energy must be dealt with. Like the rest of the Id energies, it may go too far unless the Ego realizes in time what is going on and puts a stop to it. Otherwise, the need for punishment may get the individual into trouble, sometimes through "forgetfulness" or "carelessness."

We can see now that the Id tensions are a little more complicated than we hinted at first. There are tensions of outwardly directed libido and tensions of inwardly directed libido; and tensions of outwardly directed mortido and tensions of inwardly directed mortido. All four groups are clamoring for satisfaction, and it is up to the Ego to keep them all under control. One of the most important and difficult tasks for the Ego is to see that in gratifying any of the other three tensions it does not unduly increase the tension of the inwardly directed mortido. In other words, "guilt" may cause more tension than is relieved by doing what we do, and some people who cannot control their guilt may punish themselves to a disastrous extent for some trivial trespass.

The unconscious images of the parents and their successors, incorporating the lessons learned in early life, are charged with mortido and libido split off from the rest of the Id. This system, which helps decide the individual's behavior, is called the Superego. The question of guilt and the need for punishment is complicated, because they are connected with many elements, all of which help in making decisions. The first is the Superego proper, just described. Another one is the Ego Ideal, which consists of the individual's conscious and unconscious images of what he would like to be, patterned after certain people whom he admires and would like to imitate, because they possess qualities which he regards as ideal. Another is his conscious image of what is right and wrong, which he gets mainly from his religious preceptors, schoolteachers, and other authorities; these form what is commonly known as "conscience."

For simplicity, we shall loosely include all of these three elements under the name of Superego.

Since "doing his duty" by moving his bowels properly is one of the child's first lessons in "oughtness," the period of bowel training is an important one in the formation of the Superego. This is a good example of the well-established but rather complex connection between mortido and the bowels, which we shall meet again.

It should be understood that the mortido invested in the Superego is a quantity split off from the rest of the Id energy, so that the Superego is free to work more or less as an opponent of the Id. Thus finally the Ego has at least three energy systems whose needs must be considered before acting: the Id wishes, the outside world of reality, and the Superego.

The decisions of a human being may therefore be made consciously or unconsciously. Conscious decisions are regulated, we like to think, by the Reality Principle and the conscious conscience. Unconscious decisions may be simplified and energy saved by means of habit in the case of actions which have little emotional significance. In most emotional situations, decisions depend on the result of the conflict between the unconscious forces of the Superego and the Id. Once the decision has been made without the individual's being aware of the real forces behind it, he takes upon himself the task of finding justifications for it and convincing himself and others that it has been made in accordance with the realities of the situation. This is called "rationalization."

10
To whom the good of all this?

Who is "I"? We have described the Id wishes as giving pleasure to "the individual" when gratified. We have told how the Superego guides the Ego, and punishes "the individual" for his sins. We have studied the manner in which the Ego, between these two forces, has to guide "us" through the dangers of the environment. For whose benefit are all these forces working? Is my Ego I? Or is my Id I? Or is my Superego the real I?

A woman described her Self as being something that controlled the rest of her being. She thought of herself as someone driving a donkey cart. The donkey was a part of her which took over at times and made her do things which she regretted. In such cases her Self blamed the "donkey." What was the Self she was talking about? The Self is the Ego.

The Ego is a system which can look at itself, much as the parts of the body can feel one another. This accounts for the feeling people have that they can watch their own minds at work as though they were someone else, just as they can grasp their own legs as easily as though they were someone else's. Actually, there are three parts to the Ego, and they can all look at one another at different times. Special parental images form one part, the grown-up Self which works according to the Reality Principle is another part, and in addition, every person still has in his mind the little child he used to be. Every woman has in her head a little girl and every man a little boy. The parental part, the grown-up part, and the child part form three different Selves. As long as one Self is acting independently of the others, the individual feels like one person, but if two of them are active at the same time then one looks at the other and wonders what is going on. These three aspects of the Ego will be discussed in more detail in Chapter 9.

But there is something beyond all this—some force which drives people to grow, progress, and do better. We may regard this as a fourth force of the personality besides the Ego, the Superego, and the Id. Psychiatrists and psychologists know little or nothing about this fourth part. Religious people might say it was the soul. Scientists have no answer at present. We have avoided the question so far by describing the human being simply as an energy system— a system of forces continually trying to regain or maintain its equilibrium and not trying to "please" anybody or anything or any part of itself, any more than the earth is trying to "please" anybody when it goes around the sun. But it helps to suppose that there is a system of tensions which normally pushes living things continually in the direction of "progress." We may suppose the existence of such a system in order to explain why people grow and why the human race tries to get "better," and why animals gradually become more venturesome through evolution, and why a creative love of beauty is added to the mind as that energy system becomes more complicated from the jellyfish up through the frogs and monkeys to man. We can forget the question of whose "benefit" this is for and still suppose that there is a force within us which keeps us striving to go "onward and upward."

As we shall see later, a neurosis has many advantages for the individual. If he is better off in many respects with his neurosis, what is the force which makes him "want" to get better? What is the curative force of nature which makes sick bodies and sick minds strive to become healthy again so that they can continue to grow? What makes an embryo develop? Why doesn't it just stay an embryo? Growing is hard work and uses up a lot of energy. What made some jellyfish evolve into men? Why didn't they just stay jellyfish forever? Evolving is also hard work.

For an answer we can go back more than two thousand years to a great Semite named Zeno. Zeno wandered and wondered for many years. His wandering came to an end in Athens, in ancient Greece, but his wondering did not. Zeno talked a great deal about *physis,* the force of Nature, which eternally strives to make things grow and to make growing things more perfect. The idea of *physis* was not originated by Zeno, but he did much of the thinking about it in connection with the growth and development of living things. Many philosophers since have talked about the creative force of Nature which makes all things grow in an orderly and "progressive" way.

If such a growth drive exists in the minds as well as the bodies of human beings, how can we fit it into our energy scheme, and what is its connection with the other tensions of the mind? We may remember that we have talked about inwardly and outwardly directed mortido, and outwardly directed libido, but so far we have said little about inwardly directed libido. It may be that growth energy comes from the tension of inwardly directed libido. This explanation seems too simple, however; for example, just the reverse might be true, and libido might be only one aspect of growth energy. Perhaps *physis* does not exist at all, but in spite of our inability to be definite about this subject, there are so many things which happen *as if* there were such a force, that it is easier to understand human beings if we suppose that it does exist.

We shall henceforth take the liberty of supposing that *physis* is a force to be reckoned with in studying the human mind, and avoid the question of exactly how it might be related to inwardly directed libido. We have not completely solved the problem of who is the "driver," for whose benefit the Id, the Ego, and the Superego maintain their nice balance of tensions so that the individual can grow and "progress," but we have learned that there are other possibilities in the human mind which we must not neglect to think about.

Footnotes for Philosophers, Chapter Two

In this chapter, we have ventured onto some of the battlegrounds of modern psychiatry. Our didactic purpose precludes an adequate presentation of dissenting opinions. The viewpoints chosen offer a relatively simple approach to the theory of instincts.

1. *Tensions*

It is interesting to think about the dynamics of the mind in terms of various formulations of the second law of thermodynamics, quite aside from the currently fashionable interest in cybernetics, information theory, and systems analysis. The idea that all systems tend to approach a state of equilibrium, the concept that entropy change is independent of the previous history of the system and of any particular process, and the entropy equations themselves, are all pertinent, along with Le Châtelier's principle. Since the first edition of this book appeared, Colby (1955), K. A. Menninger (1954), Ostow (1951), Szasz (1955), and others have elaborated some of the ideas mentioned in this footnote. The most detailed consideration of the problems of psychic energy can be found in:

Energy and Structure in Psychoanalysis, by Kenneth M. Colby. New York: Ronald Press Company, 1955.

2. *Anxiety*

Cf. *The Problem of Anxiety,* by Sigmund Freud. New York: W. W. Norton, 1936.

Or, for easier reading:

The Complete Introductory Lectures on Psychoanalysis, by Sigmund Freud. New York: W. W. Norton, 1966, Chapter xxxii, "Anxiety and Instinctual Life."

3. *Instincts*

The question of whether the destructive urge is primary, or is secondary to libido frustration, leaves practical psychiatry in much the same position as does the parent problem of heredity versus environment. As a test of objectivity, one may experiment with the reverse hypothesis that libido arises only as a result of mortido frustration; that in puberty, for example, genital sexual desire arises as a substitute for the desire to kill. Many people seem to be dying slowly rather than living. Such trains of thought emphasize that the subject is by no means closed either way. For psychotherapy, the pertinent question is not how much the child was born with, but how much can be modified.

For further information concerning the death instinct, see:

Beyond the Pleasure Principle, by Sigmund Freud. London: International Psychoanalytical Press, 1922.

Man Against Himself, by Karl A. Menninger. New York: Harcourt, Brace, 1956.

For a critical discussion:

New Ways in Psychoanalysis, by Karen Horney. New York: W. W. Norton, 1939. Chapter VII.

The term *mortido* is taken from Paul Federn, and is discussed in:

Ego Psychology and the Psychoses, by Paul Federn. New York: Basic Books, 1952.

Principles of Psychodynamics, by Edoardo Weiss. New York: Grune & Stratton, 1950. Weiss calls it "destrudo."

4. *Mental Mechanisms*

Cf. *Complete Introductory Lectures on Psychoanalysis,* by Sigmund Freud. Chapter XXIII.

The terms *active* and *passive* have never been sufficiently clarified in psychiatric thinking. I have taken a simple view which avoids many of the current ambiguities. The situation is actually more complicated, something like the inflections of a Greek verb.

5. *Instinctual Expression and the Ego*

For a pertinent discussion of some of these problems, see:

Language in Thought and Action, by S. I. Hayakawa, 2d ed. New York: Harcourt, Brace, & World, 1964.

Science and Sanity, by Alfred Korzybski. Lakeville, Conn.: Institute of General Semantics, 1958.

The intimate anatomy of sexual activity is described in *The Human Sexual Response,* by W. H. Masters and V. E. Johnson (Boston: Little, Brown, 1966).

6. *Psychic Growth*

Cf. *Three Contributions to the Theory of Sex,* by Sigmund Freud. New York: Dutton Paperbacks, 1962.

7. *Superego*

Cf. *The Complete Introductory Lectures on Psychoanalysis,* by Sigmund Freud. Chapter XXXI.

8. *Physis*

Our patient's "donkey cart" is similar to the "horse and rider" cited by Freud. The concept of ego states, as elaborated in the chapter on transactional analysis, removes the ambiguities from the phenomenon of self-observation. The view of *phusis,* or *physis,* used here is taken from Gilbert Murray as described in:

Five Stages of Greek Religion, by Gilbert Murray. Garden City, N.Y.: Doubleday Anchor Books, 1955.

Bergson is the best known author on the subject of creative growth, as discussed in:

Creative Evolution, by Henri Bergson. New York: The Modern Library, 1944.

Schopenhauer is among the others who have something to say on this subject. Freud, in *Beyond the Pleasure Principle,* has expressed his disbelief in the existence of such a general creative force, terming it a "pleasing illusion." He himself was none too sure at one time, however, that something like *physis* did not assist Ananke as the motive force in evolution. "This appreciation of the necessities of life," he says, "need not, incidentally, weigh against the importance of 'internal developmental trends,' if such can be shown to be present." (*Complete Introductory Lectures,* p. 355). He seemed to have much more conviction about the death instinct, and later he gave equal weight to Eros and Thanatos. The penetrating glances of some schizophrenics can see clearly the processes of decay in the lives of some of the people around them, and it is their observations which lend credence to the power of the death instinct.

3 _____

THE GROWTH OF THE INDIVIDUAL

1

What is the difference between a grownup and a child?

Grownups are much more like children than children are like grownups. To many children a truck is a Big Car. It takes them a long time to understand that a truck is made to haul goods and a car is made to haul people. Similarly, to many grownups a child is a Small Adult. They do not understand that a child carries different kinds of problems than an adult does. Though a grownup can, does, and should behave at times like a Big Child, a child is not a Small Grownup. The idea that a child is a miniature grownup we may call the *homunculus* idea about children. (*Homunculus* means a cute little fellow.)

How does a child differ from a grownup? A child is helpless. As he grows older, his helplessness grows less, but he still depends upon his parents to show him the proper way to do things. As they show him how to do some things, he has ever new things to learn, but as we have said, he cannot learn to do anything his nervous system is not ready for. The time when the various nerves, such as those to his legs and bowels, ripen depends upon the quality of the nervous system he inherits from his parents. A baby born prematurely may have to be put in an incubator until his body ripens enough so that he can enjoy living in a crib.

The child's images are vague. It is all he can do to tell the outside world from himself. His images grow sharper as he learns to pick things out. After all, grownups have had years of experience to sharpen their images and even then they are not so good at picking out the important things. The child has had no such experience, and accordingly he and his parents must endure and be patient while he is learning.

Minerva Seifuss, for example, was always an extraordinarily

clever child for her age. When she was a toddler, she occasionally upset things, as toddlers do. One time she upset an ashtray and was forcefully told that she must not do it again. To her mother, the important thing about the ashtray was that it contained ashes, but at Minerva's age, clever as she was, her attention was attracted by something more primitive: not what the ashtray contained, but the way it looked. She was eager to please, but she picked out the wrong thing to be impressed with. This particular ashtray was colored a bright blue, and Minerva said to herself, I must please Mother and never upset one of those bright-blue things again. The following day she thought nothing of going ahead and playing with a bright-green ashtray, and as a result she was thoroughly scolded by her mother, who cried: "I told you never to play with an ashtray again!" Minerva was mystified. She had carefully avoided all blue dishes, in accordance with the way she had interpreted her mother's desire, and here she was getting scolded for playing with a green one! When her mother found out what was wrong, she explained: "See, these are ashes. That is what we are interested in about these dishes. An ashtray is something that holds these gray grains. Don't upset anything that has this stuff in it!" Then for the first time Minerva understood that an "ashtray" was not a blue dish, but something that contained gray dust. After that, everything was all right.

If Mother does not appreciate the child's difficulties, and explain things carefully to him in a way that makes it clear exactly what she means, punishments may become quite senseless to him; and if this happens time after time, he may finally give up trying to be good and do as he pleases, since he feels that he will never understand what she wants anyway. He may come to regard punishments as unpredictable "Acts of God," which happen periodically no matter how he tries to behave. Nevertheless he resents them and may go out of his way to revenge himself on his mother. All this might in many cases be avoided by following the example of Mrs. Seifuss and pointing out to him clearly and unmistakably what it is that one wants him to watch out for.

An infant is mostly occupied with the basic things of life, breathing and eating, and these are his concerns before everything else. A grownup knows with some degree of certainty that if conditions are right he will eat when the time comes. The child may feel insecure because he doesn't know what the required conditions are, except that it all depends on Mother. He soon gets the idea that the first guarantee for security from fright and hunger is that his mother should love him, and he begins to make efforts toward winning her love. If he is not sure of it, he becomes anxious and afraid. If his mother does things he cannot understand at his particular age, this can upset him, no matter how clearly she may understand them herself. If she has to interrupt his feeding without a caress to take care of his sick father, it might make him just as afraid as if she had stopped because she didn't care. A frightened child is an unhappy one and a difficult one. If he sees an opportunity to revenge himself for some such scare he may do so. He cannot think clearly enough to realize that such conduct may do him more harm than good.

A child's life is full of shocks and amazing things which we cannot fully appreciate after we grow up. Imagine what a shock it must be to a child to be born! And how surprised he must feel when he first looks at writing! His mother says these black marks are "cat." Well, but he knows that a cat is a furry animal. How can black marks mean the same thing as a furry animal? What an amazing thing that is! He would like to learn more about it.

2

What does a newborn baby think about?

This is really an illogical question, because a newborn baby probably doesn't think at all. His mental life as far as we know consists only of feeling and yearning, and must resemble pure poetry.

The newborn baby has just come through one of the most trying journeys of life, namely, the trip through the birth canal into the outside world, where he is completely dependent on others for his safety and comfort and has no idea how to make his needs known until after he discovers that crying in a certain way will bring help. His heart has to push the blood around his body in an entirely new way because some of the blood vessels used after birth are different from the ones used before, and his circulation is none too efficient at first. Furthermore, he has more need for the nourishing blood, especially in his head, for his brain at this period requires extra blood food for growth. His lungs too may take time to become fully accustomed to their new job, so that breathing also may be a problem.

He must now obtain his nourishment by sucking instead of getting it automatically from his mother's blood, and here also he is handicapped at first if the nerves and muscles concerned in this act are not properly coordinated.

In this situation it helps to bring him back often as nearly as possible to his old prenatal condition. The closest he can come to this now is to be rocked in the arms of his mother while she holds him close to her breast, the source of his food. By this warmth and closeness his yearnings are partly gratified and his anxieties somewhat allayed, and by rocking and fondling him she helps his breathing and circulation.

As his brain grows he becomes more and more able to endure comfortably being away from his mother's arms, and he begins to feel more secure in the world as he understands it better. It is said that the baby who is not fondled and allowed to suck freely takes longer to develop and is more fearful than the baby who is. It is even claimed, as a result of studying the development of hundreds of infants, that the growth of the brain is encouraged if the child is well loved. In some way or another the mother who feels drawn to her child does things better than the one who doesn't. No matter how careful she is to carry out the procedures necessary for the baby's comfort, it is not enough unless she strokes and cuddles him as well. In fact, babies who are not caressed at all have been known to die of deprivation even in the presence of plenty of food and health care.

We should remember that the baby is afraid of the world and is probably yearning for a place to which no one can ever return. He cannot think and has no effective inner way for coping with his fears and desires. While his stomach can be filled from a bottle, his feeling of security and his urge to growth can best be nourished by a mother's embrace.

3

The emotional development of the nursing child

In order to understand the child's emotions during the suckling stage, one must be careful not to make the "homunculus" error by asking: "How should I feel, with my mental equipment, if I were a suckling?" One must inquire instead: "How does an infant feel, with his mental equipment?" We must remember that the child does not have any political views, nor any ideas of modesty, cleanliness, or courtesy, nor any experience of grownup pleasures. The sole guides of his conduct are his primitive yearnings and anxieties.

What is the child's image of the world at this stage? It is a changeable place where "anything can happen" and where terrifying things do happen. Somewhere is something which is warm and loving and makes him feel secure. It also allays his hunger and strokes his skin so that he falls into a refreshing sleep. His greatest security comes from being close to this warm and loving influence. When he is deserted, or his mother's admitted or hidden lack of love makes him feel deserted, he is unhappy. When he is in the arms of his loving mother or can hear her loving tones, he is happy and feels secure.

His strivings at first seem to be mainly along the lines of absorbing: he wants to absorb heat, milk, and love. His image of the world is so vague that these are almost interchangeable. If he can't have milk, he needs more love. If he can't have love, he may want more milk, and he thrives on the infrared rays that his mother's skin gives off.

Sucking is his first "social" activity, that is, the first activity after birth which involves another person for the best results. It almost seems as though each child was born with a need to do a certain minimum amount of sucking, and if he doesn't do it earlier he will do it later. (The same applies to the pecking urges of young chicks and the sucking of pups.) Sucking the breast may often satisfy more of this need in a given time than any other kind of sucking. If feeding fails to satisfy completely this desire, he may try to make up the difference in some other way, such as sucking his thumb between feedings. If that is not effective, this very early and strong mouth anxiety may remain active in later years, though as he grows older he may no longer be aware of this tension.

Conscious or unconscious, it continues to strive for satisfaction, and continues to affect his behavior through this striving. He may try to stay "on the bottle" whichever way he can that society and his own self-respect will permit, whether by sucking on a pipe or by drinking out of another kind of bottle. He may be able to keep this desire entirely out of sight in normal times, realizing deep within himself that he has not yet grown out of it, until something disappoints him. Then, if he is unable to do anything about the disappointment of the moment, he may turn back and try to make up for it by indulgence in the first great ambition of his life, his infantile desire for using his mouth. So when disappointed, many individuals turn to excessive smoking, drinking, eating, or some other mouth activity, preferably one which relieves many other tensions besides the one we are discussing.

Under good conditions, after a certain time, the minimum infantile sucking desire is more or less satisfied and the baby naturally "outgrows" the breast and the bottle. This may partly depend on the fact that he can begin to control the satisfaction of other tensions as the nervous system develops. He may begin to take more pleasure in handling things with his hands than with his mouth, for example, or the development of the nerves to his bowels and bladder enables him to experience new and strange delights from his mastery of these organs, which now give him more pleasure than sucking.

We can see that the desire to put things into the mouth and suck them is an "approach," and sucking is therefore the first manifestation of libido. The infant largely gratifies his libido through his mouth, which is also the organ he has greatest control over. We can understand that the breast makes him happier than the bottle because the more intimate a relationship is the more directly it gratifies libido. The same tensions that are gratified by being close to his mother at this stage of life will play a part in his desire to be close to other women later.

In both infancy and adult life, direct gratification of libido is accompanied by swelling of certain spongy tissues. During the first few months of infancy there are sponge-like masses present in the mouth which become swollen after breast-feeding (and rarely after bottle feeding). Physically as well as mentally there are resemblances between the libido satisfaction of the suckling and that of the grownup.

Let us now see what effect the nursing situation has on mortido. If his mother, instead of helping him gratify his libido, stands in the way of complete satisfaction by taking away the nipple or the bottle before he is contented, the infant cannot think things out, or stop to ask: "Is this trip necessary, or should she have stayed here with me?" Being thwarted, and being an infant, he immediately seeks other methods of satisfying his tensions, and if he fails to obtain libido satisfaction he seeks mortido relief. (The same applies to other frustrations.)

Lacking control of his limbs, he has few ways of doing this, and no subtlety. Whereas the adult can either run or fight, the infant can do neither. His chief possibility for passive reaction is to lie still and refuse to suck. Sometimes he may even give up trying to digest his food, leading to a dangerous state of malnutrition, even to the often fatal condition known as "marasmus." Many older physicians before the days of modern psychiatry knew by intuition and experience that the best treatment for the kind of "sulking" that caused marasmus was loving, mothering, and breast feeding.

If he reacts actively, he has to do it with the muscles at his disposal, and in the early months the chief ones he can control besides the muscles of sucking are those of breathing and stretching; so when he is "angry" he holds his breath until he gets blue, and stretches his muscles out until they are rigid, to such an extent that he may form an arch with his back.

At a slightly later age, the child may express his anger in a more aggressive way by biting. He may bite his mother's breast hard enough to make it bleed. Here mortido uses the same object as libido to obtain gratification, just as in the case of the man who murders the woman he loves. The most satisfactory way the infant can "eliminate" things at that age is by eating them. Thus, when he wants to make the offending breast disappear, he tries to bite it off (always with the idea that when it has been punished in this way it will reappear again and feed him properly). Fortunately his dental equipment does not usually allow him to get very far.

Nipple biting in some ways is like cannibalism, and this is more than a coincidence. We find that adult cannibals, too, in savage tribes eat with the greatest feeling and ceremony those organs which they consider most important.

The same fateful compulsion that applies to sucking applies also to the infant's destructive impulses. A too intense kind of frustration seems to awaken a definite amount of cruel desire, and if this is not satisfied at the time, it may remain with the Id instincts continually striving to obtain satisfaction throughout the individual's life. Such buried desires hanging over from infancy partly explain why some people can put so much time and energy into being cruel. They have an enormous ungratified mortido tension which is striving for release, and since it can never be fully gratified in civilized society, it is drained off from time to time through partial satisfactions. If an individual or a group discards the civilized veneer, the ugliness may burst out with full force.

The prevention of such unhappy personality formations, which may bring misery in later life to the individual and certainly to those around him, lies in developing methods of child-rearing, the psychotherapy of parents, and possibly partly in the science of biochemistry. Only if he frequently repeats certain forms of objectionable behavior after there is pretty good evidence that his nervous system is ready for something more advanced, should the parents begin to worry about whether something has gone wrong with the child's psychological growth.

While biting due to frustration sometimes occurs, there may be other reasons for biting. For example, the infant may bite as a sign that his biting muscles are ready for action so that he is prepared to give up sucking. It is up to the mother or the doctor to figure out in each case to what extent, if any, biting is due to resentment.

It is said that free feeding and late weaning promote generosity and optimism, and that deprivation and early weaning may encourage stinginess and greed. Richard Wright, in his autobiography *Black Boy,* tells how after a childhood of grim poverty he used to hoard food even after he was sure of getting enough. Early fears haunt and early satisfactions give perpetual confidence and gratitude.

The things mentioned in the last two sections are more fully discussed, in simple terms, in Dr. Margaretha A. Ribble's *The Rights of Infants* (New York: Columbia University Press, 1943).

This is a book which every expectant mother and every mother (and father, too) of a young infant should read.

4

How does the child learn to behave himself?

As the child's nervous system develops he seems to have an urge, which in our way of speaking is based on *physis,* to abandon his old ways of gaining pleasure and use new ones as they become available. In addition, those about him make it necessary that he do whatever he is capable of, since they leave him more and more to his own devices to cope with the problems which life places before him in ever-increasing profusion as he grows older.

If the developments described in the last section proceed normally, the child satisfies his sucking and biting urges and is ready to go on to something else. One of his most important jobs if he is to survive is to learn about the physical universe around him. He has to begin by analyzing the four dimensions of the "space-time continuum" into certain important elements, namely time, space, and gravity.

He learns about these from hard experience. Since gratifications are no longer automatic as they were in the womb, he first has to learn how to wait, and his ability to do this without distress will depend, as we have supposed, upon the efficiency of his brain as a storer of energy. His brain carries him through time.

He later learns that things which should be together in space in order to gratify his wishes are often found apart; he therefore has to learn to walk in order to gratify such wishes. His body carries him through space.

Waiting and walking (or crawling) are two of his most important lessons in the Reality Principle, with speech as a kind of short cut which helps to shorten both time and space by making his wants known to others.

Meanwhile he is also learning about gravity by continual experiment. He finds that if he knocks something over it always falls down, and never up; but sometimes he doesn't appear to accept this as the necessary order of things for quite a while. He may behave as though he thought that sooner or later he might find something that would break this rule—and of course he is right, and that is why we have rockets and aircraft.

His parents are delighted when he learns to walk and talk; there is usually no serious emotional problem here, and his progress along these lines is a matter of encouragement. It is when he is learning to control his bowels and bladder that real trouble begins. He soon realizes that whereas up to this time his parents have had the upper hand, now he is "in the saddle." He discovers that they value his bowel movements, or feces. This is no surprise to him, since he thinks quite highly of them himself. They are the first things which he himself has been able to produce, his very own creation, and therefore very, very important. And how does he know that his parents also value them highly? Simply because they beg for them.

When he sits on his little potty, he knows that his mother will be impatient if he doesn't produce, and delighted if he does. He also knows that she is beginning to get upset if he produces at the wrong time or in the wrong place. So now for the first time he has effective methods for controlling not only people's actions, but their feelings as well, and very important people, too. He can annoy them by producing these valuables at the wrong time or by withholding them when he is expected to produce; and he can please them by producing them at the right time. If we only try to put ourselves in the infant's place, remembering what he knows and does not know, we can realize how powerful he must feel. It is very much as though he had handfuls of gold and his mother wanted money. He likes the look of the yellowish metal himself, and he observes the satisfaction she too shows when it appears. We may compare him at this stage to a mischievous boy who has control of his family's fortune in cash. He can cause them distress by throwing money away or withholding it, and delight by giving it to them when they want it.

So we have the infant on his throne indulging his feelings of the moment: either playing the open-handed monarch and giving his mother what she asks for or punishing her for some real or fancied slight by withholding it or depositing it in the wrong place.

At first the situation is in his favor: he receives much enthusiasm for producing and little punishment for withholding. As he grows older he loses this advantage. Instead of winning love and approval by producing, and losing nothing by not producing, he finds that his generosity and efforts are, alas! beginning to be taken for granted, while any withholding meets with increasing disapproval (the fate of all generous monarchs). Instead of winning by producing, he now loses by not producing. How many times throughout his life is this shift to occur! Thus for the first time, at a tender age, he meets with ingratitude.

In the beginning the child complies because his mother, whose love he wants to hold, is standing over him. Later occurs one of the most amazing things in all nature. He behaves as he thinks his mother would want him to behave, even if she isn't there!* In other words, he begins to act in accordance with her directing image, so that the reality is no longer necessary to guide his behavior. At first this image may be conscious, but as the years go by it sinks deeper and deeper into the unconscious so that the bowel habits become more and more automatic.

This image of the mother waiting for the feces, which the infant gradually incorporates into his unconscious personality and which for the rest of his life has the same effect as though his mother were nearby, is one of the first items to make up the Superego. It is accompanied by an image of himself as a good boy, that is, a boy who behaves in such a way as to gratify his mother and his own growth urge, or *physis,* and this is one of the first items in his Ego Ideal, the ideal self he would like to be.

The establishment of bowel habits thus depends on the growth of the nervous system and the development of the Superego, including the Ego Ideal. Lapses will occur mostly when resentment is aroused and mortido tension becomes strong enough to overcome the regulating forces of the Superego, usually on account of some real or fancied hurt or deprivation of love. Mortido satisfaction may then be gained either actively or passively. He may be a stubborn little fellow who will actively withhold the gifts and refuse to move his bowels for days on end unless the frustration is removed or the love restored; or he may give up trying to control himself and passively allow accidents to happen. He gets an

---

* It is noteworthy that other mammals besides humans seem to have the ability to form a "Superego" by a similar process of introjection. Such animals make good pets because they can be trusted. Other animals are performers rather than pets, because they can be "trained" but not trusted.

additional satisfaction from "accidents" when he comes to know the meaning of "dirty," because he then realizes that his mother is humiliated and punished by having to clean up after him.

These two patterns of revenge and mortido satisfaction are often carried into later life by people whose personalities remain partly fixed at the bowel level of behavior, or as it is called, the "anal stage." Of course their Ego Ideals do not allow them to act as crudely as they did when they were infants, but their behavior shows the same characteristics. Such people show spite and resentment in one of two ways: either by messing things up, literally or figuratively, which is a rather easy way requiring little apparent originality, control, or determination; or by being stubborn, withholding things, and trying to control the situation in a petty way which is more annoying than threatening—as if to say, "Things will happen in just the order which I determine, even if you win in the end." If they are more determined, however, they may be the ones who win in the end.

If "anal mortido" is not able to get sufficient satisfaction in childhood, it may remain as the main driving force of the personality, instead of showing itself only on special occasions. This results in two adult types of "anal" personalities which may occur in pure form or mixed with each other: the "passive" or messy type, exhibiting untidiness and apparent lack of determination, perhaps suffering from diarrhea or colitis; and the "active" or orderly type, showing stubbornness, stinginess, too much fussiness about details in thought and action without regard to what is actually being accomplished, and often suffering from constipation.

If we compare the anal way of gratifying mortido with the "oral" way of earlier days, we can see how different are these two stages of development. "Passive" oral resentment is shown by not eating and getting sick, "passive" anal resentment by messiness; "active" oral anger expresses itself by cruel biting, "active" anal spite by stubbornness and withholding, and sometimes by its own kind of cruelty as well.

The reasons why some people are strongly attracted to one or other of these early phases of development and show thinly disguised anal or oral ways of reacting in adult life are not clearly understood. While such checks in growth can usually be connected with unsatisfied tensions hanging over from infancy, constitution also seems to play a part. This is most obvious in some kinds of anal personalities, who are typically of a decided ectomorphic build, and perhaps it is significant that ectomorphs often suffer from fallen stomach and intestines. Viscerotonics are often oral types, according to certain writers.

Old Mr. Krone, with whom we are already acquainted as one of Nana's victims, was almost a pure anal type. A decided ectomorph, he was tall, thin, and gangling, with long awkward legs and a long face. His neck was scrawny, his ears stuck out, and the corners of his mouth turned down. His posture was stiff, his movements were jerky, and his skin was thin and gray. He never had any friends, because he was more interested in his bowels and his budget than he was in other people.

Mr. Krone had a good income, but he was miserly and lived on bread and tea in a tiny room on Railroad Avenue. Every day he had the same meals at the same time in the same corner, and every day he put his dishes back in exactly the same place. His mornings he spent fussing about in the bathroom, his afternoons calculating his expenses for the previous day, and his evenings going over his old ledgers from former years and looking through his collection of magazines.

Twice a week for the last thirty years, old Mr. Krone, who was nearly seventy, had visited Dr. Nagel to complain about his bowels. He had been constipated all his life, and in his cupboard was a shelf containing rows of laxatives. The only variation in his life before Nana came to live with him was changing over to a different medicine every few days. One was too powerful, the next was not powerful enough, and another took too long to act. On each visit to the doctor he described his bowel movements in great detail, sometimes proudly and sometimes regretfully, depending upon how original and powerful he thought they were, while the physician, as the well-known medical writer Dr. Harry Beckman remarks, was supposed to be comparing them mentally with the standard bowel movement kept under glass with the standard meter stick in the archives in Paris.

Mr. Krone had a hobby, which was sorting out and mutilating with a pencil pictures of naked women in his magazines, and an amusement, which was pinching very precisely the buttocks of prostitutes. The cost of these diversions, including bus fare, he noted in his ledger along with his other expenses, and at a moment's notice he could open his cupboard and look up the exact amount he had spent on pinching in 1937. When Mr. Krone became ill, he was too stubborn to let Dr. Nagel examine him, and he finally died of cancer of the rectum.

Mr. Krone illustrates clearly the characteristics of an anal personality: stubbornness, stinginess, orderliness of a fussy kind, cruelty, and an undue interest in his bowels, which gave him his greatest pleasure.

He shows us that the bowels can be used to gratify libido as well as mortido. The infant takes an unsophisticated pleasure in his bowel movements. He enjoys his mastery of his own body and he enjoys his "creating," since this is his main "creative" activity and he can see the results. Sometimes he even likes to play with what he has created. In adults we see such frank bowel joys mainly in mental illness, when childlike interests reveal themselves more clearly, and in dreams, where the same thing occurs. Psychological analysis enables normal people to detect such tendencies in their everyday activities in disguised form. Accompanying the anal characteristics we have already described we often find certain other interests: buttocks, backs, rears of all kinds, including rear doors, and a preference for bathroom jokes rather than bedroom jokes. There is also some connection at times between anal interests and homosexuality.

The important things in this section are, first, the possibility of something going wrong during the anal stage of development in the second and third years of life which may affect the behavior of the individual when he grows up; and, secondly, the connection of the anal stage with the formation of the Superego and Ego Ideal, by acceptance of the mother's image as a guide in place of the real mother so that the child continues to behave as his parents would have liked long after they have vanished from his life. (Since it is usually the mother who gives the child his toilet training, we have spoken mostly of her. If it is the father who has this job, or if both parents take part, the same general ideas apply.) The main thing to avoid during this stage, and later on too, is giving a child regular enemas.

5

The little boy and the little girl

It now behooves us to transport ourselves to Brschiss, an eastern land full of giants, dwarfs, troglodytes, astomi, caprimulges, cynocephali, camelopards, and other wonderful creatures described by Pliny, sSanang sSetsen, Alcofribas, and Cyprian St. Cyr in his book *Letters to my Wife's Maid.*

The Brschissians are a warlike people who have slaughtered all the foreigners for a hundred miles around, and they are so inbred that their people suffer from strange afflictions. As a result of this, says St. Cyr, both sexes have the same sexual organs, but they differ in that the males have long noses and the females have no noses at all. Because of this, their religion makes much account of noses, which have become sacred objects and sacred parts of the body. For this reason, every Brschissian from earliest childhood wears a sort of half mask over the nose and cheeks, called a "cashney." Grownups are never supposed to see the opposite sex without their cashneys until they are married, and children of opposite sexes are not allowed to peek.

If the children of Brschiss ask about cashneys, they are told that they will understand when they grow up. Meanwhile they are taught not to pick their noses or fiddle with them, and are sometimes severely punished if they do. Some little boys are even threatened with having their noses cut off if they touch them.

Naturally, the children are curious about what is under the cashneys of the opposite sex. Some of them also take a special delight in breaking the rules which the adults are trying to teach them, though they feel guilty and a little afraid when they finger and pick their noses. And eventually, in spite of the strict supervision, they do get to see the difference between the two sexes. When a little boy discovers that girls have no noses, he wonders why, and the only explanation he can think of at that age is that they have been cut off for some misdeed, in the same way that his parents may have threatened to punish him. This gives him a good scare, especially if he has been breaking the rules. The girls on their part feel injured and envious, and may blame their parents for their inferior status in life. Just as a jungle man has to imagine that a hurricane is the result of something he has done to bring on the wrath of the gods, so the child explains things in terms of his relationships to the powerful beings around him, his parents, and feels that his situation depends upon their good will or ill will.

This description of the sacred nose lore of Brschiss has a kind of parallel in our own country where little boys and girls have similar noses, but different sexual organs. When they discover this difference, their feelings are often much the same as those described in the children of Brschiss. The boys may become frightened and the girls envious. Usually, they do not discuss these reactions with their parents, especially if they have been brought up almost from birth to hide their feelings about such things. The more upset they are, the more reluctant they may be to mention it, and to remember the details in later years. Often a soldier who experiences a great emotional shock in battle cannot remember without psychiatric help the details of what happened or how deeply it affected him. In the same way children, if they are deeply upset by their discoveries about the sexual organs, tend to push the whole matter out of their minds, or at least the emotions connected with their discovery. It may take a careful psychiatric analysis to reveal the hidden power of the buried fear or envy which, without their being aware of it, has been influencing their conduct. The boy may have begun to act as though his penis might be cut off if he did not behave or was too daring, while the girl may have felt resentful, as if she had once had a penis which her parents had cut off for some misdeed when she was a little baby.

Of course the boy's pride (and fear) about his penis, and the girl's envy (and resentment) vary in different individuals. But if we dig down deeply enough into the mind of a man we generally find some anxiety about the sexual organ left over from childhood, usually a fear that if he does certain things, especially things his father or father-image would not like, he may lose his penis and become like a girl; while in the woman's mind we find traces of her penis-envy—sometimes quite conscious—or perhaps of her original resentment against her parents.

It is evident that if there is such a tension as penis-envy in certain women, it can never be satisfied directly, and therefore has to be satisfied indirectly by getting something else that boys don't have. The most natural way to do this is by having babies, which, after all, are things boys cannot have; furthermore, a boy can have only one penis, while a woman can have many babies. Some women, however, avoid such feminine acquisitions as babies, and try to beat the man at his own game in order to assuage their envy, which brings them into a business or profession where they will be in direct competition with the opposite sex. If a woman's choice of occupation is based on such penis-envy, she will eventually become unhappy, because she will be frustrating the tension of her *physis,* which is urging her toward a feminine line of development.

In many individuals, especially timid men and aggressive women, such fears and envies may play an important part among the many aspects of the personality. The discovery of sex differences is another problem for the child to work out in his or her own mind. If the experience leaves little or no permanent wound it will cause no trouble in the future. If it is an emotional problem which he or she cannot solve at the time it may cause troubles in later life.

6
Getting along with people

The child is not born with a knowledge of how to get along in the world but must learn this from others. Up to the age of two or thereabouts he is so interested in getting to know his own body that he has little time or energy for paying attention to how his behavior affects other people—just so he gets what he wants when he wants it. At about that age, however, he begins to see that getting satisfaction is no longer merely a question of asking for it, but depends partly upon whether his parents are pleased with him or not. In order to find out how to handle them, he watches how they handle each other. What he learns in the next three years, from two to five, will largely determine for life how he uses his energy to handle people (unless he goes out of his way later to take lessons from his teachers, friends, wife, or psychiatrist). Though his brothers and sisters play an important part also, we shall not speak of them here, in order to keep things as simple as possible.

His parents are the handiest teachers and they are the ones the child is most anxious to get along with, so he learns most from them. If he has no parents, or only one parent, he is handicapped because later he will be competing with people who have had two parents to learn from. That is one important reason why it is a great advantage for the child to be brought up by his two parents. A child who speaks proper English all through his early years will feel more at ease with it later than one who starts to study it at the age of fifteen. Similarly a child who is brought up with a good man in the house will usually get along better with men when he grows up than a boy who is raised fatherless. The latter may make up his disadvantage later, but he has had a faulty start.

The baby is innocent of the ways of social behavior, and his fate lies with his family. If he sees them continually quarreling and grabbing, this usually encourages him to be aggressive and grabbing likewise. He says to himself, so to speak:

"I see that the way to get along in the world is to be aggressive, fight and grab." Then he is likely to grow up that way. If he finds it hard to get what he wants, he often blames the world for that, and his resentment makes him even grabbier.

If, on the other hand, he sees his parents get along by affection, generosity, and consideration, his own generosity is nourished, and he says to himself:

"I see that the way people get along in the world is by love, consideration, and generosity." So he tries it out, and if it does not always work as well as he thought it would, he may be willing to learn from experience.

Although the child may decide for himself in which ways and how much he imitates his parents, nevertheless they have it in their power to reinforce or discourage his various possibilities. They can encourage his greedy tendencies or his considerate tendencies, and his capacity to be agreeable or his capacity to be disagreeable. If he does not take the direction they think they are showing him, then the manner of his upbringing may have to be reconsidered.

The little child is the center of his own universe. If one watches him carefully one cannot help seeing that most of his affection goes to people who satisfy his immediate needs for him. This system of returning affection only for immediate favors cannot go on forever if he is to raise his own children in the most desirable way. In order to win and live happily with the prospective mother of his children in years to come, and raise his offspring in a happy household, he will have to learn to give his greatest love without hope of immediate reward. Instead of regarding people as sources of satisfaction to himself, he is going to have to love them "for themselves alone." This applies equally to both sexes. We call such unselfish love "object love," while the love which people have for things that give them immediate satisfaction is very much like self-love.

In this latter way of thinking the child behaves like a person in love with himself. This reminds us of the Greek legend of Narcissus, who fell in love with his own image when he saw it reflected in a pool of water. We therefore call libido directed inwardly toward the self, *narcissistic* libido, and libido directed outwardly toward outside objects, *object* libido. We can then say that the task of childhood should be to turn narcissistic libido into object libido. This is necessary in order to be happy living among other people, and is especially necessary for successful marriage and parenthood, since in these situations the individual is going to have to love, cherish, and take care of outside beings even at some sacrifice to himself. His Superego helps him in this unselfish task.

Thus the formation of the Superego in infancy, with its feelings of "duty" and responsibility, lays the groundwork for the later job of marriage and parenthood. After the Superego is pretty well under way there is a period from about six to about ten years of age, when the child has more or less learned how to find his place in the world, but cannot as yet take care of himself without the protection of grownups. These years he spends in learning more about the people and things around him, so that when his muscles are strong and his glands begin to work full blast at puberty, he will be more ready to cope on his own with whatever arises.

7

When does sex begin?

There are so many people who can remember distinctly sexual feelings from the age of three or earlier that there can be no doubt in the mind of anyone willing to think about such feelings that infants can have sexual experiences in the ordinary sense of the word. Those who say that sex does not begin until the first orgasm will have a hard time explaining such early thrills. We cannot attribute to mere curiosity the incidents between little boys and little girls which take place behind barns and in haystacks which they find so intriguing at the time, and often also in looking back.

The affectionate relationships of early years are similar in quality to those of later life. We can call the love relationships of the infant "sexual" even though there is no orgasm (although there often is erection). The normal voluptuous feelings of a grownup are only the fourth stage in a lifelong development.

The two earliest methods of direct libido satisfaction we are already acquainted with: they consist of sucking pleasure and bowel pleasure, which we call for the sake of convenience "oral" and "anal" satisfactions. During the third stage, gratification consists of pleasure derived from the sexual organs without the real participation of another person, that is without real object libido, and takes place commonly through handling play, which can frequently be seen in children between the fourth and sixth years. Many adults remain fixed at this stage, merely "using" their partners to obtain pleasure rather than sharing pleasure with them. Thus we have promiscuous men who merely use women as "seminal spittoons," and women who use men as "vaginal tampons"; in both cases the individual is not concerned, except from vanity, with how much happiness the partner obtains.

In lucky or wise people, the adult fourth stage of sexuality is reached, which consists of a sharing of pleasure with another person, and not merely in using a partner for the purpose of having one's sexual organs stimulated. Adult male sexual feeling consists of a desire to penetrate in order to give as well as get pleasure. Adult female sexuality is based on a desire to accept and be penetrated so that pleasure can be given as well as received. This applies also to giving and accepting material things as well as to "emotional penetration."

The difference between the third and fourth stages is more clearly shown in women. In the third stage they get their pleasure chiefly from the little penis that they have on the outside of their bodies, called the clitoris, and are mostly interested in having that organ stimulated. In the adult stage they get their greatest pleasure from the vagina, which can be used much more effectively to give pleasure to a male partner.

We also find on careful investigation that in some ways the sexual act gratifies mortido as well as libido. In the male, penetration suggests not only getting as close as possible, which is libidinous, but also destruction, which is mortidinous. In the female being penetrated also gratifies both drives.

Sometimes the mortidinous satisfactions in the sexual relationship become more important to the individual than the libidinous ones, so that he gets an abnormal amount of pleasure from inflicting or suffering pain before and during his sexual activities. If his mortido tension is on the active side he will find excuses to inflict mental or physical punishment on his sexual partner. If his mortido tension is passive, he will manage to get himself into a position where she has good reason to make him suffer mentally or physically, and will somehow encourage her to do so. If an active, sadistic man or woman meets a passive, masochistic partner, they will each have a golden opportunity to relieve their mortido tensions through consciously planned physical suffering or less consciously encouraged mental suffering. Whipping parties with actual physical flagellation are not uncommon, and are even advertised in certain magazines. Still more common, and easier to observe, are men and women who manage to arrange their love relationships so that again and again they get active or passive mortido gratification through emotional cruelty or suffering, apparently "never learning" from one experience to the next. The fact is that they do not want to learn, since if they ever did "learn," they might have to give up the gratifications.

Alecta Abel was the daughter of Prete Abel, who owned the slaughterhouse down by the Olympia freight yards. Her father had such bad luck with his marriage, his children, and his business, that Mr. Weston, the Episcopal minister, told him he must have "the mark of Abel" on his forehead, since the Lord seemed to have chosen him to be a born victim like his Biblical namesake. Mr. Abel's ill fortune, however, was always helped along by outside circumstances.

Alecta's life seemed to follow the same pattern, but with one important difference: she brought most of her troubles on herself.

Her first husband was a sober man and a good provider, but she must have found this boring, because she began to be unfaithful to him, so he left her. Alecta claimed that she was devoted to their little daughter, but she nevertheless continued to live a dissolute life, which did not help the child's emotional development. One day an old friend told Alecta that her husband was having her watched by detectives so that he could get custody of the child. Alecta was panic-stricken, but that very night she went home with a man she picked up in a bar. When the divorce came to court, her daughter was taken from her until such time as she could prove her fitness to have custody.

For her second husband, she chose Dion Chusbac, a drunkard who beat her regularly. They also had a daughter whom Alecta seemed devoted to and again, because of her promiscuous behavior, she lost custody, this time to her mother-in-law, Mrs. Chusbac senior. Her third husband was not only a drunkard and a hypochondriac, but he also had syphilis. She knew before she married him that he had the disease and was not taking proper treatment. She now spent her time between nursing him and drudging to supply him with money for liquor. Because of his condition, they had to go to Nevada, which does not require a blood test, in order to get married—a long way to go in search of misery.

Alecta Abel was not a stupid nor an evil woman. Both her reason and her ideals were in violent and continual protest against her conduct, but her inwardly directed mortido took over periodically nevertheless, leading her closer and closer to self-destruction. Dr. Nagel, who was a friend of her father's and had known her since childhood, finally prevailed upon her to go for psychiatric treatment, which, fortunately, was successful. In order for her to get better, it was necessary to give up the gruesome satisfactions of doing as her father did, and find her own way in a pleasanter kind of world. She now lives quietly in the neighboring town of Arcadia with her third child.

This is an extreme and horrifying example of "moral masochism" and self-punishment on the part of a woman, and of both physical and "moral" sadism or cruelty on the part of two of her husbands, which in milder forms make thousands of men, women, and children miserable throughout their lives. In Alecta's case, her need to destroy herself was based partly on a project to be like her unlucky father—that is, she "identified" herself with him. A careless observer might have said that she "inherited" her bad luck.

8

How does the child react to his parents' behavior?

There has been much study of the boy's preference for his mother and the girl's preference for her father. The subject is complicated because the mother is usually gentle and the father sterner, the mother indulgent and the father firm, and because the mother gives nourishment to both sons and daughters in the early stages of life and often in the later stages also. In order to understand clearly the child's true feelings toward his parents, one has to be a very keen observer or meet an unusually frank child. Another way is to dig up the adult's buried memories of his emotional development. Fortunately, the people of Brschiss live in such a way that they offer us an easier way of studying this problem.

As we remember, there are giants and dwarfs in Brschiss, and these have special households where the women are of normal size, and each family consists of a giant, a dwarf, and a woman. Each dwarf lives with the woman he loves, who returns his affection, but there are no direct sexual relationships between them. He spends most of his time in her company; he has nothing else to do, as their giant takes care of all the responsibilities.

During the day, the dwarf's happiness is quite undisturbed as he follows the woman about while she does her housework, petting her occasionally and being caressed and jollied in return. In the early evening, the trouble begins. Every day at 5:17 P.M. their giant, about nine feet tall and wearing size 24 shoes, comes tramping into the house. The lovely housewife (all women are beautiful in Brschiss) immediately "deserts" the dwarf and runs to meet the newcomer, embracing him warmly while the dwarf looks on. From that moment, the woman gives the giant most of her attention. The dwarf is sent to bed right after supper; and as he lies there he can hear the other two talking quietly to each other in the next room, until finally they too go to bed (sometimes even in the same room where the dwarf is, if they are poor or untidy). He can hear them now talking and giggling as they lie in bed together, until after a while other strange sounds take over which he does not understand very well except that they seem serious and powerful.

In some cases the poor dwarf is sadly confused by all this. He loves the woman, and he loves the giant as well, since the latter takes care of all his material needs and treats him with consideration and affection in most things; nevertheless he may be unable to help feeling resentful at the setup. In spite of his good intentions and his feeling that he is wicked for doing so, he gradually comes to feel more and more jealous of the giant and wishes that he would permanently forget to come home. There isn't a thing he can do about it, really, because that is the way people live in Brschiss, according to St. Cyr, and there is nobody he can talk to. People would either laugh or get angry at him for resenting what everybody knows is a perfectly normal and happy household. He is so ashamed of himself that he daren't even discuss it with the dwarf next door. He wouldn't know how to begin talking about it. He almost feels at times that the giant would be justified in cutting his nose off and making him look like a girl for having such ungrateful feelings. The dwarf is also jealous of little girls and boys, if any of them are born into the family.

Knowing that his feelings are wrong doesn't change them, however. In spite of himself, as the months go by and he realizes that he isn't getting any younger, he begins to get sulky and loses his appetite. The other two don't understand this. To them the arrangement seems perfectly natural, and it wouldn't occur to them that the dwarf could be jealous. They wouldn't believe he was capable of feeling that way toward them. The woman says to the giant: "I don't know what on earth has come over the dear boy lately." They try to persuade him to eat, but he stubbornly refuses. After a while they give up and ignore him, letting him eat or not, as he pleases. That only makes him feel worse. He begins to go off by himself and brood. His stomach starts to hurt every evening when 5:17 approaches. He manages to contain his feelings for quite a while, but one Saturday they explode. He begins to shout, trips and falls to the floor, and lies there thrashing his arms and legs around, screaming at the woman, the giant, and his own helplessness and shame. Then he weeps bitterly at his own undignified behavior, and that night he doesn't go to sleep until dawn, lying there listening to the other two. From then on he has trouble sleeping. He frequently has nightmares and also begins to walk in his sleep, usually ending up in the other bedroom.

This dwarf is obviously letting his feelings run away with him. The dwarf next door has the same problem, but he manages to accept things much more gracefully. Instead of kicking up a rumpus, he "adjusts" to the situation. While we are not sure just what "adjust" means, we know that it means something, since those who adjust when it is necessary are more contented and agreeable people than those who don't. Perhaps it has something to do with the flexibility of the individual's images. Adjustment is another of those things in nature, like magnetism, which we know more about from its effects than from understanding what it actually is.

Since the dwarf is so dependent on the woman for his comfort and affection, his reaction to the nightly home-coming of the giant is the most important event in his emotional life, and usually has more to do with his happiness, says St. Cyr, than money, outside success, or what he learns at school, and in the end will have more to do with his behavior and his reactions to other events, than any of these things.

The average boy in an average home in America or anywhere else reacts in much the same way as the dwarfs of Brschiss to what goes on in the household. The fact that the American giants are a little smaller, usually under six feet, and the dwarfs a little younger, only three or four years old, doesn't really change the situation much from the dwarf's point of view. Either he will have to adjust, or he will begin to lose his appetite and sulk, have temper tantrums and stomach-aches, and suffer from anxiety, insomnia, nightmares, and sleepwalking.

If he reacts in a damaging way to this early problem, we may suppose that sometimes he will react similarly to later problems, perhaps with the same pattern: loss of appetite, irritability, stomach trouble, insomnia, and nightmares; his reactions to the father-giant and the "deserting" mother may persist and leave traces in his behavior for the rest of his life. If he succeeds later in changing his images of his parents, so that the father-image ceases to be that of a giant-rival, and his mother-image is altered from that of a deserting woman, he will be able to grow beyond these problems and become interested in other things. But if he is unable to change these childhood images, and spends the rest of his life acting in accordance with them and trying to solve the situation they present, they will take up much of his energy. He may spend his time eternally seeking a woman who will not look at another man; or eternally seeking feminine conquests, like Don Juan, in an attempt to excel his father; or perhaps if the image of the father-rival is stronger than that of his unappreciative mother, he will react by beating up strangers on the barroom floor, to prove to himself and his father-image that he could have licked the old boy if he hadn't been such a coward when he was little.

We can see that there is object displacement of libido and mortido in these cases, since it is really his mother whom he wants to win and his father whom he wants to beat up. In any case, being so intently interested in proving himself, he will have less time and energy left for the world's work.

In the case of girls, though the situation is more complicated, a similar period of emotional adjustment or maladjustment has to be lived through, and the results of their solution of the turmoil show themselves in adult life in similar ways, allowing for the difference in sex. Girls spend less time with their fathers than boys do with their mothers, and therefore the problem of growing up to become interested in the opposite sex is different in the two cases. Boys associate closely with the opposite sex from infancy, while girls usually do not (leaving out the question of sisters and brothers, who add more complications). In addition, in a typical case, the boy receives nourishment from the opposite sex and stern reprimands from the same sex, while with girls the situation is not quite the same. In the long run, however, the results of bad management on the part of the parents are not too dissimilar in the two sexes, so that there are girls who flit about from man to man and girls who despise all women. Another complication has already been mentioned: boys get their chief sexual pleasure from the penis from earliest infancy, while somewhere along the line the girl not only has to transfer her affections from the same sex to the opposite one, but also has to shift her ways of gaining sexual pleasure from the clitoris to the vagina if she is to obtain complete gratification from her libido tensions.

By the time the child is four his main patterns of reacting have begun to take form; he has already shown how he is going to behave when something makes him happy or unhappy. Most children are perplexed by family life for a while, but eventually they adjust. In neurotic children, awakened mortido may be turned either outward or inward, so that the child either makes trouble for others when he is unhappy or else keeps his unhappiness inside and bothers only himself. Some express their unhappiness mostly during the day, others chiefly at night. So we have the "nasty" child who sleeps soundly, and the docile child who suffers from nightmares, bedwetting, and sleepwalking.

The earlier a pattern is established, the harder it is to change afterward. Though later adventures can make some changes in the personality, much of the child's happiness as he or she grows up depends upon how well his parents handled the ticklish "Oedipus situation" between the beloved baby and the beloved giant. If the child can be made to feel that he is one of a threesome, rather than the third wheel on a two-wheeled bicycle, he will usually make a happy adjustment. One should no more be affectionate in front of a child without letting him have his share than eat in front of him while he remains hungry. Since he cannot always be included, however, he learns to be a good sport. For example, he realizes that he really does have to get more sleep than his parents.

After childhood, the next period of strain is during adolescence. When the boy gets socially interested in girls his troubles begin anew. If he doesn't have the personality or the physical requirements to attract girls, they will desert him for other fellows who do. If he resented deeply his mother's nightly "desertion" when he was an infant, the new desertions will make him more unhappy and bitter. He may be too easily discouraged. But if his parents kept him feeling happy and wanted when he was little, though his new troubles may cause him disappointment, they will not embitter him; nor will he give up easily, for he has a good foundation. The feeling that his mother loved him will give him more confidence with the girls and he may develop himself in some way which will overshadow any drawbacks, particularly with girls of more than average good sense. The same applies to the relationships between a plain girl and the boys she meets later in life.

On the other hand, there is the case of the boy who grows up to be very attractive. In this instance, childhood bitterness at "losing" his mother may be diluted, though perhaps never washed away, by his later successes. But if both his mother, in infancy, and his girl friends, in adolescence, are won too easily, he may find it difficult to accomplish anything which requires effort. Many seductive women are of this type. They easily "won" their fathers from their mothers when they were babies, and they easily win boy friends when they grow up. The result is that some are content to sit back and let good things come to them as a consequence of their physical attractions, so that they never try to develop their personalities in a healthy way and have no genuine interests outside their own bodies. When they grow old and lose their drawing power, they are surprised and hurt if life begins to pass them by, and their old age becomes a period of frustration and failure instead of one of mellowing outlook and perfected accomplishments.

Another period of stress occurs when the individual has to begin to earn his own living and make an economic adjustment. Here again, early attitudes can be reinforced or weakened, though it is doubtful if they can be fundamentally changed. Easy money does not make truly kind men out of resentful ones, nor does hard work easily embitter loving people. But the man who was embittered in childhood by his parents or foster parents may grow more bitter when he does not do as well financially as those he envies, while the man whose parents made him happy in his infancy, if his later efforts are rewarded justly, will continue to feel happy and grateful as well.

The bitter infant who later rises through chance or talent may use his money in a bitter way, to make others envious, and his power in a cruel way, to make others suffer for his own revenge and satisfaction, while the happy infant who later cannot make a decent living because of outside circumstances may use his hardship as an example of unnecessary suffering, and seek just security not only for himself, but for his fellow men.

Marriage and parenthood are tests of personality stability and of the effectiveness of the individual's early upbringing. In wartime, situations of various kinds will reveal hidden strengths and weaknesses which have remained covered up under the ordinary opportunities and strains of civilian life. The change of life in women, and the decline of physical power in men in later years, are further periods of stress when a sound infancy will stand the individual in good stead.

Thus are secure and insecure infants strengthened and weakened as they go through life.

The clever and beautiful need not be proud, since they did nothing to earn their advantages. The slow and homely need not be ashamed, since they did nothing to deserve their fate. The hateful need not be blamed, since they did not make themselves hateful; nor need the loving be praised, for the same reason. But the hateful can be blamed for not restraining their hatred, and the loving can be praised for expressing their love.

Footnotes for Philosophers, Chapter Three

1. *Adult and Child*

An account of what is to be expected in the behavior of the child at different ages is given in various books by Gesell and his associates from the Yale Clinic of Child Development; for example:

Infant and Child in the Culture of Today, by Arnold L. Gesell. New York: Harper & Brothers, 1943.

The works of Piaget have a more Gallic charm, however, and are now easy to obtain. For example:

The Language and Thought of the Child, by Jean Piaget. New York: Meridian Books, 1955.

For an excellent selection of many different viewpoints and findings regarding human development, see:

Human Development: Selected Readings, by M. L. Haimowitz and N. R. Haimowitz, 2d ed. New York: Thomas Y. Crowell, 1966.

See also the government pamphlets *Your Child from One to Six* and *Your Child from Six to Twelve,* both put out by the Children's Bureau of the HEW Administration. These and others may be obtained from the Superintendent of Documents, U.S. Government Printing Office, Washington, D.C. 20025, for about 25¢ each, although prices may change from time to time.

2. and 3. *Newborn Infant and Suckling*

Further discussion about the inner tensions of the infant, and the beneficial effects of suckling, loving, and rocking, can be found in Margaretha A. Ribble's *The Personality of the Young Child* (New York: Columbia University Press, 1955). Compare also René A. Spitz, *No and Yes: On the Genesis of Human Communication.* New York: International Universities Press, 1957.

There is disagreement as to the instinctual meaning of infantile nipple-biting. The viewpoint presented here fits in best with the theoretical framework.

4. *Oral and Anal Erotism*

Here again the ambiguity of the terms *active* and *passive* is apparent. The classical exposition of the psychosexual development of the child is Freud's "Three Contributions to the Theory of Sex," which can be found in *The Basic Writings of Sigmund Freud,* already referred to. For many interesting ideas about the psychology of space, time, geometry, and physics, consult:

Mind, by Paul Schilder. New York: Columbia University Press, 1942. Chapters 12, 13, 14, and 22.

In regard to the libidinal aspects of space structuring, see my article: "The Psychological Structure of Space, with Some Remarks on Robinson Crusoe," *Psychoanalytic Quarterly,* Vol. 25, pp. 510–520 (1956).

5, 6, and 7.

The processes of libido development outlined in these sections are summarized in more orthodox and systematic form in Freud's readable little book, *An Outline of Psychoanalysis* (New York: W. W. Norton, 1949). The influence of cultural factors on these developments is discussed by Erikson. He also discusses the relationship between structure and function, or as he more aptly terms them, zones and modes, in instinctual development.

Childhood and Society, by Erik H. Erikson. New York: W. W. Norton, 1964. Revised edition.

What in our terms would be manifestations of mortido in young children are illustrated in:

Hostility in Young Children, by A. L. Korner. New York: Grune & Stratton, 1949.

8. *The Oedipus Complex*

The development of the Oedipal situation and the child's relationships to his parents and siblings were beautifully described in

The Psychoanalytic Study of the Family, by J. C. Flugel. London: The Hogarth Press, 1939. (First printed in 1921.)

See also: *The Oedipus Complex: Cross-Cultural Evidence,* by W. N. Stephens. New York: The Free Press, 1962.

For a study of the later psychological development of the female read:

The Psychology of Women, by Helene Deutsch, 2 vols. New York: Grune & Stratton, 1944 and 1945.

Volume 1 deals with girlhood, puberty, and adolescence. Volume 2 deals with motherhood in a variety of aspects, including adoptive mothers, unmarried mothers, and stepmothers.

See also *The Feminine Mystique,* by Betty Friedan. New York: W. W. Norton, 1963.

Years ago I used the esoteric Brschiss legend in expounding the Oedipus complex. Subsequently I discovered that a surprisingly similar tale of a child, a giant, and a woman is part of the Norse folklore, in the story of "The Blue Belt," which is sometimes included in children's books of fairy tales. Brschiss, incidentally, is a mythical land of Mongolian folklore (R. H. Bush), and sSanang sSetsen is a native historian of Mongolia.

4

DREAMS AND THE UNCONSCIOUS

1

What is the unconscious?

We have heard a good deal about the "unconscious." Let us now try to set down in one place how we can think of it.

First of all, the unconscious is an energy center, where the Id instincts begin to take form. It will help to understand it if we compare it to a factory. This factory is full of dynamos which supply energy to run the machines. Into the factory come all kinds of raw material brought from the outside. These raw materials go through the machines, which are run from the dynamos, and the finished product results.

There are two important things to notice. First, the products which come out are quite different from the machines which make them. Secondly, the parts of the product look different from the finished product. We may use automobiles as an illustration. The presses, punches, and furnaces which are used to make an automobile are quite different in appearance from an automobile. Also, any part of an automobile, such as a carburetor, looks different from a finished automobile. One would never be able to guess what an automobile looked like by looking at a carburetor. On the other hand, one would never be able to guess what either a punch press or a carburetor looked like by watching automobiles.

In the same way, the individual cannot guess how his thoughts are made by watching them go through his mind. Thoughts are the finished products, and observing them will not give anyone but an expert an idea of what their parts look like or what the "machines" look like that made them.

If, however, we allow a specially trained engineer to observe an automobile, he will probably be able to tell what parts are in it and what machines were used to turn them out. Similarly, if one lets a trained psychiatrist listen to one's thoughts, he can make a pretty good estimate as to what parts go to make them up and where they come from. Strangely enough, untrained people are often more confident that they can explain a thought than that they can explain an automobile, although a thought is much more complicated. An automobile has an end to it, that is, there are only a certain number of parts in it and a certain number of machines that are used to make it. There are a lot of them, it is true, but there is an end to them eventually. A thought, on the other hand, is made up of parts without end by processes without end. No matter how many parts one breaks it up into, one can always find more by looking farther. The thought that made Midas King have high blood pressure is a good example. Regardless of how much Dr. Treece studied it, there was always more to be learned by studying it longer. We shall demonstrate this more clearly later when we hear more of Mr. King, and discuss Mr. Meleager's dream. The study of any thought stops only because there is not enough time and not because we know all about it.

Let us return to our factory. The dynamos in the factory correspond to the energy of the unconscious, which comes from the Id instincts. These dynamos supply their energy to machines, which correspond to the images in the unconscious. The machines in the factory look different and work differently from their product. Similarly, the images in the unconscious look different and work differently from their product, which is conscious or thought images. This can be seen by thinking about dreams, which are halfway between conscious and unconscious images in form, and are a little like both and a little different from both. The conscious mind arranges things and uses logic, while the unconscious mind "disarranges" feelings and doesn't use logic. A dream, which is a glimpse of the unconscious, may look as strange to the dreamer as a punch press in an automobile factory might look to a taxi driver.

The unconscious, then, is a source of energy and a part of the mind where thoughts are "manufactured," but the way the unconscious works is different from the way the conscious mind works.

Secondly, the unconscious is a region where feelings are stored. This is not "dead storage," but very much "live" storage, more like a zoo than a warehouse, for all the feelings stored in the unconscious are forever trying to get out. Feelings are stored by being attached to images, just as electricity is stored by being condensed in something. One cannot store electricity by itself; it has to be stored in something. In the same way, a feeling has to be stored about something. When a feeling is stored in the unconscious, or "repressed," it either detaches itself from the representation which awakened it and attaches itself to an image already in the unconscious, or else it takes its own representation down into the unconscious with it. In the first case, the representation remains conscious and the feeling becomes unconscious, so that the individual is not aware of the latter; in the second case, the representation is also forgotten, since it also becomes unconscious. Thus forgetting depends on repression rather than on "wearing out." The storage of an image, that is, a feeling plus a representation, by repression, is always connected with forgetting something. This can also be said the other way round; forgetting means that a representation is being repressed. We have previously mentioned another variation of this, where the representation is repressed and the feeling remains conscious.

We remember that when Mr. and Mrs. King were planning their party, Mr. King remembered what Mr. Castor, the horseman from Hawaii looked like, but couldn't remember how he felt about him. In this case, the feeling detached itself from the representation and was repressed into the unconscious, where it attached itself to another (and unpleasant) image concerning horseback riding. Thus the representation remained conscious while the feeling became unconscious, so that Mr. King was not aware of his dislike for Mr. Castor.

Later on, after their conversation, Mrs. King repressed her feeling about Mrs. Metis, whom she was angry at, and in this case the feeling took the name of the person down into the unconscious with it, so that she forgot that Mrs. Metis even existed. When it came time to do the inviting, Mrs. King had a feeling she was leaving out someone important, but couldn't think who it was, and committed the social error of not inviting Mrs. Metis, who was the banker's wife, to her party.

Mrs. King never did recollect the name of the "marvelous Mr. What's-his-name"; in this case the feeling was not repressed, but the name was forgotten, since the representation was repressed. In all these cases we can see that repression means forgetting, and that the forgetting was due to repression.

During psychoanalysis and in dreams many demonstrations occur of the fact that forgetting does not mean "wearing out"; during such processes the individual often remembers things that he thinks he has "naturally" forgotten years ago, such as a fragment of a child's poem or an incident that happened in very early years. Mr. King, for example, had frequent dreams of horses, and during his treatment with Dr. Treece he suddenly remembered an incident that had taken place during a visit to Hawaii when he was only three years old. His father, who was a great horseman, had bought little Midas a saddle. One day when Midas was disagreeable to his mother, his father had taken the saddle away from him and sold it, which had thrown Midas into a fit of rage and grief. He had "never thought of the incident since," until he recalled it for the doctor.

One reason people do not remember much of what happened to them before the age of three is that most adult thinking is done with words or at least with images of things that have names. Before that age the individual doesn't know many words or the names of many things, so feelings have to be stored on "unnamed" images, which he has no way later of easily explaining to himself or someone else. Often all that can come to mind under such circumstances is an "unnamed" feeling about some "unnamed" thing. Nearly everyone has a few unnamable feelings about unnamable things, and usually doesn't understand where they come from. These may refer to the period of life before the individual could use words. It was a long time before Mr. King was able to explain to the doctor an unnamable feeling which he had had, and which from certain circumstances he mentioned must have dated back at least to his second year of life. He finally realized that it referred to the fact that his mother used to take his food away before he had finished eating it if he didn't eat it as fast as she wanted him to. It was this feeling which played a large part in his adult desire to get rich in a hurry and hold on to what he had, and which caused him to rush, and to get upset when things went wrong, so that his blood pressure was high by the end of the day's work.

There is a good reason why some storage place is necessary to human beings for their unsatisfied libido and mortido tensions. If every ungratified affection and every ungratified resentment which a person felt from the day of his birth were present in his conscious mind at all times, he would be unable to carry on his life. His mind would be in such a continual confusion and turmoil that he could give no attention at all to practical affairs. (Something like this actually happens in some forms of mental illness.) In order that he may be free to deal with important matters of the moment in accordance with the Reality Principle, his Ego has the ability to repress piled-up feelings into the unconscious, where they may stay out of the way.

As we mentioned, however, storage in the unconscious is not "dead" storage. It is not like putting a pile of books in the basement, where they will remain dusty but otherwise unchanged until the time comes to use them. It is more like storing a flock of rabbits. These "rabbits," fed by the feelings of the moment, breed and grow more powerful and would soon overrun the mind completely if they were not released. But just as letting out some of the baby rabbits, without touching the father and mother rabbits, would not stop the rabbits once and for all from overrunning the house, so indirect relief of Id tensions will not give permanent results and will have to be repeated again and again, to prevent the Id from overrunning the Ego. No matter how often the tension is drained off indirectly, the original "parent" tensions are still there and can breed new little tensions. Only by satisfying the original tensions directly could the Id be emptied completely (though temporarily) of unsatisfied libido and mortido. This, of course, is impossible under ordinary conditions.* Most people know that they would be very uncomfortable following such violent actions. One of the strongest tensions is the inwardly directed mortido of the Superego, which would in most cases be increased after an

* The evidence from Nazi slaughters and other mass murders is that even the most wanton killings drain off mortido only temporarily, so that shortly the individual is ready to repeat the process with more murders. In situations of complete savagery, such as the Treblinka extermination camp, a night's rest may be sufficient to renew the mortido tension, while in more civilized situations it may take a month or two before the urge to kill recurs in strength.

attempt to accomplish complete relief of the other tensions. For a while after satisfactory sexual relations with a loved one, however, the complete relief of libido tension is closely approached.

The unconscious, then, is the source of Id energy, a "thought factory," and a storage place. It cannot think, any more than an automobile factory can go on a trip. It can only feel and wish, and it pays no attention to time, place, and the laws of the physical universe, as is often seen in dreams, where the dead may be resurrected, the separated reunited, and the laws of gravity may not work normally.

Everyone is familiar with the "knee jerk" which follows a tap on the tendon of the knee. This movement is outside the will and gives some people a queer sensation, occasionally amounting to actual nausea, so greatly are they upset by the mind losing control of a part of the body. The knee jerk is carried out through the spinal cord without the assistance of the brain, and the spinal cord works quite differently from the brain. The brain works by movement patterns, with all the muscles working together to make a certain movement, such as kicking something. The spinal cord controls separate muscles, which move without accomplishing any definite purpose. The unconscious differs from the conscious in a similar way, so that the conscious mind gets a weird impression when it observes the peculiar way in which the unconscious puts things together. A dream scene of a market place is as different from a real market place as a knee jerk is from a kick.

2

What is in the unconscious?

The contents of the unconscious consist mainly of the "unfinished business of childhood" and matters related thereto. This includes tensions which have never become conscious, but are still capable of influencing behavior indirectly, and tensions which were once conscious and have been repressed. Together with these tensions are found the corresponding images: some which have never become conscious, and others which have been pushed out of consciousness.

Since imaginings, or fantasies, are just as real to the unconscious as actual experiences, many of the representations in the unconscious have little connection with reality, and yet are just as influential as realities. A "good" representation of Father may be based on memories of what he was like, fantasies of what he was like, or present experiences of his goodness, and both the memories and the fantasies may be equally important in determining the individual's attitude toward him.

The tensions in the unconscious are "unfinished business" because they have not yet been relieved, do not disappear until they are relieved, and are continually seeking complete or partial relief through their true aims and objects or through substitutes.

The chief tensions present in the unconscious minds of most people are unsatisfied oral wishes, unsatisfied anal wishes, and unsatisfied wishes of the later period of life after the fifth year. They are usually both libidinous and mortidinous, loving and hateful. They are both inwardly and outwardly directed. The outwardly directed tensions take the form of affections and hostilities. The inwardly directed ones take the form of a desire for affection and approval, and a desire for punishment. Their aims range from sexual intercourse and murder to merely looking at the object or knowing that it exists. The objects range from parents and relatives to casual acquaintances and inanimate things. Any one or more of the tensions, even contradictory ones, can become conscious if circumstances are right, and seek direct relief through the proper aim and object, or indirect relief through aim or object displacement. As many tensions as possible, conscious and unconscious, seek relief in everything the individual does or imagines.

The unconscious (as well as the conscious) tensions may be divided into two groups: those relating to the Id, and those relating to the Superego (remembering that the Superego is a split-off part of the Id, so that in the last analysis both groups spring from the Id instincts). What the individual actually does and how much he expresses himself is a compromise between these two groups of tensions, under the control of the Ego (which in turn, some doctors believe, is also a split-off part of the Id). (These splits need not be confusing. All that we need to remember is that in the grownup the Id is split, and in the very young infant it is not.)

If everyone tried to gratify all his Id wishes, anarchy would result. The gratification of Id wishes often involves suffering on the part of others, and free Id expression means the pleasure of the mighty and the misery of the weak. Many political situations in the course of history have demonstrated this.

The Superego tensions, if normal, tend to bring happiness to others. They help to make people generous and considerate. Our civilization is based largely on the triumph of the Superego over the Id, and for civilization to continue, this triumph must continue. The growth force, or *physis,* which we see evidence of in the individual and in society, if properly nourished in infancy, works along with the Superego, so that the individual has an urge to grow and to behave "better"—that is, in accordance with the principles of the adult stage of sexual development which takes the happiness of others into consideration. Both Superego and *physis,* if normal, oppose crude or brutal expressions of Id wishes. They start the individual off in not soiling his diapers, and end up in the ideals of the United Nations.

If the development of the Superego is hindered or takes place in an unusual way, there is likely to be trouble, as we shall see later. If the feelings and representations stored in the unconscious through the forces of repression become disturbed, the consequences may also be undesirable.

3

Why do people dream?

By this time, the reader should have little difficulty in understanding what a dream is. It is an attempt to gain satisfaction of an Id tension by hallucinating a wish fulfillment. Awake or asleep, the Id continues to strive for gratification. During the waking hours it is prevented from asserting itself directly by the Superego, with its stern ideas of what is right and what is wrong, and by the Ego, with its realization of what consequences may follow unwise gratification of impulses. During sleep, the Ego relaxes its repressions, and the Reality Principle by which it attempts to govern is out of commission. Thus the contents of the Id are partly freed from control. The Superego, however, does not relax much during sleep, and its effects are still felt when the Id tries to assert itself. This means that even during sleep, the Id must still conceal the true nature of its strivings for fear of offending the Superego.

Therefore, these strivings only dare show themselves in disguised form, so that the dream is rarely frank, but usually presents the Id wishes in a distorted way. The task of the dream interpreter is then to penetrate this disguise and reveal the true nature of the Id wishes which are striving for expression.

Since the individual is asleep, he cannot move about and actually obtain the gratifications he desires. All he can do is visualize them in his mind. Because the Ego with its ability to test reality is no longer in action, he is able to believe that his visions are real, and at the time they gratify him almost as much as the reality would. A sexual dream may be as satisfying to the sleeper as actual sexual relations would be in waking life. When the Ego is awake, it prefers that satisfactions be real. When it is asleep, the mind may be content with imagined gratifications.

Two apparent exceptions to what we have said in the last paragraph will help to make it clearer. First, at times the individual does move about during sleep. If we analyze an example of sleep-walking, we may find that it is related to the individual's dreams, and seems like an attempt to gain by walking what his dreams usually strive for. The dwarf of Brschiss who walked into his "parents' " bedroom while he was asleep is a good instance. During that period his wish was to separate his "parents," and his sleepwalking was a kind of attempt to accomplish this. Secondly, at times during waking life, the individual may believe in his own imaginings. This occurs in certain forms of mental illness. The example we have already given is that of the alcoholic who believes in the reality of his terrifying, mortidinous hallucinations. This means that one way alcoholism may affect the mind is by suspending the operation of the Ego's reality testing so that imagined sights and sounds seem real; when this happens, they are called hallucinations.

What is the effect (or "purpose") of dreaming? A dream is an attempt to keep the sleeper from being awakened by the shameful-ness or terrifying nature of his own Id wishes. The dream is the preserver of sleep.

When the Ego is asleep, repressions are partly lifted, and the Id tensions are released. We know that the Id is ruthless and has no morals. What would be the effect on the individual if he felt these tensions in all their power? He might immediately want to get up and bring death and sexual violence to those around him, no matter how close their relationship; in fact, his chief victims might be his closest relatives, since they are the people he has the strongest feelings about. The Id in the raw does not believe in moral discriminations and halfway measures, as we often see in criminal situations, when the repressions break down and deeds of horror are committed. It happens that the sleeper does not have to get up and carry out his desires, since he can be content with imagining their fulfillment. The reality to him of his hallucinations (dreams, that is) makes action unnecessary, so he can have his Id pleasures while he continues to sleep.

But even in sleep, if the true aims and objects of his Id tensions became known to him, the indignant reactions of his Superego would awaken him. The distortions of the dream fool the Superego so that it sees no need for indignation, and thus sleep can continue. An apparent exception again makes the situation clearer. If the Id tensions are so strong that they threaten to break through frankly in spite of the Superego and what little repression is left during sleep, the Ego half awakens and a terrific struggle follows to keep the Id from expressing itself openly and thus incurring the wrath of the Superego. If this struggle cannot be won by the Ego in its sleeping state, the alarm is sounded and the sleeper awakens, with his heart pounding and his skin drenched with sweat, panic-stricken by his narrow escape from becoming aware of the power and ruthlessness of his own Id tensions. A nightmare is a dream which has failed in its attempt to preserve sleep. If the individual senses, or learns from experience, how dangerous it is for him to relax his repressions by going to sleep, he sometimes prefers to lie awake all night rather than run the risk of becoming aware of his unconscious desires. Insomnia often results from such a fear of going to sleep. Sometimes this fear is conscious, but usually it is unconscious, and in the latter case the sufferer, not being aware of the real reason for his wakefulness, may find all kinds of other excuses such as worry, noise, etc., which satisfy him and usually his family as well.

Not only does the dream attempt to keep the sleeper from being awakened by his own Id tensions, but it also attempts to keep outside stimulations from awakening him. A familiar example of this is the man who sleeps through his wintry alarm clock. If his sleeping Ego interpreted the bell correctly, he would have to wake up, get out of his comfortable bed, put his feet on the cold floor, and go to work in the dark and frigid dawn. By "dreaming away" the sound of the bell he fools his Superego and Ego into letting him sleep on and thereby avoid this unpleasant experience. The Id, ever alert to use all kinds of opportunities for its own gratification, seizes upon the sound of the bell to use in gratifying some of its tensions. In this case, for example, it may transport him in a dream back to the happy days of his infancy, when he did not have the duty of controlling and postponing his satisfactions, and when life was more charming and pleasant. He may dream that he is hearing church bells, which is a way of saying:

"What a beautiful sound I hear. 'Tis the church bells of Olympia. How comforting it is to know that I am back there living again my carefree childhood days!"

Upon getting the subject's reaction to this dream, the interpreter may find that the church bells of Olympia remind him of his long-dead mother. Thus the dream satisfies three wishes. First, the wish to continue sleeping: since the dream allows him to believe that he is hearing church bells, and not an alarm clock, there is no need to get up. Secondly, the wish to be a child again: if he is hearing those particular bells, he must once more be a child, since that is exactly the way they sounded to him in childhood. Thirdly, the wish that his mother were alive again: in the days when he heard those bells, his mother was at his side; now that he is hearing them again, she must also be here.

In this case, he is practicing fraud or cajolery on his Superego, with its sense of duty, and on his prudent Ego, which knows that he must get to work on time. This cannot go on too long unless he wants to be a loser, and eventually he begins to stir uneasily in his sleep. Then suddenly he springs up, wide awake with the realization that he is going to be late for work if he doesn't hurry now. Reluctantly he abandons his dream world and plunges into the cold reality of the morning.

People often say that dreams are "due to" outside stimulations. This is not so. The truth is that the Id *uses* outside stimulations as handy material around which to weave its wish fulfillments. In expressing itself, the Id takes the line of least resistance, using the channels most readily available. This may be called a law, or even *the* law, of the Id. It applies not only to dreams, but also to neurotic symptoms. Thus we have wish-fulfilling dreams based on, but not "caused by," indigestion, and wish-fulfilling neuroses based on, but not "caused by," old bodily injuries. For example, the pain of indigestion may be used by the Id in forming a dream of "anal" satisfaction. Since anal satisfactions are often horrifying to the Superego of the grownup, a fearsome internal battle may follow, and such a dream may therefore take the form of a nightmare.

Besides trying to express the anal wishes, the dream attempts to gratify the wish to go on sleeping, so that it has to deal with the pain itself as well as with the increased Id tension which the pain activates. By "using up" the pain as material in a wish-fulfilling dream, the same soothing effect is obtained as in the case of the alarm clock. If the alarm were perceived as an alarm, the subject would waken; if the pain were perceived as a pain, the subject would waken. But if, for example, the subject's mother used to massage his abdomen when he was constipated as a child, the pain may be "dreamed away" in a pleasant hallucination of having his abdomen rubbed by a woman resembling his mother, in which case he can go on sleeping blissfully in spite of the pain. If the idea of such a massage offends the Superego, then the dream will be turned into a nightmare, and will fail in its purpose, so that the dreamer will awaken anyway. The following is an example of such a nightmare.

Wendell Meleager dreamed one night, after eating a large and fancy dinner, that an ugly woman giant was chasing him with a blazing object resembling a rubber roller such as is used in massage parlors. The dream was so terrifying that he awoke in a panic.

Mr. Meleager had come to the psychiatrist because of the symptoms which followed his uncle's death. When the treatment began, he complained of shakiness, palpitation, insomnia, nightmares, exaggerated fears, depression, inability to concentrate, and impotence. Throughout his life he had suffered from lack of confidence and from constipation, both of which he felt were relieved by frequenting massage parlors.

Mr. Meleager's "associations" to his dream were as follows: the woman giant did not look like his mother, but somehow she reminded him of her. Then he remembered that she had the same kind of hands as his mother and wore the same kind of wedding ring. He went on to recount some of his pleasant experiences at the local massage parlor. Suddenly he remembered something he had not thought of since early childhood: that when he was constipated as an infant, his mother used to massage his abdomen. More than that, he recalled something which startled him even more, and that was the *feeling of pleasure* he had had on such occasions. At that moment, in the doctor's office, he went through the tremendous experience of reliving that feeling in all its meaningfulness, including his fear of his mother.

The dream can be reconstructed as follows: the underlying wish was that his mother should massage his abdomen, which would have brought his Id much gratification. Such a dream was quite unacceptable to his Superego, since it revealed too plainly how much he formerly enjoyed and still desired physical contact with his mother, and how much this procedure and the satisfaction it brought had encouraged his tendency to be constipated in childhood. In the work of "manufacturing" the dream, therefore, his mind had disguised the nature of the Id wish it fulfilled. First, it had disguised his beautiful mother by turning her into an ugly giantess, so that his Superego would not recognize the real object of the dream. Secondly, instead of visualizing the actual massage in the dream, he had "symbolized" it by the picture of the blazing rubber roller in the giantess' hand. This meant instead of "She is massaging you," rather "She is going to massage you," which, though less satisfying, was at least a fair substitute and might have brought some gratification with less guilt if the deception had worked.

Unfortunately for Mr. Meleager, however, his Superego was in this case not fooled by the indirectness and the disguises of the dream, and began to protest violently, resulting in the panicky feeling of the nightmare. When the Id threatened to break through completely and let the giantess capture him and perform the massage (as is not unusual in nightmares, he was unable to run despite his fear, so that she was in a fair way to catch him), his Superego was in danger of losing control. The alarm was sounded, and he woke up. His Ego also probably felt this dream as a threat, because he was actually quite scared of his mother when he was little.

This dream and its interpretation by means of Mr. Meleager's associations marked a turning point in his treatment. It opened up such a rich mausoleum of long-buried feelings and memories that rapid progress was made from that time on. The important thing to notice about the process of interpreting this dream is that without Mr. Meleager's associations it could not have been done effectively. The interpretation hinged on the sudden memory of his childhood pleasure, which had been unconscious for nearly forty years and was only recalled during the "free association" of psychoanalysis, which we shall discuss further in a later chapter. Without this association, the dream would have meant little to either Mr. Meleager or the psychoanalyst. The doctor might have guessed its meaning in a general way, and his guess might have helped him understand Mr. Meleager better, but it would not have helped Mr. Meleager understand himself better. Only when he recalled by free association the actual *feeling* of the experience upon which it was based, could he profit greatly from the interpretation.

It should be said that this profitable opening up of his childhood emotional life, which gradually led to a beneficial reorganization of his personality, only began after six months of daily visits to the analyst, and it required many more months to work it out completely. As Mr. Meleager told his friends, however, his increased efficiency in the long run enabled him to earn more in his law practice, so that his eventual freedom from symptoms and the new-found relaxation of himself and his family really didn't cost him anything financially, since he earned back the money he had invested in his treatment.

In this section we have learned that the function of dreams is to preserve sleep, and that dreams are wish fulfillments in disguise. We have seen that it is necessary to obtain the dreamer's associations in order to interpret a dream properly, and that such interpretations reveal the dreamer's unconscious wishes to such an extent that dreams have been called "the highroad to the unconscious."

It is probable also that dreams have another function, and that is to assist in healing the mind after emotional wounds and distressing emotional experiences. As the reader will see later, the terrifying battle dreams of Si Seifuss probably represented an unsuccessful attempt to accomplish this healing after his damaging war experiences. There is now evidence to show that even ordinary emotional experiences have to be "digested" in some way through dreaming in order for the individual to feel well. A person deprived of the opportunity to dream may become quite confused; many psychoses are preceded by a period of prolonged lack of sleep, and hence lack of opportunity to dream. It may be that the mass of "undigested" emotions which results has some effect in bringing on the psychosis.

4

Interpreting dreams

We have just given an example of the method used in interpreting dreams. Briefly, the material used in the interpretation is obtained as follows: after relating the dream, the subject tells exactly what comes to his mind when he thinks of what he has dreamed without any attempt to censor his thoughts or to put them in order.

The purpose of the interpretation is to find out which Id tensions are trying to find expression in the dream, their true aims and objects, and their meaning for the individual. These factors are called the "latent content" of the dream. The dream itself, as the dreamer experiences it and tells it, is called the "manifest content." The interpretation is an attempt to trace back from the manifest content to the latent content. Without the subject's associations, an experienced dream interpreter might be able to guess from the manifest content alone which Id tensions were trying to find expression in the dream and even what their true aims and objects were, but he could not tell the most important thing of all: the significance of these things for the individual. And until the dreamer realizes significances by *feeling* them, the interpretation is of no immediate value to him except as an interesting scientific study. Only by making associations to the dream can he experience these all-important feelings.

It is a common error to suppose that *finding out* the meaning of the dream is the important thing. This is not so. The meanings must be felt, and these feelings must be put into proper perspective with other past and present feelings of that particular person, for the interpretation to have any effect in changing the underlying Id tensions, which is the purpose of the procedure.

The interpreter has to remember that a dream is a disguised attempt to picture a feeling during sleep. Factors which influence the formation of the manifest dream from the latent content are as follows:

1. During sleep, the Ego is largely out of commission. Thus the dream is formed without much help from the Ego in "arranging," and without the full benefit of the Ego's experience in learning from reality. Therefore the dream may appear strange to the Ego after the dreamer awakens. It may seem absurd, unarranged, and even disorderly, nor is it bound by any of the demands of reality: time, space, gravity, death, and other basic factors which the Ego has to take account of in waking life, may have no logic in the content and action of the dream.*

2. During sleep, the Superego is partly out of commission. Therefore the dreamer does things in his dream which he would never dare to do or, perhaps, even think of doing in waking life.

3. Among the influences which the Ego keeps more or less inactive or at least under control during waking life, but which have freer expression in the dream, are the three "absolutes." In his dreams, the individual is always immortal (if he pictures his death, he survives as a spectator); his charms are irresistible (he can and does make love to any woman he wants to); and his thoughts are omnipotent (if he thinks he can fly, he jumps, and lo! he flies).

4. The task of the dream is to show complicated feelings in pictures. A feeling cannot be shown directly in a picture. Only the act which signifies the feeling can be shown. There is no such thing as a picture of fear, but an expression of fear, or the act of running away can be pictured. There is no such thing as a picture of love, but approaching, giving, adoring, or a sexual act can be shown. There is no such thing as a picture of hate, but destroying, casting out, or injuring can be visualized. Sometimes the dream has the task of condensing all three feelings into a single picture and, in addition, disguising the feelings so that the Superego will not know

---

* In the experience of the author, a slow-motion picture is the nearest thing in dynamic reality, and the paintings of Salvador Dali are the nearest thing in static reality, to the unreality of a dream.

what the picture represents. Furthermore, the aims and objects of the feelings may also be condensed and disguised. That is one reason why sometimes the analysis of a single feature of a dream may take a whole session.

In Mr. Meleager's dream, the principle of "disguise by opposites" was very active, as well as "disguise by symbolization." When Mr. Meleager finally *felt* the meaning of his dream, *he* told the *doctor* (and not vice versa) that it expressed a long-forgotten desire to have closer physical contact with his mother. The disguises were then revealed. His beautiful mother was disguised on the principle of opposites as an ugly woman; instead of running to her, on the same principle, he ran away from her; instead of his having the male organ, she had it. The male organ was symbolized in disguise by the rubber roller, and the heat of his passion even as a child was symbolized in disguise by the flame.

The figure of the giantess was a good example of "condensation" of several items. First, she represented his mother. Secondly, she represented two large and ugly masseuses who held a strange sexual fascination for him. In addition, her ugliness represented the ugliness of his desires, her fearsomeness represented the fear they aroused in him, and her enormity represented their enormity. He told the analyst these things with great feeling, so that his heart pounded and he sweated as he talked.

5. Above all, the interpreter bears in mind that the dreamer writes his own scenario. The dream is the sole product of his individual mind. Like the author of any scenario, he can put in any characters he pleases and do with them as he will. He can take his heroine and marry her, kill her, impregnate her, set her up in business, enslave her, beat her, give her away, or do anything else with her which his fancy dictates and his sleepy Superego will permit. If he feels passionate he can caress; if he feels envious he can plunder; if he feels guilty he can punish himself; if he feels angry he can kill; and if he has unusual desires he can gratify them. But whatever he does, or to or with whomever he does it, and whatever disguises he cloaks them in, the dream is the product of his own mind and not of anyone else's. The manifest dream will be a compromise between the policing of the Superego and the unsatisfied wishes of the Id, and the analysis of the dream will lead back to the latent thoughts which arise from these two forces. It

may be said that the influence of the Ego can also be noted in "secondary" arranging of the manifest dream elements.

5

What is sleep?

There is more to dreams than just their psychological interpretation. Since Freud's day, a great deal has been learned about the connection between dreams and sleep. During sleep, as in wakefulness, the brain sends out electrical impulses which can be recorded by a machine called an electroencephalograph. These impulses show that sleep occurs in four different depths or stages. The most interesting thing is that in one of these stages, where the brain waves take a certain special form, the eyeballs begin to move around rapidly under the closed lids. By waking people in different stages of sleep, it is found that nearly all dreams occur during this particular stage, which is called "rapid-eye-movement" sleep, or "REM," sleep. The other stages are called "non-rapid-eye-movement" sleep, or "NREM," sleep.

During REM sleep, the body may actually be more active than in waking life, even though the individual remains in the same position in bed. The heart may beat faster, the blood pressure goes up and down more quickly, the breathing becomes irregular, and the muscles of the arms, legs, and face twitch. The supply of blood to the brain is higher than during waking life, and in men the penis frequently becomes erect. In one study, 80 per cent of REM periods were accompanied by an erection. This is a remarkable confirmation of Freud's idea that nearly all dreams are sexual in origin. Freud arrived at this conclusion through psychological intuition and interpretation, and had no way of checking it experimentally. It is only now, seventy years later, that experiments prove he was right, at least as far as men are concerned, and there is no reason to doubt that it applies equally to women, although in their case it is more difficult to confirm.

A normal night's sleep consists of NREM sleep interrupted by periods of REM. These periods occur every ninety minutes, three to five times a night, and each one lasts about twenty minutes. Both kinds of sleep are necessary for the individual to function normally. For example, if a person is deprived of REM by waking him every time he goes into it, he may become very disturbed after a few nights. As soon as he is allowed to sleep as he wishes, he will make up all the REM time and have all the dreams that he missed during the experiment. The electroencephalograph shows that other mammals besides humans have REM sleep—cats, cows, dogs, and even the opossum, which has survived on earth for more than a hundred million years.

Sleeping and waking depend on a certain part of the brain called the "reticular activating system," or "RAS" for short. When the RAS is active, the person is awake; when it is inactive, he goes to sleep. When certain hormones act on the RAS during sleep, an animal begins REM; when another substance acts on the RAS, it will cause NREM sleep. By knowing all this it is possible for scientists to learn more and more about sleep and dreams. Suggestion, isolation in a room, and LSD increase the REM time and hence the amount of dreaming. Barbiturates, alcohol, and certain tranquillizers decrease the REM time. But whether the REM episodes are shortened or lengthened, they still continue to occur about ninety minutes apart. Interestingly enough, these studies confirm one piece of folklore about dreams: cheese sandwiches really will make people dream more, because cheese contains a substance which increases REM sleep, and hence the amount of dreaming. The actual length of a dream is from one to eighty minutes, and the actual duration is just about the way it seems in the dream: a "quick" dream happens quickly, and a "slow" dream actually takes a long time.

Nearly all the experiments confirm what Freud said about dreams: not only their sexual nature, but their independence of outside events and of what the dreamer does just before he goes to sleep. Outside stimuli, such as sounds, lights, or a spray of cold water, do not start dreams, but are blended, usually in a symbolic way, into dreams that are already there. Also, the events of the previous day influence dreams much more than the doings of the evening before going to sleep. In other words, dreams go their own way and they happen during REM sleep, which occurs every ninety minutes regardless of what is going on outside the body; even the stomach, which is inside the body, does not have much influence over REM sleep. The dreamer, however, does have some control over his dreams. For example, one subject was afraid that his dreams would reveal too much about him, and the tracings showed that his REM periods stopped almost immediately after they began instead of lasting the usual twenty minutes. This meant that even while he was asleep he was cutting off his dream period as quickly as he could. In the morning he said that he had dreamed of a TV set which someone turned on, then he turned it off and the screen went blank.

Those who call themselves poor sleepers are actually sleeping a large percentage of the time when they think they are awake, but this is NREM sleep. What they feel they are missing is REM sleep. Bed-wetting, sleepwalking, and night terrors in children occur only during NREM periods, while teeth grinding, head banging, and nightmares occur during REM.

The official record for staying awake, 264 hours (11 days), was set by a seventeen-year-old high-school boy in San Diego. He suffered no aftereffects. In most people sleep is regulated by the clock, as is shown when they travel long distances by jet. They get sleepy when their watches tell them to, rather than when the sun tells them to at their new destination. This 24-hour rhythm is called a "circadian" rhythm (from the Latin *circa diem,* "about a day") The circadian rhythm regulates not only sleeping and waking, but also body temperature, heart rate, blood pressure, and the formation of urine, all of which go up and down in a regular day-night cycle. One interesting experiment in this regard was carried out with cockroaches, whose circadian clocks are controlled from a special part of the brain. If this part of the brain is transplanted from one cockroach into another, which has had his own clock removed, the receiving cockroach gets along fine if the new clock in his head keeps the same time as the old one. But if the two are out of phase, the receiving cockroach gets cancer and dies. This is a remarkable result, the meaning of which is not yet clearly understood, but it does show how important rhythms are in keeping the body functioning well.

Footnotes for Philosophers, Chapter Four

1. and 2. *The Unconscious*

Korzybski's influence may be seen here.

For further information about the topics discussed in these sections, see:

An Elementary Textbook of Psychoanalysis, by Charles Brenner. New York: Doubleday Anchor Books, 1957.

Facts and Theories of Psychoanalysis, by Ives Hendrick. New York: Alfred A. Knopf, 3rd edition, 1958.

3. and 4. *Dreams*

There is no substitute for Freud's work "The Interpretation of Dreams," which can be found in *The Basic Writings of Sigmund Freud.* Part II of his *Complete Introductory Lectures on Psychoanalysis,* and the revision of his dream theory in Lecture XXIX may also be read.

Freud's study of dreams is so subtle that some trained psychoanalysts reread "The Interpretation of Dreams" periodically, each time gaining further enlightenment.

5. *Sleep*

For summaries of recent developments, see:

Sleep, by G. G. Luce and J. Segal. New York: Coward–McCann, 1966.

The Psychology of Sleep, David Foulkes. New York: Charles Scribner's Sons, 1966.

The dream substance in cheese is tyramine. See D. Horwitz et al. *Journal of the American Medical Association,* Vol. 188, p. 1108 (June 29, 1964).

Part Two

ABNORMAL DEVELOPMENT

5

NEUROSES

1

How can emotions cause physical disease?

There are millions of unhappy people all over the world who suffer from headache, backache, stomach-ache, loss of appetite, excessive belching, nausea, heavy feeling after eating, pain in the chest, pounding heart, dizziness, fainting spells, breathlessness, weakness, and pains in the joints, without ever finding out what is the matter with them. Year after year they go from one doctor to another, getting X rays, urinalyses, gastric analyses, electrocardiograms, and blood sugars, and taking vitamins, hormones, electric treatments, elixirs, and tonics, and sometimes undergoing one operation after another. If they have been in the army or navy of their native land, they have been labeled "psychoneurotic," and many a man who has boldly faced machine-gun fire has quailed at the sound of this word. Some of them dislike doctors and go to chiropractors and naturopaths, because they feel that medical doctors think their troubles are imaginary.

When a doctor, after doing all the tests and examinations and finding them negative, says that these troubles may be caused by emotions, he does not mean that they are imaginary. Everyone has heard of people getting headaches from worrying, which gives us the expression "This job is a headache!" Those who have had such headaches (as many doctors have) know that they are not imaginary. The happy little Gremlin who is driving red-hot rivets into the backs of the victim's eyeballs may be imaginary, but the pain isn't.

Anyone who has seen a robust man or woman faint at the sight of blood knows that such fainting spells are not imaginary either, and whoever has seen a child vomit from excitement after coming home from the circus knows that such vomiting is real enough. In these cases, the headaches, fainting spells, and vomiting are all caused by emotions. There is no disease of the head, heart, or stomach, but the trouble happens just the same. There is nothing to get angry about if the doctor says that the patient's symptoms are emotional. He does *not* mean that they are imaginary. Emotions can cause mild illnesses, serious illnesses, and death.

A hundred years before there was any scientific psychiatry, the famous English physician John Hunter had a heart attack which nearly killed him. Being a good physician, he knew even in those days that the heart could be affected by strong emotions. When he recovered, he said: "My life is in the hands of any rascal who chooses to annoy and tease me!" He was unable to keep his temper, however, and one day he became angry and dropped dead. Though his death was caused by his emotions, it was not imaginary. His temper brought on a very real blood clot in the wall of his heart.

If we study what goes on inside the chest of an animal or human being under an anesthetic, we can understand how the heart can race and cause pounding, or slow down and miss a beat, without anything being wrong with the heart itself. There are two nerves of different kinds which go to the heart. These nerves can actually be seen with the naked eye and picked up with the fingers. They are like pieces of white string which run from the heart to the lower part of the brain. We can call one kind the S nerve (for Sprinting) and the other the P nerve (for Plodding). If the S nerve is touched with an electric battery, a current goes down the nerve and the heart begins to sprint. If the P nerve is touched with a battery, the heart slows down and begins to plod. This can be repeated again and again. Anybody can do it, because the nerves are right there for anyone to see. Thus one can make a perfectly normal heart pound or slow up without even touching it.

There are similar nerves which affect the blood pressure. If electricity is sent along one of these, the blood pressure goes up; if it is sent along the other, the pressure goes down. We have only to remember that fainting is caused by a fall in blood pressure to understand how a person can faint without anything being wrong with the heart.

Normally, of course, there is no electric battery in the chest, but there is something similar in the lower part of the brain where the

S and P nerves end. There is some "electric" tissue there that can send a current down the S nerve to speed the heart up, or down the P nerve to slow it. This can be tested easily by putting two wires on the S or P nerve and connecting these wires to a galvanometer, which is something like the ammeter in an automobile. It has a needle which shows when an electric current passes between the two wires which run out from it. In this way we can show that when the heart speeds up from excitement a current is coming from the brain down the S nerve to the heart; and when the heart slows down for an instant from fear (many people faint when they are afraid, because slowing contributes to a sudden fall in blood pressure) current is passing down the P nerve.

If one uses a tomcat in this experiment, and a dog is shown to the animal after it comes out of the anesthetic, the current can be demonstrated passing down the S nerve. If the cat's feelings are stimulated in a different way, the current passes down the P nerve. This shows that the cat's emotions can determine which way the current flows, and the heart can be seen accordingly to speed up or slow down without anyone's touching it. It is the same with a human being. When a man gets angry, his heart speeds up; when he is afraid, it may slow down for a few moments. The rate of his heart at such times depends on his emotions and has nothing to do with the condition of the heart itself. When his mind grasps what is happening, an electric current goes from the upper part of his brain to the lower part of his brain. If it passes by way of the anger or "pounding" complex, it will arrive at the S nerve center, and a current will then go down the S nerve. If it passes by way of the fear or "fainting" complex, it will reach the P nerve center, and a current will then go down the P nerve.

What determines whether the current goes by way of the anger complex or the fear complex? The same thing which determines the path of any electric current. It follows the path of least resistance. If the person is irritable and aggressive, the anger path has a lower resistance; if he is timid and fearful, the fear path has a lower resistance. Thus the things in early life which determine whether a person's attitude toward the world is a belligerent one or a timid one determine which nerve the current will pass down and how the heart will react when emotions are aroused.

We can see that the reactions of the heart to emotion are

important and often useful to the individual. It is important and useful for an angry man to have a strongly beating heart, for he may get into a fight and his muscles will then need plenty of extra blood pumped into them. If the heart slows down in a tight spot, on the other hand, this is important, but not really useful, as the person may then faint and be at the mercy of whatever danger threatens. We can recognize here two old friends, "active" and "passive." The brain uses the S nerve in connection with an active, fighting response, and the P nerve in connection with a passive, fainting response. The theory that the brain can store energy explains how a person can remain calm while things are happening and only feel his heart pound or faint after the excitement is all over. In such a case the energy is not immediately released down the S or P nerve, but is stored until the situation has been taken care of.

We notice then that emotions can cause electric currents to go through the nervous system in various directions. These currents can be studied without exposing the nervous system, by means of various electrical devices, including the brain-wave amplifier, which we shall hear more about later.

The patient who comes to the doctor complaining of palpitation may have one objection to all this: he may say that it is all very well for such things to happen to people who are angry or afraid, but that his heart begins to pound when he is lying quietly in bed at night and doesn't feel either emotion.

The answer to this, of course, is that just because he is unaware of the nature of his tensions does not mean that they do not exist. The very fact that his heart, though normal, pounds when he is lying quietly is one of the best proofs that they do exist. There is no reason to suppose that people are aware of all the tensions of their libido and mortido. Quite the contrary. We know that it is perfectly possible for a person to have ungratified tensions without being conscious of them. Many people are in love, or angry, or afraid, for ten, twenty, or thirty years without being aware of it until they come to a psychiatrist. They may not know that they are angry, but their hearts know it, and act accordingly. The reason such feelings are called unconscious is that the person is not aware of them. Therefore, it is not logical for a person to say that he has an unconscious feeling, or to deny that he has it. If he knew that he had it, it would no longer be unconscious.

Some doctors and psychologists, it is true, maintain that we are conscious of all our mental energy imbalances, and claim that if we are not conscious of a libido or mortido tension, it does not exist. So far they have not been able to prove their point effectively enough to convince other doctors, such as psychoanalysts, who specialize in studying Id tensions.

After all, we breathe because of energy imbalance, but no one would say that the wish to breathe did not exist because the individual was not always conscious of it. By a simple procedure such as holding his breath he can quickly become aware of it. It is a little more complicated to become conscious of unrecognized libido and mortido tensions, but it can be done. Because an individual is not aware that he is acting affectionately does not mean that he has stopped loving.

What has been said about quickening or slowing of the heart applies also to the rise and fall of blood pressure, which can cause pounding sensations or fainting spells.

In the case of the stomach, the story is even more interesting. From time to time one finds a man with a wound of the abdomen which will not heal properly, so that for years he has a little window in his belly which looks in on his stomach. Some of these men, for money or for the sake of humanity, have let doctors watch their stomachs in action. The most famous case of this kind occurred in the 1820's, when a man named Alexis St. Martin was hired and observed by Dr. William Beaumont, and to these two we owe much of our early knowledge as to how the stomach works. Other examples have been observed since that time.

From such studies we learn that as in the case of the heart, many of the stomach's reactions depend upon the emotions and in much the same way. There are two kinds of nerves going to the stomach, the S (for Sponge) and the P (for Pale) nerves. If a battery, or the nerve center in the lower part of the brain, sends a current through the S nerve, the blood vessels in the wall of the stomach expand and soak up blood like a sponge; if the current passes down the P nerve, the blood vessels shrink and squeeze most of the blood out, so that the organ looks pale. It happens that when an individual gets angry, the current goes down his S nerve. His face gets red and so does his stomach. Though the individual does not know that his stomach is red, he often notices that it feels heavy. This is perfectly natural. It feels heavy because it *is* heavy, just as a sponge is heavier when it has lots of water in it than when it has only a little bit.

If a man is afraid, on the other hand, whether he is conscious of it or not, the current goes down the P nerve and the stomach turns pale. At the same time the nerve current slows it up so that it squeezes less efficiently than usual and takes longer to digest food, which lingers in the stomach and begins to ferment. This causes belching and loss of appetite, since, for one thing, no room has been made for more food by the time the next meal rolls around. So people with unsatisfied mortido tensions, which may be expressed at times through the S nerve and at times through the P nerve, often complain of heavy feeling in the stomach, excessive belching, and loss of appetite, for ten, twenty, or thirty years.

In addition to becoming congested if the mortido current goes down the S nerve, something more serious may happen to the stomach. The digestive juices may become too powerful and burning. It is one of the great mysteries of life why the stomach doesn't digest itself. If a man eats a piece of tripe, which is cow's stomach, his digestive juices will digest that piece of dead stomach, but they don't usually digest his own live stomach. If his digestive juices get more powerful than usual, however, while at the same time the stomach wall gets congested and soggy, it may happen that he *will* digest his own stomach, or at least a little piece of it. This has been seen in the cases referred to above. So sometimes when a man has an unsatisfied tension over a long period, conscious or unconscious, a little of the inside layer of his stomach wall may get digested off and leave a raw place. What do we call such a raw place, whether it be on the leg, the gums, or the stomach? It is called an ulcer. The man's tension may partly relieve itself by discharging electrical impulses down his stomach nerves until he digests himself off a stomach ulcer. A long way back we said that the necessity for the human energy system to postpone the relief of certain tensions had a connection with why some people get burning pains in the stomach, and we also said that repressed Id energy may affect the individual's body adversely so that some bodily illnesses are disguised expressions of Id wishes. We now see how such things come about.

Diet will do little to prevent a stomach ulcer, but it does help ulcers heal more quickly. The idea behind this applies to ulcers anywhere on the body. If a man had an ulcer on his leg and put salt and pepper into it three times a day, together with some coffee and hamburgers, it would take quite a while to heal up, whereas if he covered it carefully with milk poultices it would heal pretty quickly. In the same way a milk diet often helps a stomach ulcer. If in addition to the milk we pour in some alkaline powders to neutralize the overly powerful acids of the stomach, that helps it along too, although this has to be done cautiously or unforeseen complications may arise.

How long does it take a stomach ulcer to heal? It may take only a few weeks.

Mr. Edgar Metis, president of the First National Bank of Olympia, became very angry when Dr. Nagel told him that his latest X rays showed he didn't have a stomach ulcer.

"You local doctors," he muttered, "don't know one end of the intestine from the other, especially that X-ray man. I had X rays taken two months ago at the University Hospital in Arcadia, and they definitely showed an ulcer."

"Let me tell you a parable," said Dr. Nagel. "A man once came to me and said: 'Doctor, I cut myself while shaving and I have an ulcer on my left cheek. Can you cure it for me?' I looked at his cheek and found it smooth and healthy. I told him so and he got very mad. 'I know I have an ulcer there,' he insisted. 'In fact I have a picture of it.' So he pulls a photograph of himself out of his wallet, and there on his left cheek, sure enough, was a large ulcer. 'There!' he said. 'The picture *proves* I have an ulcer.' 'Yes,' I said, 'but when was this taken?' 'Oh,' says he, 'about two months ago!' "

An ulcer in the stomach under favorable conditions may heal just as quickly as an ulcer anywhere else.

The moral of all this is that psychiatry can prevent many stomach ulcers by keeping the stomach from getting red, soggy, and overly acid because of unsatisfied Id tensions, and can help ulcers heal quickly by making the stomach wall a nice healthy pink instead of an angry red. This ceases to be true after a certain length of time, because sooner or later an ulcer will go deep enough and get dirty enough so that it cannot heal by smooth repair like a shaving cut, but will have to heal by means of scar tissue. Scar tissue is permanent, and furthermore it contracts. Many people know how in a bad burn of the face, as the months and years go by, the scar tissue contracts and pulls the face over to one side, sometimes interfering with chewing, speaking, and turning of the head, so that the scar has to be cut away by a surgeon. The same thing happens in the stomach. Once scar tissue begins to form in an ulcer, healing will be slow, and later the scar may contract and deform the stomach and its passages. Then the individual has to have part of the stomach cut out, or a new passage made, by a surgeon.

Psychiatry can often prevent or cure certain kinds of heart trouble, stomach trouble, and high blood pressure, as well as some kinds of asthma and eczema, as long as no scar tissue has formed, but psychiatry cannot ever change scar tissue. Once the scar stage is reached, psychiatry can only attempt to prevent the condition from going further. The time for psychiatry in such conditions, therefore, is before any scar tissue has a chance to form. In other words, a man is wiser to bring his unconscious tensions under control and keep his stomach than he is to have his stomach taken out for the sake of proving that he does not have any unconscious tensions. Unfortunately for them, many people would rather lose their stomachs than their tensions, so they find excuses for not going to a psychiatrist, and in some cases, alas, their family doctors or surgeons encourage this pathetic attitude. Every American citizen feels that he has a "constitutional" right to give up his stomach if he so desires.

Thus we see that physical diseases may result from emotional tensions because the various organs are connected to the brain by means of nerve cords. Some methods for the partial discharge of repressed Id tensions through the body organs may not result, even over long periods, in such serious conditions as those we have described, but they may cause milder afflictions which result in embarrassment and a waste of time and energy. Diarrhea is rarely an asset in any practical situation. Neither is an urgent desire to urinate or the sudden onset of a menstrual period or menstrual cramps. All these conditions may result from conscious or unconscious tensions.

2

How can emotions cause physical pain?

We have seen that emotional tensions over a long period may play an important part in diseases of the stomach and heart, and that there is nothing imaginary about such diseases. Now let us look at some of the more common and less sinister types of pain.

How can an emotion cause a headache? This can be studied during a spinal tap. A spinal tap is in many ways similar to a blood test. In a blood test, a needle is put into a vein in the arm and some blood is withdrawn. If it is desired, a harmless measuring instrument called a manometer can be attached to the needle to measure the pressure of the blood in the vein. In a spinal tap, or lumbar puncture, a needle is put into the spinal canal in the back and some of the fluid which surrounds the brain and spinal cord is withdrawn for study. This fluid acts as a cushion and as a nourishment for the nervous system, and is not much different from tap water or mineral water. There is enough of it that it is quite harmless to remove the few drops required. Usually the pressure of the spinal fluid is measured in the meantime with a manometer.

Let us take an individual who has many unsatisfied libido and mortido tensions. When the needle is inserted into his back, the pressure of the fluid shows in the glass measuring tube. If the patient is lying down and is fully relaxed, the fluid will rise up normally about five inches, or 120 millimeters, and that is the pressure of the fluid as it surrounds the brain inside the bony skull, just as the pressure of the air in the atmosphere as shown by a barometer is normally about 30 inches, or 760 millimeters.

We now watch the water level in the tube and ask the individual some simple question which will not make him emotional, such as "What is four times four?" or "What does the Fourth of July celebrate?" As he answers, we see that the pressure in the tube hardly changes. Thus, answering a question does not in itself change the pressure around the brain. Now let us ask him a more personal question, particularly one which hits a sore spot, such as: "Do you love your lawyer?" Usually there is a pause before he answers such a question, and as we watch the pressure gradually rises to 150, 180, or 200 millimeters. After he answers the question, the pressure may slowly fall again, or it may stay up for an indefinite length of time, depending upon how much the individual is stirred up.

Thus we can show that emotional disturbances can increase the pressure of the fluid around the brain. If this increase in pressure is maintained, the contents of the skull will be squeezed by the fluid and a headache may result. So we can see with our own eyes how an emotion might cause a headache. On the other hand, if an experienced psychiatrist is unable to get a rise in pressure by asking personal questions, he might assume that the individual probably does not have headaches from this cause.

It is possible that some low back pains are also caused by emotional tensions. The back is a balanced mechanism, more delicate in some cases than in others. In some people this balance probably has to be kept just right for the back to be able to perform the tasks imposed upon it.

In such individuals, if the female sexual organs or the male prostate become congested with blood like an angry stomach, the soggy organs may affect the muscles and ligaments of the back so that they begin to ache. This often occurs when the congestion is caused by inflammation due to disease. There is also a normal cause for such congestion, namely, sexual excitement. Since people are not aware of all their unsatisfied libido tensions, it could happen that an individual's sacroiliac would be painfully conscious that he was sexually excited without his realizing it himself.

Ambrose Paterson, the electrician, began to have backaches when he was fourteen years old. At the same time he began to have a discharge from his penis which was not due to venereal disease. For years, whenever he became excited, sexually or otherwise, his backache and his discharge would both get worse. The worst backache Mr. Paterson ever had occurred on the day he married Barbara Dimitri, but during the following week it gradually got better and then he was free of both backache and discharge for a long time. Eventually, however, both symptoms returned.

The day after he went looking for Loki Farbanti with his gun (an incident which we shall hear about later), Mr. Paterson had not only a backache and a discharge, but for the first time in his life he had the hives, and a few days later, hay fever. He was now going to three doctors: one for his back, one for his discharge, and one for his hives and hay fever. The doctors all got together one day at the hospital and decided that the best thing to do was to send Mr. Paterson to Dr. Treece, the psychiatrist. Dr. Treece liked difficult cases, but for a long time he shook his head whenever he thought of Ambrose Paterson. After a long course of psychiatric treatment, however, lasting almost two years, all Mr. Paterson's symptoms cleared up. After all, this is not so astonishing. Although his symptoms sound very different from each other, actually, they were all due to the same thing: changes in the blood vessels in various parts of the body: the prostate, the skin, and the nose; and we know how easily the emotions can affect the blood vessels, as in blushing, sexual excitement, and anger. It will be noticed that before he went for psychiatric treatment, Mr. Paterson's symptoms got worse whenever there was an increase in his ungratified libido or mortido tensions.

Another painful condition which may sometimes come from unsatisfied Id tensions is arthritis. This may be due to disturbances in the blood supply to a joint. In this case we have to know that the blood vessels which supply the muscles around a joint also supply the joint itself. If the blood supply to the muscles is altered over a long period, so is the blood supply to the joint. The tissues in the joint are then affected accordingly. (A good example of how the blood supply to a limb may affect the growth of the bones is seen in cases where a child has a large birthmark full of blood vessels on one leg. The bones in the affected leg may grow longer than those on the other side because of the increased blood flow.)

Well, how can we suppose that the blood flow is altered in the muscles and joints of an arthritic arm?

The body is always kept in readiness to gratify conscious and unconscious tensions. The stronger the tensions, the more prepared the body is kept to gratify them. A person with strong ungratified mortido tensions, such as often hang over from childhood, may always be in a condition of readiness to gratify those tensions, even if he is not aware that they exist. Direct satisfaction of mortido tensions involves mainly the muscles of the arms, legs, and back, which are used in running and fighting. We may suppose, therefore, that a person with strong repressed aggressions and hostilities might keep one or more of his limbs tense as though in readiness to satisfy these unconscious mortido tensions. In other words, he might not know that he was angry over a period of years, but his arms might, and be kept tense as though always in readiness to hit someone; or his legs might, and be kept tense as though ready to run away. Because certain muscles were tense, their blood supply might be altered, and this might affect the bones and other tissues of the joint, resulting in the painful condition we call arthritis.

In connection with arthritis and other conditions where a combination of infection and emotional tension might be the cause of a disease, the following medical principle should be kept in mind: disease germs tend to settle in those parts of the body where the blood vessels are abnormally widened. Since we know that the chief changes which are caused in the body by the emotions consist of widening and narrowing of blood vessels in various places, we can see how an emotion, especially one which lasts over a period of years, might make disease germs especially apt to settle in the particular part of the body concerned, be it the stomach, the prostate gland, the neck of the womb, or one of the joints.

We have tried to show some of the ways in which emotions might contribute to the occurrence of physical pains in various parts of the body. In connection with headaches we have described some actual observations concerning the spinal fluid, and in connection with backache we have mentioned some facts concerning infections of the organs contained in the lowest part of the abdomen. The rest of what we have said is half speculation, supported by what facts are known. There is no doubt that certain cases of headache, backache, and painful arthritis can be benefited by psychiatric treatment. Suggestions for further reading on this important subject are given in the notes at the end of the chapter.

3

What is psychosomatic medicine?

The things we have discussed in the two previous sections, that is, the connection of the emotions with physical disease, together with the effects of physical disease on the emotions, are often spoken of as "psychosomatic medicine." This term often means thinking of a human being as consisting of two separate parts, a mind and a body. The idea is then that a sick mind may affect a healthy body, and a sick body may affect a healthy mind.

If we think of the whole human being as a single energy system, we can understand that anything which affects the body will always affect the emotions as well, and anything which affects the emotions will always affect the body. In other words, all diseases are "psychosomatic." There is no such thing as a disease of the body which does *not* affect the mind sooner or later. Even such a simple thing as an ingrown toenail can influence people's dreams. The same applies to a cold in the head. The simplest operation, such as squeezing a blackhead, can have a strong emotional effect, as shown by dreams, while the anxiety aroused by having a tooth pulled can be very disrupting. Similarly, there is no emotional disturbance which does not affect the body, and all mental illnesses are accompanied by some physical effects.

Thus there are not three kinds of medicine, as the word "psychosomatic" might lead one to think. It is not a question of mental medicine, in which only the psyche is involved, somatic medicine, in which only the body is involved, and "psychosomatic" medicine, in which "sometimes" both are involved. There is only one kind of medicine, and it is *all* psychosomatic. Medicine is just medicine. It is not either psychosomatic or nonpsychosomatic. It is true that some doctors are more interested in the mental aspects of disease, and some in the physical aspects, but every disease is both "mental and physical." The diseases don't care whether the doctor knows this or not, they go ahead just the same. The real problem of the doctor is whether a certain patient who is experiencing a certain illness in a certain way at a certain time will be more easily cured by psychiatric methods or physical methods, or by a combination of both.

The harmfulness of the word "psychosomatic" lies in the fact that it may mislead some people into thinking that in certain cases one doesn't have to treat the mind aspect of the human energy system, but only the body aspect, as though to say: "Let some doctors go ahead and practice psychosomatic medicine, but let some stick to nonpsychosomatic medicine." There is no non-psychosomatic medicine.

4

What is neurotic behavior?

We have seen how mortido tensions which have not been able to find relief through their natural objects may accomplish their damaging aim by turning inward upon the individual himself and causing physical pain or disease. Libido tensions also seem to be naturally intended for outward expression, and if they are turned back upon the individual, they too may cause unhappiness. In addition to their physical effects, long unsatisfied Id tensions may cause mental difficulties, such as insomnia, inability to concentrate, restlessness, irritability, sadness, sensitivity to noises, nightmares, unsociability, and a feeling of being talked about. Besides such symptoms of chronic anxiety from which anyone may suffer at times, there are particular individuals who have special kinds of symptoms, such as the hysterics, who suffer from paralysis, blindness, inability to talk, and a host of other afflictions which imitate physical diseases; and the compulsives, who complain of continual doubts, inability to make decisions, strange fears, persistent thoughts, and inability to keep from doing certain things over and over, such as counting, washing their hands, stealing, and retracing their steps.

All these abnormal ways of partially relieving Id tensions when they overflow have certain things in common.

1. They are all inappropriate; that is, none of them uses energy in such a way as to give final relief to the tension. The energy is used for some purpose which does not satisfy the Id instincts in the way they want to be satisfied, and which in the end may result in harm or unhappiness to the individual.

2. They all waste energy. Instead of the energy's being put under the control of the Ego, it is spent to no good purpose in spite of all the Ego's efforts to prevent this. The Ego, guided by the Reality Principle, normally uses energy to change the surroundings in such a way as to make possible the satisfaction of libido and mortido. In these abnormal conditions, from stomach ulcer to compulsions, the Ego has lost control of part of the mental energy.

3. They all result from too long unsatisfied Id tensions, "the unfinished business of childhood."

4. They are all disguised expressions of Id wishes, so well

disguised that in all the history of human thought, it was not until eighty years ago that they were first clearly recognized for what they were.

5. They all employ over and over again the same useless or damaging methods for this disguised expression. This is called the "repetition compulsion." The individual seems to be compelled to relive the same patterns of behavior again and again when the Ego loses control.

6. They usually result from inwardly directed Id energy which really requires an outside object for complete satisfaction; in any case, there is always object displacement, whether the false object be the individual himself or merely something closely related to the real object.

Any *behavior* which has these earmarks is called neurotic. A neurosis, or psychoneurosis, results when there is so much of this behavior that it interferes with normal living and impairs the individual's efficiency, happiness, and ability to get along with or love other people. "Neurosis" is a medical diagnosis, a condition due to misguided attempts and persistent attempts to satisfy Id tensions in ways which are inappropriate, waste energy, result from unfinished business of childhood, express the wish tensions in disguised instead of direct form, use the same pattern of reaction over and over, and employ aim and object displacement. A little later we shall discuss at greater length the difference between neurotic *behavior,* which is simply a method all members of the human race use for getting rid of their excess wish energy in disguised form, and an actual *neurosis,* which is a *disability* characterized by *too much* neurotic behavior.

Normal behavior uses energy efficiently in a way which is appropriate to the situation of the moment to satisfy easily recognized Id tensions by effective behavior toward the proper objects in the surrounding environment. Planning for future financial security, raising healthy children, or the conquest of nature are examples of this. Neurotic behavior uses energy inappropriately and wastefully to satisfy old disguised Id tensions by means of old patterns of behavior directed toward substitutes for the real object or toward the individual himself. Examples of this are gambling, overconcern about bowels, diet, and appearances, sexual promiscuity and a compulsion to "conquer" members of the opposite sex, a hunger to collect possessions and objects which have no practical or aesthetic value, smoking, and drinking. From these examples it will be seen that in a mild form much neurotic behavior is harmless, socially acceptable, and "normal"; only when it becomes damaging to the individual and those around him is it called a "neurosis," or some similar medical name.

We have to consider with special care those cases where the neurotic use of energy involves one of the individual's body organs as a false object. If the patient has complaints which seem to come from his stomach, heart, thyroid, or one of his other organs, but nothing can be found wrong with that organ by physical examination, X rays, or laboratory tests, such complaints are called "functional," because they are due to the way the organ functions rather than to any demonstrable change in its structure. If there is evidence from physical, X-ray, or laboratory examination that the organ has been changed in appearance by physical, chemical, or bacterial action, such changes are called "structural," and the complaints "organic."

A good many people use "functional" to mean the same thing as "neurotic," and "structural" to mean "not neurotic." This is not strictly correct, because there are many functional changes which are normal. Any emotion, such as sexual desire or anger, will cause functional changes throughout the body in preparation for the gratification of Id tensions. In such cases, the reactions do not have the characteristics of neurotic behavior described above; they are appropriate and efficient preparations for the gratification of immediate, undisguised Id tensions in accordance with what the Reality Principle calls for in different situations with the proper object. "Functional," therefore, does *not* mean neurotic; nor does "structural" mean "not neurotic," since, as we have seen, neurotic reactions often lead to structural changes in various organs such as the skin or stomach.

5

What is a neurotic symptom?

The fact that a certain amount of energy finds expression in a neurotic manner does not by itself make a neurosis. People who suffer from functional disorders such as headaches, stomach upsets, or constipation are not necessarily "neurotics" if, aside from the actual pain or inconvenience caused by the symptom at the time it occurs, they feel well and are able to carry on their everyday lives efficiently. Certain types of migraine and hay fever are particularly good examples of this. These conditions may result from piled-up Id tensions, and during the attack the individual may be uncomfortable, but between the attacks he may feel perfectly well; even during an attack he may carry on with his affairs, though not as efficiently as usual.

It is only when the battle between the Id instincts and the other forces of the mind takes up so much time and energy that the individual feels poorly for long periods, or is unable to work efficiently, meet people openly, and love well, that we have a true neurosis. This is the distinction between neurotic behavior and an actual neurosis. As we have mentioned, smoking is neurotic behavior according to our standards, but this does not mean that everyone who smokes suffers from a neurosis. Smoking may be beneficial from the point of view of mental efficiency, since it satisfies tensions which might otherwise hamper the individual. A true neurosis is accompanied by a feeling of unhappiness, disappointment, and frustration.

Neurotic symptoms are complicated to unravel because they result from not one, but four tensions striving for relief, and the symptom tries to take care of all of them at the same time: inwardly and outwardly directed libido, and inwardly and outwardly directed mortido. This means that each symptom must meet the following specifications: it must in some way gratify the individual's self-love, as by attracting other people's attention; it must give him some external libido satisfaction in disguised or symbolic form, as by giving him an excuse to call people; it must punish the patient, as by causing physical pain; and it must harm others, even if only in a disguised or symbolic way, as by making them tiptoe around the house.

The unconscious, being a natural system of forces, automatically takes care of all these tensions at once without having to do any figuring; just as a cloud floats through the sky without thinking, its course being determined by a number of factors—wind speed and direction; rotation of the earth; altitude; temperature; density of the cloud; etc. If we stop to think about all these factors, and use them to try to figure out where the cloud is going or where it came from, it looks complicated, but it isn't complicated to the cloud; it just goes where the resultant of the acting forces carries it. Similarly, the forces in the human mind act together to produce a symptom, and that symptom is the automatic outcome of all circumstances acting at any given moment; if the circumstances change, so may the symptom. If we try to figure out the forces behind a symptom we have the same trouble as in the case of the cloud, but because something is difficult to explain does not mean that it has trouble happening. It *has to* happen.

There is one more specification which the symptom must meet: it must disguise the Id wishes sufficiently so that the Ego and Superego do not recognize their true nature. If recognition occurs, the symptom may disappear, because it no longer meets this requirement; that is one way in which analysis of a symptom may cure it. If the individual does not find a different way of handling the tensions behind the symptom, however, they may simply find another and better disguise, and a new symptom arises.

We may state these requirements of a symptom in another way by saying that a symptom is a defense against certain urges becoming conscious, while at the same time obtaining some gratification through the symptom. Thus, a symptom is (a) a defense (b) a symbolic or indirect expression of an Id wish. Anything which has to do with the mental image concerned in gratifying the wish can serve as a symbol of that gratification. For example, we have already indicated that the infant's image of comfort has at least three clear elements: love, warmth, and milk. If a symptom should arise from a wish relating to this early stage of life, it might take the form of an unquenchable thirst for milk. This would symbolize the individual's discontent with his present life, and his wish to get some of the comforts of the nursing infant.

Lavinia Eris was Ludwig Farbanti's secretary when he owned the Olympia Cannery. Lavinia's three sisters were all married by the time she was thirty, but she stayed on at home and took care of her mother. Every time Lavinia got serious about one of her boy friends, her mother would have a "heart attack," and then Lavinia would have to give up any idea of marriage so that she could stay home and take care of her ailing parent. When Lavinia was forty, Midas King bought the cannery. She stayed on at her old job, but she had a hard time at first. Mr. Farbanti was quiet and never showed that he was excited, but Mr. King was irritable and was always shouting at Lavinia, who was very sensitive.

About this time Lavinia's mother had another heart attack and took to her bed for good, so that Lavinia had to stop going out with Mr. McTavish, who owned the drygoods store and whom she had hoped to marry. Lavinia began to feel a nervous strain, and suddenly acquired a great desire for milk. She drank several quarts of it every day, and began to put on weight. The doctors could find nothing wrong with her physically, nor did injections of calcium and vitamins have any effect. After a few months, the desire gradually diminished. It was not until she had a nervous breakdown seven years later that she went to Dr. Treece and found out the meaning of this symptom.

Her neurotic craving for milk satisfied her tensions in the following symbolic and indirect ways:

Inwardly directed libido: Up to that time it was always her mother who got all the attention, with her heart attacks. Now that Lavinia was "sick," she got some attention too.

Outwardly directed libido: In a symbolic way, it brought her close to the comfort of infancy and her early loving relationship with her mother.

Inwardly directed mortido: By getting fat and less attractive she punished herself.

Outwardly directed mortido: Since she was sick, she neglected her mother for a while; she also told her mother by her attitude: "See, it is you who made me sick and unattractive to men with your demands!" (Which was true enough actually, since her mother literally took great pains to keep Lavinia from getting married, so she would not lose a good provider and nurse.)

At the same time, her symptom was so mysterious and so far removed from direct satisfaction of her real cravings, that she had no need to admit any of these underlying tensions. Nearly all of them would have horrified her if she had had to face them directly. The symptom relieved these desires and at the same time was a defense, or a way of concealing their real strength. At that time the defense was successful. After the tensions had been partly relieved by the mechanisms described above, her craving gradually diminished. Later, under the new added stress of her approaching fifties, she was unable to defend herself successfully by means of neurotic symptoms and broke down completely into a *psychosis,* when the Id took over control of the personality from the Ego. (In the next chapter, we shall learn what a psychosis is.)

This illness was called a neurosis rather than merely "neurotic behavior," because during the time she was complaining about the symptom, Lavinia's efficiency was lowered, her social life was broken off, and she felt unhappy, disappointed, and frustrated.

6

The different kinds of neuroses

We are already familiar with some of the results of the neurotic use of energy and the damage it can do. We saw how Nana Curtsan's neurotic drive for seeking affection eventually led her to become a prostitute. Nana suffered from a "character neurosis," that is, a neurosis which did not cause any obvious symptoms, but weakened her character so that she was unable to get along in the ordinary way of life. Midas King's inwardly directed Id instincts affected his circulatory system, so that his blood pressure went up and down from time to time, until at length it remained constantly at an abnormally high level. Edgar Metis's inwardly directed tensions laid the foundation for an ulcer of the stomach. Ambrose Paterson's neurosis also affected certain special organs, including his skin, back, and prostate gland.

While these are good examples of the neurotic use of energy, the types of neuroses most commonly spoken of by psychiatrists are somewhat different and fall into several groups, the best known of which are compulsion neurosis, phobias, conversion hysteria, anxiety neurosis, hypochondriasis, and neurasthenia. Let us study examples of some of these, starting with compulsion neurosis.

Ann "Nan" Kayo, the only daughter of Enoch Kayo, the chief of police of Olympia, had a hard time going through college, especially after she broke her engagement with Hector Meads. Her asthma interfered with her studies, but worse than that was her feeling that she never did anything right. Even when she went for a walk, she was beset by doubts. She had to step on all the cracks in the pavement wherever she went, and often upon getting home, she would begin to wonder if she hadn't missed one somewhere. On several occasions she had even got out of bed late at night, after lying awake worrying for an hour or two, to go back over her route and do the whole walk again to make sure she didn't miss a crack.

At times when she went out she felt as though there were a rope tied to her which she paid out as she went along, and if she didn't return the same way it seemed as though this "rope" had gotten tangled. Even if she did return the same way, she would sometimes doubt her own memory of the journey, espccially if she was feeling bad for some other reason, and would lie awake wondering if she should do it over in order to make quite sure that the imaginary rope was untangled.

The problem of doorknobs also took up a lot of her time. She could only permit herself to turn doorknobs to the north or west. If a room faced in the wrong direction, she would not go in unless the door were open. This phobia changed after she fell in love with Josiah Tally. Then she had a compulsion to turn all the doorknobs she could find. She was obsessed with the idea that every time she turned one, she was transmitting "love power" toward Josiah, and making their relationship more secure.

This brought on a new difficulty, however, since now, every time she touched a doorknob, she felt that she was getting her hands full of germs, and that the only remedy was to wash and dry them four times. Furthermore, she often doubted her memory of her counting after this cleansing process was finished, and then she would have to do it all over again. If she didn't, her doubts would bother her for hours until they became unbearable. She was passionately jealous of Josiah and was obsessed by the idea that if she omitted to do things the way she "had to," he would go out with some other girl. She often lay in bed imagining that he was making love to some other woman, fascinated by torturing visions she could not get out of her mind.

If everything was going well, she got along better. But the minute things went wrong, or if she had to worry about some change in her routine, even such a small thing as going home for the weekend, her doubts would become worse and then also her asthma was likely to come on. At such times she was unable to make up her mind about anything, and it would take her hours to get dressed for the twenty-mile drive to Olympia.

It should not be supposed that Ann was unintelligent. She realized only too painfully how unreasonable her phobias, obsessions, and compulsions were. Her Ego exerted every ounce of will power to conquer them, but to no avail. It was a problem to eat, sleep, and concentrate on her studies, and only by letting her compulsions have their way was she able to accomplish these things.

Such compulsion neuroses are very difficult to cure, but after a few weeks of treatment Dr. Treece made her life easier to a certain extent so that her studies improved. She got so much confidence in him that she no longer had to retrace her steps after going somewhere. She felt that if she had come home the wrong way, or neglected to step on a crack, somehow the doctor would take care of it for her. She told him:

"I feel as though you will fix it up personally with whoever or whatever it is that threatens to punish me when I don't make sure of carrying out every one of those rituals in detail, and then I can go to sleep without worrying about it any more."

At the bottom of Ann's troubles, including her asthma, were a raging anger against her mother and some mixed feelings toward her father, whom she loved dearly but also despised for his lack of self-confidence. In spite of his aggressive occupation of police chief, at home he was unsure of himself and leaned on Ann's mother, letting her decide even things relating to his office. Ann's anger and contempt, together with the three "absolute ideas" we talked about in a previous section, were the important factors in her illness, and when she became fully aware of them and sorted them out carefully, she improved. Her belief in the "omnipotence of thought" showed in her feeling that through doorknobs she could influence her lover and strengthen their love, while her belief in the "irresistibility of her charm" expressed itself in a twisted way through a wish that all the other women in the world would die so that she could have all the men. In the main, her symptoms were connected with powerful death wishes directed against her own sex.

Death wishes are distressing to people of good conscience, just as sexual desires used to be to many people in the Victorian era. If they are strong, and are strongly repressed, they continually agitate for release and gratification, sometimes causing sym`toms which are quite out of the control of the Ego, since the Ego has banished the tensions which give rise to them. We may compare such death wishes to the death-dealing Nihilists whom the Tsar of Russia banished from his empire. Once they left the country they were out of his control and were able to carry on their work unhampered, though they could only express themselves indirectly. Since the unconscious is outside the boundaries of the conscious Ego, wishes which have been banished to the lower regions are out of the Ego's control, and if they make trouble there is little the Ego can do about it until they are brought back.

Compulsions such as hand washing, phobias such as fear of germs, and obsessions such as self-torturing jealousy are very commonly found together.

Conversion hysteria is a different type of neurosis, and usually has its most dramatic effects on some part of the body rather than on the emotions.

Horace Volk hated his father, but he never said anything about it to anybody. His father was a Baptist minister who raised Horace and his three older sisters very strictly. Their mother died while they were all still small children, and their father from then on did not spare the rod.

Horace was eighteen when his oldest sister, Mary, became pregnant. When she came to her father for help, he ordered her never to come into his house again. When Horace came home from work that night and heard what had happened he started to protest, but one look at his father's fiery eyes, and he was struck dumb. He remained unable to speak above a whisper for about six weeks, and then his voice returned.

When his second sister ran away from home two years later, Horace again lost his voice. After a few weeks, it came back as it had before.

When his third sister found out she was pregnant, she took the precaution of getting married before she told her father about it. She and her brand-new husband came to the house on the evening of their marriage and announced what had happened. Reverend Volk listened to their story, and then raised his hand slowly and pointed to the door. He ordered them never to enter his home again. Horace tried to say something, but once more his voice had gone.

This time it did not get better. After about two months, Horace went to the family doctor, who tried to cure him by injecting Sodium Amytal. While he was under the influence of this drug, Horace was able to talk, but as soon as its effects wore off, his voice sank to a hoarse whisper again. After three trials of this treatment over a period of a month, the doctor sent Horace to see Dr. Treece.

Dr. Treece was able to "cure" him without using drugs or hypnotism. Horace had been in quite good spirits while his voice was lost, but after it returned he became depressed and was unable to sleep. When the doctor removed his symptom of dumbness, which was the only way his repressed Id tensions had of expressing themselves, they had to find a new way, which was accomplished partly by forming an overly emotional attachment for the doctor through the mechanism we described in the section on "images," and partly by making Horace depressed and keeping him awake. Dr. Treece had expected both these new symptoms and proceeded with the second part of the treatment, which consisted in dealing with the underlying Id tensions that caused all the different symptoms. During this period they uncovered not only Horace's primitive feelings about his family, but also the origin and nature of his childlike admiration of the doctor. Eventually, after a year of treatment, Horace was in good enough shape to become firmly attached to a girl and get married himself.

In this case we see that the mortido tensions which were connected with the illness were conscious, while the libido tensions were unconscious. Horace was perfectly aware that it was his hatred of his father, suddenly fanned into new life, which had caused him to be struck dumb. What he did not realize was that each time he lost his voice he not only had new reason to hate his father, but had also lost one of his beloved sisters; that is, he had lost a libido object, leaving a large amount of libido with no outside object for release. This libido had turned inward, and for reasons which came out later, had affected his ability to speak (rather than his stomach, or his arm or leg muscles).

Such sudden cripplings of special parts of the body are characteristic of hysteria. Hysterics suffer from inability to use the arms, legs, or vocal cords; they may suffer from wry neck or spasms of the body muscles which keep them bent over; they may lose one of their senses, such as smell, taste, sight, or hearing, or they may lose the ability to feel in one part of the body such as an arm or a leg. In fact, almost any medical condition can be imitated by hysteria. While it can be imitated, however, it is not duplicated, so that the doctor can nearly always tell that the symptom is functional. As we have previously remarked, hysteria is accompanied by a change in the individual's image of his own body, and since he acts and feels in accordance with his images instead of in accordance with what his body is really capable of, the symptoms correspond to the altered body image rather than to any change in the body itself. The task of the psychiatrist, then, is to change the altered body image back to normal, rather than to change the body. The change in body image which causes the illness is due to a suddenly awakened rush of libido or mortido which cannot for various reasons find outside relief. It therefore turns inward and distorts the body image in the manner described. Because such a neurosis depends on the conversion of mental energy into a bodily symptom, it is called conversion hysteria. There is always a special reason why one part of the body is affected rather than another. Horace, for example, remembered since early boyhood a desire to shout his defiance and tell his father he wanted to kill him. His dumbness was a perfect mask for this frustrated mortido tension, which is why he "chose" this symptom rather than any other.

Because individuals who are overly dramatic in their behavior and overly emotional in their responses are especially apt at some time or other to suffer from hysterical conversion symptoms, such people are commonly called "hysterical." If they displace their dread of their own inner urges onto outside forces, they may also suffer from abnormal fears, called phobias.

Let us now turn our attention to anxiety neurosis. Septimus Seifuss ran a bookstore and artists' supply shop on Thalia Lane. His son Simon, or Si, was the oldest of his five children, the other four being girls. Simon worked in the post office until a war began, and then he enlisted in the army. Simon had always helped his sisters with their lessons and done other things for them that a good big brother should do, so he was used to looking after people. This soon became apparent to his captain, who gradually promoted him until he was a sergeant in charge of a platoon.

When his outfit went into combat, things happened in a hurry, and Simon didn't have as much time as he would have liked to see that each of his men dug his foxhole in the proper place and in the proper way. A shell landed on their position before they were ready and killed ten soldiers. It also knocked Simon out, but luckily he was only on the edge of the blast. When he came to, he was in the hospital, and somehow he heard about the ten men who had been killed.

Simon wasn't wounded, and he might have been discharged from the hospital almost immediately if he hadn't become a "nervous wreck." The slightest sound would make him jump and set his heart racing. He couldn't eat, he had hot and cold sweats, and he slept poorly. Everything got worse at night. He had night-mares about battle—almost the same nightmare every time. He would go through all the events of the attack until he could hear the fatal shell coming over. Then he would wake up screaming and shaking, in a cold sweat, with his heart pounding.

Simon had to be moved back to the United States, where he spent some months in a general hospital before he was fit for duty again. For a long time he had the same dream every night, and just as the shell came over he would wake up screaming. This not only frightened him but also worried him, because he woke up some of the other men in the ward every time. Under proper treatment, however, he recovered from this part of his illness and as treatment continued he calmed down more and more.

With the psychiatrist's help, Simon began to understand the feelings at the bottom of his neurosis. He was a conscientious man and as so many conscientious people do, he blamed himself for things that weren't his fault. It soon appeared that he felt that if he had been more careful to watch where his men dug their foxholes, they wouldn't have been killed. His guilt about this was much stronger than he realized. Of course, this feeling was unreasonable, for if the men had dug their foxholes elsewhere the shell might have landed elsewhere too, and actually there was nothing he could have done about it.

Simon was the victim not only of his feeling of "guilt," but also of a blocked fear tension. He had been so busy taking care of other people that he had had no time to prepare himself for the shock which followed. He was knocked out so quickly by the shell that he hadn't had time to feel the fear which it aroused when he knew it was coming. In other words, he didn't have time to "feel through" and live out his natural fear. With the doctor's help, he was able to go through with the "living out" in a kind of hypnotic state, and relieve the pent-up fear tensions. He and the doctor crawled on their hands and knees under the table, pretending it was a foxhole. When Simon "saw" the shell coming over, he screamed again and again:

"Oh, God! *Get* in your foxholes! Oh! God! Hit the dirt, for *Jesus'* sake. Oh, God! *Get* in your foxholes!"

This was the way he would have relieved his fear tension at the time if he hadn't been knocked out before he could do it. After a few sessions of this, ending with Simon putting his face in his hands and weeping as he "saw" the men being killed, his dreams stopped.

Why did Simon have this dream? It was apparently an attempt to "live out" his fear in his sleep. If he had been able to carry the dream through to completion, it might have stopped by itself. One reason why he couldn't do this was that he blamed himself so much for his "carelessness" (as he thought of it) that he felt that he, instead of his men, should have been killed by the shell. To have carried his nightmare to completion might have meant being killed in his dream. For some reason which we do not understand, inwardly directly mortido is rarely if ever allowed to express itself completely in dreams. The terrified dreamer who falls off a cliff always wakes up before he hits the ground; the panic-stricken girl who cannot move while the giant with the big knife rushes toward her always wakes up before she is caught; or if she is caught, it turns out that he is not going to kill her after all. This is in contrast to dreams of outwardly directed mortido or libido, which often go on to completion in murder or orgasm. Since Simon couldn't finish himself off in his dream, he had to stop dreaming at the critical moment. With the doctor's assistance, however, the business he could not finish in his natural dreams was completed; the dammed-up energy was released, and he became a free man again.

The psychiatrist did not stop at this point. On further study he and Simon both became aware that the whole situation had been a repetition of some unfinished emotions of childhood, regarding some similar supposed "carelessness" while he was taking care of his young sisters, when one of them had been slightly burned during the big fire in Olympia many years before. By the time the treatment was finished, this had also been worked out, and Simon was relieved of this additional tension which had been buried in his mind for years, and which even before he went into the army had caused some nightmares and palpitation.

Milder forms of this neurosis occur even in people who lead an apparently quiet life and have suffered from no emotional shocks that they can remember, the symptoms consisting of jumpiness, restlessness, excessive sweating, fast heart, insomnia, nightmares, and a haggard feeling and facial expression. These symptoms resemble those of hyperthyroidism so closely that in any case where there is possible doubt, a surgeon, an internist or gland specialist, and a psychiatrist may have to get together to decide which it is. A further resemblance is the fact that an emotional shock often marks the beginning of thyroid disease, as in the case of Polly Reed, whose father ran a record shop next door to the Seifuss Book Store. When she was twenty-six, her father died, and immediately afterward her thyroid gland began to enlarge and she acquired many of the symptoms described above. These symptoms disappeared after the diseased gland was removed. Thus it is sometimes very difficult to distinguish between a disease of the thyroid gland and an anxiety neurosis, since the two may resemble each other in many respects.

While it is possible to say in a general way that there are different types of neuroses, such as those we have been discussing, actually there are as many neuroses as there are patients, so that it is really artificial to speak of compulsion neurosis, hysteria, anxiety neurosis, etc. The dreams of Simon Seifuss were obsessive in a way like Ann's thoughts, while Horace's hysteria turned into a mild anxiety neurosis after his conversion symptom was taken away from him. To be accurate, one should really speak of Simon's neurosis, Ann's neurosis, and Horace's neurosis, instead of calling them by the names of different conditions. For convenience, however, since most patients seem to favor a certain type of symptom over a long period, classifications are made so that psychiatrists will understand each other when they say that a patient's symptoms "fell mostly into the compulsive group," or "mostly into the hysterical group," or "mostly into the anxiety group." But psychiatrists always remember in dealing with a patient that they are not dealing with an example of a disease, but with a certain individual who has gone through certain experiences which caused certain tensions, resulting in certain measures to get partial relief of the tensions; and that each individual has his own special way, which may change from time to time, of handling his tensions.

Hypochondriasis and neurasthenia are two other classifications which should be mentioned. Anyone who complains unduly about his health is commonly called a hypochondriac, but a true hypochondriac is relatively rare. A true hypochondriac not only complains about his health, but uses his complaints in a shrewd way to control his environment. These patients suffer from an excess of inwardly directed or narcissistic libido. They use their energy to "love themselves." They continually observe the reactions of their bodies and take alarm at the slightest irregularity, much in the manner of Mr. Krone or Mrs. Eris. They call a doctor or visit their favorite quack on the smallest pretext. Their rooms are full of strange medicines and weird contraptions for giving themselves treatment; many a quack makes his whole living from feeding the fears of these people and flattering their self-love. Their households are run entirely for their own comfort no matter what sacrifice this means for the other members of the family, and they will cause an upheaval for the most trivial reasons. Hypochondriacs are very difficult to treat, since they are so much taken with themselves that they bridle at any hint that their feelings are abnormal, and if anyone dares to suggest that they go to a psychiatrist they become infuriated. It will be seen, however, that their behavior fulfills the requirements of a neurosis. Even if they *appear* to cooperate, they are almost incurable. It would have been easier to cure Romeo of loving Juliet than it is to cure a hypochondriac of loving himself.

Neurasthenia is an old term which is sometimes still used to describe people who are tired, depressed, lackadaisical, slightly irritable, and who cannot concentrate on anything and like to lie around without much responsibility. A good many psychiatrists nowadays prefer to classify such cases with either the anxiety neuroses or the neurotic depressions.

In this section we have discussed different types of neuroses, but it should always be remembered that each "neurotic" has to be treated as a special individual and not as an example of some form of disease. Symptoms change from time to time, and each person experiences his symptoms in an individual way.

7

What causes neuroses?

A neurosis depends, first of all, on the strength of the Id impulses and their opportunities for expression either directly in some decent way or by healthy methods of displacement. A person who has been enraged or sexually stimulated since early childhood may simply not be able to handle the piled-up excitement with the normal methods available, and it will interfere with his happiness and efficiency unless he has outside help. Some people, on the other hand, cannot handle even normal amounts of excitement without getting into trouble because of an overly strict Superego, an Ego and storage capacity which have not been encouraged to develop properly, or unusually bad outside circumstances.

If a person has trouble in handling his piled-up tensions, a change in any of the factors mentioned above may bring on a neurosis. He may get along all right until circumstances either increase his Id tensions (increased resentment or sexual excitement), increase the severity of his Superego (guilt feelings), weaken his storage capacity (physical disease), or deprive him of ways for healthy expression (confinement), and then a breakdown results.

The Superego is very important in determining how much tension the individual allows himself to relieve and how much he must store up. If it is easygoing, it will permit free relief and little storage will be required; if it is strict it will allow little relief and much tension will pile up, putting a strain on the individual's storage capacity. This does not mean that the way to avoid neurosis is to give free expression to one's impulses. In the first place, such behavior may lead to so many complications with outside energy systems, such as nature and other people, that further relief will become impossible and in the end more tensions will pile up than ever before. For example, a man who scolds his wife whenever he feels like it may lose her, and then he will be left without anybody who will permit herself to be used as an object for either mortido or libido, and he will suffer accordingly.

In the second place, it is wiser to exercise restraint than to risk offending the Superego, since the latter is a jealous master whose punishments are difficult to avoid. For example, a woman may decide that her Superego will permit her to have an abortion without punishing her for it afterward. At the time, if she is unable to judge her true feelings properly, it may seem all right to go ahead; but if she has misjudged herself, as is sometimes the case, she may begin to feel guilty many years afterward, and perhaps break down when she is forty or fifty under the long-continued reproaches of her Superego.

Another important factor in neurosis is the amount of unfinished business left over from childhood. The greater the amount, the more likely a neurosis is to occur in a given situation, and the more severe it is likely to be. Thus among three patients exposed to the rigors of army life together—whose fathers had died when the patients were two, four, and eight years old, respectively—the first man had the most severe breakdown, the second had a less severe one, and the third had the mildest. The first man had the most unfinished "father business," the second man had less, and the third man had least of all. The severity of their neuroses corresponded to the degree of their emotional experience—or lack of it—in relation to older men, this relationship being an important factor in army life, where the officer must play the role of a father in many ways. A man with few emotional hangovers from early years can stand much more strain in later life without breaking down than a man with many unsolved childhood problems.

It is very common among neurotics to say, "My mother and father were nervous, so I am nervous. I inherited it."

This is not true. Neurosis is not inherited; but its foundations may be laid in early infancy as a result of the parents' behavior. Neurosis depends upon how the individual uses his energy. Some of his *tendencies* may depend upon his inherited constitution, as we saw in the first chapter, but his actual development is influenced mostly by what he learns from watching his parents. As an infant, whatever his parents do seems like "the natural thing" to him, since he has few chances to compare their behavior with other people's. We have already described how he imitates them by being agreeable and affectionate or hateful and greedy. If he sees that they meet difficulties by flying off the handle instead of coping with reality according to the Reality Principle, he will imitate this behavior. If they use their energy in a neurotic way, he will have a tendency to do likewise, since whatever his parents do seems "necessary" to an infant. Thus, if his parents are neurotic, he may grow up to be neurotic also, but not because he inherits neurosis, any more than they did. They also learned it from their parents.

It is possible that the strength of the Id drives, the ability to go through the processes required to form a stable Superego, and the storage capacity of the mind may be inherited, but what the individual does with his natural endowments depends upon his early training. It seems that some children from birth find it more difficult than others to develop a normal personality, which is an added burden for their parents, who in such cases have to be particularly prudent in their own behavior. If this fails, it is then up to the psychiatrist to go through the process of correcting the neurotic behavior patterns, however long they have been present, with due regard to whatever assets and liabilities the individual came into the world with.

Footnotes for Philosophers, Chapter Five

1. and 2. *Emotions and Disease*

Precision and detail have been sacrificed somewhat for the sake of clarity, particularly in regard to the workings of the sympathetic and parasympathetic nervous systems. The explanations for backache, arthritis, and "stomach ulcer" are offered more as paradigms than as scientifically tested hypotheses, although there is literature to support them. The fact that microscopic particles collect in areas of vasodilatation was well demonstrated by H. Burrows (1932). An interesting exposition of the so-called "psychosomatic" viewpoint more than a hundred years before the advent of modern psychiatry can be found in contemporary biographies of Dr. John Hunter.

The following references are suggested for those who wish further information on the subjects covered in these sections:

Mind and Body, by Flanders Dunbar, Revised edition. New York: Random House, 1955.

Human Constitution in Clinical Medicine, by George Draper and others. New York: Harper & Brothers, 1944.

Emotions and Clinical Medicine, by Stanley Cobb. New York: W. W. Norton, 1950.

3. *Psychosomatic Medicine*

The problem of the psychosomatic approach in relation to the general philosophy of "etiology" is discussed by T. Lidz in *American Handbook of Psychiatry,* edited by S. Arieti (New York: Basic Books, 1959) Chapter 32. Chapters 33–39 discuss psychosomatic disorders of various bodily systems in detail.

4. *Neurotic Behavior*

See *American Handbook of Psychiatry,* Chapters 79–83. Also *Encyclopedia of Mental Health,* Volume 4, pp. 1312–23.

5. *Neurotic Symptoms*

For further reading on this subject see: *Complete Introductory Lectures on Psychoanalysis,* by Sigmund Freud, especially Chapters 17, 18, 22, and 23.

6. *Nosology*

The complexities of diagnosing and labeling are shown by the fact that the *Diagnostic and Statistical Manual for Mental Disorders,* published by the American Psychiatric Association, is a book of about 130 pages listing various names for such disorders.

Some of the most readable and easily understood formal descriptions of the different kinds of neuroses can be found in the textbook of W. A. White.

Outlines of Psychiatry, by William A. White, 14th ed. New York: Nervous & Mental Disease Publishing Company, 1935.

While the case of Si Seifuss is descriptively an example of anxiety neurosis, some clinicians might prefer to call it technically a "traumatic neurosis." For more cases similar to his and their fuller explanation, the reader may consult Grinker and Spiegel's study of war neuroses:

Men Under Stress, by Roy R. Grinker and John P. Spiegel. New York: McGraw-Hill Book Company, 1963.

7. *The Causes of Neurosis*

I have selected here those items and that point of view which seem most useful and enlightening to the layman. For further information about the psychoanalytic point of view, the reader may consult:

An Elementary Textbook of Psychoanalysis, by Charles Brenner.

I have not discussed "cultural factors," because I believe on the basis of my own published studies that their influence has been overemphasized. See my articles "The Cultural Problem: Psychopathology in Tahiti," *American Journal of Psychiatry* 116 (1960), 1076–1081, and "A Psychiatric Census of the South Pacific," *Ibid.,* 117 (1960), 44–47; also "Cultural Factors in Group Therapy," *International Mental Health Research News Letter* 3 (June 1961), 3–4.

6

PSYCHOSES

1

What is insanity?

In most people the Ego is able to keep the Id reasonably well controlled, so that mental energy can be applied to useful purposes and emotional life can proceed normally. In some individuals, if the Ego is weakened or the Id is stirred up, energy is wasted, because the Id instincts manage to obtain partial gratification in disguised form in ways which interfere with welfare, efficiency, and happiness. Such warped expressions are called neurotic behavior; if they occur regularly and seriously hamper the individual, they constitute a neurosis. In some unfortunate individuals (about one out of every two or three hundred people), the Ego retreats completely and the Id takes over. The repressed images then become conscious and lead to strange forms of behavior which are called psychoses.

In order to make clearer the actual effects of such a complete retreat of the Ego, let us examine a case of one of the commonest forms of psychosis, namely, schizophrenia, in which the illness went through four different stages of development before the healing process began.

There was in Olympia, living down on the mud flats by the river, a young fellow who should have been a shepherd. Alone with his sheep, he could have lain on his back in the grass, arms outstretched, dreaming his dreams as he gazed at the fleecy clouds. He was full of heavenly aspirations. With his sheep for subjects and audience, he could have played at being a king and philosopher. Unfortunately, Cary Fayton worked in the Meat Department of Dimitri's Grocery, where he had to take care of dead sheep instead of living ones. When he lay on his back, all he could see was the cracked ceiling of his room in a cold-water flat near the Olympia Cannery.

Cary spent a good deal of time lying in his room. He was never able to get along with other young people, and girls, whom he very much wanted to be with, found him too strange and silent. Most of his life was wrapped up in his daydreams, and he couldn't bring himself to talk about those; and since he didn't have much else to talk about, conversation was difficult.

One time he did tell a girl named Georgina Savitar about his daydreams: how he would be a great man when he grew up and would save her life sometime when some man got too fresh with her. But the next day Georgina whispered to the other girls in school what she had encouraged him to tell her; after that, they always giggled when he passed by, and he felt so small that he couldn't bear to come near any of them and would cross the street to avoid meeting them. He once walked home with Minerva Seifuss, a kind and intelligent girl, who tried to tell him in a helpful way that she thought he was a nice boy but because he was so shy people and especially other girls thought he was funny, and why didn't he try to get interested in sports and things so he could be like other boys? Cary knew she was trying to be kind, but what she said only made him feel worse and more helpless. He always avoided Minerva after that, though at home he secretly wrote poetry about her.

When Cary was lying on his bed in the evening while his divorced mother was entertaining her boy friends, such as old Mr. Krone, he often thought about the various women who came to the butcher shop during the day and how some day they might get into trouble and he would come up and rescue them and then they would fall in love with him. There was one woman especially whom he liked to think about because she had very long thin legs and he was particularly fond of that kind of legs. He always watched her carefully when she came into the shop to see if she gave any sign of noticing him particularly. One day she smiled at him in a friendly way and then he decided that she must be in love with him. He figured out that she had been in love with him for a long time and that she had been afraid to tell him about it because her husband would beat her if he knew her secret thoughts about Cary.

Cary knew that the woman was Georgina Savitar's sister and the wife of Alex Paterson, the druggist. He found out where she lived and began to loiter on the corner, hoping that some time she might come out and then he could speak to her alone, which he could not do in the store. He wanted to tell her how much he loved her, and also that the butcher shop was beginning to worry him and that he wanted to leave it. He hoped that she might run away with him and leave her husband, whom Cary imagined to be treating her cruelly. One time she did pass by but when the big moment came he couldn't say what he wanted to and lowered his eyes so that he didn't even say hello to her. Finally he decided that the only way to tell her he knew about her suffering was to write her a note. He wrote the note and kept it in his pocket for weeks before he had the courage to put it in the parcel when he wrapped her meat.

When Mrs. Paterson got home that day she found the note, which read as follows:

DEAREST:

I love you. I would like us to go away together. I know how you are suffering. I will kill the beast. I am tired of the butcher shop. When I look at the meat I feel dizzy and don't know if I am alive or dead. It all seems like a dream. I have been here before. My face is changing. They will get us both if we don't watch out. They will make your legs change. Good-by darling. I'll meet you at the usual place.

CARY

Mrs. Paterson didn't know what to make of this note. She and her husband talked it over. They thought of going to Cary's mother to tell her about it, but they were both timid people and she had a reputation for being belligerent when she was drinking, so they went to the police instead, or rather, Mr. Paterson did. When he walked into the police station he was surprised to find Cary there too. Cary was asking for protection. He said people could read his thoughts and that they followed him down the street making signals about him which caused his face to change. He wanted to have someone arrested. He said it was a plot, though he didn't know who was at the bottom of it. Mr. Paterson walked out of the police station without saying anything and came back later. When the police sergeant read the note, he called Chief Kayo. They decided that it was a case for Dr. Treece, so they went down to Mrs. Fayton's house and brought Cary to the hospital.

Dr. Treece found that Cary had had some strange experiences. The Lord had appeared to him and told him that he was to be King of the World. He had given him a certain sign, a cross with a circle under it, which was to be his sign. Voices kept talking to him, telling him what to do. Sometimes when he went to do something like lifting a piece of beef, the voices would tell him just what he should do. They would tell him to bend down, put his hands under the beef, raise his arms, put the beef on his shoulder, and so on. When he went out in the street, the voices would warn him that everybody was making faces about him and that they were out to get him.

Everything seemed like a dream. The people who were after him used mental telepathy to change his appearance. He would spend almost an hour sometimes in front of his mirror wondering just how much his face had changed in the last few hours. Everything he did seemed to have happened before. All these feelings got worse when he was around the butcher shop, and sometimes they were so bad when he was actually handling meat that he got sick to his stomach. He said that his only hope was in Mary. Mary was what he called Mrs. Paterson, though her real name was Daphne. He said that they were after her too, and that he was the only one who could save her, by using his magic sign. When he was asked about his mother, he replied: "I don't have any mother."

When his mother came to visit him, she was weeping and sobbing. He didn't even say hello to her. He just smiled at her and asked: "Do you like porridge?" He didn't seem to recognize her, and paid no attention to her weeping or to her statements that she was his mother and could make him better. He looked at her as haughtily as an ancient king might have looked at a peasant, gave her a piece of paper with his magic sign written on it, and then walked away and stared at the tips of his shoes with a puzzled frown.

The next day began a period during which Cary just lay in his bed and didn't move. This lasted for more than two weeks. He didn't talk, open his eyes, or show any signs of recognizing anybody. He refused to eat, and in order to keep him from starving to death food had to be put into his stomach through a tube which the doctor slid gently down his gullet. He didn't take any care of himself at all. He didn't care what happened in his bed. If the doctor took his arm and raised it in the air, it would stay there for a long time, sometimes a few minutes, sometimes over an hour. His arm and hand could be bent into any position and they would just stay that way, as though he were a wax image that could be bent into any shape.

One day Cary came out of this state and began to speak again. He didn't complain any more about the people who followed him. Now he said they couldn't touch him. He would sit in a chair in a corner and tell how he was King of the World and the world's greatest lover. All the children in the world were fathered by him. No woman could have any more babies without his help.

He still didn't recognize his mother. No matter what she said or how she behaved, he showed no response. He went right on telling her what a great man he was, just as he did with the doctors and nurses, without any emotion, as though the whole world knew it except the person he was talking to. If anyone tried to argue with him about this, or ask him how he could be a king if he was sitting in a corner in a hospital, he would just listen and then go right on telling what a great man he was as though no one had spoken to him.

Dr. Treece didn't try to argue with Cary nor did he give him any special treatment at that time, because he had a feeling he would eventually get better by himself, which he did after seven months. Only when he seemed to be well again did Dr. Treece begin to talk things over with him.

After he was discharged from the hospital he got along well, seeing Dr. Treece about once a month. Because Dr. Treece was taking care of him, Mr. Dimitri gave him a job again, but not in the meat market on Main Street. Mr. Dimitri also owned the Depot Market on Railroad Avenue North, and Cary worked with the grocery stock there. Mr. Dimitri thought he was taking a chance with the customers by having him work there, even though Cary never had to serve anybody, but he said the boy deserved as much of a chance as anyone else and that as long as he did his work well he would keep him, since Dr. Treece said it was all right. Dr. Treece worried about Cary, though he never let on to anyone that he did. He just kept close tabs on him. He believed that if Cary had any sick feelings he wouldn't hesitate to come right to the doctor and tell him about them, even before he went home from work, which is what he told Cary to do.

Cary's breakdown happened about twenty years ago, before the discovery of the new "mind-clearing" drugs, and before group therapy was used very much. His case is described here to show the "natural history" of schizophrenia, that is, the stages it can pass through if it is not treated by modern methods. In many backward countries it still happens the way it did with Cary, because they do not have the mind-clearing drugs available and they do not have psychiatrists properly trained to do group therapy. Some doctors still use electric shock, insulin, carbon dioxide, or brain-cutting for severe cases of this type, but these methods of treatment are going out of style as more and more is learned about medications and group therapy. All this will be discussed at more length in the sections on treatment. At any rate, when Cary began to have trouble again a few years later, Dr. Treece put him into a therapy group, which helped to put him back and keep him on an even keel. It was even easier to do this when the new drugs came into use. Whenever Cary felt upset, Dr. Treece would prescribe one of these for a while, and when Cary felt comfortable again he would stop taking it. In this way, Cary never had to go back to the hospital again. He kept his job at the grocery store and eventually got married. With group therapy he got better and better and was eventually able to stop treatment altogether.

And now back to our study of the various forms of schizophrenia as shown by the progress of his original breakdown. What happened in this case? It is evident that Cary was different from the other boys and girls around him. He never formed any friendships or attachments for anybody. He was not even close to his mother, which may be attributed to the kind of life she led. Certainly if he *had* any ability to form human relationships she did not make it easier for him. On the other hand, neither did he ever actively express enmity or resentment against anyone. All his expressions of both mortido and libido took place in his daydreams. In real life he neither kissed nor punched anybody, while in his fantasies he had intercourse and killed people.

He was so inexperienced in the realities of human contacts that on those rare occasions when he tried to approach another person he bungled it. He had little opportunity to learn from experience to form accurate and useful images of human nature in accordance with the Reality Principle, as people with normal parents do. He put himself in an embarrassing position with the scornful Georgina and her mocking friends without having a clear image of the consequences; and his images of Daphne Paterson and her husband were definitely warped.

Finally, he had enough loneliness, embarrassment, humiliation and trouble on his hands to bring things to a head. His ungratified object libido and mortido became so strong that they overwhelmed his Ego; his mind gave up the Reality Principle entirely and his Id took over all his images and changed them according to its own desires and its own picture of the universe. We remember that the Id acts as if the whole universe centers around the individual who, in the image of his own Id, is immortal, all-powerful in matters concerning both libido and mortido, and able to influence anything in the world by merely wishing or thinking about it.

The changes in Cary's images became more and more obvious as the Ego lost control. His image of his face changed, as well as his images of the people around him, of his place in society, and even of the meat in the butcher shop. Instead of being something he handled, the meat became something personal that frightened him to the point of nausea. During the struggle between the Id and the Ego's reality testing, his images became so confused that he could no longer tell the difference between a new image and an old one, and between the images of his daydreams and those based on reality. The result was that he didn't know whether or not he had seen things before; he felt as though things were happening for the second time when they were happening for the first time; and he couldn't tell half the time whether he was dreaming or not.

At the same time, all his tensions, which so far had received only make-believe relief through daydreaming, suddenly exploded outward, but in a very unrealistic and unreasonable way. Instead of expressing them through healthy loves and hates toward other people, he put his own wishes into the minds of others and felt as if they were directed toward himself. It was like projecting his feelings on a screen so he could sit back and watch them as though they were someone else's. It was like having them turned into a movie called *"Love and Hate,* starring Cary Fayton," and he was watching that movie. After all, that is what he had done all his life anyway in his daydreams, which consisted of movies of "Love and Hate" inside himself, with himself as the star, in which he made love to beautiful women and killed his wicked rivals. In a way, the only difference now was that he was projecting these movies outside himself.

Because he was a sick man, however, he didn't recognize his own feelings in these movies. He thought that they belonged to the other actors, and didn't realize that he was the author of the scenario. Because he didn't recognize this strange movie as his own creation, it frightened him with its powerful and dramatic libido and mortido drives, just as it might have frightened anyone else who saw it as plainly as he did. But no one else could see it, and that is why no one else could understand his agitation. Perhaps if the desk sergeant saw the world as Cary saw it at the time he was in the police station, he too would have asked for protection.

Cary's sickness at this stage, then, consisted in not being able to recognize his own feelings when he saw them, so that he imagined that they were other people's feelings directed toward him. Psychiatrists call this "projection," just as in the example of the movie. It might also be called "reflection." Instead of his mortido and libido being directed toward other people in the normal way, they were projected toward others and reflected back toward himself. In order to hide the fact that he wanted to kill people, he imagined others wanted to kill him; to justify his illicit love for someone, he imagined she was in love with him. Thus he avoided the guilt which would have arisen if he had been the aggressive one in either case. It got to the point where his Id instincts had to express themselves outwardly somehow, and he couldn't express them directly without first "getting permission" from his Superego. This he did with the false belief that others had made the first move. Projecting love and hate, and then returning the imagined feelings in kind, is an interesting way to avoid guilt, but what a price he had to pay for adopting such a roundabout method of expressing his loves and hates! It resulted in his being hospitalized for the better part of a year, until with Dr. Treece's help he was able to push his Id instincts back where they belonged and put his Ego in control again. And by keeping it that way, with whatever help was required from time to time, Cary was able to live a normal life.

A neurosis, as we have said, consists of a troublesome but successful way of relieving Id tensions in a disguised form. When all methods of controlled expression break down, the Ego is overwhelmed by the Id, and we call the condition a psychosis. In Cary's case, the first defense was a general paralysis of all outward expression of the Id instincts, so that they were permitted to obtain relief only in daydreams. In the first chapter we have already mentioned this type of "inhibiting" personality, with a weak "barrier" between the unconscious and conscious parts of the mind and a brittle "barrier" between the conscious mind and outward action, and have noted that these people wisl. that the world would change to correspond to their images while they do nothing to bring about such a change. It is evident from Cary's case why the barrier between daydreams and action in such individuals was described as "brittle." When it breaks, it does not give way gradually but shatters completely and suddenly, so that the Id pours out copiously and unhindered.

As long as his unconscious only broke through in daydreaming, nobody was harmed except Cary, who lost time and energy in this profitless occupation, which did not make his spirit grow stouter or increase his usefulness to himself or society. But when the barrier between fantasy and action broke down, he became a danger to himself and to others and had to be kept where he could not harm himself or others socially or physically. He had to be protected by society from the scandalous desires of his Id until he was once more strong enough to protect himself.

At the beginning we mentioned that there were four stages in the development of Cary's illness.

1. First of all, during most of his life, he suffered from a "simple" inability to make human contacts through either libido or mortido. He neither loved nor fought. His tensions were locked up inside of him. He never got to master any of his jobs. He never got so he could love any situation or person. He just drifted through life, through jobs, and through people, without showing any outward feeling for any of them. Such a way of experiencing is called "simple schizophrenia." We might say that he acted as though he had neither libido nor mortido to spare for anything outside his

daydreams. He appeared to suffer from an insufficiency of mental energy, just as an anemic person seems to suffer from an insufficiency of physical energy. This appearance was false since we know that, underneath, his feelings were piling up. What appeared to be a "simple" insufficiency was a complicated inability to express his feelings in a normal way.

2. When his acute breakdown arrived, heralded by many strange feelings, both libido and mortido were projected in large quantities. He saw his own feelings reflected from others, and just as a light reflected from a mirror might appear to a confused mind to come from the mirror itself, so he thought that he was loved and hated by people who hardly knew him or knew him not at all. He heard voices and saw visions which confirmed his projected feelings. An important part of his illness besides his delusions, or false beliefs, was a tendency to misjudge "significance." He would think that the slightest careless movement on the part of another person had great personal meaning for him and was connected with the way he felt. Everything about him had too much "significance." The meat in the butcher shop looked more significant than usual, so significant that it made him nauseated. A person lighting a cigarette or licking his lips in a restaurant seemed to be doing it for the purpose of conveying to him a significant personal message or threat. All these new significances confused him.

Such a mental state, involving projection and reflection of feelings, and increased significances, we call "paranoid," especially when the person feels that people are doing everything they do for mortidinous reasons, that is, to warn, threaten, insult, or harm him. A "paranoid schizophrenic" feels persecuted and usually hears voices, as did Cary, confirming his feelings. The voices, of course, were only another kind of projection and reflection: they were his own thoughts being spoken back to him. That somehow he vaguely knew that he himself had written the scenario is shown by his feeling that his mind was being read, that other people could see his thoughts, and so on. We should note that during this stage both his libido and mortido were in action. One person loved him, others hated him.

3. In the third stage he lay for a long time almost as though dead. In such a state patients often show sudden, unpredictable outbursts of great violence. They will appear to be completely

uninterested in their surroundings and then suddenly lash out murderously at someone standing nearby. There is practically no outward sign of libido activity in such a state, and everything that can be observed seems to come from inwardly and outwardly directed mortido. What is called the "tone" of the muscles is also changed, since the limbs can be placed in any position and will stay there indefinitely without tiring, as though the individual had been given a tonic which made him stronger than usual. At the same time, his interest in what happens to him and around him seems to have completely vanished. This emotional catastrophe and the tonic state of the muscles help us remember that this condition is called a catatonic state of schizophrenia.

4. In the fourth stage there was no more evidence of mortido. Cary seemed agreeable and docile. Everything, he said, was fine. He was now the greatest man in the world, the procreator of all children, and the source of all sexual energy. He appreciated himself to the fullest as a benevolent king and a great lover from whom all gifts came to men and women. At times he passed out scraps of paper to the other patients and to the staff as tokens of his generosity; at other times, when he fancied some insult, he withheld his gifts. Once or twice he wrapped small pieces of his feces in the paper as a sign of special favor. He loved all the world and especially himself. His libido was going full blast, and now no longer projected, but mainly turned inward. The similarity of his behavior at this stage to that of the infant who sits kinglike on his throne and donates or withholds his gifts of feces is evident.

During this stage, Cary would want and do opposite things from one minute to the next, without seeming to notice how contradictory he was, as though one part of his mind didn't know or care what another part was up to. He acted as though his personality was split into separate pieces, each acting independently of the others.* This disconnected behavior with a somewhat sexy tinge often occurs in adolescence—*hebe* is the Greek word for youth, and since these patients seem to be in a frenzy (or "phrensy," as it was formerly spelled) and are very often in their teens, they are called *hebephrenics*.

Cary's mind was split in another way, besides being cut up into

* See the section on Transactional Analysis.

separate pieces each acting as though the others didn't exist. The sights which met his eyes and the sounds which came to his ears were split off from his feelings so that reality did not call forth the normal emotional responses. His mother's sobbing no longer made him feel sympathy, nor did the kindness of his nurses awaken gratitude. His feelings seemed to have no connection with what went on around him. His mind was split two ways, so to speak, up and down, and also across. These splits remind one of the up-and-down split in the Church during the Middle Ages, which was called the Great Schism, and of how a certain rock called "schist" splits across when it is under stress. The schisms in such frenzied minds is what leads us to call all such conditions "schism phrensies," or *schizophrenias*.

Schizophrenias are often accompanied by what looks like a split, partial or complete, between what happens to the patient and how he feels about it, so that his feelings have little or no connection with happenings as far as we can see. Cary showed this kind of split when he smiled at his sobbing mother instead of weeping with her at his sad plight. Before an actual split occurs, it is often noticed that events do not affect the prospective patient as much as they do his normal companions. His feelings seem flat instead of being in sharp contact with what is going on. So we speak of things affecting the patient in a flat way, and call this type of response flattened or inappropriate affect. Such individuals are more interested in their daydreams than in what goes on around them, and because their emotions depend more upon what goes on inside their minds than upon what happens outside, a normal person has an eerie feeling when in their company. Schizophrenia is just an exaggerated example of the principle that people feel and act in accordance with their inner images rather than in accordance with reality.

We can now summarize what we have learned about schizophrenics. First of all, they show flat or inappropriate affect, with splitting of feelings from events and, later, splitting of the mind into pieces which seem to act independently of one another.

Secondly, they can be put into four main classes. The patient may show all four types of behavior mixed up, or they may occur one after the other, as in Cary's case; or he may show only one kind of schizophrenic behavior throughout his illness. The first is the simple type, shown by inability to become emotionally attached to anything or anyone, so that the individual wanders about from place to place and from person to person. Many vagabonds and prostitutes, amateur and professional, who are forever changing places and people because they don't care where or with whom they are, are simple schizophrenics. This does *not* mean that everyone who changes jobs and companions frequently is schizophrenic. Only a trained person can judge properly if there is a true psychosis present or in the making.

The second type is the paranoid schizophrenic, characterized by projection and reflection of Id wishes, reflections of thoughts into voices and visions, and feelings of heightened significance.

The third type is the catatonic, who shows stoppage of almost all muscular movements, queer changes in the behavior of his muscles, and impulsive violence.

The fourth type, the hebephrenic, behaves and talks queerly and expresses many fantastic ideas with a rather sexy and often religious tinge.

In the old days, schizophrenia was called "dementia praecox," because the individual was supposed to become completely demented eventually, and the psychiatrists of that time felt that this was a precocious condition, since they thought that dementia was properly a condition of old age.

Fortunately, we know now that these patients do *not* become demented, though after being sick for a long time many of them may seem so to the inexperienced observer. In addition, a large percentage of them recover with modern methods of treatment, or even without them. Also, the disease does not always begin precociously; in fact, paranoid schizophrenia is in many cases a disease of late middle age. The term *dementia praecox* is, therefore, a worn-out and discouraging one which had better be discarded. Such illnesses should always be called schizophrenia, meaning a "split mind," which we can hope often to put together again, and never dementia praecox, which means to many people a hopeless condition of confusion.

Cary was insane. This means (1) that he no longer knew the difference between right and wrong in many matters and would have been incapable of doing right if he did know; (2) that he was a danger to himself and others and likely to cause a public scandal;

and (3) that he was not responsible for unlawful acts which were the products of his mental illness. Therefore it was necessary to place him in a hospital under the supervision of experienced doctors, nurses, and attendants in order to protect society and to protect him from himself. Insanity, however, is only a legal term, and has no standing as a medical word, though it is still used as though it had by many people. In fact, even legal authorities are not agreed as to the definition of insanity, so that (1), (2), and (3) above are all legal definitions, which vary from state to state and with different tribunals.

The proper way to describe Cary is to say that he was psychotic. It made little difference to a doctor trying to cure him, or to Cary, once he was in the hospital, whether he knew right from wrong. There are many psychotic people who need psychiatric treatment even though they know right from wrong, and there are some people who don't know right from wrong who should be treated by means other than psychiatry. Once society and the patient are protected, the doctor is not primarily interested in whether his patients know right from wrong. As far as medical science is concerned, it doesn't matter. The problem for medical science is how much the Id is overwhelming or threatening to overwhelm the Ego; and whether the specific wishes which might win control are acceptable to society or not is a side issue as far as cure is concerned.

A psychotic is a person whose Ego has almost completely lost control of his Id.

The cure for psychosis is to strengthen the Ego or diminish the amount of energy piled up in the Id; if the proper balance is reached the patient gets better. Then the doctor can help him make his recovery permanent. Anything which severely weakens the Ego, such as a prolonged high fever, or the excessive use of alcohol, may make it easier for a psychosis to occur in a susceptible person. Fortunately, in some cases, as with Cary, recovery takes place spontaneously, perhaps because the free expression of Id tensions during the illness restores the energy balance to its former state.

While "psychosis" is a medical term and refers to loss of control of the Id, "insanity" is a legal term which refers to the patient's inability to obey the law. "Lunatic" is an outdated word which shouldn't be used at all. The old idea of a lunatic was an individual whose mind was affected by the moon. Mental hospitals are full of people who are not visibly affected by the moon (though some aspects of the weather do seem to affect them). Psychotics are forlorn people and have troubles enough without being called names which are either meaningless or out of date or both.

2

The different kinds of psychoses

There are three great groups of psychoses: the schizophrenic, the organic, and the manic-depressive. The case of Cary Fayton illustrates well the different types of schizophrenia. The organic psychoses form a more varied group.

Anything which causes structural changes in the brain may confuse the Ego. If some of the brain cells get damaged or burned out, the nerve circuits do not work properly and reality testing begins to fail. In addition, the Id tensions start to break through the Ego's controls, causing still further confusion. The result is an organic psychosis. Among the things which may cause such changes are infections of the brain resulting from diseases like syphilis, meningitis, and tuberculosis; also infections in other parts of the body which are very poisonous or cause high fevers, such as blood poisoning, pneumonia, and malaria. The picture of the delirious (psychotic) explorer lying prostrated with fever in the jungle is familiar to every boy and girl who reads adventure stories. Alcohol and drugs can poison the brain temporarily or permanently and cause psychoses such as delirium tremens and methedrine deterioration. Wounds and tumors of the brain, hardening of its arteries, old age, and *serious* prolonged vitamin deficiency, such as occurs in prison and concentration camps, may also seriously affect the Ego's function.

In the most severe cases, an organic psychosis may take the form of a delirium in which the individual sees terrifying animals, people, or insects and is full of dreadful fears and forebodings. Most organic psychoses are curable if the condition which is damaging the brain can be remedied.

We can now turn our attention to the manic-depressive group.

Janus Land was the youngest of the five children of Alfred Land, the Olympia real-estate and insurance agent. Jan was usually much jollier and more easygoing than the rest of the family, but at times he would get sluggish and irritable. He would then stop seeing his many friends and spend his spare time reading sad philosophers.

Jan entered law school somewhat doubtfully in order to fulfill the ambitions which his father had for him. He himself would have preferred to be a salesman, but he had gradually been persuaded by his parents that he should do something more decorous than selling clothing wholesale. So he began to study hard and did well in his midterm examinations.

After the examinations were over he went out with his friends to celebrate. The others went back to classes the next day, but Jan didn't, because his father was due to pass through Arcadia on business and Jan was going to meet him at the hotel. Just before he left his room, however, he received a telegram saying that his father had changed his plans and would not come after all. Jan, who was still feeling happy from the night before, wanted to go right on celebrating. He had a few drinks and then went downtown and ordered himself a new suit. After lunch, he thought he might as well do things properly, so he bought himself three pairs of shoes, four hats, and a dozen shirts. He took a fancy to the girl who waited on him in the department store, and spent the rest of the afternoon standing around the shirt counter telling her jokes in a loud voice, somewhat to her embarrassment, although she thought some of them were really funny and liked his jolly manner. He didn't have enough money to pay for everything he bought, but his father was well known in Arcadia, which was only twenty miles from Olympia, so his credit was good.

That night he took the salesgirl on a round of the night clubs, where they did things in a grand manner. They drank nothing but champagne, and at each place they came to, Jan bought drinks for everyone in the house, signing his father's name to the check. Then he and the salesgirl went to an auto court, where they spent the night.

The next day Jan still didn't go to classes. Instead, he went to all the clubs he had visited the night before and demanded to see the checks he had signed. At each place he complained loudly of being overcharged. He finally went to a lawyer with his complaints, who told him he had better think it over. Jan went to another lawyer who said he would have to see the checks in order to decide what could be done. Jan wanted immediate action, however, so he went to the police and demanded that a policeman come with him and look into the situation. While he was at the police station, he was so jolly and boisterous that they almost arrested him for being drunk, but he challenged them to smell his breath, and they had to admit that it didn't have any odor of liquor. He slapped the sergeant on the back and, forgetting what he had come for, walked out singing loudly. He sauntered down Main Street, winking at all the girls, until he came to Harry's Haberdashery. He strode into the store and insisted on buying all the gloves they had in the place. The proprietor was suspicious, but he let Jan have six dozen pairs of men's gloves after Jan signed a paper saying that his father would pay for them before the first of the month.

Jan took his armful of gloves and climbed onto the back of a small truck which was parked nearby, where he began to give a sales talk. He shouted out the wonderful qualities of the gloves and a crowd gathered, but no one would buy any. This irritated him, and after a while he began to make sarcastically clever remarks about the tightwads of Arcadia.

A bird began to sing in a tree nearby and Jan stopped talking and listened to the bird. Then he began to whistle loudly in imitation. After a few minutes, a pretty girl walked by. Ignoring the crowd, Jan jumped off the truck and dashed after her, thrusting several pairs of gloves upon her. Just then a police car drove up. Jan saw the officers coming toward him and began to laugh heartily. Then, as quickly as he could, he took the gloves out of the boxes and scattered them among the crowd.

At the police station they again had to admit that he wasn't drunk, so they called his father and told him the story. Mr. Land brought him back to Olympia, where he was put into the hospital.

He quickly recovered from his exuberant state, but Dr. Treece advised his father that he needed a long rest. Jan, however, was ashamed of his behavior and determined that to make up for it he would go back to college and study harder than ever. His father, who was anxious to have a lawyer in the family, favored this idea,

especially since Jan appeared to him to be perfectly well. Against
Dr. Treece's advice, Jan went back to Arcadia. His friends had a
different attitude toward him, but he kept out of their way and
didn't seem to be too upset by the way people gossiped about him
on the campus. He lived quietly and studied hard, avoiding night
clubs and the department store where he had met the girl.

Because he had missed almost two months of the term, Jan
sweated a good deal during the examinations at the end of the
session. He felt uncertain as to how he had done, and he knew
that if he failed his father would find it hard to forgive him. The
day after the examinations were finished, instead of packing to go
home as the other students were doing, he sat in his room and
brooded. Now that it was over, his anxiety began to grow worse by
the hour. He had been feeling overworked for the past six weeks.
He had been having difficulty falling asleep at night, and would
wake up before dawn in the morning, feeling more tired than when
he had gone to bed. He couldn't eat, had no sexual desire, and no
interest in being with people, who irritated him. His thoughts had
slowed up and he had been having much difficulty in concentrating
on his studies. He didn't seem to have a normal interest in what
went on around him, and he wept easily. Noises made him jumpy.
His eyes tired quickly, he was constipated, and he suffered from
belching and heartburn. Now he began to think of the things he
had done after midterm, and things that he had done when he was
younger that he was ashamed of, and it seemed as though everybody knew about them and stared at him on the street.

That night Jan tried to hang himself with a necktie. Fortunately
it broke and he fell sprawling to the floor.

He didn't pack the next day either, and the second evening he
tried to asphyxiate himself by plugging up all the cracks around
the door and windows and turning on the gas. Luckily some gas
leaked out and his landlady found him in time. He was again
removed to the hospital in Olympia and this time his family agreed
to everything Dr. Treece said. Jan was in the hospital for six
months and continued to see the doctor frequently for over a year
after that. Even though he passed the examinations, he did not go
back to college but went to a city upstate and became assistant
manager of a men's clothing shop. For the most part he has
remained in good health through the years, but he still sees a

psychiatrist once a month, and when he starts to have an elation or a depression the doctor prescribes an appropriate medicine and he is able to continue living and working on a more or less even keel.

It may seem surprising that two illnesses with such different manifestations could occur in the same person and be part of the same psychosis, but if we think about the two episodes we can see that they have one most important feature in common: they were both due to the sudden release of large quantities of ungratified Id tensions. During the first illness he was overly sociable, overly generous, sexy to the point of being careless, and also at times irritable, critical, and belligerent. These actions resulted from an explosion of pent-up libido with a small amount of mortido, outwardly directed and so powerful that it overwhelmed his good judgment and his reality sense.

During his second illness, there was another explosion of Id energy, but with two differences: first, it consisted mostly of mortido; and, secondly, it was directed inwardly instead of outwardly. In individuals who are subject to such explosions, we find all sorts of combinations of constructive and destructive energy. Usually the libido is outwardly directed, resulting in what is known as a manic episode, and the mortido inwardly directed, causing a depressive or melancholic episode. Since both conditions frequently occur in the same individual, this type of illness is called a manic-depressive psychosis. In some people there is a long depression without much manic phase, or a long mania without much depression. In others, manic and depressed episodes alternate without any normal period in between. In Jan's case there was a period of fairly good health between the two phases. Mixed types also occur in which the explosions of libido and mortido come at the same time instead of one after the other.

Once the explosions are over, the individual is as well as he ever was. This illness, unfortunately, tends to repeat itself as the years go by, and it was to prevent such repetitions that Jan continued to see a psychiatrist for such a long time after he was well. In this respect a psychosis is much like tuberculosis: when the individual recovers, he still has to be careful and should continue to see a doctor at regular intervals to make sure that he stays well.

In our country, in peacetime at least, most people are encouraged by church and by upbringing to turn most of their libido outward and most of their mortido inward. During a psychotic explosion of mortido, therefore, the patient chooses to relieve his tension by suicide rather than by murder, so that the suicide rate is more than double the homicide rate. In some other countries, where mortido is not so strongly directed inward, there is more tendency to hurt others, and the same applies to some groups in this country. Among certain Mohammedan people in the Far East, individuals may suddenly run amok and try to kill as many people as possible, sometimes with "justification," meaning that the Superego allows the person to direct his death wishes outwardly instead of inwardly. Although a great deal is written about running amok in other parts of the world, it also occurs in America, and the record number of killings has probably occurred here. Besides individual massacres, there are also numerous kinds of mass killings which are not regarded as psychotic: wars, extermination, racial and religious massacres, and banditry, some encouraged, some condoned, and some fought by the authorities.

It is sometimes difficult to distinguish between schizophrenic and manic-depressive psychoses. The important thing in labeling such illnesses is not what the patient does, but how he does it. A manic-depressive may get the same ideas of persecution as a paranoid schizophrenic, and many schizophrenias begin with episodes of melancholia. To distinguish in doubtful cases between the despairs of a schizophrenic and the depressed feelings of a manic-depressive may require years of training and practice. The diagnosis may be important in deciding which kind of medication to prescribe.

3

What causes psychoses?

We know little about this, except that schizophrenia may have something to do with the chemistry of the brain cells, and manic-depressive psychosis with the glands. There is also evidence that a simple chemical in the blood, lithium, is in some way connected with manic-depressive psychosis. But at present we know more about the effects than about the causes of psychosis.

A neurosis is a defense. In a neurosis, the troublesome tension is corralled into one part of the personality, so that the rest is left free to develop as best it can in its crippled condition. By crippling himself in one respect, the patient leaves himself more or less free to develop in other respects. In the psychotic, on the other hand, the whole personality is involved in a surge or an oozing of Id impulses and childlike thinking. *Physis,* the growth force, is blocked. The Reality Principle is suspended. The individual acts in accordance with badly warped images, so that if he sets out to do something he may need a lot of luck to be successful. Thus in his first illness, Jan succeeded in attracting a woman of poor judgment, but a more sensible woman would have realized that something was wrong and he would have failed. Even Cary might have succeeded in attracting a sufficiently confused woman with his hectic note.

Psychosis, like neurosis, is the result of a conflict between the Id and the inner forces which restrain it, but in neurosis the restraining forces win by a compromise, while in psychosis the Id wins.

Footnotes for Philosophers, Chapter Six

1. *Insanity*

Factitious etymologies were used in this section for their mnemonic value. As for "flattened affect" and "split personality," there is some question as to how these terms apply to schizophrenics as one sees them in the clinic, but an attempt is made to present these popular concepts here in such a fashion as to satisfy nonprofessional curiosity.

For a detailed discussion of the legal difficulties in defining insanity, and the various rules adopted by different jurisdictions in this connection, see the article "Law and Psychiatry," by B. L. Diamond, in *The Encyclopedia of Mental Health,* Vol. 3, pp. 908–29. In fact this article gives an excellent account of the whole field of forensic psychiatry.

2. *The kinds of psychoses*

The material in this chapter should be well digested by the layman before he attempts to apply it to his friends, otherwise he is likely to make false judgments, in view of the prevalence of schizoid and cyclothymic personalities in our "normal" population, and our national tendency to psychological hypochondriasis.

For further study, some of the most readable formal descriptions of the psychoses can be found in White's *Outlines of Psychiatry.* The classical personal account of mental illness is *A Mind That Found Itself,* by Clifford W. Beers. New York: Doubleday, Doran, 1948. See also:

Symbolic Realization, by M. A. Sechehaye. New York: International Universities Press, 1952.

I Never Promised You a Rose Garden, by Hannah Green. New York: New American Library, 1964.

For further reading, some excellent technical and literary descriptions of psychoses can be found in *The World of Psychology,* edited by G. B. Levitas. New York: George Braziller, 1963, Volume I, pp. 330–439. This includes some of Kraepelin's original lectures, which are difficult to find elsewhere. It also includes stories by Conrad Aiken and Guy de Maupassant.

For a discussion of "running amok" among Filipinos, see:

"Cultural Aspects of a Multiple Murder," by Eric Berne. *Psychiatric Quarterly Supplement,* Vol. 24, pp. 250–269 (1950).

For a general discussion of the problem of suicide, see:

Symposium on Suicide, edited by Leon Yochelson, M.D. Washington, D.C.: George Washington University, 1967.

7

ALCOHOL, DRUGS, AND SOME BEHAVIOR DISORDERS*

1

The different kinds of drinking

Thalia Lane was a tiny thoroughfare opposite Court House Square, one block long, running between Wall Street and Leonidas Street. There were three narrow houses on one side, and three little stores on the other. The stores belonged to Mr. Seifuss, the bookseller, who also dealt in spices; Mr. Reed, who owned the music shop; and Sam Chusbac, the wine merchant. The neighbors said that Mrs. Chusbac really ran the business, while Sam liked to chat with the customers and give them advice. Mr. Chusbac loved his wines, and he always had a small glass of something special to sip with his meals (1).† Sometimes his daughter Thalia (named after the street where she was born) was allowed to have a sip too, especially on special occasions or holidays, and in this way she learned to drink sensibly (2).

Sam Chusbac had two brothers, Van and Dan, who worked in the steel mill in Arcadia. Sam, the youngest, was slightly built and soft-spoken. Van and Dan were different; they took after their father, who had been a heavy drinker. They were a burly, noisy pair, and rather than having a few glasses of wine to taste during the day, they preferred regular doses of whiskey. Van took a good slug every morning before he went to work, and another in the

---

* I am indebted to Claude Steiner, Ph.D., supervisor of group therapy at the Center for Special Studies in San Francisco and a Teaching Member of the International Transactional Analysis Association, for assistance in bringing this chapter up to date, and for writing the section on transexuals and transvestites.

† The numbers in this story refer to the discussion at the end of the section.

evening when he came home (3). Dan handled it differently. He
was a big man, and everyone in his family was afraid of him.
Almost every weekend and some week nights, Dan would go out
with "the gang" to one of the downtown taverns and play cards
and drink whiskey. Usually when he came home he was somewhat
intoxicated and although he never really hurt anyone, he would
often embarrass his wife by singing and cursing loudly. Occasionally, he shoved around some furniture or pushed one of the
children (4).

His elder son, Dion, followed his father's example and also
pushed the other children around. This would anger their mother,
who was a teetotaler and did not allow whiskey in the house (5).

Just before Dion went off to college, his father took him to his
favorite tavern and ordered him a glass of whiskey, saying "Your
mother wouldn't like this, but now that you're a man, you might as
well start to drink." Dion had been drinking on the sly (6) for the
past two years with his high-school friends, so he drank the
whiskey down without any trouble, at which his father nodded
approvingly and expressed his admiration.

At college Dion really learned to drink. Although he walked
with a swagger, he actually was shy and had trouble being sociable
when he went to parties. He soon found that a few shots of
whiskey gave him a nice glow and then he could talk to the girls as
well as any of his fraternity brothers could (7).

Dion was a clean-cut, good-looking fellow, and he did not have
much difficulty getting a job and a girl friend when he came back
to Olympia to settle down. In spite of being by nature a little
touchy, he became genial enough after a few drinks to become
quite a good salesman (8). Mr. Land, the real-estate man, put Dion
in charge of his insurance business, since the Land boys had all left
Olympia.

Dion used to worry sometimes because he didn't really make
friends with people. When he was in company he could hardly say
a word until he had had a few drinks. Afterward, though, he would
become talkative and lovable, and in this way he became good
friends with Marilyn Land and Mrs. Land. Soon he was going
steady with Marilyn. They had fine times together. Sometimes they
would stay home and drink with Mrs. Land. More often they
would go to a bar or a night club in Arcadia and spend the evening

drinking and talking, either alone or with some friends they would meet there.

When Marilyn became pregnant, neither she nor Dion was very upset, though of course it was an accident that had happened one night when they both had had too much to drink. They quietly got married, and soon it was an open secret around town that they had been married for some time. Finally, when things looked right, they set up housekeeping.

Both of them liked good whiskey, and usually they had a few drinks every day. They would have cocktails before dinner, and then one with dinner, and afterward they would spend the evening sitting around, talking and drinking (9).

After the baby came, though, things were different. Marilyn couldn't nurse him and he was put on the bottle. The doctor advised Marilyn not to drink for a few months. Dion tried not drinking too, but he found it difficult to have any fun without it. He wasn't as fond of the baby as he had thought he was going to be, and sometimes he got impatient with Marilyn for spending so much time with him. He also began to find other things wrong with her. Above all, he found that when he wasn't drinking, she bored him. They tried to talk it over several times, but it didn't do much good. Marilyn then discovered that if she drank with him, he would stop complaining. So it gradually got to be a habit with them to drink together every evening, and many nights Dion would pass out on the couch and Marilyn would barely be able to take care of their child.

This went on for about three years and it soon got so that both of them woke up with hangovers. Then Marilyn got pregnant again, and this upset Dion so much that he began to drink as soon as he got up and would continue while he was at work. Marilyn thought that this was going too far, so she refused to drink any more and told Dion that if he kept on, she would have to divorce him. He managed to stay sober for a couple of months at a time, but always backslid, until Marilyn finally did divorce him. Everyone thought she was foolish to do that because he had the reputation of being a charming fellow. Marilyn moved into her mother's house with the two children and resolved to stop drinking, which she did with little difficulty (10).

After his family broke up, Dion was so sad and lonely that he drank more heavily than he used to. Sometimes he would get too drunk, and then he wasn't so charming. There were always some friends, however, to see him home when he couldn't make it. If he was shaky in the morning he would take a big snort, and afterward he would be all right for the rest of the day (11). People began to worry about him; sometimes he even worried about himself, so he tried to stop drinking. He managed to go for several weeks without touching liquor, and then, having shown himself and everybody else he could do it, he decided to celebrate his victory, and went on a bender that lasted four days. He was very much ashamed of himself for having missed work, but he didn't let on to anybody that he was. He steered clear of liquor for a few weeks again after that. He didn't sell as much insurance as usual during those weeks, though, which worried him. He got so worried that one night he took a drink to cheer himself up. Then he took another, and a few more on top of that, and finally wound up on another four-day bender, during which he didn't eat and got hardly any sleep (12).

During the next three years he married and divorced Alecta Abel, and meanwhile things went from bad to worse. If he didn't drink he couldn't sell, and if he did he went off on a bender and lost out on his work altogether. He began to think that drinking might end his career, so he went to Dr. Treece. It didn't do much good, because Dr. Treece said he would have to come for treatment for a year or two, and Dion thought the doctor was just trying to make a good thing out of it, since the treatment would have cost more than he was spending for liquor, which was a lot. So he went right on drinking, but he began to be pretty sensitive about it. When Mr. Land would say something to him about missing time from work, he would reply: "I still sell more insurance than anyone else in town!" Mr. Land wasn't satisfied with this, because he felt that pretty soon Dion was going to slip 'way below par. Other people tried to talk to Dion, but it wasn't any use. He would only get angry at them (13).

One day when his mother scolded him a little bit, he said: "Dammit, everybody is against me! Can't a man do as he pleases any more, without a lot of blabbing women interfering?" This thing that he said stuck in his mind, "Everybody is against me!" He would lie awake at night sometimes and say to himself: "Everybody is against me!" After a while when his work did fall below his former standard, he didn't even feel guilty any more. He just said it was because everybody was against him. "Look at me," he would say to himself. "I'm well-educated, kind of good-looking, smart, and I know the insurance game. If I don't make a go of it, it's because people are against me. No wonder I drink. Who wouldn't if he was trying his best and everybody looked down on him?" That was what he said to himself the day Mr. Land told him he would have to go (14).

Mr. Paluto, Mr. Land's competitor, had some misgivings about Dion, but when Dion promised that if he was given a break he would make good, Mr. Paluto gave him a job without telling him about his doubts. Dion thought Mr. Paluto was a swell fellow and told him so. Dion felt that anybody who could see that he was the best salesman in the game, if he was given a break, was a smart apple, and he, Dion, admired anyone with such good judgment. He swore off liquor for good.

After he had been about three months with Mr. Paluto, not drinking, Dion realized he wasn't doing so well anyway. A good many of his old friends were taking their business elsewhere. One night he got so sad thinking about the injustice of this that he decided he needed a snorter, just one (12). This time his bender lasted seven days instead of four, and he ended up in the hospital with delirium tremens. Dr. Treece pulled him out of it all right, though it wasn't easy. Dion hadn't eaten for a whole week, and an important part of the treatment consisted of a heavy diet with lots of vitamins, calories, and carbohydrates. After a few days the shaking ceased, the fears went away, and Dion stopped seeing things whenever he closed his eyes. Dr. Treece preferred to use old-fashioned drugs, such as paraldehyde, in the treatment of this condition, rather than tranquilizers and other new drugs.*

When Dion went back to the office, Mr. Paluto wasn't at all agreeable. He didn't want to take a chance with his business reputation by having a man like Dion working for him, and had resolved mentally when he hired him that the first time he went on a bender he would fire him, which he now did.

Dion cussed him out plenty. "You can't fire me!" he said. "I

* The reason for this is discussed in the note on delirium tremens at the end of the chapter.

resign! I knew you were a faker the first time I set eyes on you. You too! The whole world is against me. No wonder a fellow takes to drink!" That was the end for Dion. Now that he was sure everyone was against him, there was no use trying any more. So he gave up and became a real bum. Marilyn and Alecta had both remarried, so they couldn't help him much, but his mother, his cousin Thalia, or Mrs. Land always took care of him, no matter how bad his condition was. Dr. Treece's opinion that Dion would kill himself with drink within two years frightened them, but it didn't scare Dion, because he knew that if he got the breaks he could stop drinking any time (15). Every time he ended up in the hospital he would promise Dr. Treece and himself that that would be the last episode, but he always went back. Once in a while he would just give up and say to the doctor: "What's the use anyway? Everybody is against me and I don't get any breaks anywhere. What if I do die? Everybody will be happy when I'm gone, even my own mother!" But Dion's mother was very sad indeed, and so was his former wife Marilyn, and so was Dr. Treece, when Dion died a couple of winters later from a combination of delirium tremens, liver disease, and pneumonia which he caught from lying all night in the gutter.

Let us discuss the various kinds of drinking which took place among the Chusbac brothers, who were born in Europe, and their children, who were born in the United States.

1. Sam Chusbac liked to drink a little wine with his meals. This is a European equivalent of our American habit of drinking coffee and the English habit of drinking tea. A little wine with meals acts as an appetizer and cheers everyone up. For those who are brought up that way, it rarely becomes a bad habit. The signs of this kind of drinking are the sipping of the wine rather than the drinking of it, and the enjoyment of its taste and aroma as much as the effects of the alcohol. In this case wine is an appetizer and beverage rather than an intoxicating substance, and is associated with food taking.

2. There is considerable evidence that alcohol addiction is rare in certain kinds of families because the children learn to associate drinking, and especially wine drinking, with special occasions and thus learn to drink with appropriate moderation. In such families, heavy drinking, rather than being regarded as a sign of strength

and masculinity, is looked down upon as a weakness. Research has shown that in the United States, Italian, Jewish and Greek families introduce their children to wine and that these groups tend to have a significantly lower incidence of alcoholism among them. The signs of this kind of drinking are the same as above.

3. Van Chusbac liked a slug of whiskey before and after work every day. Physical workers with a certain attitude toward drinking can sometimes get away with this without becoming alcohol addicts or getting into a brawl every Saturday night. This practice is not uncommon in Europe. Travelers in Yugoslavia, for example, cannot help but notice the large number of people whose breakfast begins with or consists of one or two glasses of *sljivovica,* or plum brandy.

4. Not everyone who abuses alcohol is an alcoholic. Dan Chusbac is a good example of a man who abused alcohol, but because his drinking never became progressively worse and because it did not greatly interfere with his work or his family life, he cannot properly be called an alcoholic.

5. Dion's mother's uncompromising aversion to alcohol tended to promote alcoholism, because it prevented "teaching" the appropriate use and consumption of alcohol to her children.

6. A large number of alcoholics get started in their drinking careers during high school. Teen-age drinking is often promoted by the confusing attitudes of the adults in a community in regard to drinking. Teen-agers who see their elders abusing alcohol are in effect being encouraged to drink. Dion is a good example of a teen-ager who was secretly being encouraged to drink by his father while his mother tried to pretend that the problem did not exist and refused to deal with it.

7. During Dion's college days, he indulged in typical American social drinking. Americans like to go to new places and meet new people. It is important for their enjoyment of life that they learn to make friends quickly and converse readily. A few drinks in the course of an evening keeps people loosened up. For shy people, this may seem especially necessary, as otherwise they might be wallflowers a good part of the time. Such drinking, however, may be a danger for these very people. It is such an easy way out of their shyness that it is liable to become a habit and a crutch, and

prevent them from undertaking the harder job of being happy in society by learning to enjoy. If excesses can be avoided, this kind of drinking, in the American way of living, may be a help on special occasions, although drinking would seem to be less desirable than trying to attain a sounder and more permanent foundation for social living.

8. Occupational drinking—that is, drinking to make business relationships easier—is not good. A businessman is in business every week of the year and if he comes to rely on help from liquor he is likely to be drinking every day. He may soon come to believe, perhaps rightly, that he will lose business if he doesn't drink to help things along, and so it gets to be a regular habit; and being easier than trying to develop a sound way of carrying on under his own steam, it may then be leaned on too heavily. In addition, some people don't like to do business with a man who has the odor of alcohol on his breath.

9. Dion's drinking with Marilyn may have been a subtle form of insult. It may have meant as it so often does: "When we're sober we're bored with each other. We had better keep on drinking because then we can stand each other." An affection for and an image of one's life partner formed in a retort of alcoholic fumes will seldom stand up under stress, and Dion's didn't. Married couples who spend their evenings drinking often end up in one of two ways because of the ever-present danger that they will find out how little they have to offer each other. If they stop drinking, as Dion and Marilyn did, they may soon begin to feel this boredom, and a separation is likely to result. If they go on drinking, they may have to drink more and more as time passes, because the longer they know each other, the more strongly they bore each other and the more liquor it takes to cover it up.

10. Marilyn was evidently not an "addictive personality." She drank to keep Dion company, and as soon as she was removed from his influence, drinking ceased to be a problem. Many persons go through periods of heavy drinking which eventually become obviously harmful to them, and decide to stop, without further signs of addiction. Dion, however, is a good example of an "addictive personality" who drinks not so much because of external influences as because of an internal need.

11. Nearly everybody agrees nowadays that when a man begins to take a morning drink to cure the shakes or hangover of the night before, he is well on his way to becoming an alcoholic.

12. If a man can't stop drinking after the first one, when he has previously made up his mind to, he is an alcohol addict, since his craving now controls him, instead of vice versa. When his drinking becomes the only activity he engages in, to the exclusion of sleep and food, the process of physical deterioration begins. Because alcohol has only calories and no other food value, the person is basically starving himself to death. In addition, the concentration of alcohol in the liver causes the deterioration commonly known as *cirrhosis*. The wasted parts of the liver become hardened, and when most of the liver is gone the person dies. An alcoholic with most of his liver wasted away will get drunk on less and less alcohol because his liver is no longer capable of breaking down the alcohol so that his body can eliminate it.

13. When a man sacrifices more for a drink than any drink is worth, he is called an alcoholic. If he is willing to lose his job, or let his children go hungry or without good clothes in order to satisfy his craving, he is an addict. We define the condition by its results. If the results of his drinking are seriously harmful or distressing to himself or to others, a man is an alcoholic (no excuses accepted).

14. When a man loses his perspective to the extent that he blames others for what he brings upon himself, he starts to become a burden to those who love him.

15. If he keeps on drinking in the face of medical advice that he will seriously injure his system by doing so, we see plainly what we saw less clearly before: that chronic alcoholism is a slow form of suicide. It is a way of evading the growth force of *physis,* and the prohibition which normally keeps inwardly directed mortido from causing the death of the individual. Drinking is a pleasanter way than hanging oneself, and it does not arouse the same feelings that a deliberate attempt at suicide would. Chronic alcoholism is suicide, even though the drinker may pretend that his death drive is "unconscious."

But there are other kinds of drinking too. People who suffer from cycles of depression may start to drink when they feel a depression coming, without realizing why they do it, using this method of trying to conceal their condition from themselves. In the old days, women who used to have depressions with their menstrual periods would take large quantities of certain "vegetable compounds" which contained a high percentage of alcohol and were really nothing more than cocktails; but because they were labeled as medicines, even the most prudent spinster, who wouldn't have dreamed of taking a "drink," could allow herself to take these wonderful "compounds" which magically made her menstruation seem so much gayer and more hilarious than it used to be.

Drinking cheap wine to the exclusion of other forms of alcohol is the mark of the "wino." Wine is the cheapest available way to get drunk. Many people, when talking about alcoholics, think of skid-row "winos." Most alcoholics, however, are not "winos" or bums. Only about seven per cent of alcoholics in this country live on skid row. The rest, about five million of them, are found in homes, factories, and offices.

It often happens that two alcoholics marry each other under the illusion that because they are afflicted by the same difficulties they understand each other and will be able to help each other. This is a bad risk for both of them, since more often than not they will encourage each other to continue drinking.

Perhaps the few people who become nauseated from drinking before they reach the stage of intoxication are more fortunate than their fellows in the long run, in spite of their embarrassment.

2

What is a narcotic addict?

There are certain drugs which are normally prescribed by doctors in very small quantities. The best known of these come from the juice of the Oriental poppy plant. After an operation, the doctor makes the patient comfortable by giving him an injection of morphine which weighs about one quarter as much as a grain of corn. This is enough to put the average person to sleep even in the face of severe pain.

Some people find the products of the poppy plant a very pleasant thing and start to use them without a doctor's order, either to experience pleasant dreams and visions, or to calm their jangled nerves and make it possible for them to sit still. Since such use is against the law, the narcotic is taken by these people in whatever form they can obtain it illegally. In some places they find that peddlers can sell them opium which they can smoke or swallow, while in other places they can get only morphine or heroin, which they inject under the skin by means of a needle.

After they have been taking these drugs for a while, two things often happen: first, their tensions increase because of their guilt feelings; and, secondly, their Egos are weakened by the drug. They have all their old troubles, and in addition, maybe a sneaky feeling that they are breaking the law and associating with criminals in order to get what they want.

In this way a bad circle is set up: their Id tensions become more and more frightening, and their Egos become less and less able to cope with them. Such users thus require increasing quantities of the drug to make them feel safe, calm, and controlled. They become "addicts of the mind."

Not only are their minds in a turmoil when they are without the drug, but they also become "addicts of the body." An addict deprived of morphine suffers from all kinds of aches and pains, sweating, pounding of the heart, stomach upsets, shakiness, and, in general, "the screaming meemies." In order to quiet his body and his mind, he may require eight, sixteen, or even forty times the normal dose, quantities which would kill a normal person but are just enough to keep the addict from being miserable.

Such doses, obtained illegally, cost a great deal of money, and addicts gauge the magnitude of their addiction by how much money it costs them daily. It is not unusual for an addict to have a fifty-dollar-a-day habit, and since without his drug he is a trembling mass of nerves and aches, he will go to considerable extremes to get it. That is why the narcotic addict is so often forced to turn to crime, usually prostitution or theft.

By far the most common crime is theft, and some addicts become expert at walking through large apartment houses, trying every doorknob, and making a thirty-second raid of each unlocked apartment, picking up everything valuable that fits into a pocket. Young people who turn to prostitution as well as people who turn to theft become an additional source of income to the syndicates which sell them their narcotics and may also control prostitution and the sale of stolen goods. In addition, almost every addict becomes himself a "pusher" to support his habit. And so he becomes increasingly enmeshed with the underworld. Since the syndicates know that he has to have the drug at any price, he is completely at their mercy. They will charge him all that they can get and cheat him whenever they feel like it. The illegal drug traffic is a dirty business in which everybody concerned, with few exceptions, will double-cross everybody else at every opportunity.

Some people who become addicted to narcotics do not get sucked into the circle described above, especially if they have enough money to support the habit without financial strain. But in any case a true addict is a person who is miserable without his drug, who will sacrifice anything to get it, and who requires larger and larger doses to keep him comfortable so that eventually he may take quantities which would kill several average people.

It should be said that some who have studied these matters very carefully think that there is no such thing as an addict of the body, and that all addiction is of the mind.

3

The things people can become addicted to

The most serious forms of drug addiction (aside from alcohol) involve cocaine, and opium derivatives such as morphine, heroin, and opium itself. These are the most dangerous drugs, since addiction to them can occur very quickly, sometimes in less than one week. In fact, in some cases it takes only one dose to awaken the terrible craving which may lead to addiction. This does not occur when the drugs are taken for a short period under a doctor's orders. Occasionally, people become addicted to other medications if they take them over a long period.

Nowadays almost everybody has heard of phenobarbital, Nembutal, and other sleeping powders, capsules, and pills which doctors call "barbiturates," and which street users call "downers." These are being used habitually in increasing quantities, so that more and more people are going through life half "doped up."

Most of the barbiturates leave more or less of a hangover the next day, and while it may be so slight that the individual isn't aware of it, nevertheless his efficiency is lowered. These drugs should be taken only for limited periods under a doctor's supervision, and people who take them on their own initiative are asking for trouble. The cure for insomnia lies in emotional tranquillity and not in the drugstore.

Probably the most harmless and effective sedative there is (for hermits or patients in a hospital) is an evil-smelling and foul-tasting drug called "paraldehyde," which is excreted through the lungs. People, especially alcoholics, may become addicted even to this unappetizing (but otherwise almost perfect) sedative.

Another kind of drug that almost everyone is acquainted with is "pep pills" or "diet pills." These drugs are known medically as "amphetamines." Amphetamines are stimulants, and their effects are the opposite of sedatives. They are called "uppers" because they produce insomnia, lack of appetite, increased activity, and a feeling of competence and exhilaration. They can be taken by mouth but are sometimes injected with a hypodermic needle. They are often taken by athletes, entertainers, students wishing to cram for examinations, and busy people who need to stay awake for long periods of time. The dangers of such pep pills are that the taker will not sleep and may not eat, and if he takes enough of the drug for a long enough period of time he will develop a psychosis in which he has hallucinations and may feel that people are trying to kill him. The stimulant drugs first came to the attention of the traffic police when it was found that truck drivers who were taking them in order to stay awake on a long driving run, would go berserk and drive off a cliff or through a busy intersection in an attempt to shake some imaginary persecutor.

The worst of the amphetamines is the one called "speed," or methedrine, which can cause rapid addiction and rapid deterioration in the user, a fact which is known to both the users and the drug peddlers. In some areas, the drug syndicates supply large quantities of the drug free of charge to young people in the hope of hooking and rooking some of them. Even among "hippies," who are very favorably disposed toward the use of drugs, methedrine is frowned upon, since it is becoming more and more evident that the deterioration caused by its use may be permanent. It is possibly due to brain cell damage and the effects of the high blood pressure caused by continued abuse.

Bromides are drugs which can be obtained either in pure form by prescription or in various mixtures in patent medicines. They were formerly very popular for the treatment of epilepsy, but are now rarely used for this purpose. They are still used, however, as a self-prescribed treatment for headaches or hangovers, and they are easily available for this purpose in the form of patent preparations sold at soda fountains. Such preparations often contain other drugs which may cause poisoning, along with the effects of an overdose of bromide. The trouble here is that bromide poisoning causes insomnia, the very condition the drug is supposed to "cure," and the natural reaction of most people to this condition is to take even more of the drug, resulting in more poisoning and worse insomnia. Any doctor who has watched a bromide psychosis or who has seen a man turn sky-blue all over from taking too much "morning-after" soda-fountain fizz, becomes very conservative about prescribing these preparations. Such drastic results, however, are likely to occur only after prolonged and intensive use of bromide preparations.

Marijuana does not cause a true addiction, because it does not leave any craving. Many people find it pleasant to take and use it for solace and enjoyment. Since it interferes with the individual's efficiency in most occupations, it is medically a harmful drug in the same way that alcohol is. It can be indulged in after working hours to some degree without any apparent ill effects, but if it is used excessively, it may interfere with the individual's normal way of living. At one time it was thought that the use of marijuana inevitably led into the use of narcotics. This is not so. Nevertheless, the possession of marijuana is just as illegal as the possession of hard drugs such as heroin.

One reason for the many disagreements about the effects of marijuana is that they vary with the personality of the user, and a second reason is that the effects also depend on the kind of people the user associates with. A third reason is that the drug as sold to its users in this country varies in strength and composition. The marijuana plant often grows wild and can be easily cultivated almost anywhere. Its street name is "pot" or "grass," and in America it is usually smoked. The leaves come from Indian hemp, which is used in making ropes. It was growing well in this country before 1632. It is difficult to know precisely from which plant illegal dealers obtain their drug unless they should happen to be deteriorated professors of botany, and even then they might argue among themselves as to whether it was the true *Cannabis sativa* or the false *Apocynum cannabinum,* also called Indian hemp.

Another class of drugs which has recently become the object of a great deal of attention is that described as *psychedelic.* In this group the most highly prized among users is *L.S.D.* (from its chemical name, *d-lysergic acid diethylamide*) or, as it is colloquially called, "acid." Other psychedelics are *mescaline,* which comes from the peyote cactus, and *psilocybin,* which come from a mushroom. Marijuana is also included in this class. Recently two new chemicals have appeared on the illegal market: *D.M.T.,* which gives a quick-acting, short-lasting "trip," and *S.T.P.,* which causes a long and dangerous two- or three-day "trip." These drugs are also called "hallucinogenic," because they cause the users to see, hear, and feel things that he would not ordinarily experience. These hallucinations differ from dreams and the hallucinations of psychotics because the drug user realizes that they are caused by the drug and that they are not real. The psychedelic drugs are the cornerstone of the "hippie" social movement.

While the short-range effects of psychedelics are fairly well understood, their long-range effects are still not known for sure, except in the case of marijuana, which has been used for a long, long time in the United States and numerous other countries throughout the world. The consensus seems to be that it has little if any long-range effect. L.S.D., the most popular "psychedelic" at this time, is praised by its users as consciousness-expanding and highly beneficial in the long run; but medical and psychological authorities are becoming increasingly wary and concerned about the possibility of physical and mental damage, for which there is some evidence.

We have defined an addict roughly as a person who has an unnatural craving for some particular thing and will sacrifice almost anything to gratify it. By this standard, there are many addictions which do not involve drugs, the two commonest being gambling and overeating. Gambling is a serious family and police problem, while addiction to food is a medical problem affecting a considerable portion of the population in this country. The normal masturbation of adolescence often gives the feeling of an addiction during that sensitive period of growth and experience.

4

How can an addict be cured?

Curing an addict is the easiest thing in the world—*if*. All we have to do is find something that will interest him more than the thing he is addicted to. We can cure any alcoholic *if* we can find something that will interest him more than alcohol does. So far nobody has found any such thing that will work in all cases.

The most important thing is that an alcoholic rarely has a two-way relationship with anybody. He may become attached to somebody he can lean upon, just as Dion Chusbac leaned upon and was fond of Mrs. Land, but this was the same kind of attachment an infant has for his mother. He loved her because of what she did for him and not for herself. In this way, as in many other ways, alcoholics are childlike in their emotional behavior—childlike not in a nice way, but in many respects like badly brought up babies. In fact, it is no joke to say that an alcoholic is a person who has never been weaned from the bottle.

This gives us a clue as to one method for attempting to cure an alcoholic: by getting him to form a more stable relationship with another person. This can sometimes be accomplished by a skillful psychotherapist who uses his influence to guide the patient into changing his behavior.

In a very rare case, the right woman can do the same thing as the psychotherapist by getting the alcoholic to love her more than he loves his liquor. This happens so rarely that no woman should count on it. Usually the alcoholic marries a woman for what she gives him, and not for herself. If his own mother couldn't wean him from the bottle, how does a mere wife think she can do it? The fact that an alcoholic chooses a certain woman to marry, or allows her to "persuade" him to marry her, nearly always means that she does not threaten him with having to form a healthy relationship with her. If she did, he would avoid her, since it would mean too much sacrificing of his established satisfactions. The same is true, of course, for other addicts as well, whether they be addicted to drugs, food, gambling, or some more unusual pleasure.

Curing an addict is a two-stage process. First, and most important, the addiction of the body has to be arrested. That is to say, the addict has to stop taking the drug, recover from the withdrawal effects, if any, and clear his brain of the mind-altering effects of the drug. This makes it possible for his Ego to engage in the second part, which is to find something that will interest him more than the thing to which he is addicted.

Some addicts can decide to stop taking the drug all by themselves, but most of them need the strength and encouragement provided by a professional practitioner or by a group of people who play the parts of strict and watchful parents to the addict. Different substitute parents will use different approaches. Some medical practitioners use medications. A drug called Antabuse is useful in the treatment of alcoholics. If a person drinks while taking Antabuse, he will become violently ill; therefore once he starts taking it, it is unlikely that he will have anything to drink. For about four days after taking an Antabuse pill, an alcoholic has "a hammer hanging over his head in case he feels like getting smart," as one man described it. (A similar drug is now available for narcotics addicts. It is called cyclazocine. Methadone may also be used for this purpose.)

Once the addict is without the drug he can begin to look objectively at his situation. The first thing he usually notices is that his life seems empty without the drug, and that he does not love anybody, not even himself. He finds that although he may be a "great lover" and a very sociable person, his relationships with people tend to be twisted or unpleasant. He finds that he attaches himself to some people because he needs them and uses them as props for his weaknesses, while other people use him to fulfill some need of their own.

Thus, the second part of the treatment, which involves finding something more important and more interesting than alcohol or the drug that the person has been taking, has to do with seeing people differently. If it is successful, the addict may decide that people are indeed more interesting than drugs. The drug addict finds that he has been using drugs instead of people, and that for his own well-being he needs to learn to appreciate people instead of drugs. This project of substituting people for drugs can be helped by a psychotherapist, preferably in a treatment group where the people that the addict needs are right in front of him. This can also be accomplished by organizations such as Alcoholics Anonymous, Narcotics Anonymous, Synanon, and other self-help groups which devote themselves to the problems of addicts.

A device which is sometimes successful with a drug or alcohol addict is to make a missionary out of him. The one thing which may interest him more than taking the drug is to spend his time preventing others from taking it. Some of the individuals who are rehabilitated in Alcoholics Anonymous seem to recover on this basis. They become as fanatic in their missionary zeal as they were in their drinking. While these individuals are better off and more useful to society under these circumstances, the problem is that their sobriety depends upon the existence of "active," drinking, alcoholics. The danger is that if all the available alcoholics in the town have been "converted" and there is no more new blood to do missionary work with, many of the "cured" backslide. This is recognized by sophisticated members of Alcoholics Anonymous, and so they try to involve themselves in other activities.

The best hope for those who are addicts lies in group treatment coupled with individual psychotherapy or self-help groups such as Alcoholics Anonymous and Synanon. Psychoanalysis has not proved its usefulness in this field, and many therapists think that transactional analysis is preferable.

Rules which have been found by experience to be wise are:

1. Such treatment should start off "cold turkey" (complete abstinence immediately).

2. Complete abstinence is only a beginning, since abstinence by itself has no lasting effect. Unless there is something to take the place of the drug, little is accomplished. Treatment is lengthy. The process of substituting people for drugs is likely to take at least one year, so that abstinence for less than that period is no guarantee of recovery.

3. No one should marry an alcoholic to reform him. If the addict wants to marry badly enough, let him (or her) reform first for at least a year and preferably two. No more pathetic creatures come into a psychotherapist's office than the once gracious and beautiful young ladies who are beaten down and old before their time as a result of marrying an addict to reform him.

5
What about delirium tremens?

It seems strange, on the surface, that a disease which formerly killed many of its victims should be a subject of joking among the very people who are most liable to get it. It is not strange if we realize that for self-destructive people, death is a welcome joke. Delirium tremens, or "the D.T.'s," is a psychosis which sometimes occurs following a prolonged alcoholic binge in people who have been drinking excessively for a number of years. It is a torturing and strenuous experience which may leave the marks of strain on the heart and brain as well as on the mind. Its victim is in a state of acute fear and trembles all over. He imagines that he sees all sorts of horrible creatures, such as snakes, bugs, and small animals, coming after him or crawling over his skin, or that he is faced with endless and desperately monotonous tasks, such as washing millions and millions of dishes, or walking up an endless hill. These experiences are very real to him and he reacts accordingly. Contrary to the popular idea, the animals seen by these patients are usually small and horrible, rather than large and benevolent creatures, such as pink elephants. The fact that delirium tremens has become a joke, like much that has to do with alcohol in our country, shows how confused and childlike is the American attitude toward drinking. School girls giggle about sex, and grown men giggle about whiskey. The unfortunate effect of this is that alcoholics and other drug addicts encourage each other by their gigglings and by laughing about things which they know will make them suffer, such as D.T.'s or drug withdrawal. This encouragement comes not only from the addicts or potential addicts themselves, but from the people around them, especially in the case of alcohol, where advertisements, movies, television and humor all seem to favor the drinking environment.

The facts are that even nowadays with the best facilities and treatment, delirium tremens leads to fatal heart disease, pneumonia, or convulsions in five or ten per cent of cases. Of course, the dead ones do not go back to the old hangout and the ones who live do, so people see only the survivors, which is one reason they do not realize how damaging the condition may become. Actually the experience is so terrifying that it often marks the beginning of serious attempts toward recovery. Even if it does not kill, delirium tremens may injure, and each attack may diminish the individual's physical and mental capacities. As has been said before, delirium tremens, as well as Korsakoff's psychosis (long-lasting confusion, sometimes with paralysis), seems to be partly the result, in many cases, of lack of food, besides the amount of alcohol consumed. People who are on a bender cannot seem to spare the time or money for eating. Vitamin B seems to be the important factor in this connection. A good rule for a heavy drinker, therefore, is to be sure to eat more vitamin B than usual while on a spree. If he is unwilling to eat, he should at least buy a big bottle of thiamine chloride or vitamin B tablets before starting out and keep eating them as long as he continues on his binge. If the patient survives several attacks of delirium tremens, he may end with the condition known as "wet brain," which has a very high mortality rate.

Among the other psychiatric effects of alcohol is its tendency to exaggerate paranoid tendencies and epilepsy. Both paranoia and convulsions may make their first appearance during an alcoholic bout. We saw how over a long period drinking brought out Dion Chusbac's paranoid tendencies more and more openly. In some people this may happen quite suddenly, with an acute onset of paranoid panic and hallucinations. Alcoholic homicidal mania is another condition which may result even after light drinking, and is particularly apt to occur after drinking cheap liquor.

Alcohol weakens the Ego and the Superego and allows the Id to express itself more freely. People tend to show their true emotional urges when they are drinking. If a man is disagreeable when he is drunk, he is likely to be the same way under stress when he is sober, no matter how charming he may appear on the surface in his normal state.

6

What is a sociopath?

There is a certain type of behavior disturbance which in the past was called "moral insanity" or "moral imbecility." Until recently, people who showed this form of behavior were referred to by practitioners as psychopaths. The term *psychopath,* however, has been replaced by a more accurate word, *sociopath.*

The word *sociopath* refers to individuals who are basically anti-social and, because of this, are always in trouble, never seeming to profit from the unpleasant experiences and punishment which their behavior causes them to suffer. These people appear to have none of the usual loyalties to the community, their parents, or any of the people around them. They do not seem to have any particular defect when it comes to talking or reasoning about anything; rather the defect seems to be in their inability to conduct themselves with decency, responsibility, and respect for the rights of other persons. In short, they are socially defective.

In the common neuroses, the individual afflicts mostly himself with his neurotic behavior. Sociopaths make other people do most of the suffering. The neurotic does not allow his Id instincts to be expressed but rather turns them inward. The sociopath turns them outward to obtain relief of his tensions. When the Superego fails to keep the Id instincts under control, the individual can either find some outside influence to help keep the Id in check, or he can let it go ahead and express itself freely. In the first case, he may let some stronger personality guide him, such as the leader of a party or a religion. Or, he may become interested in the law and feel that as long as he has the law on his side, he is sufficiently in the right regardless of what he does. In the second case, every wish, no matter how trivial or impractical, is gratified regardless of the consequences.

One of the main characteristics of a sociopath is that no matter how wrong his acts seem to other people, he himself does not feel guilty about them; hence it appears as though he had no Superego. Nevertheless, the very people who are capable of committing such outrageous acts as killing in cold blood, lying, exploiting defense-less persons, and assaulting their parents, wives and children, will feel guilt in relation to certain other acts which seem wrong to them. For instance, in prisons the thieves and robbers may feel morally superior to the murderers, and vice versa. Each has his own special kind of standards, so instead of saying that their Superegos are weak, it is probably more accurate to say that they are selective.

In general, there are two kinds of sociopaths. The first type, the latent or passive sociopath, behaves fairly well most of the time by accepting guidance from an outside source, such as religion or law, or at times by attaching himself to a stronger personality and accepting him as an ideal. (We speak here not of those who use religion or law as an instructor to inner conscience, but of those who use such doctrines *instead* of an inner conscience.) Thus, they are guided not by the usual considerations of decency and humanity, but only by their obedience to their interpretation of what the "book" says. "Christians" who discriminate against others, and unethical lawyers who advise criminals how they can break the laws of human decency and still keep out of jail, are interesting examples of latent sociopaths.

The second type, the active sociopath, has neither inner nor outer restraints, even though he may curb himself temporarily and put on a good front, especially in the presence of persons who expect him to behave in a decent and responsible way. These people, however, choose not to restrain themselves the moment that they are out of the range of the grownups or the authority figures who demand good behavior.

There are many kinds of sociopathic behavior. Some of it is spectacular, though infrequent, such as sexual attacks on little children or women, giving a young person a venereal disease, committing coldblooded murder or cheating unsuspecting people. Less dramatic but more common, are people who drive recklessly, lie down on the job, or deliberately gum things up. These persons are unconcerned about how much danger or extra work this may mean for others, or how much of value they may destroy.

The range of a sociopath's activities depends upon his intelligence and his opportunities. If he is wealthy and powerful, he may cause trouble on a magnificent scale, something like the Roman Emperor Caligula, who sank festive barges full of people to amuse himself.* Or he may satisfy his whims in the most tragic and inhuman way, as history tells of prison guards who spent their time devising tortures for their victims. If he is poor but intelligent, he may specialize in swindling people; if he is poor but unintelligent,

---

* Although he stands as a memorable example of "conscienceless behavior," similar to that of a sociopath, actually Caligula is thought to have been a schizophrenic. The distinction between sociopathy and schizophrenia is often not easy to make.

he will do things requiring little originality, such as playing practical jokes, driving cars destructively, beating up innocent people, or wantonly damaging property. Many gossips are of this type, giving vent to their destructive impulses by spreading scandal.

Most people have built into their Superegos very strong prohibitions against promiscuous sexual activity and the use of illegal drugs. Therefore, they never get close enough to these activities to become endangered by them. A certain number of sociopaths, whose Superegos lack prohibitions against these activities, find that illegal drugs make life pleasant for them and proceed to use them and thus become addicted. Likewise, a sociopath who has no prohibitions against uncontrolled sexual activities, will expose himself and others to the dangers of venereal disease and will often make his sexual partner pregnant and later fail to take responsibility for his offspring.

Let us follow the career of an intelligent sociopath and see what havoc he leaves behind him.

Ludwig Farbanti, Olympia's undertaker, had once owned the Olympia Cannery, and it was largely because of the doings of his only child Loki that he had had to sell it to Midas King.

Loki was a problem from infancy. He was difficult to handle when he was nursing, and his toilet training was almost impossible. When he started school all the little girls were terrified of him because of his cruelty. One day he found a penknife and jabbed it through the hand of Minerva Seifuss, who sat next to him. After that he had to be put into a private military school but the instructors there couldn't do much with him either. Punishments did not avail except to make him run away. He was above the average in intelligence, however, and managed to pass his examinations in spite of all this. At college he was always in debt, and began to forge his father's name to checks. Since Mr. Farbanti always made good in the end, out of respect to him none of the tradesmen of Arcadia complained to the police.

During his summer vacations, Loki spent his time traveling in idleness from one city to another, and he never managed to live within his generous allowance. He was always trying to impress someone and had to have a large wardrobe, stay at the best hotels, and entertain large numbers of people. He didn't choose his companions with very good judgment, however, and during these jaunts he caught gonorrhea twice and was in jail many times for drunkenness. Finally his father, unable to keep up with his lavish expenses, declared for the last time that he would no longer make good any bad checks that Loki passed. This time he meant it.

This did not deter Loki. If he saw something he wanted, he bought it. He was so well dressed and was such a good talker that he had no trouble in pushing checks. He never saved enough money to buy a car, but he always had one somehow or other, and being a free spender he was popular with the girls. He got several of them into trouble, but it was not until Ambrose Paterson, the electrician, came after him with a gun for trying to seduce his younger sister Daphne, that Loki left Olympia and Arcadia for good, leaving it to his parents to clear up the expensive difficulties he left behind.

Loki went to Los Angeles, where he talked himself into a job as a radio announcer by claiming that he had had a lot of experience. Here he first learned how really effective his voice was, and he began to use it to impress people. One night for amusement he went to a religious meeting with a rich middle-aged divorcée with whom he was living. The size of the collection was a revelation to him, so he studied the matter and decided to set himself up in business with the aid of his lady friend. He read a few books on Theosophy, Spiritualism, and Christian Science, and made up a cult called "You Are Glad." With his friend's financial and social backing, and his own eloquence and persuasive power, he soon became a popular preacher and evangelist, and after a while he was even able to start branches in several Western cities. As time went on, he made a rule that his true followers must turn over all their money to his church. He bought some apartment houses and allowed his disciples to live in them—at a price. He organized a cooperative restaurant in each house and charged a liberal amount for meals. By this and other methods, most of his disciples' earnings as well as their capital ended up in the church fund, which was all in his name.

One day he decided that he was getting tired of putting up a preacher's front, and that for other reasons the time had come to leave. Without giving them any inkling that he was actually leaving, he subtly prepared his followers for his departure so that they would not become alarmed too quickly. He turned into cash as many of his church's assets as he could, decamped with the money and went to Germany, where he and an American bank-robber named Maxie lived high for a while. After Maxie died, Loki got interested in the National Socialist Party. When World War II began, Loki was writing anti-American propaganda for the Nazis, under an assumed name.

Some of his followers saw the light when he disappeared, and they went to the police. Many of them, however, still believe in him, because of the way he had prepared them for this event. To this day, some of them swear that it happened at one of his meetings, and that they saw with their own eyes the angels raise him up to Heaven. The mother of the sixteen-year-old girl he took to Germany with him and later introduced to a procurer for a Buenos Aires brothel, committed suicide when one of Maxie's friends, as part of a swindle scheme, told her what had happened to her daughter.

Loki's story illustrates many of the things we have said about sociopaths. It is obvious that Loki's conscience did not deter him from doing what he wanted to do when he wanted to do it. It is also clear that his intelligence did not deter him either. When he wanted to drink or to have sexual intercourse, he did it, regardless of the consequences. If either his conscience or his intelligence had controlled his impulses, he would not have caught gonorrhea or gone to jail, or taken the risks he did in cashing bad checks. His behavior is a little different from those who form a conscience and then behave badly in order to defy it or to revenge themselves on their parents. Loki's behavior was bad from the beginning and never showed any signs of improvement. In many situations he injured himself more than he did other people.

Certain of the events in Loki's life are typical, and can be found in the life histories of many sociopaths. They are nearly always badly behaved in infancy and at school. If they attend a well-run school, they are nearly always expelled. They run up debts, trade on their family's good name if it exists, wander around the country, show off as extravagantly as they can arrange for, catch gonorrhea, go to jail, get into trouble with women, fool people by glib talk, flee from discipline of every kind, and cause grief to almost everyone with whom they come in contact. So much are these things a matter of course in the lives of such people that if the worried parents finally come to a psychiatrist for advice, the doctor, after listening to the beginning of their tale, can often guess the rest.

Some people prefer to think that sociopaths are born that way, while others maintain the evidence shows that their behavior is subtly encouraged by their parents. The latter view, which makes considerable sense, implies that even though the parents of sociopaths complain and do not like the bad situations in which their offsprings' misbehavior places them, some part of them actually enjoys their children's unruliness and lack of control. Therapists often find that when children misbehave one or both of their parents find their misbehavior amusing or charming. Unfortunately, it often happens that these children go from this charming misbehavior to seriously destructive and sociopathic behavior. In this manner, Dan Chusbac, the father of Dion, the alcoholic, would have enjoyed hearing about Dion's heavy drinking during the time he was in college having a good time and being a hearty fellow. Yet Mr. Chusbac would have protested if anyone had suggested that his very strong encouragement had led to Dion's later self-destruction.

The treatment of a young sociopath who is still dependent on his parents requires the cooperation of everyone concerned. If, as is likely, his misbehavior is being subtly encouraged by the parents, then the parents need to be involved in the treatment, and if the problem is inborn, then it is much more likely that his sociopathic tendency will be cured with the cooperation of the parents than without it. Psychiatrists nowadays insist that the parents come along, and may even see the whole family at once in a "family therapy group." Sociopaths do not often come for treatment voluntarily, but if they end up in prison they may then become more interested and often benefit from the group therapy which is supplied in many prison systems.

It is interesting to think, in this connection, how much the attitude of "wild" animals, which seem to be unable to form anything resembling a Superego, and can be "tamed" only through fear, resembles the attitude of the sociopath; while the attitude of those animals of which we make house pets, which do seem to be able to form something resembling a Superego, is much closer to that of a socialized human being.

7

What is sexual perversion?

In the normal course of growth *physis* directs the individual toward the opposite sex of adult human beings as his true libido object. Only if something goes amiss will he select another object for his affections, such as members of the same sex, little children, old people, or animals. In the same way *physis* directs him toward vaginal sexual intercourse as his preferred aim, so that libido may accomplish its biological end of uniting the sperm and the egg to create a new individual; but if something goes wrong he may adopt a special method for the greatest satisfaction. Thus some people prefer unusual objects for sexual gratification, some prefer unusual methods and some are unusual in both respects. All these people find that either society, their own Superegos, or perhaps their thwarted *physis* makes them unhappy. Such unusual preferences are called sexual perversions.

Perversions are usually the result of not growing away from some childhood way of obtaining sexual pleasure. Children are often seen in sexual play with members of the same sex or animals, and we have noted that infants get pleasure from sucking, anal activity, or playing with their own sexual organs. An individual who does not grow away from these will try to get relief by similar methods in adult sexual life. Since human beings are experimenters at heart, it should be understood that mere experimenting with unusual sexual activities is not perversion. Only when an unusual activity is *consistently preferred* to the conventional ones should it be called a perversion.

8

What is masturbation?

Masturbation is sexual satisfaction in which the individual has no partner at all, or only an imaginary one. Sometimes when two people of the same or opposite sexes cause each other to have an orgasm with their hands, this is called "mutual masturbation." Because Americans usually marry late, long after the sexual glands are fully developed and the libido, not satisfied with indirect relief, is clamoring for sexual orgasms, most boys and girls in this country go through a period of a few years during which they have to find sexual satisfaction outside of marriage. Usually they find it partly in masturbation which they accomplish by stimulating their sexual organs in various ways. Nearly all boys and at least half of all girls go through a period of such activities while they are growing up, in addition to the stimulation of their sexual organs during early childhood which serves a similar purpose.

Masturbation does *not* cause insanity, nervousness, weakness, impotence, frigidity, tuberculosis, pimples, slime under the heart, or any of the other things which young folks hear about from various people, young and old; and a drop of semen is *not* equal to a quart of blood, as some gentlemen have been known to tell their young charges it is. A normal person who masturbates unwisely may feel a little washed out for a day or two afterward, but that is all. It is true that nervous people and people on the verge of a breakdown sometimes masturbate more than usual, or more than other people, and are sometimes more sensitive about it, but this does not mean that masturbation causes their nervousness or their breakdown. In such cases excessive masturbation may be an attempt to diminish the nervousness or prevent the breakdown by relieving the Id tensions which are causing the trouble or are threatening to overwhelm the Ego. Such a method of treatment cannot be conscientiously recommended, however, as it may make matters worse by increasing the tension of the Superego, among other things.

The chief harm of masturbation, besides the self-reproaches and the washed-out feeling which follow it in many people, has to do with later love life. Masturbation is easy and doesn't require any courting. The masturbator can have anyone he or she desires for an imaginary partner without having to go to the trouble of winning trust and affection, and can do pretty much as he or she pleases with this partner without regard to the "partner's" feelings; and, above all, the masturbator doesn't have to wait for satisfaction. Later on, however, in normal courtship and marriage, the individual may have to do things he doesn't like to do and make sacrifices in order to win the one he loves. He will also have to consider his partner's feelings during their sexual activities. In addition, he will have to wait for his satisfaction until the partner feels that the time is ripe. The courting and waiting period may seem boring and difficult to the masturbator, instead of being a delightful time of anticipation. Like the infant, he wants what he wants when he wants it, without regard to anyone else's feelings. The result is that he may be unable to go through with a normal courtship, and when he is married and has to respect the desires and delicacy of his partner, he sometimes feels thwarted and does not enjoy the relationship.

In other words, he may get so he would rather do things *to* an imaginary partner than *with* a real one, and so he may remain a bachelor or become an unhappy married man or divorcé. Good sex is not doing things to somebody, but doing things with somebody. Doing things to somebody, even a real partner instead of an imaginary one, is merely a form of masturbation with another person present, and is different from the experience of mutual sexual pleasure that comes from an adult sexual emotion. The undesirable feature of masturbation, then, is not that it stunts physical growth, which it doesn't, but that it may become more attractive than sexual intercourse (even in marriage), as it is to some people.

The best "cure" for masturbation is to marry the person one loves—the *right* person. On the other hand, the riskiest remedy for any kind of unhappiness is to marry the wrong person.

9

What is homosexuality?

Homosexuality is love of the same sex. Some people can get almost equal pleasure from making love to either sex. These people are called bisexuals.

Many beautiful things have come out of homosexual relationships, such as some of the philosophy of Socrates. Nevertheless, happy homosexuals are uncommon. Homosexuality nearly always means a thwarted *physis* and a troubled Superego. It is contrary to the customs of our society and so makes social difficulties even under the best circumstances. Also, it is often against the law for men and therefore can lead to real disasters. Curiously enough, while nearly every state has laws against male homosexual activities, there is none* which has laws against homosexual activities in females.

Homosexuals obtain their sexual satisfaction in whatever ways their imaginations can devise and their consciences permit. Homosexuality occurs in both sexes, and may be overt, with actual love-making, or latent and hidden. If it is latent but conscious, the individual has to restrain himself from trying to do what he would like to do because of the possible consequences in regard to society and his own conscience. If it is latent and unconscious, and the individual is not even aware that he has such desires, he then has to obtain his satisfaction in disguised form through displacements and sublimations. Nearly everybody has homosexual desires of which he or she is not aware. Usually they are well repressed and cause little trouble, but in some people they are so strong that it requires a continual struggle to keep them from coming to the surface, and this may keep the individual in a perpetual turmoil for no reason that he can determine. The last defense against such desires becoming conscious is usually a mental illness, and such illnesses of the type called "paranoid" are often the result of a struggle to keep homosexual feelings repressed.

It is said that some homosexuals are biologically different from heterosexual men, even though the actual chemical difference has not been detected. All men have both male and female sexual hormones in their blood but in normal men the male hormones predominate. Some experimenters maintain that in certain men the balance may be upset so that the female hormones get the upper hand and cause homosexuality. One may suppose that a corresponding upset may occur in women. The above has not been satisfactorily confirmed and therefore it does not mean that we can cure homosexuality by injecting appropriate hormones. However, the notion that some male homosexuals may be biologically different from heterosexual males is strongly suggested by studies of twins. It has been found that with monozygotic twins (twins that

* As far as the author and his friends in the legal profession can ascertain.

come from the same egg), if one of the twins turns out to be homosexual, the other one is very likely to be a homosexual as well. On the other hand, the dizygotic twin (a twin from a different egg) of a homosexual is a great deal less likely to be homosexual himself. This suggests that it is possible that in some circumstances homosexuality has biological roots. This makes some homosexuals pretty resentful against nature, since they rightfully feel that their condition is an unjust affliction.

When one examines the developmental histories of homosexuals, they seem to fall roughly into four categories. The individual may show signs of peculiar sexual behavior from early childhood, by dressing frequently in his sister's clothes, for example. When such boys grow up they may look quite feminine and affect feminine mannerisms. Men like this are usually in a great deal of conflict since they are resented by other males, whom they make uneasy by stirring up latent homosexuality, while women hate them or at least find them hard to understand. This type of homosexual can generally sense just how close to the surface overt or latent homosexuality is in any other man. The corresponding development may take place in girls, with similar consequences. The above-mentioned childhood sexual peculiarities do not always develop into homosexuality. In some cases, it is likely that they are only temporary and in other cases they develop into transvestism or transexualism. It should be pointed out here again that children are curious and tend to experiment and, as a consequence, it is important to realize that cross-dressing (dressing in the clothes of the opposite sex), and occasional homosexual play or experimentation are not necessarily indications that the child or adolescent is heading for homosexuality or any other unusual sexual development.

There are some men (and all this applies conversely to women) who seem entirely usual until they grow up, and then they find to their surprise and anxiety that men interest them more than women. Nothing in their backgrounds indicates with certainty that this development is likely to take place.

A third kind of homosexual development occurs in prisons and other places where there are no women available. As libido piles up, people get less and less particular about their sexual objects, and if the preferred one is not available they will often take whatever they can get. A girl that a man would not walk down the street with in his home town may seem like a glamorous beauty if she is the only woman on an island in the Pacific, because the strong libido tensions mold her image into such a form. Experiments with marijuana show that a usually normal man may even try to kiss a bridge lamp if his libido becomes aroused sufficiently and there is no reasonable outlet available. It is not surprising, then, that where there are no women, men will sometimes turn to each other for sexual satisfaction, and similarly among women who are cut off from the opposite sex.

There is a fourth way in which a girl or boy may develop overt homosexuality, and this is by seduction. Seductions are not too uncommon in boys' and girls' boarding schools, and the seducing teacher has been a theme for plays. Some homosexuals were deliberately raised that way. A boy who has lost his mother occasionally finds himself living with a father who turns to homosexuality for consolation, and occasionally parents farm out their children to homosexual couples, two men or two women. The child of a female homosexual may be raised in a homosexual household from birth when the father takes off after the mother gets tired of experimenting with men and goes back to her girl friend.

Among homosexuals of both sexes there are four types of lovers. There is the man who acts as a man, the man who acts as a woman, the woman who acts as a man, and the woman who acts as a woman. There are also, of course, mixed types and alternating types, men who act as men sometimes and as women at other times with their male partners, and similarly among women. Thus there are male male homosexuals, and female male homosexuals; female females, and male females. Groups of homosexuals are found in certain night clubs in every large city. Some saloons cater almost exclusively to homosexuals, some to males, some to females, so that a "straight" person feels out of place in them. As a result of this getting together, homosexuals of each sex have evolved special customs, etiquettes, and vocabularies, complete "sub-cultures," each with its own magazine to promote its own interests. An unsophisticated visitor to one of these saloons might be surprised to find a large number of athletic, masculine-looking men, some of them in fact ex-football players; and on the other side, some of the most beautiful and feminine-looking women to be found anywhere in the city; both of these types mixed in with the obvious "queers" and "dykes." Some homosexuals are always on the prowl, "cruising" at all hours of the day and night. On the other hand, there are the quieter relationships of homosexuals who find mates and pair off to form sexual friendships or "marriages," occasionally blended with highly spiritual feelings which may result in works of art and literature.

From what we have said, the possibility of "curing" homosexuals is fairly apparent. The man or woman who has taken this direction since childhood is the most difficult to treat, while the man or woman who has turned to homosexuality because of lack of available heterosexual partners is the easiest. If a homosexual wants to be "cured," it is possible with enough treatment. Most homosexuals who come to a psychiatrist, however, do not want to be made heterosexual, but want to be relieved of the symptoms which often occur among homosexuals, such as headaches, diarrhea, and palpitation. Many of them are "oversexed," and cannot resist the temptation to "cruise" and pick up anybody they can at any time and in any place. Some bisexuals carry this so far that even if they are in the company of their spouses and children in some public place, they will take off for a "quickie" if they spot a likely partner.

What is society to do with homosexuals? Their lives are confused enough as it is, and punishment is not indicated. The best thing one can do is treat them as politely as one would anyone else. They on their part, of course, should be expected to abide by the ordinary rules of decency such as apply to relationships between men and women: namely, they should not seduce minors, nor force themselves on people who are not interested in their company; they should not flaunt their desires in public by dressing in clothes of the opposite sex or otherwise; and they should not embarrass those around them by making love or talking about it in public. If they behave themselves and control themselves as discreetly as people with heterosexual desires are expected to do, their private lives should be no more concern of anyone else's than should a "straight" person's. Putting them in jail often (or even usually) results only in providing them and the other prisoners with added opportunities for sexual activity. Many people now-

adays feel that the laws concerning homosexual activities should
be changed, as they have been in England.

10
What are transexuals and transvestites?

A transvestite is a person, usually male, who derives sexual
satisfaction from wearing clothes, often only underwear, of the
opposite sex. These persons are, more often than not, heterosexual
in their sexual interests, but have an overwhelming desire to cross-
dress. They feel that they are men rather than women, and they do
not desire sexual relationships with other men. The difficulties that
they get into are largely due to other people's disapproval of their
activities. It is because of this that female transvestites are not
considered to be a problem, since no one will think anything of a
woman wearing men's clothes, while a man who walks down the
street in high heels and a skirt is actually breaking the law in most
states. When a transvestite becomes interested in treatment, it is
usually possible to "cure" the condition through psychotherapy.

An unusual type of person that has come to popular attention in
recent years is the transexual. Transexuals, again mostly men,
are individuals who as far back as they can remember, have
wanted to be women, and have abhorred their male sexual organs
or anything that reminded them of the fact that they were men. As
soon as they are able, they attempt to assume female identities,
and so intense is their dislike for their manly sexual characteristics,
that they almost always yearn to have their male organs removed.
Transexuals are often able to obtain female hormones. These
hormones, by decreasing their facial hair growth, possibly creating
a certain amount of breast development, and heightening the pitch
of their voices, seem to give them great psychological relief. There
have been a number of notorious cases of transexuals who have
had their sexual organs removed and who are now living as
women, and have even married. It is interesting to note that
transexuals are not homosexuals. They do not want to have
sexual relationships with homosexual men, but wish to be women
and to marry heterosexual men. It seems that as long as a
transexual has to live as a man, he is unhappy, and that as soon

as he is able to assume a female identity, he feels a great deal better. Psychological treatment of transexualism has, to date, been unsuccessful. Some authorities feel that the only way to treat a true transexual is to allow him to assume female identity and to grant him an operation. Most of these operations are performed abroad, but a few are done in the United States after thorough investigation of each case.

Finally, there is the condition *hermaphroditism,* which means that the person has both male and female sex glands—that is, both a testicle and an ovary, so that theoretically a true hermaphrodite is able to fertilize himself. This condition is very rare, and most of the people who are called hermaphrodites are persons who have deficiencies of their external genital organs, such that they seem to have both a penis and a vagina, but biologically they are really either male or female. For these cases, corrective surgery is often able to reshape the genitals to match the true biological sex of the person so that he or she can live a fairly normal sexual life.

Footnotes for Philosophers, Chapter Seven

1. *Alcoholism*

   The well-known work of fiction, *The Lost Weekend,* by Charles Jackson, can be read with benefit by everyone who has an alcohol problem with himself or in his family. For some facts about alcohol, consult: *Alcoholism,* by E. N. Blum and R. H. Blum. (San Francisco: Jossey-Bass, 1967.)

   The Blums cover quite adequately most of what is known about alcoholism to date. They do not, however, give adequate coverage to group treatment, which in this writer's opinion is the preferred therapeutic approach for the treatment of alcoholics. Nor do they mention the fruitful findings of transactional analysis. See:

   Games People Play, by Eric Berne. New York: Grove Press, 1964.

   The most recent developments can be found in two articles by C. Steiner, "The Treatment of Alcoholism," *Transactional Analysis Bulletin,* Vol. 6, pp. 69–71 (July 1967), and "The Alcoholic Game," Ibid., Vol. 7. pp. 6–16 (January 1968).

   For an account of the beneficial effects of wine, see Salvatore P. Lucia, *The History of Wine as Therapy.* New York: J. B. Lippincott, 1963.

2. *Drug Addiction*

   Those who wish to read further on this subject are referred to Marie Nyswander's chapter in the *American Handbook of Psychiatry.* The Alcoholism and Drug Addiction Research Foundation of Ontario, 24 Harbord Street, Toronto 5, publishes a series of pamphlets on addiction, of which the most comprehensive, *Man and Chemical Comforts*, gives a good presentation of the drugs being used and abused nowadays.

3. *Psychedelics and Other Drugs*

For the "official" medical position on some of the more prevalent drugs mentioned in this section, see the reports of the Committee on Alcoholism and Addiction and the Council on Mental Health of the American Medical Association, published in the *Journal of the American Medical Association* as follows:

"Dependence on Barbiturates and other Sedative Drugs," Vol. 193, pp. 673–77 (August 23, 1965); "Amphetamines and Other Stimulant Drugs," Vol. 197, 1023–27 (September 19, 1966); "Cannabis (Marihuana)," Vol. 201, 368–71 (August 7, 1967).

Historically marijuana is perhaps the most interesting drug known to man, as noted by Marco Polo and by Edward FitzGerald in his introduction to *The Rubaiyat*. One of the best books about it is still:

Marijuana, by R. P. Walton. Philadelphia: J. B. Lippincott, 1938.

During the past two or three years a number of popular books on "pot," most of them favorable, have appeared on the newsstands. The best botanical and agronomical article is "Hemp," by L. H. Dewey, *Yearbook*, U.S. Department of Agriculture, 1913, pp. 283–346.

For an article on the other psychedelic drugs see: "The Hallucinogenic Drugs," by F. Barron, M. E. Jarvik, and S. Bunnell. In *Scientific American,* April 1964.

4. *Treatment for Alcoholics*

Any alcoholic sincerely interested in overcoming his or her habit, or any relatives or friends of any alcoholic, have four resources available. The names of private psychotherapists can be obtained from the local medical or psychological societies. If there is a city clinic for alcoholics, its location can be ascertained from the city or county department of public health. If neither of these are available, there are two national organizations that devote themselves exclusively to this problem: Alcoholics Anonymous and The National Committee on Alcoholism. In addition, Synanon Foundation, which was organized primarily for drug addicts, has residential centers that will accept alcoholics for treatment in a number of cities in California and elsewhere in the country. For information, write:

Synanon Foundation, 110 Lombard Street, San Francisco, California.

The local branch of Alcoholics Anonymous will usually be listed as such in the telephone directory. If it is not, the location of the nearest branch can be obtained from General Service Headquarters, Alcoholics Anonymous, P.O. Box 459, Grand Central Annex, New York, N.Y. 10017. The other organization may be listed in the telephone directory as Committee on Alcoholism or Alcoholism Committee Information Center. If it is not, write or telephone the National Committee on Alcoholism, 2 East 103rd Street, New York 10029.

Alcoholics Anonymous chapters vary in their quality and in their experience, and the whole organization is often mistakenly judged on the basis of one or two chapters. Most practitioners recognize the value of Alcoholics Anonymous as an adjunct to psychotherapy. Group treatment is becoming accepted as the preferred approach to alcoholism and is being used increasingly in municipal clinics, such as the one in San Francisco.

For information about cyclazocine and methadone, see A. M. Freedman et al. *Journal of the American Medical Association*, Vol. 202, pp. 191–194 (October 16, 1967).

5. *Delirium Tremens*

Tapering off is usually practiced in smaller sanitariums which "cater" to their clientele. With the advent of new drugs such as Librium, Dilantin, and chlorpromazine and its derivatives, the treatment of delirium tremens and other alcohol withdrawal syndromes has changed considerably during the past ten years. The death rate has fallen, but these are still serious diseases. Interestingly enough, the most recent study of these conditions advocates a return to the older drugs, paraldehyde and chloral hydrate, claiming that they are more effective and less dangerous than the newer drugs or than the continued administration of alcohol itself. Hence Dr. Treece's treatment of Dion Chusbac. See:

"Comparative Evaluation of Treatments of Alcohol Withdrawal Syndromes," by T. M. Golbert, and others. *Journal of the American Medical Association*, Vol. 201, pp. 99–102 (July 10, 1967).

6. *Sociopaths*

The distinction between "latent" and "active" sociopaths is useful in clinical thinking. It is easily understood in the language of transactional analysis as a function of early transactions with the parents, without the dubious necessity of postulating masochism and a desire for punishment as primary driving forces in "sociopathic" behavior.

The manner in which parents encourage their children into antisocial acts is described by A. M. Johnson and S. A. Szurek in "The Genesis of Anti-Social Acting-Out in Children and Adults," in *Psychoanalytic Quarterly*, Vol. 21, pp. 323–343 (1952). This article is the predecessor of transactional thinking in this area. For case histories and a more orthodox view of the dynamics of sociopathy, see:

Wayward Youth, by August Aichhorn. Cleveland: World Publishing Company—Meridian Books, 1955.

For the transactional viewpoint see the "Script Analysis Number" of the *Transactional Analysis Bulletin*, Vol. 5, pp. 150–156 (July 1966), with articles by P. Crossman, D. Kupfer, I. L. Maizlish, and C. Steiner. Also *Transactional Analysis in Psychotherapy*, Chapter 17.

7. *Sexual Perversion*

The expression "get relief" is used here not because sex should be experienced as "getting relief," but because in terms of psychic economy that is what happens—tensions are relieved.

For an understanding of how sexual perversions come about, Freud's "Three Contributions to the Theory of Sex," can be read in *The Basic Writings*. Chapters 20 and 21 of his *Complete Introductory Lectures* are easier reading, however. For a different viewpoint, see *The Meaning and Content of Sexual Perversions*, by Medard Boss. New York: Grune & Stratton, 1949. For a description and discussion of various perversions with many case histories, Havelock Ellis is the classic: *Studies in the Psychology of Sex,* by Havelock Ellis. New York: Random House, 1940. For statistical information the well-known works of Kinsey and his associates should be consulted.

8. *Masturbation*

The American Medical Association (535 North Dearborn Street, Chicago, Ill. 60610) publishes a series of pamphlets on sex education, one each for: little children; ten-year-old girls; high-school boys; high-school girls; young men and women. For a short article designed to assist the general practitioner in dealing with this problem in his patients, see: "The Problem of Masturbation," by Eric Berne. In *Diseases of the Nervous System,* Volume 5, pp. 3–7 (October 1944).

A general discussion of sex education problems for parents and teachers can be found in *Sex Facts and Attitudes,* by M. O. Lerrigo and H. Southard. New York: E. P. Dutton, 1956.

9. *Homosexuality*

For further information, the works of Freud, Havelock Ellis and Kinsey may be consulted. Stekel gives extensive case histories. For a study of homosexuals in the American setting see:

All the Sexes, by George W. Henry. New York: Collier-Macmillan, 1964.

The Overt Homosexual, by C. W. Socarides. New York: Grune & Stratton, 1968.

Homosexuality, edited by Irving Bieber. New York: Basic Books, 1962.

Bieber claims that 20 to 50 percent of homosexuals of various types are "curable" with psychoanalytic treatment.

10. *Transvestism and Transexualism*

The recognized authority on transexualism in the United States is Harry Benjamin. See:

The Transexual Phenomenon, by H. Benjamin. New York: Julian Press, 1966.

For an up-to-date comparison of transvestism and transexualism, see:

"Transvestism and Transexualism in the Male and Female," by Harry Benjamin. In *The Journal of Sex Research,* Volume 3, No. 2 (May 1967).

Part Three _____

METHODS OF TREATMENT

8

PSYCHOTHERAPY

1

What is "going to a psychiatrist"?

"Going to a psychiatrist" means going to a physician who specializes in the study of human emotions. Going to a psychiatrist can help people become happier and more efficient and better able to cope with themselves and with the people and things around them. A psychoanalyst is a psychiatrist who specializes in one form of psychiatric treatment, namely, psychoanalysis, which, as we shall see later, is the study and readjustment of the patient's Id tensions. Other psychiatrists use various other methods of treatment—different forms of psychotherapy, drug prescriptions, hypnosis, and shock treatment. Some psychologists are specially trained to do psychotherapy, although they are not permitted to prescribe drugs or give shock treatment. They are called "clinical psychologists." Some social workers are similarly trained. Professionally trained people who use psychological methods of treatment are called psychotherapists.

Whenever one person goes to another over a long period for advice or help, a powerful and complicated emotional relationship arises. This happens whether the adviser and the client are aware of it or not. It may show itself in conscious feelings of like, dislike, gratitude, resentment, admiration, or contempt. Some of these feelings may be natural and understandable, but often they are much more powerful than the situation calls for, because part of their power and energy is derived from childhood feelings which are left over in the Id and are now transferred to the adviser. These feelings which are transferred from childhood are called "transference." One of the psychoanalyst's chief aims is to analyze and dissolve the transferred feelings, while other psychiatrists and psychotherapists often prefer to leave transference alone, because the patient's strong feelings of attachment may be helpful in carrying out the treatment; for example, a patient with a great admiration for his psychiatrist, even if it is exaggerated by childhood feelings, will be more apt to take his medication regularly.

Psychotherapy includes those methods of treatment which depend for their effect on the emotional relationship between the patient and the doctor. One of the great scientific problems of all doctors is to determine how much the result of their treatment depends upon this emotional factor, and how much is due to the actual physical or chemical methods employed. Even the most impersonal surgical procedures are affected by such emotional factors. The amount of anesthetic required and the rate of wound healing after an appendix operation may be influenced by the patient's attitude toward the doctor.

There are several kinds of psychotherapy: unconscious and conscious, informal and formal. In unconscious psychotherapy the doctor and, usually, the patient are overlooking the fact that the treatment is influenced by emotional factors, as is sometimes the case in dental and surgical operations. In conscious psychotherapy the doctor, but not always the patient, is aware that he is using his emotional power in the treatment. In informal psychotherapy the doctor is aware of what he is doing, but makes up his treatment as he goes along; this is the kind of treatment that is used by the family doctor in certain situations. In formal psychotherapy there is a carefully thought-out plan to use the emotional situation for the patient's benefit according to a definite method; this is the kind of treatment which is given by a psychiatrist or psychoanalyst. When we speak here of psychotherapy, it is the last kind we are referring to.

Each psychiatrist naturally chooses the kind of psychotherapy that will give the best results in the shortest time, and this depends on the doctor's personality as well as the patient's. Thus, a few psychiatrists like to use hypnosis, because they do their best work with it, but most feel that they do better without it.

The frequency of visits and the length of treatment depend upon the method used and the needs of the patient. A psychoanalyst likes to see his patients almost every day, or at least several times a week, and this may go on anywhere from one to five or ten years. On the other hand, in treating Cary Fayton and Janus Land after they recovered from their breakdowns, Dr. Treece saw them only once a month. He did not think it wise to probe too deeply into their minds, which had already been too active; his aim in their cases was the modest one of seeing that they were getting along all right with themselves and with the world from month to month, at least sufficiently to carry on their occupations. In some cases, such "preventive psychiatry" may go on for the rest of the patient's life. Mild conditions may require only one or two visits altogether. The commonest schedule of all is one individual session a week, or one group-therapy session a week, for about three years; and this is probably the minimum for cure of a neurosis or a psychosis. Indeed, a psychotherapist who cured a neurosis or a psychosis in that number of visits would be entitled to feel quite proud of himself.

There are many methods of psychotherapy. First, there is the great division between individual psychotherapy and group therapy. In individual therapy, the great division is between psychoanalytic and other methods. Psychoanalytic methods are split into formal psychoanalysis, and "psychoanalytic psychotherapy," which uses the ideas of psychoanalysis, but is not as concentrated nor as standoffish. Some of the other special methods, such as transactional analysis, are related to psychoanalysis but look at things differently. The most common ones will be discussed farther on. In addition to the methods which require special training, every psychiatrist is skilled in reeducation and persuasion, which attempt to teach people how to handle their emotional reactions better, without trying to readjust their Id tensions. These are similar to suggestion, which is an attempt to use the doctor's authority to change the patient's images without seeking their origins in the Id.

The main division in group therapy is between psychoanalytic group therapy and transactional group treatment; other methods are also used to a lesser degree.

Fees for psychotherapy range from one dollar per visit for group therapy at some public clinics to fifty dollars per visit to some of the senior psychotherapists who have been in practice for many years. Twenty-five dollars per session is a frequent fee among psychiatrists in private practice.

In state hospitals, private sanitariums, government hospitals, and other places where people live during their psychiatric treatment, there are specially trained people who help the patient to loosen up mentally and physically and to use his time to the best advantage. Social workers are particularly useful in helping him solve some of his practical problems, such as those concerning money and his family affairs; they also act as psychotherapists if they have the proper training. Occupational therapy attempts, among other things, to relieve some of his inner tensions by encouraging his Id and his Ego to work together to produce something concrete in carpentry, metalwork, pottery, weaving, painting, or other arts and crafts. Industrial therapy trains his Ego in reality testing by assigning him useful tasks which require some skill and which will be used for the benefit of the whole institution, such as making furniture, repairing equipment, or doing office work. Music and dance therapy attempt to influence the disturbed patient's way of feeling and thinking by programs carefully selected for his special needs and those of the groups he is with. Since all these activities are performed with the cooperation of other patients, they have some of the advantages of group therapy, as well as their own special benefits.

Most psychiatrists use a mixture of methods according to the individual patient's needs. This is especially true of sanitarium treatment, where facilities are at hand for all forms of activity. It should always be remembered, however, that the skill of the psychiatrist is far more important than any amount of fresh air, sunshine, and golf. Very few psychoses or neuroses are due to lack of golf. A well-mowed lawn makes the patient's family feel comfortable and impresses his banker, but it is not a substitute for psychiatric skill. A sanitarium should be chosen with only one thing in mind: that the doctor in charge shall be good at being a psychiatrist. Whatever his other qualifications, they are less important for the future of the patient.

The job of a psychotherapist, whatever his professional background may be, is to observe, predict, and influence human behavior. He has to know what he is dealing with, and for that he needs training; know what is likely to happen, and for that he needs experience; and know what to do about it, and for that he needs competence.

2
What is psychoanalysis?

First of all, psychoanalysis is a method of treatment, and almost every analyst nowadays is first a physician. He tries to relieve his patients of their complaints and to send them forth free of unnecessary doubts, unreasonable guilts, distressing self-reproaches, faulty judgments, and unwise impulses. Psychoanalysis tries to untangle the personality, and not merely to comfort the patient. But the analyst is only a guide and observer, and the patient, or "analysand," has the responsibility in the end for the finished product.

Secondly, analysis is a method for the scientific observation and study of the personality, especially in regard to wishes, impulses, motives, dreams, fantasies, early development, and emotional distortions.

Thirdly, analysis is a system of scientific psychology. This means that the observations and ideas of psychoanalysis can be used in an *attempt* to predict human behavior and the outcomes of human relationships, such as marriage and parenthood.

The system of ideas we have set forth up to this point is mostly the result of psychoanalytic observation. We shall now deal with psychoanalysis as a method of treatment.

3
How psychoanalysis is carried on

The process of psychoanalysis consists in the study and reorganization of the personality in order to enable the individual to store tensions with more prudence and less discomfort until the appropriate time for relief, and also to express freely without doubts or guilts, in accordance with the Reality Principle, tensions whose relief is permitted or demanded by a situation. For example, it tries to enable him to control irritation when it is wise to do so, and express anger when it is proper to do so, at the same time eliminating irrational sources of irritation and anger.

Psychoanalysis attempts to do this by studying the Id tensions of the individual, opening avenues for relief when it is practical, and bringing them as much as possible under conscious control. To complete the process requires sessions lasting about an hour, three to six times a week, for at least a year. If the study lasts less than a year, or there are fewer than three sessions a week, it is almost impossible to carry it through effectively. If the extent of the treatment is cut in either of these two ways, the psychoanalytic method may be used, but the individual probably will not have been psychoanalyzed. A complete psychoanalysis is always a long process.

In order to make the unconscious conscious, and to bring under observation the unsatisfied tensions which have collected in the Id since earliest childhood, the patient usually lies on a couch, at the head of which sits the analyst out of the patient's sight. Thus the patient's mind is free to work without distractions. He cannot see the doctor's face and so is not disturbed by the latter's facial reaction, if any, to what he says. This avoids some interference with the free flow of thoughts, since the likelihood is that in most cases if he had an idea as to what made the analyst look pleased or displeased, he might tend to regulate what he said accordingly, and might be influenced more than was desirable by observing the doctor's behavior. The doctor can also relax better and concentrate harder on what the patient says, since he is not under continual scrutiny. Many patients, however, are disturbed just because they cannot see the doctor's face.

The method used is called "free association." By this is meant the free expression or a free flow of ideas not hindered or changed by the usual conscious censoring forces: the conscious Ego Ideal (politeness, shame, self-respect), the conscious conscience (religion, education, and other principles), and the conscious Ego (orderliness, reality testing, conscious desire for gain). Indeed, the very things the patient would usually not say are often the most important ones for the analysis. Thus, he will sometimes underline the significant things by his very hesitancy. It is the things the patient feels are obscene, wicked, rude, irrelevant, boring, trivial, or absurd, which the analyst frequently pays special attention to.

In the freely associating state, the patient's mind often becomes crowded with desires, feelings, reproaches, memories, fancies, judgments, and new viewpoints, often in an apparently disordered jumble. And yet in spite of the seeming confusion and lack of connection, every utterance and gesture has its bearing on some ungratified Id tension. As the hours go by, day after day, meanings and connections begin to appear out of the disordered skein of thoughts. Gradually there may develop over a long period some central themes referring to a series of ungratified tensions from early childhood, long buried from conscious recognition, which are at the bottom of the patient's personality structure and from which his symptoms and associations arise. The patient's experience during the analysis may be a feeling of jumping from one thing to another without rhyme or reason, and often it is difficult or impossible for him to see the common threads running through them all. This is where the skill of the analyst performs its function, by detecting and pointing out the underlying tensions which bring forth and hold together the seemingly disconnected associations.

The analyst keeps a strictly neutral attitude toward his patients, even though his life is bound up with theirs daily for a year or more, and he relives with them in minute detail their current and past experiences.

Since the analyst's job, in a way, is mostly to point out to the patient when he is fooling himself, the doctor must maintain a continual attitude of self-criticism to make sure that he is not, out of sympathy or irritation, allowing the patient to fool the doctor as well as himself. An uncalled-for emotional attitude on the part of the analyst toward the patient is called *countertransference*. The analyst must be just as skillful in detecting and handling such feelings in himself as he is in detecting and handling the patient's attitude toward him, which takes the form of *transference*.

This is one of the chief reasons why it is necessary for an orthodox psychoanalyst (that is, a member of the International Psycho-Analytical Association or one of its recognized societies) to be analyzed himself before he starts to practice, for if he did not understand his own tensions thoroughly, he might unwittingly allow his judgment to be influenced by some countertransference of his own mood or sympathies of the moment, and he might lose sight of or damage the long-term effect of the treatment. The purpose of analysis is not to make the patient feel comfortable while he is with the doctor, but to enable him to handle his own problems independently of the doctor in the long years to come. A misplaced word might encourage a self-damaging attitude or seem to justify the patient's errors in judgment, which it is the purpose of the treatment to teach him to avoid; or on the other hand, it might increase the patient's already bothersome guilt feelings. This does not mean that the analyst lacks human feelings or sympathies. It only means that he has to be able to recognize his own feelings clearly, so that he will not regard in a prejudiced way what the patient says. The patient comes to the analyst for understanding, not for moral verdicts. The doctor remains neutral for the patient's good, and not necessarily because he is cold-hearted.

Analysis does *not* make the patient dependent upon the doctor. In fact, it deliberately takes pains to avoid this, by analyzing and carefully dissolving this very bond (the relationship between the doctor and the patient) so that the patient will be a free individual, independent and able to stand on his own feet. This is the very purpose of analysis.

The reader will now understand that contrary to popular belief, when a parlor psychologist, or even a professional psychiatrist, fixes someone with a gimlet eye and says: "My, but you are an introvert!" this is *not* psychoanalysis. Psychoanalysis is a very special and definite method of observation and psychotherapy, and it takes a long, long time.

4

What happens during an analysis?

During analysis, the image of the analyst tends gradually to become charged with all the piled-up energy of ungratified Id wishes which has collected since the patient's earliest infancy. Once this energy has been corralled in one image, it can be studied and redistributed, and the tensions partly relieved by analyzing the patient's image of the analyst. In ordinary language, this means that after a while the patient may become very emotional about the analyst. Since in reality he knows very little about the doctor, he must be acting and feeling in accordance with an image he made up himself. The analyst remains neutral throughout the treatment, and actually presents himself to the patient as not much more than a guiding voice. As there is no reasonable basis for loving or hating a neutral person, the feelings which swirl around the image of the analyst must not have been aroused by him, but by other people, and the patient, with his permission and under his observation, uses the analyst as a scapegoat for tensions he could not relieve on their proper objects. He transfers his libido and mortido from these objects to his image of the analyst. That is why the attitude of the patient toward the analyst is called transference.

We may say this in still another way: during the analysis, in a manner of speaking, the patient may attempt to finish the unfinished business of his childhood, using the analyst as a substitute for his parents, so that later he can devote most of his energies to the business of being an adult.

Of course, this is an attempt which is never completely successful. The patient has to give up his defenses, painfully erected over a period of years, and meet his disagreeable and unacceptable Id impulses in the open and wrestle with them. He is willing to do this for the sake of getting better, for the sake of the money he is paying, and for the sake of the analyst's approval. It is sometimes an uncomfortable, distressing, and painful experience; at other times it is a cozy protected relationship with the doctor. This cozy feeling, combined with his unconscious (and later conscious) reluctance to part with his old friends, his symptoms, and the attention and other advantages he may get from them, act as a drag on the treatment. The analyst may devote considerable attention to this surprising reluctance, or *resistance,* as it is called, when it begins to emerge, otherwise the analysis might go on forever.

Analysis attempts to change emotions, not merely to call them names. It is a talking treatment because words are the best way the patient has of expressing his emotions to himself and to the doctor. If he expresses them in other ways, such as by gestures and movements, words are still the best way to make clear what they mean and where they come from. The important things are the feelings and what happens to them, and not the scientific words used to describe them.

The idea that analysis consists of deciding which adjectives to apply to a patient is incorrect. Adjectives do not cure neuroses. It may be interesting, and perhaps reassuring, to be told that one is a thymergasic extroverted pyknophilic endomorph with an inferiority complex and disharmonious vagotonic borborygmi, but it is not curative.

Lavinia Eris, at the beginning of her analysis with Dr. Treece, asked:

"Doctor, at the end of this treatment, will you give me a written description of my personality?"

To which Dr. Treece replied:

"Madam, if at the end of the treatment you still wish to have a written description of your personality, then the treatment will have been a failure!"

There is one thing above all that we must learn—namely, that happiness depends upon the fluid and dynamic urges and feelings of the human spirit, and not upon the answers to questionnaires which have only to be inserted like slices of bread into the right computer for the toast of life to emerge neatly browned and buttered. Unfortunately, popular magazines, and many legitimate psychologists as well, encourage such a theory of personality. Most psychiatrists and psychoanalysts leave to others the answers to such questions as "Are you intelligent?" "What is your charm quotient?" and "Are you a typical wife?"

Psychoanalysts are concerned with the problem, not of which statistic fits, but of Who is You? Or perhaps it was even better put by a long-forgotten movie comedian many years ago, when he kept asking people: "You are who?" Intelligence, for example, is a tool, and not really a part of You, and the important thing is whether the Id allows the individual to use this tool properly.

We often hear people say: "I could do it if I wanted to!" The answer to this is, "Of course you could!" Anybody can do almost anything if he wants to badly enough. History is full of examples of this. Among the most impressive are one-legged men who become expert jitterbug or rock-and-roll dancers, and blind men who become good musicians. The important question is not "Could you?" but, "Do you want to as much as you think you do, and if not, why not?" Analysis is concerned mainly with desires and only incidentally with capabilities. Perhaps the question the analyst silently asks the patient can best be written thus: "How much are you willing to give up in order to be happy?" It will be seen that this has little to do with intelligence, charm, or statistics.

5
Who should be psychoanalyzed?

Psychoanalysis was originally devised mainly for the treatment of neuroses. As time went on, it was found that many other people besides frank neurotics benefited from it. Among the most common types of neurosis, which we have previously discussed, psychoanalysis is most useful in hysteria and the anxiety neuroses. It is often efficient in the character neuroses, and can do a great deal for compulsion neuroses, depending on how interested the patient is in getting the most out of the treatment. For hypochondriasis it is less reliable, and for phobias it may have to be modified.

Psychoanalytic methods are being used more and more in the treatment of psychoses and especially in the prevention of recurrences. It requires special training, talent, and effort to use them in these conditions, and doctors who are fully competent to treat psychoses by psychoanalytic methods are very uncommon.

As for "normal" people being analyzed, this is happening all the time. Many well-adjusted psychiatrists are being and have been analyzed for training purposes. Many social workers and psychologists also go through an analysis so that they will be able to understand people better and cooperate with psychoanalysts in treating others. In spite of the expense and hardship which younger people with limited incomes must go through to accomplish the task, most of these "normals" consider analysis an excellent investment because it helps to make them happier, wiser, and more efficient human beings. Everyone has ungratified tensions stored up from infancy, whether these tensions express themselves in openly neurotic ways or not, and it is always a help to have one's unsatisfied Id energies reorganized and partly relieved through analysis. It is certainly an advantage to those who have children to raise.

The question often arises, Is psychoanalysis harmful to some people? The greatest danger lies in treating a patient who is on the verge of a psychosis when the analyst does not realize his true condition. The analyst must also be careful to distinguish neuroses from certain brain diseases and glandular disorders, such as hyperthyroidism, which may cause similar symptoms, so that he will not treat by psychological methods alone patients who should have surgery or special medications. In order to avoid such errors, psychoanalysts nowadays are required to have a thorough training in medical psychiatry before they are accepted by the American Psychoanalytic Association. Nonmedical psychoanalysts deal with this problem by calling in consultants and by requiring a thorough medical examination of the patient before treatment begins.

Occasionally a patient will make a career of analysis, remaining in treatment year after year without any appreciable improvement, depriving himself of all but the barest necessities in order to do so. This is particularly likely to happen with professional people such as social workers. Anyone who has been in analysis for more than two years without any decisive results is certainly entitled to consult with another psychiatrist or psychoanalyst to evaluate the situation. Sometimes an overzealous analyst will encourage divorce without having a clear picture of the marriage, which he could easily obtain by interviewing the spouse and the children involved. A large percentage of neurotics are suicidal; one of the chief contributions of psychoanalysis is the saving of many people who would otherwise kill themselves.

Another kind of danger comes from people who break off an analysis in the middle, against the advice of the doctor, and then advertise the fact that they were psychoanalyzed by so-and-so (which is untrue since they did not go through with the treatment) and that it made them worse. This is much like a patient getting off the operating table before he is sewed up and then claiming that the surgeon made his wound bigger. Psychoanalysts hesitate to start treatment when they suspect that an individual is more interested in this kind of showing-off than in getting better.

6

Who was Freud?

Like all great doctors, Sigmund Freud, the discoverer of psychoanalysis, was interested in curing sick people and in finding out what made them sick so that similar sicknesses could be prevented from occurring in other people. To these purposes he devoted his life, trying to help people just as William Osler, the great physician, and Harvey Cushing, the great brain surgeon, did, and trying to find something which would enable others to help them, just as Alexander Fleming, the discoverer of penicillin, and Paul Ehrlich, the discoverer of salvarsan, "the magic bullet," did. Like nearly all great doctors, he was a dignified gentleman who was not interested in publicity, riches, or pornography. Since one of his most important discoveries was the significance of sexual tensions in causing neurosis, however, and since he made so bold as to publish his observations, publicity came to him in spite of his desire to live a quiet studious life.

He is usually talked about as though he personally had discovered sex, and his name has even become a synonym for second-rate writers to use when they mean "sexual." It should therefore be said that sexual ideas are not "Freudian," but belong to the person who is thinking them. What *is* Freudian is understanding how the sexual feelings of children can be transformed, under certain circumstances, into symptoms of neurosis in the grownup. One of the great wonders of scientific discovery is Freud's insistence that nearly all dreams, however unsexy they may appear on the surface, are fundamentally sexual. When he announced this, before 1900, he was greeted with intense opposition and derision, but he stuck to his guns, although he came to this conclusion purely by psychological insight and intuition. As we noted in the section on sleep, it took seventy years to prove that he was right.

Even if he had not discovered psychoanalysis, Freud would have been a great man because of his other discoveries. He was the first to make a sensible and clear scheme of classification of the neuroses, doing for them what the great and respected Dr. Kraepelin did in classifying the psychoses. Thus, any doctor who makes a diagnosis of anxiety neurosis is practicing Freudian psychiatry, however much he might be horrified at the idea (as some doctors still are).

Freud was also a pioneer in studying cerebral palsy in children and discovered the probable way in which this disease comes about. Perhaps his greatest contribution to medical science, aside from psychoanalysis, was his connection with the discovery of local anesthesia. The development of local anesthetics, upon which a good deal of modern surgery is based, may be said to have started in large part from Freud's experiments with cocaine. An eye doctor named Koller is generally given credit for the discovery of local anesthesia, and in his first painless operation he used a cocaine solution which his friend Freud had prepared and given him in a little bottle. People who go to dentists as well as people who go to psychiatrists, therefore, owe Freud a debt of gratitude.

Thus, even before he had fully developed psychoanalysis, Freud had elevated himself to a position of eminence in medicine and psychiatry. Some of the doctors who criticize him are not aware of the other things he did, and they have not themselves had a thorough psychoanalysis or thoroughly analyzed many patients according to his method. Many of these people say that they have analyzed patients, but admit that they have not quite followed his method; yet they blame him because their treatment did not work. This is like a critic of Thomas Edison building a model of one of Edison's machines, but leaving out some of Edison's ideas and putting in a few of his own, and then criticizing Edison because the machine didn't work!

Freud's discoveries in psychology rank with Darwin's discoveries in biology and perhaps have done more to change the thinking and viewpoint of people all over the world. The quality of the men who follow Freud's ideas and apply them carefully, methodically, and sincerely is a good testimonial to their value. The group of his older and respected followers includes men and women of great perception and integrity. Among the younger people who enter the study of medicine, Freud's ideas have a great attraction for many of those with the greatest intelligence and human understanding.

7

Freud and his followers

Sigmund Freud was born in 1856 in what is now part of Czechoslovakia, and he died in England in 1939. He spent most of his life in Vienna, where he acquired a brilliant group of followers, who felt that by using his ideas they could do more to help neurotic patients than by any other method. These men spread his ideas throughout Europe and America. After a while, some of them broke away from the original Psychoanalytic Society and founded schools of their own. The best-known of these dissenters are Alfred Adler and Carl Jung.

About 1910, Alfred Adler began to turn his attention to certain conscious factors in the personality and gradually veered away from Freud's basic ideas, namely, the importance of the infantile libido and the driving force of the unconscious Id. After a while Adler himself realized that his ideas were getting farther and farther away from those of Freudian psychoanalysis, so he dropped this word and called his system "Individual Psychology."

His best-known idea is the "inferiority complex." By this he means the feelings which center around an evident physical or mental handicap. Lameness, short stature, and stuttering are examples of such handicaps. "Inferiorities" arouse an intense desire to make up for them and gain power and prestige in some other way. At times this is done by developing some other organ than the one affected, but often it is accomplished by giving the inferior function special attention until it is developed beyond the average and can be used to raise the individual to a superior position in society. Thus we have the lame Byron becoming a famous swimmer, and the stuttering Demosthenes becoming a celebrated orator; while the undersized Napoleon got his compensation by becoming a powerful leader of fighting men.

The reactions started by the inferiority complex strengthen the "will to power," resulting in a forceful "masculine protest"—that is, an attempt to prove superior manliness. This striving for power, according to Adler, causes the symptoms of neurosis. Sometimes the masculine protest produces exceptional ability, as in the cases of Byron and Napoleon, but too often there is no way for the individual to prove his superiority in the world of competition, so he expresses his protest in a way which wastes the time and energy of himself and those around him. According to Adler, since women have a harder time asserting their masculine will to power, they have more neuroses.

Psychoanalysts feel that the methods of treatment advocated by Adler, which are based largely on reasoning with the patient, do not go deep enough to affect permanent changes in the individual's way of handling his energy, and that they are therefore more useful for guidance than for actual treatment.

Carl Jung's earlier books, especially those dealing with the psychology of schizophrenia and with word-association tests, are highly regarded by psychiatrists. In 1912, however, he published a book on the psychology of the unconscious in which it appeared that his ideas were taking quite a different track from those of psychoanalysis. He began to call his system "analytic psychology," to distinguish it from psychoanalysis. Jung traveled in India and Africa, and after these journeys became especially interested in the mystical aspects of the mind. As time went on, his ideas became more and more different from his teacher's, and he began to stress heavily some teachings which he imported from the Orient and which are difficult to fit in with scientific psychology as we know it in the Western world. In addition, he gives less attention than the psychoanalysts to the relationships between the mind and the body, so that it is more difficult to fit his ideas into the framework of modern medicine. Many of Jung's ideas are striking and thought-provoking, however, particularly his approach to the question of images, and to the meaning of life.

Karen Horney was another discontented member of the Freudian family. Adler, Jung, and Horney (as well as Rank and Stekel) all were thoughtful psychotherapists with considerable experience, and what they have to say must be taken seriously and carefully considered before any opinion can be expressed as to the value of their ideas. No one can deny their observations, and they are entitled to their own interpretations of what went on with their patients. The only problem at issue is whether shifting the emphasis from the ungratified, unconscious Id tensions of early infancy to the various other factors which these authors are interested in is always to the greatest benefit of the patient, and whether these other factors are more important than the things Freud stressed. The orthodox psychoanalysts say that they are not.

Horney tends to emphasize the conflicts of the individual with his surroundings of the moment, rather than the residues left over from infancy. Orthodox analysts feel that she makes an error here, and that treatment directed mostly toward solving current conflicts will not have the lasting results which come from relaxing earlier tensions. Nevertheless, they appreciate the fact that, like Adler, she has made a useful contribution in giving special study to certain aspects of the personality.

One of Horney's chief attempts to introduce new ways into psychoanalysis was concerned with self-analysis. Psychoanalysis is a long and expensive procedure, out of reach of most people, and any valuable method of shortening the time required and reducing the expense would be a great contribution to the field of psychiatry. Dr. Horney felt that in some cases the patient might be able to continue analysis without the close guidance of the doctor, once he or she had learned the method. She claimed that some people could get a clear understanding of their unconscious tensions without the supervision of a professional analyst. Judging from what she wrote, the qualifications that a patient must have to carry on self-analysis successfully include a college education, complete freedom from the usual moral prejudices, and a high degree of "psychological intuition."

Many psychoanalysts have conducted experiments in an attempt to cut down the time required for "psychoanalysis," sometimes to only a few visits in the course of a week or two. By using psychoanalytic principles, they have sometimes succeeded in relieving patients of one or more symptoms in a remarkably short time, but it remains to be seen how deep and long-lasting these results will be, and whether they will hold up under such strains of later years as retirement and the menopause. For those who cannot afford psychoanalysis, or who are suffering from conditions for which psychoanalysis is not suitable, there are other psychotherapy approaches available which give better results in many cases.

8

What is hypnotism?

An Indian yogi once demonstrated before the Calcutta Medical Society that he could stop his pulse beat. The doctors suspected some trickery, so they placed the man before an X-ray machine and looked at his heart through a fluoroscope. They found to their astonishment that his heart had indeed stopped beating and that he was able to stop it for as long as sixty seconds at a time while they looked at it through the X-ray screen. Many yogis after years of training are said to be able to do things which are almost as remarkable, such as sticking needles through their cheeks, pulling out their colons to wash them in the Ganges, and developing their tongues to such a length that they can touch their foreheads with them.

In the Middle Ages, and even now, hysterical young girls have been able to show stigmata—that is, designs written on their skins in raised wheals. There are many reports of girls having cross-shaped blotches appear on the palms of their hands.

In some freak shows there are men who can be stuck with hatpins without apparently feeling any pain. Many people remember seeing Houdini stick pins through his cheeks without bleeding or showing signs of pain.

People who are hypnotized can often be made to do some of these things. They can be made not to feel pain and not to bleed when pins are stuck into them or through their cheeks. They can be made to have wheals appear beneath strips of court plaster pasted on their arms.

The action of the heart, bleeding, the appearance of wheals, and probably to some degree the feeling of pain, can all be controlled by the same P and S nerves we became familiar with in discussing the relationship of emotions to disease. These nerves belong to a part of the nervous system called "autonomic"—which means much the same as *automatic*—because it cannot ordinarily be controlled by will power; it takes care of the automatic responses to emotions without the individual's thinking about them. Thus, when we are enraged our hearts automatically beat quickly, our skins flush, and we feel pain less than usual. When we are afraid, our hearts may skip a beat, our skins turn pale, and we become sensitive to the slightest pain.

This gives us a definition of hypnotism: hypnosis is a state wherein the autonomic nervous system is brought under partial control so that its reactions can be willed. It may be under the control of the individual himself as in the case of the yogis, or under the control of another person, as in the case of a hypnotized subject. In the latter case, the subject falls more or less asleep before unusual things can be made to happen at the suggestion of the hypnotist. Since the autonomic system is related to the emotions, we may say that hypnotism is a way of temporarily affecting the emotional responses, physical as well as mental, through conscious suggestion and willing.

This enables us to understand how neurotic symptoms can sometimes be influenced under hypnosis. Since such symptoms come from images, they can be affected by changing the images concerned. For example, the neurosis of Si Seifuss was based on an image of himself as "a wicked man who was responsible for the deaths of ten others." When this image discharged its energy under hypnosis, he got better. Symptoms can be produced under hypnosis by the same method of image changing which cures them. In the case of a hypnotized subject who forms a wheal under a piece of court plaster, the hypnotist describes to the subject a new image of himself in which he has a wheal on his arm, and his body changes to correspond to the new image.

With a suggestible patient, whose images are easily molded by an outsider, the cure of the symptom may be permanent. More often it is only temporary. If the unrealistic image has been warped through long years of *inside* stress, the effect of the treatment will soon wear off, since the twig was early bent and so the late tree cannot easily be straightened, but only twisted into a shape that may look straight for a while. If the symptoms are brought on by a later *outside* stress, such as starvation, infection, combat, fear, injury, or uncertainty, the relief obtained by hypnosis may be more permanent. In other words, if the symptoms are based mainly on the unfinished business of childhood, they will be more difficult to cure by hypnosis than if they develop principally from the unfinished business of recent times. The more recent the tensions, the more lasting the cure. That is why the results with hypnosis during a war are better near the battlefield than after the patient gets back home.

Is hypnosis the best way to remove neurotic symptoms in a hurry? Much depends upon the personality of the therapist. Some do better with ordinary psychotherapy because their curative powers come out to best advantage in a psychiatric interview rather than in a hypnotic séance. The success of any psychiatric treatment probably depends upon the relationship of the patient's Id to the therapist's, whether they both realize it or not, and it happens that some therapists influence the patient's Id most easily through hypnotism, and others by talking and listening. Whichever method brings out the most powerful response when used by any particular psychiatrist, will be that doctor's most effective way of treating people.

There is more to hypnotic therapy than just hypnotizing the patient and changing his images. The changed images must be fitted into his waking personality. This usually means sessions of discussion after the hypnosis is over. Most psychiatrists feel that they can cure the same symptoms in the same length of time without hypnosis and get a better result, since from the beginning the changed images become a part of the patient's normal personality; and, in addition, which is not often the case while the patient is under hypnosis, the cure of the underlying neurosis, as well as of the symptoms, can be begun. They think they can do the patient more permanent good while they are removing hysterical hoarseness in a fifty-minute interview than while they are removing it in a fifty-minute hypnotic session.

There is a danger in hypnotism that the therapist may remove the symptoms without offering anything in return. Since neurotic symptoms are substitutes for Id wishes which cannot be gratified, removing the symptoms sometimes weakens the individual rather than strengthening him, though he appears better off to the inexperienced eye. We remember that when Dr. Treece was able to restore Horace Volk's voice, Horace became anxious and depressed. An affliction which affected only his talking was replaced by one which affected his whole personality and made him less able to carry on than he was before. Dr. Treece, being an experienced psychiatrist, was not proud of his "cure" when he made Horace talk, since he realized that the most important part of the treatment was still to come: he had yet to find a way for Horace to relieve the tensions which caused the symptom.

Nature's solution is usually the best, and if we take this away from the patient without offering anything in return, a new symptom is apt to appear which may make him worse off than he was before. Thus, a hypnotist may "cure" a hysterical stomach-ache, only to have the patient go "blind" a few weeks later. This can sometimes be prevented by using the information gained under hypnosis or in subsequent interviews to find a less damaging way for the patient to relieve his tensions. In some cases the support given by the image of the psychiatrist may make him feel more secure than his symptom previously did, and then he will remain free of obvious symptoms as long as he knows that the psychiatrist is there to help him if he needs it.

Much of the interest in hypnotism nowadays centers around its use as a method of anesthesia. It has been successfully used as a painkiller in childbirth, dentistry, and in minor surgery. Since the usual dangers and discomforts of an anesthetic are absent, it is a valuable tool in the hands of those who can use it effectively, and their number is increasing. Its use in major operations and even in childbirth is risky, however; it is likely to be uncertain, and it cannot be used on everyone, since the depth of sleep necessary for success cannot always be induced. In addition, there is the possibility of bad aftereffects if it is used on people who are already emotionally disturbed.

Hypnotism has always taken the public fancy, because it is dramatic and mysterious. That is why some patients are more impressed by it than by more thorough but less theatrical treatment. It can be used as a stage and parlor trick by those whose minds work that way. It is said that some Indian fakirs can hypnotize groups of people all at the same time, and this is also done in this country on the stage and on radio and television. Some more respectable hypnotists use group hypnosis in treating their patients, but this is an experimental procedure whose value remains to be demonstrated. It is certainly not to be recommended for most people, since in some cases, particularly paranoids, it may end up making them more confused than ever.

Certain questions which are commonly asked about hypnosis can now be answered in the light of our present knowledge as follows:

1. Some subjects can be hypnotized without their knowledge and without their consent.

2. Subjects who can "do things better" under hypnosis can also do them better without hypnosis, with proper motivation.

3. Hypnosis can be used for antisocial and criminal purposes.

4. Some people do not come out of the trance state, particularly if they are on the verge of a psychosis when they are hypnotized.

5. As already noted, relief of a symptom by hypnosis may result in the appearance of much more serious symptoms.

The solution for all these possibilities is that hypnosis should only be performed by someone with adequate psychiatric, medical, or psychological knowledge, training, and ethical standards to prevent unfortunate occurrences. Hypnosis should always be prescribed as the treatment of choice by the psychiatrist or physician, and never at the request of the patient.

9

Other approaches

Transactional analysis, which is one of the most rapidly growing methods of treatment at the present time, will be discussed in detail in the next chapter. Two other approaches to psychotherapy have been in use for some time. Many of the older generation of American psychiatrists were trained under the "Meyerian" system of psychobiology, which was developed by Adolf Meyer, late professor of psychiatry at the Johns Hopkins Medical School. Psychobiology stresses the importance of getting a complete history or biography of the individual, mental, moral, and physical, starting with his ancestors and the day of his birth.* Psychodrama, which was developed in Vienna by J. L. Moreno and is now widely used in many parts of the world, is based on the purposeful relationship between the patient and the people around him.

Psychodrama is really a form of group therapy in which one person, called the "protagonist" or "subject," acts out an individual problem (or a problem which has arisen in a group such as a hospital ward), preferably on a small stage, which in some hospitals is provided for just that purpose. Other patients or trained assistants, called "auxiliary egos," are instructed by the protagonist as to how to play their parts. The therapist acts as a director, deciding from his knowledge of the patients' personalities which role it would be most helpful for each one to take.

In the case of a schizophrenic who is having hallucinations, for example, the protagonist plays himself, while the auxiliary egos may play the parts of the voices he is hearing. The patient explains

---

* This approach requires strict clinical training and is too complex in language and concept to outline briefly. For bibliographical references, see the notes at the end of this chapter.

to them exactly how the voices sound or what the people were like whose voices he hears. On the other hand, the patient may take the part of one of the voices, while one of the auxiliary egos plays the part of the patient. In another case, severe emotional stresses may be re-enacted so that the subject can express himself fully and completely and thus become aware of his pent-up fears and guilts.

Psychiatrists with a certain type of personality can obtain excellent results with some types of patients in this way. Other psychiatrists, who try psychodrama "out of the book" and are not really built to be casting directors, may not do so well with this approach. Thus, the results seem to depend, as in many forms of psychotherapy, first on the personality of the psychiatrist; secondly, on how thoroughly he is trained; and thirdly, on his skill and experience.

The many new methods of psychotherapy that have been developed in recent years include existential therapy, Gestalt therapy, reality therapy, nondirective therapy, and behavior therapy.

Existential therapy is based mainly on the ideas of certain European philosophers. While the ideas reach back more than a hundred years, their use in psychotherapy has been developed mainly since World War II. It uses many long philosophical words which are difficult to define, as well as some which are a little easier to understand, such as "confrontation" and "encounter." It deals with the patient in his confrontation with three aspects of the world: first, the environment and the biological possibilities of a human being; secondly, the world of his relationships with other people; and thirdly, the world of his own inner experience. It is best suited to people with a knowledge of philosophy, who have a knack for understanding philosophical matters.

Gestalt therapy is similarly based on philosophical ideas, but these have to do with ways of seeing, hearing, touching, and moving, and so are easy for the patient to understand. For example, Gestalt therapy stresses the hidden meaning of unconscious bodily movements. Such movements are really devices to keep from becoming too aware of oneself and to protect oneself from going ahead with the unfinished business of childhood. Gestalt therapists are unusual in that they deliberately touch their patients, even going so far at times as to wrestle with them, all with the object of making the patient more aware of himself. Shy people are particularly enthusiastic about Gestalt therapy because it allows them to become intimate with other people quickly in a way they may never have experienced before. Sometimes, in fact, they proceed too quickly and become terrified at their own forwardness. Gestalt therapy is an excellent way to loosen people up, but the therapist must use good judgment to keep some of them from flying apart completely.

Both existential therapy and Gestalt therapy pay a great deal of attention to what is going on "here and now." Reality therapy also starts from "here and now," but talks about what is likely to happen in the future, thus making the patient consider in a realistic way the results of his behavior. Reality therapy is particularly useful in dealing with people who get into trouble and try to talk their way out of taking responsibility for what they have done or what they are planning to do.

In nondirective therapy, the therapist remains noncommittal, sometimes merely repeating what the patient himself has said, on the theory that if the patient becomes more aware of what he is saying, he will get a new picture of himself and that picture will enable him to go ahead on a new basis. In practice, this approach seems best suited for dealing with minor difficulties of young people and to help them with certain predicaments which young people get into, such as not being able to make it at college. It is of doubtful value for true neuroses or psychoses.

None of the approaches mentioned above can be called scientific, since none of them is based on a well-tested theory of personality, and there tends to be a certain hit-or-miss quality in their application. This is in contrast to psychoanalysis and transactional analysis, which are based on carefully checked theories which have been tested on many patients. Thus it is possible with either of these approaches to predict in advance what is going to happen with an individual patient, and even to decide whether it is worthwhile to go ahead. Hence the other approaches are interesting to people who do not need or do not like clear-cut ideas, while psychoanalysis and transactional analysis appeal more to people who like precision in their thinking and behavior.

A third approach which is based on a carefully tested theory is behavior therapy. Behavior therapists believe that neurotic symptoms are conditioned reflexes and that the same procedures which are used to "extinguish" conditioned reflexes in animals can be used to extinguish neurotic symptoms such as phobias. Claims made by behavior therapists are much more sweeping than those made by other therapists. They maintain, for example, that fifty per cent of neurotics will improve with any one of the standard methods of treatment, and a large percentage without any treatment at all, while with behavior therapy, they hold, recovery will occur in eighty to ninety per cent of the cases. They do not claim to cure psychoses. It may be that behavior therapy is the best treatment for curing certain special symptoms of neurosis, such as abnormal fears, but this conclusion is not accepted by the majority of conventional psychiatrists at present.

Since all the newer treatments mentioned in this section are still questioned by a great many experienced psychiatrists, it is hard for a layman to choose intelligently among them. Anyone who wishes to know more about any of them will find a helpful list of books in the notes at the end of this chapter, and he should consult with a trusted adviser before making any decision about selecting one for himself.

10

What is group therapy?

In individual treatment the doctor can make detailed observations on how the patient behaves when sitting in a room with one other person, and a special kind of person at that: a therapist who has complete control of the situation, much as the patient's parents had when he was little. In this situation, the doctor gets his picture of how the patient behaves with other kinds of people from what the patient tells him. These stories are always one-sided because they give only the patient's viewpoint, which is usually slanted for better or for worse and may overlook important details. This limits to some extent the value of individual therapy.

It is simple for the therapist to see for himself how the patient behaves with a variety of other people, and this information may be very valuable in hastening the patient's cure. To do this, the doctor introduces the patient to a group of other patients who are trying to work out their problems together in a therapy group.

Some doctors feel that even if the patient seems well in individual therapy and in his outside activities, he cannot really get well until he has spent some time in such a group. Others are even more enthusiastic; they feel that group therapy does more for the patient in the same amount of time than individual treatment can do. In any case, there is no doubt that a patient who has not been in a therapy group has missed a valuable therapeutic experience.

There are different kinds of group treatment, each with its own benefit for the patient. The simplest kind consists of *lectures* and *pep talks,* which give the patient information and encouragement that may be helpful to him, particularly if there is a discussion period in which the patients exchange ideas. Next in order of complexity comes *supportive treatment,* in which the patients, under the guidance of a therapist, encourage each other and share their experiences. In this way they gradually get a feeling of belonging which is very gratifying, particularly to people who have been isolated for long periods, or even most of their lives, because they had no one to talk to or because one symptom of their mental illness was to stay away from other people. In *permissive treatment,* the individual learns to give free expression to his thoughts and feelings, so that he no longer fears them so much or fights them so hard, and in addition he relieves himself of the burden of pent-up tensions.

It is known, however, that while relieving one's feelings is temporarily relaxing, it does not cure the underlying mental conflicts. This can be accomplished in a group by the use of some form of *analytic treatment.* There are three main types of analysis which are used in groups.

The first, which developed principally in England, is called *group analytic therapy.* Here the happenings in the group are related to the state of the whole group at any given moment, so that the individual learns how the people around him influence his behavior from minute to minute.

The second is *psychoanalytic group therapy,* which uses many of the principles and techniques of psychoanalysis, such as free association, dream interpretation, and the analysis of resistances to getting better. It attempts to study unconscious as well as conscious images and feelings and to effect a deep reorganization of the emotional drives of the individual. Here the theory and technique are borrowed from individual therapy and are applied to what goes on when many people are present instead of just the doctor and the patient. This is perhaps the most widely used form of group treatment at present.

The third type is *transactional group treatment*, in which the transactions between patients are analyzed into their ego states, and sets of transactions are analyzed to see which games are being played. The theory on which this is based, and the way it is used in practice, will be discussed in the next chapter. While transactional group treatment is growing in popularity, the number of people trained to do it properly is limited, so that its use is confined to a few localities at present.

Which kind of psychiatric treatment is best? As with any form of treatment, this cannot be settled by talking about theories and using big words, but is demonstrated entirely by the results. The better treatment will cure more patients in less time, the cures will last longer, and the patients' ability to work well and love well will be greater the better the treatment. By these standards the results of analytic group therapy stand up very well against the results of individual therapy, and the results of transactional group treatment seem particularly promising.

The conditions for group treatment are often set by outside factors. For example, in prisons or social agencies, "the authorities" may decide where the group meetings will be held, how many people will be in a group, how often they will meet, and how long they can continue in the group. The group therapist then has to make the best of these conditions. In private practice, however, it is possible to set up the groups in the best possible way to obtain the best results for each patient. The ideal number for a therapy group is six to eight patients. Before he enters the group, the patient's physical condition is checked and he has a private interview with the therapist, so that the doctor can find out about his background and what he wants to be cured of. This also gives the patient a chance to become acquainted with the doctor and what he has to offer. Most groups meet once a week, although sometimes, if it can be arranged, more frequent meetings may be desirable. Some doctors like to have another psychiatrist, a psychologist, a psychiatric nurse, or a psychiatric social worker to act as a "cotherapist."

Group therapy may be carried on along with individual therapy. Thus the patient may have from one to four individual sessions per week and also go to a therapy group once a week. Sometimes he only has a private interview on special occasions when either he or the doctor feels that it is desirable to settle a particular problem. In some cases there may be two therapists, one for private sessions and one for the group. A group may be set up to run for a definite number of sessions, or it may go on indefinitely. The patients may all start at the same time, or a new patient may be put into an "open" group. In an "open" group, as one patient drops out he is replaced by another, so that the group itself continues indefinitely with gradually changing personnel as members get better or withdraw for other reasons.

There are several stages in all three types of analytic group therapy. First there is a stage of getting acquainted, where each patient learns how the others react and how they respond to his behavior. The second stage is that of group feeling, when the patients start to get over their fears of each other and to mean something to each other, so that the group meetings give a feeling of "belonging." After that, the patients begin to see more clearly their difficulties in getting along with others and themselves, and learn to adjust their behavior so that it will get better results and they will feel good about themselves and the others after the group meetings. This leads into the stage of individual dynamics, when the patients become more and more aware of the reasons for their behavior toward various other individuals in the group. They begin to see each other more as real people instead of figures with whom they have to work out their childhood problems or play their games.

One of the commonest reactions of patients when group therapy is proposed is to say they could never talk in front of strangers, or that they feel ill at ease in groups. These are just the kinds of problems that group therapy is designed to deal with, so that the very people who make such objections are the ones who may benefit the most from being in a group. The rule of most analytic-therapy groups is that anyone can say anything he likes at any time with no exceptions, although any physical contact or physical violence is prohibited. Most people are irked by what they consider a lack of freedom, and in the group they are given complete freedom to talk. They then discover, much to their surprise, that instead of enjoying the freedom they have been longing for, they are frightened by it. But as they learn to trust the others in the group more and more, they are able to enjoy this freedom more and more, and they discover that straight talking, contrary to their expectations, makes friends rather than enemies.

Nowadays, group therapy is used for a wide variety of conditions, including psychoses, neuroses, addictions, and sexual difficulties. It has also been found effective in "psychosomatic" conditions, such as obesity, allergy, stuttering, and skin diseases. Indeed, the first application of systematic group therapy at the beginning of this century dealt with groups of patients suffering from tuberculosis.

Group therapy is now widely used in Army, Navy, and Veterans Administration hospitals, as well as in psychiatric hospitals, psychiatric wards, psychiatric clinics, prisons, industry, and homes for the aged and for unmarried mothers. In some mental hospitals it has largely replaced the use of isolation rooms, restraints, drugs, and shock treatment. Often schizophrenics who have been in the hospital for many years and have never taken part in any of the activities of the hospital and have not been able to benefit from individual therapy, start to talk and make friends when they find themselves in a well-run therapy group. Through its careful use, distressing symptoms can be cleared up temporarily or permanently, and changes in the individual's emotional make-up and in his behavior toward other people take place. What he learns about himself and how to get along with other people stays with him and is useful for the rest of his life.

As is often the case in individual therapy, the process of improvement seems to continue between meetings and after the treatment is terminated. Failures in group therapy occur for the same reason as in individual therapy. The patient is not ready to get better or he cannot tolerate what is happening to him and the changes that threaten to take place within him.

For private patients, group therapy not only may offer more rapid progress, but in most cases the cost is less than half that of individual treatment. Its value is sufficiently well established to warrant the assertion that any psychiatric hospital which does not employ group therapy in an earnest effort to reduce the use of drugs, shock treatment, and brain-cutting operations is behind the times—and unfortunately this is the case in many states and countries which do not have a sufficient number of well-trained psychiatrists. Group therapy is even more desirable from society's point of view than from the individual's. There are millions of neurotics in this country who are prospective or actual parents. Every neurotic individual who has children is likely to bring them up to be neurotic, so that for this reason alone, disregarding any other factors which might encourage neurosis in the world today, the number of neurotics is likely to increase. Every time a psychiatric patient is cured, or at least given knowledge of his or her condition so that he can change his behavior, the next generation benefits.

It would be impossible for the limited number of well-trained psychiatrists in this country to make a significant reduction in the total number of neurotics in the population through individual treatment. Group therapy enables each psychiatrist to treat five or ten times as many patients as he could individually; even if all the members of his group are not cured, they may at least become better parents through what they learn about human beings and about themselves. From the point of view of the nation's future and the world's future, it is more important to become a better parent than to be cured oneself. This is where group therapy may have its greatest value.

Besides the specific benefits of the analytic forms of group treatment, there is something about "groupishness" itself which is curative. Therefore, any *well-conducted* group of any kind can have a therapeutic value. Even a person who does not have psychiatric training can be trained in a short period to be a good group leader and to give his charges the considerable benefits which come from being in the same room with other people who are interested in human behavior and are willing to examine their own behavior. Clergymen and people who work in prisons, for example, often have to deal with behavior problems, and they usually find that group sessions are the most effective way of doing this in their particular situations. If they do not have the professional training to be therapists and cannot find a trained person to take care of all the disturbed people they are responsible for, it is either group meetings or nothing. If the group is well run, the members will know when to call a halt and will not be backward in pointing out when the leader is going beyond the scope of the group. In this way many group leaders learn from their members how to do better and better.

11

What is family therapy?

Besides the "small group" consisting of individual psychiatric patients, there are several other forms of group therapy now in use. A great many child psychiatrists nowadays will not accept a child for treatment unless the parents also come, because they feel it is no use getting the child better during the treatment hour and then have him go home to the same surroundings that may have caused his problems. A convenient way to see the whole family is in a family group (sometimes called a "conjoint" family group). In such a group the patient is called the "identified patient," and all the other members of his family attend—his parents and his brothers and his sisters, and his uncles and his aunts and his grandparents too, if they are living in the same house. This is amazingly effective, because the difficulties which the members of the family have with each other very quickly become apparent when they are all seen together.

Having two or three families in the same group is even more effective. There the parents discover, for example, that there are certain problems that most parents have in common, while there are other problems which are quite different in each family. This helps them sort things out better in their minds. The same applies to the children. The rule in family therapy has to be, of course, that all the members have the right to speak freely and that no one may be punished for anything he says in the group. If the group is successful, not only will the identified patient improve, but his brothers and sisters, whose troubles may not have been quite so obvious or quite so annoying to the parents, will benefit as well. The parents will also learn more about each other. In the long run, a family group may have a tremendous influence on how the grandchildren will be brought up, so the benefits, rather than being confined to the identified patient, may be distributed among three generations.

Marital therapy is similar to family therapy in that the husband and wife go to the same group. Sometimes this is a general group with individual patients, and sometimes it is a special group for married couples only. The object of such a group is not counseling, which is the job of a marriage counselor, but psychiatric treatment. The counselor acts sometimes as a referee and sometimes as an adviser; the marital group therapist is interested in the underlying psychiatric problems which may be causing difficulty between the spouses. Married couples who have been to marriage counselors are well aware of this difference, and do not expect refereeing or advice from a psychiatrist, but realize that they each have psychiatric problems to solve.

Another form of group therapy is common on hospital wards, where all the patients meet together with the whole staff in order to thrash out problems which concern the ward, and also to get acquainted with one another, particularly with new patients. This is the policy of "therapeutic community" wards.

Very popular nowadays are group meetings or weekends spent together by people who are not patients, but who work in the same place or go to the same church, or have something else in common. These are called T-groups, or sensitivity-training groups. The idea here is that if people talk frankly to each other they will get to know each other better and also know themselves better. Such groups tend to use a special language with words such as *communication, self-actualization, integration,* and a sprinkling of psychoanalytic terms such as *identification, dependency,* and *hostility.* Since some of these terms are vague and cannot be defined scientifically, and others tend to be used improperly, the value of such groups is open to question. One of the criticisms of T-groups is that they merely expose people to a series of insults and insights which they are not ready for, so that people get taken apart, as it were, and there is no one there to put them together again. One definition of a sensitivity group is that it is a place where sensitive people go to have their feelings hurt. Many psychiatrists, the writer included, have an unfavorable impression of such meetings, particularly if they are conducted by someone who may not have sufficient training to cope with the bad or even psychotic reactions which may result. Fortunately, the long words offer a shield which sensitive people can hide behind if the going gets too rough.

A recent development is the "marathon," or overnight group, which is a group therapy meeting that lasts from twenty-four to forty-eight hours. Some therapists feel that going through the night without sleep makes people drop their guards, so that the results are better. Others feel that it is preferable to take off for the night and sleep, so that the group can start fresh in the morning. Most patients who attend such marathons come out feeling very enthusiastic, and it is sometimes difficult to determine whether this is because the marathon was a kind of "trip," or because it was of real benefit. In any case, the long-term results remain to be evaluated, so that the actual therapeutic effects of marathons will not be known for another five or ten years.

Footnotes for Philosophers, Chapter Eight

1. *Psychotherapy*

For further information about most of the topics mentioned in this section, there are two reliable sources containing articles written by carefully selected leaders in each field. Both of these have been cited previously.

The Encyclopedia of Mental Health is written for intelligent laymen.

The American Handbook of Psychiatry is intended for practicing psychiatrists.

2. *What is psychoanalysis?*

Two of the best books on the subject matter covered in this chapter are *An Elementary Textbook of Psychoanalysis,* by Charles Brenner, and Freud's *Outline of Psychoanalysis*. The simplest, most readable, and most pleasant introduction to the psychoanalytic approach in general is *Delusion and Dream,* by Sigmund Freud (Boston: Beacon Press, 1956).

3. and 4. *The process of analysis*

Those who are particularly interested in the subjects covered in this and the following sections, including the question of what is and what is not psychoanalysis, may consult *Practical and Theoretical Aspects of Psychoanalysis,* by Lawrence S. Kubie (New York: F. A. Praeger, 1960).

5. *Who should be psychoanalyzed?*

If Medea had gone to her therapy group that afternoon in ancient Greece, the whole bloody business would never have happened.

6. *Freud*

Interested readers will turn to Jones's biography of Freud, which literary critics have called one of the best biographies in the English language.

The Life and Work of Sigmund Freud, by Ernest Jones, 3 vols. New York: Basic Books, 1953, 1955, 1957.

An excellent shorter account is *The Psychoanalytic Revolution: Sigmund Freud's Life and Achievement,* by Marthe Robert (New York: Harcourt, Brace & World, 1966).

Another interesting work contains Freud's letters.

The Origins of Psychoanalysis. New York: Basic Books, 1954.

For Freud's own account, see his *Autobiographical Study* (New York: W. W. Norton, 1963).

7. *The Dissidents*

An excellent series of essays on both the orthodox and dissident viewpoints, by their respective founders, can be found in *An Outline of Psychoanalysis,* edited by C. Thompson, M. Mazer, and E. Witenberg. New York: The Modern Library, 1955. (This is not the same as Freud's *Outline.*)

For additional information about Adler's ideas, see:

The Individual Psychology of Alfred Adler. New York: Basic Books, 1956.

A condensed account of Jung's theories can be found in:

The Psychology of C. G. Jung, by Jolan de F. Jacobi. New Haven: Yale University Press, 1963.

There is a personal controversy over Jung, because there is considerable evidence that he actively cooperated with the Nazis as far back as 1934 ("Dr. C. G. Jung and National Socialism," by S. S. Feldman, *American Journal of Psychiatry,* Vol. 102, p. 263 [September, 1945]). An attempt at refutation was published by Dr. Ernest Harms (*Psychiatric Quarterly,* Vol. 20, pp. 199–230 [April, 1946]).

The most concise and readable account of Horney's views may be found in:

Are You Considering Psychoanalysis? edited by Karen Horney. New York: W. W. Norton, 1946.

This book contains several statements which it is difficult to resist the temptation to correct. For example, it is stated that according to Freudian concepts, the desire to grow is "an evidence of something sick." This is not so. Among orthodox Freudians, the patient's desire to grow is (and was at the time the book was published) regarded as a valuable indicator of his ability to get well.

I am indebted to Dr. Jack L. Rubin of New York for further clarification of Horney's viewpoints and their development since her death in 1952. The following statements are taken out of context.

"In effect, her contribution to psychoanalytic thought is a culture-based, growth-oriented, holistic and dynamic theory of neurotic process. Freud's libido theory and its derivatives . . . are rejected. . . . The topographical theory of psychic organization is also rejected as tending to reify functions which are transitory, dynamic, and subjective. Neurosis is redefined . . . [Developments during the past seven years have crystallized into four areas.] First, ideas have been clarified. . . . Second, gaps existing in the original theory have been filled. . . . Third, clinical applications of the theory have been [extended to include additional diagnostic categories and newer clinical settings] such as in group analysis. . . . And fourth, principles of the psychoanalytic process have been investigated, such as the doctor-patient relationship, the nature of insight and interpretation, and the negative therapeutic reaction. . . ."

For further details, see "Holistic (Horney) Psychoanalysis Today," by Jack L. Rubin (*American Journal of Psychotherapy*, Vol. 21, pp. 198–219 [1967]).

For an account of a shorter form of psychoanalysis, see:

Psychoanalysis and Psychotherapy, by Franz Alexander. New York: W. W. Norton, 1956.

The reader may be curious as to how it happens that some doctors are "Freudians," some "Jungians," some "Horneyites," some transactional analysts, and so on. This is because the doctor has the responsibility of actually treating patients, and has to make a clear-cut decision as to what form of treatment he is going to give each individual in order to give him the greatest benefit in the long run. The psychiatrist makes his decision in the same way as a surgeon, basing it on his own past experience, his reading, and the experience of those colleagues whom he most respects. After trying various approaches, each of which seems effective for a time at least, he may end up choosing one particular one because, after a fair trial, in comparison with other methods it appears to give the best results in his particular practice.

8. *Hypnosis*

Most popular books on hypnotism are highly misleading. For accurate information on this subject, the two reference books mentioned at the beginning of these notes should be consulted: *Encyclopedia of Mental Health* ("Hypnosis," by H. Rosen, Vol. 3, pp. 800–817), and *American Handbook of Psychiatry* ("Hypnotherapy," by L. R. Wolberg, Vol. 2, pp. 1466–1481).

The powers of the yogis, as confirmed by the Calcutta Medical Society, are recounted in:

The Mysterious Kundalini, by Vasant Gangaram Rele, 2nd ed. Bombay: D. B. Taraporevala Sons, 1929.

9. *Other Approaches*

Dr. J. L. Moreno, originator of psychodrama, informs me that the best introductory article on this subject can be found in *American Handbook of Psychiatry*, Vol. II, Chap. 68, "Psychodrama," by J. L. Moreno, pp. 1375–96. In the same place, pp. 1317–32, will be found an outline of the Meyerian psychobiological approach by Wendell Muncie.

For an introduction to existential psychology see the paperback *Existential Psychology*, edited by Rollo May (New York: Random House, 1965). For a detailed discussion of Gestalt therapy, see the paperback *Gestalt Therapy: Excitement and Growth in the Human Personality*, by F. Perls, R. E. Hefferline, and P. Goodman (New York: Dell Publishing, 1951). Reality therapy is discussed by its originator in *Reality Therapy*, by W. Glasser (New York: Harper & Row, 1965).

The text for nondirective therapy is *Client-Centered Therapy,* by C. R. Rogers (Boston: Houghton Mifflin, 1959). An easily accessible book on behavior therapy is the paperback *Behavior Therapy Techniques,* by J. Wolpe and A. A. Lazarus (New York: Pergamon Press, 1966). Behavior therapy is based on pioneering studies on conditioned reflexes which are described in *Lectures on Conditioned Reflexes,* by I. V. Pavlov (New York: International Publishers, 1963).

In addition, some of the approaches discussed here, together with a variety of others, are described by authorities in their respective fields in *Contemporary Psychotherapies,* edited by M. I. Stein (New York: Free Press, 1963), and in *Active Psychotherapies,* edited by H. Greenwald (New York: Atherton Press, 1967).

10. *Group Therapy*

For a more detailed discussion of group therapy and a comparison of some of the principal approaches, see my book *Principles of Group Treatment* (New York: Oxford University Press, 1966).

11. *Family Therapy*

The most readable book on family therapy is *Conjoint Family Therapy,* by Virginia Satir (Palo Alto, Calif.: Science and Behavior Books, 1967). N. W. Ackerman's book, *The Psychodynamics of Family Life* (New York: Basic Books, 1958), may also be consulted. For various views on marital therapy, see B. L. Green, *The Psychotherapies of Marital Disharmony* (New York: Free Press, 1965). For an advanced approach to "therapeutic community" meetings, see my article "Staff-Patient Staff Conferences." (*American Journal of Psychiatry,* Vol. 125, October 1968, in press).

9

TRANSACTIONAL ANALYSIS
by John M. Dusay, M.D.*

1

What is transactional analysis?

Transactional analysis is a newly evolved method of treating emotional disorders. While it is a form of psychotherapy, doctors using this method occasionally prescribe medication and other forms of somatic treatment. Many transactional analysts are physicians, but other well-trained professionals in mental health fields also use this method of treatment. A great deal of attention is focused on the troubles that patients get into with other people, and their inability to form satisfactory relations with others. There is less emphasis on unconscious mental processes. Because of this, the doctor† is active and direct and does not remain anonymous. It is this very involvement of the doctor that is one of the distinguishing differences between this new form of treatment and orthodox psychoanalysis. Transactional analysis historically grew from psychoanalysis as a way of doing group treatment; recently, however, it has been utilized by a few experienced doctors in individual, family, and marriage-counseling sessions.

A theory of personality has developed based upon observations that although a person may say one thing he may be saying or implying something quite different in a hidden or disguised way. An individual has many parts to his personality, and one part may trick another just as he tricks other people in his life. How human beings can fool themselves and others, sometimes with tragic con-

---

* Dr. Dusay is an instructor at the University of California School of Medicine and a Teaching Member of the International Transactional Analysis Association.

† "Doctor" refers not only to psychiatrists but also to other qualified transactional analysts.

sequences, and tend to do it over and over again, is explained by principles of transactional analysis which have gradually evolved by careful looking at what people do to other people.

2

What are its main theories?

It is well known that people speak differently under varying conditions. The young business executive will speak with one tone of voice when he is making a report to his manager, another tone of voice when he returns home in the evening and is asked by his wife to take out the garbage, and yet another the next morning when, just as he is about to leave for the office, his three-year-old son spills a glass of prune juice on his freshly pressed business suit. Not only does his tone of voice change in these different experiences but the look on his face, his feelings, his actions, and his thoughts also change. Careful observation of patients has led to the discovery that there are three basic ways that an individual may exist at any one time. These are called ego states. An ego state includes the way a person is thinking, feeling, and behaving at any one time. The three ego states available to any person are called the Parent, the Adult, and the Child.* Regardless of how old a person is (except in the case of a very young infant), he exists in one of the three ego states.

The Parent ego state is essentially copied from the real parents or authority figures. Sometimes the nourishing and loving qualities of the parents are seen in a person who is in the Parent ego state, and at other times punitive, unfair, prejudiced attitudes of the real parents may come out. Patients are often surprised when certain attitudes and gestures of their own are traced back to origins in their parents, especially if they have spent a great deal of energy in rebelling and separating from their real parents. They overlook many of their parents' basic characteristics which they incorporate, almost habitually, as their own.

---

* When written with capital initial, Parent, Adult, and Child refer to ego states, and when written with small-letter initial, parent, adult, and child refer to actual persons.

The Adult ego state is essentially a computer. It is that part of the individual which is rational and logical and mainly processes data much like a huge electronic brain; therefore, feeling and emotions are not part of the Adult. The Adult is seen when a scientist presents research data to a group of colleagues or when a housewife adds up the bank account. This is the part which does work. The mental process necessary for a carpenter to hammer a nail is Adult. When he slips and hits his thumb the Adult gives way to another ego state. The Adult is not always the best ego state to be in, however; at most parties the Adult would be very boring.

The Child ego state is that part of the personality which is preserved from actual childhood. Children can be naughty* or nice, very happy or very sad, stubborn or flexible, and any person, regardless of his chronological age may have the same feelings, thoughts, and behavior that he once did as a child. Children have the ability to see through needless or absurd social conventions (Parent) and don't like to take time to figure out everything logically (Adult). There is a spontaneous, creative, and intuitive quality to the Child ego state. Older people (more than three years of age) who are intuitive are experiencing childlike qualities; for example, a child will stare at any part of a person's body that interests him, while the parents will discourage this type of behavior. Seeing new or interesting things, the individual is more like a child and less like a parent. The intuitive person is said to be Child and not Parent. Children also seem to have all the fun, and people who habitually enjoy themselves have a very active Child ego state.

The three ego states are referred to as the structure of the personality, and diagnosis of the ego states is called "Structural Analysis." This is usually the first part of a Transactional Analysis. The action begins when two people get together. Every individual has a Parent, Adult, and Child ego state, so when two people are alone in a room there are actually six people who can suddenly appear.

A transaction is a stimulus from one person and a related

---

* Children are born frank and free. Early transactions with their parents shape the personalities of older children.

response from another.* Many transactions are simple and straightforward; for example:

> Boss: What time is it? (*Stimulus*)
> SECRETARY: Four o'clock. (*Response*)

This is a straightforward Adult-Adult transaction. The answer could be from a different ego state and the situation becomes more complicated.

> Boss: What time is it? (*Adult stimulus*)
> SECRETARY: What's wrong with your watch? (*Parent response*)

If the boss is good-natured, the secretary may still be working for him next week; however, he did not get his question answered, because she responded as a parent would to a child. Her Parent ego state transacted with his Child. His original Adult stimulus was crossed up by her response, and they could go on this way forever without the boss ever finding out what time it was.

> Boss: I left it at home. (*Child*)
> SECRETARY: My, you're forgetful. (*Parent*)
> Boss: But I was in a hurry. (*Child*)

And so on.

Another possibility exists in which the secretary responds to boss's Adult stimulus with a Child response; for example:

> Boss: What time is it? (*Adult*)
> SECRETARY: Wouldn't you like to know! (*Child*)

Many interesting transactions may follow this, but the boss probably will not find out what time it is until much later.

---

* This is also called *communication,* and nothing else is called communication by a transactional analyst, although this term has been very popular recently and is used to mean many things.

It is readily apparent in the above example that people don't always behave in the manner which seems socially appropriate. The boss may be thought of as a boss on the social level, but psychologically he may be a little boy, or a playmate. Transactions can become even more complicated and hidden than in the above examples, and many readers will be able to recall situations in which a person talks on one level but has a hidden transaction on another. The hidden, double-level transactions give rise to games.

A game has three specific parts: first, there is an orderly series of transactions; second, there is a gimmick (which means that the transactions are double-leveled and one level is hidden from the other); and third, there is a payoff. Nothing else satisfies the definition of a *game* for a transactional analyst.

The very first psychological game discovered was the game of Why Don't You, Yes But. Its main characteristics are well known by transactional analysts, and the following example demonstrates how it occurred in a therapy group:

> HARRY: How can I get my term paper finished on time this semester?
>
> MARY: Why don't you start tonight?
>
> HARRY: Yes but I was up all night last night.
>
> LARRY: Why don't you start tomorrow then?
>
> HARRY: Yes but I have to go to Chemistry Lab.
>
> CAREY: Why don't you do it on the weekend?
>
> HARRY: Yes but I have to visit my family.
>
> JERRY: Why don't you ask the prof for an extension?
>
> HARRY: Yes but he has already said, "No exceptions."

This game is usually met by silence when all of the others give up and Harry wins. Although he seemed to present a straight Adult request for information, he successfully rejected all suggestions, like a little boy getting all sorts of parental advice none of which satisfies him. He later admitted that he had already thought of the suggestions himself, and the hidden level of his game became apparent. Harry's Child was tricking the Parent of the other group members into paying attention to him on the hidden or psychological level. His payoff was that he again proved that the Parent can't tell him anything new.

Like all game players, Harry knew his own game well and could play either side. Frequently he would take the Parent position with his girl friend, Mathilda, who also plays Why Don't You, Yes But, and she would take the Child position; they could switch back and forth with ease. People choose to associate with others who will play their game or a complementary game, so they can gain the advantages of game playing.

The newborn human infant cannot survive without receiving physical contact from his mother or a mother substitute. A famous child psychologist has proved that babies who get little attention or human contact have a much higher actual death rate than those who get more physical contact, even though physical contact spreads germs. This form of early nourishment given from the mother to the infant is known as *stroking*. The need for strokes continues throughout life, although the forms of stroking change and seem to become more sophisticated. Harry was getting verbal attention instead of physical strokes, but the words from the Parents of the other group members to Harry's Child were the equivalent of physical strokes. Strokes are so important in later life that all sorts of elaborate means are devised to get them. Sometimes adolescents have to steal automobiles or break street lights before they can get stroked, and this indicates that negative strokes are better than no strokes at all.

Harry's game illustrates another important advantage (payoff) of playing games. Harry was reassured of the correctness of an early decision, which he is now unaware of, that his parents could not tell him anything meaningful. This decision, which has determined so much of Harry's later life course, was based on the fact that his mother died when he was less than five years old and his father remarried a stepmother who regularly "missed the point." Harry felt that his father never understood him either, because first of all he brought home a substitute "mommy" who was not as good as the real thing and secondly his father never stayed around long enough to find out what was bothering him. He was convinced at a very early age that his father and stepmother were paying more attention to themselves than to him, and were not discussing the real basis of his loneliness and misery. The Why

Don't You, Yes But game reinforced his basic decision because, sure enough, the Parents of other people he met in later life, such as those in his treatment group, could never say anything meaningful to him either about what seemed to his Child to be a real concern. It was not surprising that he also complained that Mathilda, his girl friend, did not really understand him, nor did any other girl whom he dated. He also said occasionally that the doctor could not understand him or say anything meaningful.

Because games are based on early childhood decisions, they can be unlearned, and the patient can make a re-decision. Games can be given up altogether or exchanged for less destructive ones. The doctor surprised Harry when he tried to start a new Why Don't You, Yes But at a following session:

> HARRY: I never can get out of bed on time in the morning.
>
> DOCTOR: You do have an interesting problem, don't you?

Rather than jumping in with a new series of suggestions, all of which would be rejected, the doctor refused to enter into Harry's game and gave Harry the idea that he might be able to find some other way of relating to people. This challenged Harry's basic decision, and when he finally abandoned Why Don't You, Yes But, he was a changed person.

Another advantage of playing games is that as long as games go on between two or more people, intimate, straightforward situations may be avoided. This at first seems tragic, which it is, but it can be understood by looking back to childhood experiences. Harry feared intimacy with Mathilda; this may be why he chose her—because the first woman in his life with whom he was intimate abandoned him at an early and relatively helpless age. This deep fear created by his mother's untimely death was still with Harry, and rather than risk abandonment he preferred to play games with Mathilda and thus avoid intimacy.

Human beings have devised many such psychological games, all having in common the orderly series of transactions, the gimmick, and the payoff, but some game-players play more seriously than others. The game of Rapo, a sexual game, illustrates this. Rose, a pretty young lady at a cocktail party, sits in just the right position in her strategically located chair so that Henry, who is having an intelligent Adult-to-Adult discussion on modern art with her, can just glimpse the right amount of thigh as her skirt slowly inches upward. Intrigued, Henry disregards his Adult and asks, "May I take you home tonight?" Rose abruptly answers, "What makes you think I'm that kind of girl?" Henry is then entitled to feel foolish, and Rose is entitled to feel indignant. Henry did not know it, but when she was only six years old Rose, because of unfair treatment by her father, decided that men were no good. She proved it again tonight as she has many times in the past and will many times in the future, unless she appears at a psychiatrist's office complaining that she just doesn't seem to get along well with men. Henry felt foolish only for a little while; it won't hurt too long and he'll recover to be a victim of Rapo again. This is "first degree" game playing, and both Rose and Henry will seek out other "first degree" players. Some players prefer to play games a bit harder, and in the case of Rapo, the victim gets his face slapped and the indignant lady is entitled to announce to her friends what a fiend he was; this is "second degree." The really hard game-player, "third degree," plays for keeps. In the case of Rapo, the third-degree victim goes to jail, and the indignant lady is entitled to scream loudly, get a free trip to the hospital, and explain the whole thing to a police officer. People seldom change the "degree" of their games, but most games have "hard" and "soft" players.

Games are so predominant and deep-rooted in society that they tend to become institutionalized—that is, played according to rules that everybody knows about and more or less agrees to. The game of Alcoholic, a five-handed game, illustrates this. The "victim," the first hand, is the one who is "it." In most cities there is an area known as "skid row," with its own rules and values, where alcoholics can feel comfortable and the victims collect as they go downhill. The second hand, the "persecutor," is typified by the wife who has informal coffee gatherings where she and other wives compare how horrible their husbands are. There is also a formal organization known as Alanon for wives and families of alcoholics. The "patsy," the third hand, is the reinforcer, who encourages the one who is "it" to continue the game. He is the man who meets

the victim in the friendly neighborhood pub after work and hears
his tale of woe:

> Victim: The boss piled all of the work on my desk
> . . ." (*et cetera*)
> Patsy: Oh, that's terrible.
> Victim: Then when I got home Claudia started holler-
> ing at me . . ." (*et cetera*)
> Patsy: Let me buy you a drink.

The fourth hand, the "source," is big business. In some states
the most influential lobbies in the legislatures are working for the
alcohol industry. The "rescuer," the fifth hand, has organizations
such as Alcoholics Anonymous. This is an example of the fact that
some games are so popular that social institutions have developed
to bring the various players together. Generally, the one who is
"it" comes on Child, thus provoking the Parental ego state (critical or protective) of the persecutor or rescuer and the Child ego
state of the provocative patsy.

Games are part of the ongoing course of life. From the early
transactions between mother, father, and child, a life plan evolves.
This is called the script. If a mother says to her child on one level,
"Be a success in life," and on another level, "But don't leave me,"
the youngster will develop a basic set of games to fulfill mother's
early injunction. Gerald was an example of this. He would appear
to be a "success," or at least have the potential, then at the last
minute he would flop and come running home to mother ("Don't
leave me!"). Gerald may be entitled to a free depression or even
suicide if he collects enough failures, and the script will have a
tragic outcome.* Some people seem to be winners at almost everything they do, and when setbacks occur they take them in stride
and return to win again. Losers can manage to lose in the most
favorable situations and sometimes exercise a good deal of in-
genuity to insure failure. Tragic as it may seem, they are following

---

* The author recently had a patient whose mother presented this type
of script to her son and finally told him directly, "If I were like you, I
would commit suicide!"—which he is seriously contemplating.

the life plan set down in early life. Fortunately, scripts can be changed, since they are not inborn, but learned.

3
What happens in transactional analysis?

Structural analysis (the diagnosis of the Parent, Adult, and Child), analysis of transactions, game analysis, and analysis of the underlying scripts are all distinct phases of treatment, but are included under the more general term *transactional analysis*. Usually all phases of treatment are carried out at the same time, as opportunity permits, but some well-trained doctors analyze only one phase at a time. Transactional analysis originally was developed as a technique of doing group treatment, and it seems to be the most clear-cut approach to group treatment at the present time. Groups are fertile ground for playing games, because there are so many opportunities available for transactions.* As previously noted, two people in a room together are really six, and when eight people are together there are twenty-four ego states present, so it doesn't take long to find someone with whom it is easy to play a game.

It has been noticed, in treatment groups as well as in social, family, business, and other situations where two or more people come together, that playing games is only one of the six things that can happen. When people are together they all face the question: What are we going to do with our time now?† Occasionally this becomes the predominant concern of a person who is shy and insecure and who, upon entering a group, tends to *withdraw*. This is one way to behave when in a group, and it can be accomplished by having private fantasies, like Huckleberry Finn thinking about the "ole fishin' hole" when the teacher is talking about arithmetic. A patient can have even more elaborate fantasies, and rather than reveal their contents he may choose to say nothing. Sleeping in the presence of others is another popular form of withdrawing.

---

* This is one distinct advantage of group treatment over individual treatment, since it gives more information to work with.

† People who can answer this question are richly rewarded by their society. A television performer who will take care of a whole hour for millions of people is often paid thousands of dollars.

Rituals are stereotyped series of transactions prescribed by society. Some are formal, such as wedding ceremonies, circumcision rites, or death ceremonies.* Informal rituals are very common. The nature of rituals may be understood by examining the greeting ritual so well known in contemporary America:

> JOE: Good morning.
> MOE: How are you?

In both of these ritual statements Joe strokes Moe and Moe strokes Joe. There is almost a syllable-for-syllable giving of strokes in the above example—each gave the other three syllables. Or it might sound like this:

> JOE: How have you been, Moe? Haven't seen you for a long time.
> MOE: Hi!

This will never do; Joe said a whole sentence, and Moe gave back only one syllable. Moe owes Joe several strokes, and Joe will feel cheated. Or:

> JOE: How are you?
> FLO: Well, not so good. I had a headache this morning, but no fever, and somehow that new medicine for constipation . . . (*et cetera*)

This doesn't work either, as Flo is giving Joe more strokes than he bargained for, and he will not likely be talking to her again soon. Transactional analysts occasionally use informal rituals at the very beginning of a treatment session to warm people up, but they avoid prolonged rituals.

Working is a third way of filling or structuring time in groups, and transactional analysts call the task that is performed an *activity*. (What takes place in most offices between nine and five

* Funeral arrangements are quite complex rituals, and people pay large sums for having their time structured when personal loss occurs.

involves a much smaller percentage of work than most people are willing to admit.) In hospitals, for example, the staff unites to perform an operation, or the patients get together for occupational therapy, and the specific task is called the group activity.

Pastimes are another type of group behavior, being just what the name implies. Since people must do something with their time, they may discuss harmless but interesting topics to fill the interval. Unlike the game player, the pastime player doesn't get a payoff. Pastimes are specific to different groups with similar social and educational backgrounds. For example, assembly-line workers at a factory will frequently pass the time at the morning coffee break with "General Motors." In this pastime Sam says, "I like a Chevy [or a Plymouth or a Ford] better than a Plymouth [or a Ford or a Chevy] because . . ." (Fill in with twenty-five words or fewer.) Gus then replies, "Well, I like a Ford [or a Chevy or a Plymouth] better than a Chevy [or a Plymouth or a Ford] because . . ." (Fill in with another set of twenty-five words or fewer.) Both Sam and Gus are able to use up several minutes of the coffee break in this way and don't have to sit back silently. Just one pastime may take care of the allotted time; but, if not, they may also engage in "Baseball" or "Did ya see . . . [that broad]."

At cocktail parties in large metropolitan areas the intuitive hostess will escort the new arrival to the small group which has an enjoyable pastime for him. People huddle in different circles according to the pastime that is going on. They proceed from one circle to the next until they find their favorite: If they can't find a good one for them, they will go home muttering, "That was a lousy party." "Psychiatry" is a favorite among intellectuals and takes two forms. "Introjective Psychiatry" (or "Let's Talk about Me") goes like this:

> PHYLLIS: I can't seem to make a decision.
>
> GEORGE: Your ambivalence comes from your father.

Many hours can be passed with this, and incidentally a good deal of useful information may be conveyed in this way. "Projective Psychiatry" (or "Let's Talk about You [or Them]") goes like this:

WILSON: The lack of fathers is causing the race riots.
ANDREW: And another thing is the police force's representation of authority—in a totalitarian manner.

Some other pastimes which are well-known are "P.T.A.," usually played by housewives with children of school age; "If It Weren't For————" (fill in current husband's name); "Weather," a favorite in rural communities; "Ever Been to————" (some exotic place), or the adolescent type "Ever Taken————" (some exotic drug); "What Became of————" (an old acquaintance, or a onetime celebrity); and so on. Readers will recall other forms of pastimes from parties they have attended. One advantage of pastimes is that they form a platform from which games can be launched, and the game seeker can survey the opportunities.*

Games also take care of time and have specific, individually tailored payoffs, like Harry's, and they offer protection from intimacy.

The only other way of existing in a group of two or more is by attaining *intimacy*. This is very rare, usually is private with just two individuals, and is a straightforward, game-free relationship; it is free also of withdrawal, rituals, activity, and pastimes. Many people live their entire lives without intimacy. When intimacy does occur it can be recognized immediately without much question. Poets have been writing about it for thousands of years, and they probably come as close as anyone to conveying the feeling of it. Intimacy almost never occurs in psychotherapy or social groups. It is most commonly found between lovers who feel no need to put each other down or exploit each other, and thus feel perfectly free to talk straight and act without subterfuge or concealment.

Withdrawal, ritual, activity, pastimes, games, and intimacy are the six ways that people can structure their time with other people. Transactional analysts carefully observe the group to determine which type of time structuring is occurring. They do not prejudge

---

* Transactional analysis groups are ideally composed of people of widely different backgrounds, ages, and illnesses so that they won't all engage in the same pastime.

whether any type is good or bad in itself, but rather determine what is good for what. A shy, withdrawn girl who doesn't know what to say to boys on dates may profit from exercising pastime behavior, while a loud, socially outgoing salesman may benefit by some degree of withdrawal and introspection.* Rituals tend to warm things up, but become useless if prolonged, while activities are best left for occupational therapists. Pastimes are usually the most difficult for any group to give up. They could keep a group going for years with no results, and the group members would be justified in saying, "My, that's an interesting group"—for years and years.

Results are important to transactional analysts. From the beginning the doctor seeks to form a treatment contract with the patient.† This is initiated by asking the patient, "What do you want?" or "How will you know and how will I know when you have gotten what you came here for?" Although this seems like a simple question, many psychotherapies have been conducted for years without its ever being asked. Many patients enter treatment, take time away from their jobs, pay a sizable fee, and make an emotional investment, and then tell the doctor, "Well I don't know why I'm here; what do you think?" The transactional analyst recognizes this as being a Child asking the Parent to tell her what is best for her. This may lead to the playing of games, if the doctor is careless and responds with some Parental prejudices. In that case, the Child of the patient may end up rebelling. This type of action is exciting, but it does not help the treatment. Such undesirable situations are avoided by making an Adult type of contract which will consider objectively the patient's individual needs:

DOCTOR: What will make you happy?

PATIENT: Having a true friend.

DOCTOR: What is a true friend?

---

* One extremely extroverted person of the author's acquaintance attains a calmness which lasts for days by sitting silently in front of a blank wall every Saturday morning.

† The contract is not made as a legal document, but the four basic requirements of any contract also apply to the treatment contract: (1) mutual assent, (2) consideration, (3) competency, and (4) legal goal.

PATIENT: Someone I can talk to, spend some time with, and have dinner with.

DOCTOR: I see. Have you ever had a true friend?

PATIENT: No, I have trouble meeting people.

DOCTOR: Okay, then if you develop a true friend you will have what you are consulting me for.

PATIENT: That's right.

These are the essential transactions of an Adult-to-Adult contract. Both the doctor and patient know what they are working for and have a reasonable idea as to what will be different with the patient if the treatment is successful. In order to accomplish this goal, some important personality changes will have to take place. Contracts are stated simply and clearly in well-defined words. Other contracts read: "I want to make $100 or more per week"; or "I want to be potent in my sexual life." With such contracts the patient either gets what he's coming for or he does not, and both parties can tell what is happening.

If the patient is unable to form an Adult contract, this inability becomes the chief concern in the treatment. Occasionally a patient is hospitalized or coerced into treatment against his will when things have gotten out of control. For a short period of time the doctor will assume many parental functions and accept the responsibility of the Parent-Child situation—for example, "It's time to eat now, George." Every effort is made to establish contact with the patient's Adult and form a treatment contract. Then treatment can proceed more rapidly.

Structural Analysis is an early and ongoing phase of treatment when the doctor and the patients in a group begin to distinguish whether the Parent, Adult, or Child is the active ego state. Sometimes this is easy to see.

HORACE: (*trying to be Adult*): Let's talk this over calmly, Molly.

DOCTOR: Why were you pointing your finger at Molly when you said that?

HORACE: She's being childish.

Horace's Parent had come out, not his Adult. Gestures such as a pointed finger often reveal the ego state. Behavior, words, tone of voice, feelings, all help to diagnose ego states, and group members may become astute at detecting hidden clues.

Two particularly common problems occur with ego states. The first is *exclusion*. This occurs when one ego state takes over and won't allow any other to come out. If the Adult takes over and excludes both the Parent and the Child, the person will be quite rational and objective but will have neither values nor beliefs, and will not be able to have fun. A fixed Parent usually spends his time stamping out anything that resembles childlike fun,* perhaps calling it sin. The fixed Child who excludes Adult and Parent may have a lot of fun, over and over and over, but he may end up without any resources, not even enough to eat. Because ego states are natural, each performs a specific, necessary function. It is a question of which ego state is best for a particular situation.

Contamination is the second important ego-state problem. This happens when two ego states fuse and the patient doesn't know which one is operating. A six-year-old girl awakens from her sleep and cries, "Mommy, Mommy, the big, bad wolf is in my closet; I heard it!" Mommy comes into the girl's room, turns on the lights, gives her daughter a hug and says, "Don't be afraid; everything will be okay!" (Parent). She then proceeds to perform a scientific experiment. She pulls the covers off the little girl's head and says "There's no wolf there." She opens the closet door and says "Let's look." (experimentation), and ends up with "See!" (conclusion). This scientific examination strengthens her daughter's Adult, while her reassurances and hugs strengthen the Child. The daughter was dreaming and awakened with a fantasy (Child). This fantasy was so strong that it contaminated her Adult and she was convinced that she heard noises in the closet. If her Adult were not contaminated, she would have known that the noises were familiar sounds from somewhere else, such as falling leaves or a dog. When her mother came in and paid attention to both her Child and Adult, they were strengthened and able to exist separately; and she fell off to sleep.

---

* Grant Wood's "American Gothic" is a striking portrait of two people with fixed Parents.

This situation occurs also with patients of any age where Child fantasies contaminate the Adult computer. For example, the patient may fearfully believe that he is being followed by some sinister character. This Child-Adult contamination is known as a delusion, and the doctor proceeds in very much the same manner as the mother did, by recognizing and talking to both the Child and the Adult, each in a different way, which allows them to separate. The patient can then say, "That was an odd idea I had, about people following me." Sometimes in treatment this structural ego-state analysis is all that a patient wants or needs, and when that is successfully completed, he may resume his usual activities and home life, with only an occasional follow-up visit to the doctor. Most patients, however, go on to game analysis.

Games are played in transactional analysis groups for two reasons: first, because the doctor does not allow the group to pass the entire session in pastimes or withdrawal; and second, because games have many advantages (payoffs), especially when the going gets rough. Games are first diagnosed, then treated if this is called for by the patient's contract. The experienced doctor does not pounce on all games, because he knows that everyone needs games from time to time, and some are relatively harmless. But if a game is harmful, the doctor steps in.* Mr. Holmes, the patient whose contract is to have a friend, plays the game Now I've Got You, You Son of a Bitch (*NIGYSOB*). In this game he overlooks all of the nice things that a person may say to him and waits patiently for the victim to say or do something wrong, at which point he triumphantly points out the mistake. He is an expert at finding flaws, even when nobody else seems to notice, and makes the most out of them. This will not help him in his project of forming a friendship.

Whenever the doctor recognizes a game in progress, he has four basic ways of responding. He may (1) expose the game; (2) play along with the game; (3) ignore it completely; or (4) offer an alternative game.

1. In the case of Mr. Holmes, the doctor decided that exposure was necessary. Holmes played NIGYSOB with the doctor:

---

*Sometimes astute patients provide the important transactions which will stop the game that is being played, and the doctor learns from them.

HOLMES: Last week you said you were going to start the meeting ten minutes early, but you didn't do it.

DOCTOR: Now you've got me!

HOLMES (*laughing*): I'm always trying to get you.

DOCTOR: Yeah.

This is an intuitive response to the game, by the doctor's Child. The doctor could also have exposed the game by going into the details objectively with his Adult. Since the doctor was intuitive, he did not have to spell out all the details, and Holmes caught on quickly.

2. Fanny made a recovery from a very serious disturbance in which she killed one of her children, and spent years in the back ward of a large state mental hospital. She was now leading the life of a quiet housewife and seeing the doctor for follow-up treatment. Her contract was to remain at home and not go back to the hospital. She maintained herself by playing Gee, You're Wonderful, Doctor. The doctor chose to play her game and accepted her endorsement of his talents. The result was that she followed his advice, took her medications, and otherwise conducted herself well. These are the types of choices the doctor continually makes in a transactional analysis group.

3. Richard complained that his parents would unfairly beat him physically when he was a child. During a group session, he told an obvious lie, which was easily detected by the doctor because it did not match with another story he had told previously. The doctor was tempted to expose the lie, but controlled this urge because he realized that Richard was playing Kick Me and *wanted* to be exposed and embarrassed. Richard could, and did, get kicked almost everywhere else, so he didn't need it from his doctor. If the doctor had played the game, Richard would probably have left the group after that.*

4. The doctor decided to start an alternative game in the case of Rose, who had undergone extensive treatment previously, including long- and short-term hospitalization, drugs, and electroshock.

---

* Patients who get just the same old response in the group that they can get anywhere else tend to get bored with treatment.

None of these affected her very primitive game of Uproar, during which she complained violently that everything that was said to her was unfair. In one group session, she was especially loud, and the members thought that she should go back to the hospital, whereupon the doctor said, "Rose, you're making an ass out of yourself." She was surprised, and could not believe what she heard. She abruptly halted the Uproar, and went into a game of hurt feelings, Why Does This Always Happen to Me? She pouted and told the doctor how unprofessional he was, but now she decided to control herself. She left the office calmly and avoided an unnecessary trip to the hospital.

When a patient finally gives up an important game, he is in a unique position. He has given up an "old friend," because he knew his game well and it did so much for him. At this time, there is usually a period of despair. This is something like a depression, but is different in that it comes on rapidly and has elements of frustration and bewilderment. This despair is a reaction of the Child and is similar to what happens to a real child when his best playmate moves away. He is lonely and doesn't know what to do. A few days later, he may be seen joyfully playing with some new friend. Patients giving up games are in a similar lonely position, but they are also free to choose new friends.

This is a time of decision. The responsible transactional analyst never abandons the patient at this point, but continues through the period when the patient, free of his old encumbrances, is deciding what to do now. Rather than repeat his old patterns, he tests new ways in the group. The Child of the patient now seeks help from the Parent in the doctor. The Doctor, having prepared for this moment, is ready to respond.

In Gerald's case, his mother had said to him when he was a child:

> MOTHER (*on one level*): Be a success in life.
> MOTHER (*on another level*): Don't leave me.

At this point, the Doctor says:

> DOCTOR (*on one level*): Be a success.
> DOCTOR (*on another level*): You may go now.

In some respects, there is a healthy competition between the real mother and the Parent ego-state of the Doctor. The responsible doctor recognizes the strength of his influence and has prepared himself for this responsibility by knowing his own Parent, Adult, and Child well. In some instances the patient who gives up his games attains intimacy, the most pleasurable and gratifying of experiences.

4

Transactional analysis in action

The following are the highlights of a typical transactional analysis, illustrating some of the features emphasized in the clinical use of this approach. The numbers refer to the discussion at the end of the section.

Amber Argent came to Dr. Treece following her discharge from the new psychiatric ward at the Arcadia General Hospital, where she had been sent because she had been very depressed, and Dr. Nagel, her family doctor, thought she was suicidal. In referring her for psychiatric treatment, Dr. Nagel mentioned that she had not paid her bill, even though she earned a good salary as a secretary at her present place of employment. Rather than press for payment, Dr. Nagel had decided to cross it off his accounts.[1]

Miss Argent arrived punctually for her initial appointment with Dr. Treece, friendly, outgoing, attractively dressed, and not nearly so sad as he expected from Dr. Nagel's account.[2] She started for a convenient chair in the office and managed to trip slightly over a foot-stool. She didn't get hurt, nor did the furniture, but the look on her face seemed to imply that Dr. Treece was at fault for leaving the stool where it was. Dr. Treece didn't respond to the incident, but quickly got down to the question of "Why are you here?" She replied in a very straightforward manner, "I keep getting fired from my jobs and I must be doing something wrong." Dr. Treece agreed when he found that she had been fired from more than twenty-five jobs. To be fired twenty-five times is an accomplishment, but to find new jobs with such a record is even more remarkable. She did have outstanding secretarial skills; ability was not her problem. The contract was readily established: "I want to keep a good job for more than one year." The doctor agreed that this seemed like a suitable contract and said that he would be glad to explore her job problem with her and work toward her goal of keeping a job.[3]

While Dr. Treece was getting more details about her life, she suddenly looked at him and said, "Where did you get *that* neck-tie?" A few minutes later, she decided to change chairs, and in the course of moving the furniture around, she bent over directly in front of Dr. Treece. He felt that she was deliberately exposing herself in this way.[4]

After careful discussion of her physical condition and emotional problems, Dr. Treece prescribed group treatment. She was briefed on the basic principles of transactional analysis in a following session[5] and then invited to a group session composed of eight members, meeting once a week for one and one half hours.

By this time, Dr. Treece had decided that Miss Argent was a lonely girl, and that her favorite way of relating to people was to play the game called Kick Me, in which she would try to provoke people into criticizing her or saying mean things to her, as a substitute for a more pleasant or loving relationship. This was confirmed at the very first meeting, when she met Rex Bigfoot, another group member, who was especially talented in the game of Now I've Got You, You Son of a Bitch (*NIGYSOB*). She interrupted him when he was discussing his favorite subject, his hatred of his mother, whereupon he turned and said, "Why don't you keep still until you know more?"

It took only a few minutes for Miss Argent and Mr. Bigfoot to team up in game-playing, because Kick Me and NIGYSOB are complementary.[6] The Child in her desired kicks, and the Parent in him enjoyed kicking, just as in early life his mother used to punish or "kick" him unfairly.[7] Rex was not the only one who ended up wanting to "kick" her, however. The other members spent the last half hour of the session discussing whether or not Amber was a suitable patient for group treatment and for their group in particular. Dr. Treece noticed that she was smiling slightly during this discussion,[8] and he spoke to her about that.

> DR. T.: You seem to be enjoying the situation.
>
> MISS A.: They don't scare me.
>
> MR. BIGFOOT: You're not worth scaring, baby!
>
> DR. T.: How did that feel?
>
> MISS A.: He's awful.

At this, the others relented and decided to be patient with her. At a later session she told of her constant problem of being "kicked out," of being expelled and suspended from school—how it started in first grade and persisted through college, where she also managed to get expelled because of a persistent argument with the administration. She also managed to be expelled from the Girl Scouts, and was divorced by two husbands. Regarding her situation with the family doctor, she said that just before her depression began he had discussed her bill with her and suggested that if she could not afford his treatment he would refer her to a low-fee clinic and end his treatment with her. She knew very well that she would get just such a kick from him if she presented herself as a well-employed person and did not pay her bill. She said that this was the last blow before the onset of her depression.[9] Dr. Treece thought that this was a good time to start breaking up the game.

> DR. T.: You seem to get kicked by everybody.
>
> MISS A.: You're right.
>
> DR. T.: How are you going to get me to kick you?
>
> MISS A.: (*laughing*): But I don't want you to.
>
> DR. T.: Why don't you pay your bill in advance?

The doctor let her know that by doing certain things she would not be in a position to be kicked. Her Adult recognized this, and she told Dr. Treece that she would pay in advance to avoid Kick Me in regard to money, the game which had succeeded with Dr. Nagel. Nevertheless, she continued to play the game in other arenas. She would have a special provocative look on her face when she interrupted someone, spilled coffee on the man next to her, or engaged in similar disruptive maneuvers.[10] Dr. Treece thought that she was like a little girl trying to look innocent when everyone could see that she was guilty. One of the other group members remarked intuitively, "You look like you just dirtied your diaper."[11]

> DR. T.: When was the first time you felt this way?
>
> MISS A.: I don't remember dirtying my diaper, but I do remember messing things up around the house. One time I knocked an ashtray full of cigarette butts on the floor, and my mother got very angry.
>
> DR. T.: How old were you then?
>
> MISS A.: Three.

This, she said, was her earliest memory of childhood.[12] She went on to say that the only way she could get attention from her mother was to do something naughty in her presence, and then her mother would scold her or punish her physically. She continued this policy in later life, getting unfavorable attention as a substitute for love. This gratified her, in a gruesome sort of way, and made her feel that at least she was alive, but it was an unhappy way to live. Actually, her Child was counting the Kicks, saving them up as some people save trading stamps, and it was clear that some day she intended to "cash them in" for a suicide, which she had almost done with Dr. Nagel. For this reason, Dr. Treece felt that the game would have to be stopped. He suggested to her that she not speak in the group unless she had something positive to say. She said she would try, and the result was that she hardly spoke at all for two weeks. Then one day she criticized Rex Bigfoot again. He started to answer, but Dr. Treece interrupted him and said to Amber, "Well?"

"Oh," she exclaimed. "There I go again!" She started to laugh and the others laughed with her.[13] Then she looked bewildered and asked, "How else can I get attention if I don't say something to get booted?"

Rex, in a good mood that day, suggested, "There must be another way," whereupon Amber said: "You know, you're really not so bad, Rex, you just talk tough sometimes." At this, Rex looked embarrassed, as though he had been caught doing something bad.[14]

From this first uncertain insight, Amber began to make rapid changes. She dressed in brighter and more attractive clothes, and reported that several men in the office had taken to spending more time around her desk and that she had been asked out for dates for the first time in several years. At the end of a year she had attained her goal of continued employment. She continued in the group, nevertheless, to find out more about herself.[15] Her script, or unconscious life plan, was based on an early decision that "Negative attention is better than none at all." Her mother had said to her on one level (out loud), "Get married and be happy," but on another hidden level, "Mess up, and then I'll pay attention to you." She said that Dr. Treece was getting something different across to her—"You don't have to mess up." She was also learning from the other members of the group that people could be interested in her for her good points and that she did not have to be objectionable to get their attention. And she was now able to accept positive "strokes" rather than only negative ones. Her Child had "permission" to have fun in new ways, and she had a new view of life: "People will like me when they see how pretty I am."

The problem of her "messing up" now became the center of attention.[16] After a year and a half of treatment, she felt that she could continue her new way of life on her own. Toward the end, she asked the group if they liked her better this way, and they all said "Yes." Her pleasant smile at this approval marked her new-found ability to accept positive strokes (or "gold trading stamps," as they are called in transactional analysis groups) in place of verbal kicks (called "dirty brown stamps"). She could see that dirty brown stamps were only good for tragic prizes such as suicide, while gold stamps could be traded for happier prizes.

In this account we have not described how Amber Argent learned to distinguish Parent, Adult, and Child ego states in herself and others, and how to analyze transactions into their respective ego states, and how she learned to detect the hidden gimmicks in the apparently innocent transactions that went into games, but we have brought in some special features of interest about transactional analysis treatment, following the numbers in the text.

1. Dr. Treece made a point of finding out why she stopped going to her previous doctor, since this gave him valuable infor-

mation about her favorite games and what to expect in her treatment with him. In Amber's case, one of the important features was a money game, so he prepared himself to deal with that.

2. With depressed patients, a period of hospitalization or an attempted suicide often cheers them up temporarily, since in this way they "cash in" some of their old trading stamps and can make something like a fresh start until the difficulties pile up again. They may also cheer up because they have decided to cash in their stamps in the near future, so that they may act better while they are actually preparing for suicide.

3. It is unusual for a patient to have such a clear-cut goal at such an early stage, and a hopeful sign for the outcome. Because the contract was so clear, neither the doctor nor the patient had to spend time on irrelevancies or preparation.

4. By noting the patient's behavior, the doctor comes to see the games quite clearly. One provocative maneuver alerts the doctor, two give him grounds for a tentative opinion, and three give him a feeling of confidence that he knows what the game is.

5. Transactional analysts make a point of teaching the patient, because this strengthens the Adult and helps the patient feel more at home when she is in a group of experienced people who understand what is going on.

6. It is amazing to see how quickly people pick out those who play the same game or a complementary game.

7. In diagnosing ego states, the doctor must demonstrate that the conditions really existed. To establish that Rex had a "kicking Parent," it was necessary to show that one of his actual parents actually "kicked" people.

8. When the patient smiles in a certain way, especially when the smile is out of place, one can safely assume that the patient is playing her favorite game.

9. If the favorite-game diagnosis is correct, it will be found that the patient plays the game outside as well as in the group.

10. If the patient stops playing the game in one situation, she may still continue to play it in others. In order to cure her of playing it, the whole game system must be uprooted.

11. This is done by tracing it back to its earliest roots in childhood.

12. This does not happen all at once. The "earliest memory"

first recalled may be a screen. It is then necessary to use psycho-analytic methods, such as free association, to find the original learning situation—in this case, probably in toilet training.

13. The "laugh of insight" occurs when the patient's Adult realizes what she has been doing, and how her Child has been conning her most of her life. This laugh is a very good sign.

14. This shows the value of group therapy. While Amber was getting better, her new attitude toward Rex made him realize that his toughness was merely a mask whose purpose was to hide some underlying embarrassment.

15. After the original contract has been fulfilled, the patient may want to make a new one in order to go farther.

16. At a certain point, transactional analysis merges with psychoanalysis in its interest in the very early experiences of the patient.

5

The history and future of transactional analysis

Transactional analysis began with the discovery of the Child. Dr. Eric Berne, who had been involved with orthodox psycho-analysis for about fifteen years, reported a case in which he was working with a highly successful lawyer. The lawyer told him a story about an eight-year-old boy who was vacationing on a ranch and was dressed in his cowboy suit to help the hired man. The hired man said when they were finished, "Thanks, cowpoke!" to which his assistant replied, "I'm not really a cowpoke, I'm just a little boy."

The lawyer went on to say that when he was doing his professional work he was very much an adult. He was successful in the courtroom and in raising his family, and did much useful community work. At certain times, however, he would say, "I'm not really a lawyer, I'm just a little boy." This was noticed by Dr. Berne during the course of treatment when the lawyer's mannerisms, gestures, and love of noise were exactly those of a small boy, the boy that he had once been. It was recognized that the little boy, the Child ego state, was very important in the troubles that he got into. This ego state, or Child, was recognized as being different from the Id. While the "unconscious" Id is a hypothetical idea, the Child is observable and can easily be consciously experienced. Observation of other cases following this verified that the observable Child was only one part of the personality, and the Parent and Adult were also seen as observable parts of the personality. The Parent, Adult, and Child ego states offer a new and realistic way of viewing the personality of any human being.

A small group of psychiatrists, psychologists, and social workers who all had a common interest in group therapy began meeting regularly at Dr. Berne's office in San Francisco in the late 1950's to share their clinical experiences to better understand how people in trouble could gain control of their disturbed behavior.* They soon agreed that most of their patients' troubles were due to conflicts between the Parent and Child ego states, and began studying how these two related to each other. The game of Why Don't You, Yes But was the first game to be discovered, and by 1962 a whole range of games had been delineated.

There was no textbook to guide the early transactional analysts, since nobody had done this type of analysis before. As they discussed cases and listened to tape recordings of their groups, they noticed that the therapist himself would have a tendency to play certain games. When these were carefully discussed, the therapist could give better treatment. They found that in order to give his patients the best chance of recovery, the therapist had to be aware of what his own Parent, Adult, or Child was doing at any one time in the group. A rigorous training program evolved, including attendance at weekly seminars and a period of supervision by well-experienced transactional analysts. This extended training lasts from one to three years or more, and is followed by an oral and written examination by a special examining board of senior transactional analysts. Only after successfully completing training does a qualified professional become a certified transactional analyst. This training is undertaken in addition to the regular training that professionals undergo. Although transactional analysis had its beginning on the West Coast, the original small group

---

* The early group became organized under the name of "San Francisco Social Psychiatry Seminars," later changed to "San Francisco Transactional Analysis Seminar" as its aims became more specific.

has grown into an international organization known as the International Transactional Analysis Association, with more than four hundred members practicing in thirty states and several foreign countries, and about twenty local branches.

Advanced seminars presently conduct regular meetings to examine the older theories and explore new ideas about human problems. An especially promising area of investigation at present is the detailed examination of how mothers and fathers give their children permission to either succeed or fail in life. These permissions lead to the life scripts which, it has been found, can be changed or re-written. Transactional analysts are constantly expanding and examining their theories and ways of doing treatment.

Footnotes for Philosophers, Chapter Nine

1. *What is transactional analysis?*

Transactional analysis is a new way of looking at the things that people have been doing to others for centuries. Some critics have said that this is just another way of saying the same thing that psychoanalysis says. Of course all doctors have been observing the same types of problems, and therapists tend to make similar observations, but nowhere else has the concept of actual Parent, Adult, and Child ego states been documented. The theory of pathological development which most nearly approaches transactional analysis is that of the "double bind." This was developed by a group studying the interaction of families with schizophrenic children. See: "Toward a Theory of Schizophrenia," by G. Bateson and others, *Behavioral Science*, Vol. 1, pp. 251–264 (1956). These studies point to the concept of double-leveled messages, but lack the specificity of transactional analysis.

The most recent comparison of transactional analysis with other forms of treatment can be found in *Principles of Group Treatment*, by Eric Berne (New York: Oxford University Press, 1966, Chapter 13).

2. *What are its main theories?*

The first complete presentation, and still the fundamental work on transactional analysis is *Transactional Analysis in Psychotherapy*, by Eric Berne (New York: Grove Press, 1961). This work furnishes a basic understanding of transactional theory in both its simplest and its most complex aspects.

Transaction analysts have colloquially declared that people play games "to keep their spinal cords from shriveling up." This is traced back to Spitz's classical work on infants in foundling homes in which he discovered that infants who received more human contact (actual physical strokes) and less medical care had a much lower mortality rate than infants who had good medical supervision but little human contact. Children who did not get strokes would die of general debilitating conditions, marasmus, and intercurrent infections. Older people prevent such wasting away by playing games. See:

"Hospitalism: Genesis of Psychiatric Conditions in Early Childhood," by René Spitz. *Psychoanalytic Study of the Child,* Vol. 1:53–74 (1945).

Ego states seem to have an actual anatomical representation in the human brain because certain total states are reproduced in certain epileptic conditions, and also when the cortex is electrically stimulated. See:

Epilepsy and the Functional Anatomy of the Human Brain, by W. Penfield and H. Jasper. Boston: Little, Brown and Company, 1954, pp. 127–47.

Games People Play, by Eric Berne (New York: Grove Press, 1964), is a glossary of games which have been discovered in the several years that transactional analysis principles have been applied. This popular work has found wide acceptance by the lay public as well as by professionals for whom it was written.

Scripts are mentioned in the earlier works but are being studied in more detail. See:

Transactional Analysis Bulletin, Vol. 5, No. 19 (July 1966).

Dr. Claude Steiner, who is most active in examining and explaining scripts, has provided an essential detailed list of questions pertaining to scripts.

"A Script Checklist," by C. Steiner. *Transactional Analysis Bulletin,* Vol. 6, No. 12 (April 1967).

3. *What happens in transactional analysis?*

Principles of Group Treatment, by Eric Berne (New York: Oxford University Press, 1966), is a general textbook for professionals doing group treatment of all types and contains the only systematic treatise on the use of transactional analysis in groups.

A detailed examination of groups and organizations is found in *The Structure and Dynamics of Organizations and Groups,* by Eric Berne (Philadelphia: J. B. Lippincott, 1963). This work discusses what happens in all types of groups due to the special properties of groups.

Therapeutic interventions are detailed in "Response in Therapy," by J. M. Dusay. *Transactional Analysis Bulletin,* Vol. 5, No. 18 (April 1966).

4. *Transactional analysis in action*

The continual acquiring of payoffs is likened to collecting trading stamps. When a person gets enough, he can exchange them for a prize. See:

"Trading Stamps," by Eric Berne. *Transactional Analysis Bulletin,* Vol. 3, No. 10 (April 1964). For a discussion of the basic psychological positions, see his article on "Classification of Positions," *Ibid.,* Vol. 1, No. 3 (July 1962).

5. *History and future of transactional analysis*

The International Transactional Analysis Association, as well as its affiliates, the Transactional Analysis Seminars and Study Groups in various cities have kept a good record of their discussions and have published these in the quarterly *Transactional Analysis Bulletin,* and the history of transactional analysis can be traced through its pages. A bound copy of back issues (Vols. I–V) has been made available by Transactional Pubs., P.O. Box 5747, Carmel, California, 93921.

Berne's curiosity about the phenomenon of intuition was first brought to attention in 1949 prior to developing the principles of transactional analysis. See:

"The Nature of Intuition," by Eric Berne. *Psychiatric Quarterly,* Vol. 23 (1949), pp. 203–26. Several other articles followed, and this culminated in his 1962 presentation of his views of intuition in transactional analysis terms.

"Intuition VI. The Psychodynamics of Intuition," by Eric Berne. *Ibid.,* Vol. 36 (1962), pp. 294–300.

Especially important is his first thorough discussion of the Child ego state:

"Ego States in Psychotherapy," by Eric Berne. *American Journal of Psychotherapy,* Vol. XI (1957), pp. 293–309.

The following articles indicate some of the continuing trends in the application of transactional analysis:

"The Use of Transactional Analysis in Prison Therapy Groups," by F. H. Ernst. *Journal of Social Therapy,* Vol. 8 (1962), No. 3.

"Psychiatric Treatment of the California Felon," by F. H. Ernst and W. C. Keating. *American Journal of Psychiatry,* Vol. 120 (1964), pp. 974–79.

"Job Finding for Court Wards," by Paul McCormick. *Journal of the California Probation, Parole and Correctional Association,* Vol. 3, No. 2 (Fall 1966).

"Games in Marital Group Therapy," by I. L. Maizlish. *Voices: The Art and Science of Psychotherapy,* Vol. 2 (Fall 1966), pp. 77–82.

The Doctor-Patient Relationship, by K. Browne and P. Freeling. Edinburgh and London: Livingstone, 1967.

"Transactional Analysis and Acting," by Arthur Wagner. *Tulane Drama Review,* Vol. 11, No. 4 (Summer 1967), pp. 81–88.

10

ALLIED PROFESSIONS

A. Psychiatric Social Work
by Mary Edwards, M.S.W.*

1

What is a psychiatric social worker?

Psychiatric social workers, like psychoanalysts, psychiatrists, and clinical psychologists, are professionally trained to treat people with emotional problems. When a patient arrives for his first interview at a psychiatric clinic, he often finds that his therapist is a psychiatric social worker; statistics show that throughout this country the majority of patients seen at psychiatric clinics are treated by psychiatric social workers. Social agencies, such as Family Service and the various parent-child counseling agencies, are staffed and administered by psychiatric social workers, with psychiatrists available to prescribe medication and serve as consultants. In mental hospitals psychiatrists evaluate patients and determine treatment methods; if psychotherapy is indicated, the therapist may well be a social worker. Although most psychiatric social workers are employed in psychiatric hospitals, clinics, or social agencies, many also treat patients in private practice. All of this surprises some people, because they think of a social worker as a "welfare lady" or, in the old-fashioned stereotype, as a spinster in flat heels and longish skirts who goes around "doing good" by taking food baskets to the needy.

* Mrs. Edwards is chief psychiatric social worker, Monterey County Psychiatric Clinic. She is a Clinical Member of the International Transactional Analysis Association.

2

What is psychiatric social work training?

After receiving a bachelor's degree in psychology or social work, the student begins a two-year professional graduate school program, leading to a master's degree in social work. During these two years he studies community agencies and resources, and environmental stresses, such as poverty, prejudice, and social class pressures. Primarily, however, the psychiatric social worker learns about emotional problems and how to treat them. In most graduate programs, Freudian theory is emphasized, but he also studies other theories of psychopathology, including recent advances in family diagnosis and treatment. During these two years, half his time is spent in a clinic or a hospital, where he learns by actually treating patients under the supervision of his instructor and the professional staff. During this period he may also seek psychotherapy or psychoanalysis for himself, in order to increase his awareness of his own emotional functioning and to resolve any problems that might otherwise hinder his effectiveness with his patients. After completing his training, he is expected to work under the supervision of a senior psychiatric social worker and usually also a psychiatrist for two more years; he will then be eligible for membership in the Academy of Certified Social Workers. Most psychiatric social workers attend postgraduate seminars and continue psychiatric consultation for at least another three years before entering private practice.

3

How does a psychiatric social worker differ
from other psychotherapists?

His training places some restrictions on his practice. Although he has studied psychoanalytic theory, only a psychoanalyst is trained to practice psychoanalysis. Most psychoanalysts and all psychiatrists are physicians, and therefore they alone can prescribe medication or other medical techniques, such as electric-shock treatment. Usually the psychologist administers and evaluates psychological testing. The psychiatric social worker has more detailed knowledge of public and private agencies and how to make referrals to them; also he has been taught to be aware of social and economic factors involved in emotional disturbances.

Practitioners from several disciplines (psychiatrists, psychologists, social workers, and others) use psychotherapy as a method of treatment. Many articles have been published in an attempt to prove that each professional discipline has some unique way of doing it. Social-work professors, for example, often label the psychiatric social worker's brand of therapy "casework" and write articles listing special "casework" techniques. In actuality, these "differences" in technique remain on paper, simply because theories and techniques that have evolved in the past seventy years have become part of a common body of knowledge, available to and used by all disciplines. Also, in clinic and hospital work as well as in teaching, exponents of these disciplines work and study together, sharing their skills.

There are differences in therapeutic style, based on the personality of the therapist. Some therapists are quiet, some more dramatic, and some work best with a crisp, intellectual style. In addition, there are differences in techniques that stem from different theoretical frameworks. The transactional analyst, whether psychiatrist, psychologist, or social worker, emphasizes details that the Freudian ignores; the Gestalt or the existential therapist approaches patients' dreams differently from the Jungian. However, all psychotherapists will focus on the present reason for entering treatment, the present conflict within the patient, and often use the tools of psychotherapy in order that the patient can resolve his emotional conflict without necessarily having to make extensive personality changes. Therapists and patients work to achieve increased spontaneity, awareness, and, as Freud put it, "ability to work and to love."

B. Psychiatric Nursing

by Hilma B. Dickson, R.N., B.S.*

1

What is a psychiatric nurse?

A psychiatric nurse is a registered professional nurse who has chosen psychiatry as her special interest, as some nurses choose surgery or the nursing of children.† All nurses study psychiatry as part of their curriculum in nurses' training, and any registered nurse is actually prepared to go into the field. Those who do usually receive additional on-the-job training. The psychiatric nurse may work in a hospital that specializes in mental illness or she may work in a general hospital that has a psychiatric ward. Her job is to work with the doctor to get each patient better and back to the community.

A patient who is admitted to a psychiatric ward is entering an entirely new living situation. The psychiatric nurse is probably the first person he will meet, the one to introduce him to his surroundings, answer questions, and "just be there" if he is frightened. After she gets to know him better, the nurse sets up goals toward which she will direct her efforts to help him. Perhaps he needs someone to talk with him, to help him differentiate between what is real and what are his imaginary thoughts, or to calm him down when he feels like exploding.

The psychiatric nurse is with the patient twenty-four hours a day, whereas the psychiatrist may see his patient only an hour or a half hour each day. Thus, the psychiatrist must depend on the nurse to tell him about the patient's daily progress. One of her roles, then, is to observe changes in the patient's behavior and report these to the doctor.

---

* Mrs. Dickson is Head Nurse of the Inpatient Adult Service at the Mc-Auley Neuropsychiatric Institute of St. Mary's Hospital in San Francisco.
† The feminine pronoun is used here only for convenience.

She also takes care of the patients' day-to-day needs. She must see that they get adequate nourishment, even if it means feeding them with a spoon or with intravenous fluids. She must see that they sleep at night, whether it means giving them another sleeping pill or separating a patient from his snoring roommate. Sometimes her main concern may be to keep the suicidal patient alive. This she does primarily by conveying to the patient the conviction that she cares about him and will do all she can to prevent him from killing himself.

The nurse is able to teach the patient through her own example. He can see how she talks to people—both her superiors and those under her supervision; how she organizes her time in order to get her jobs done; how she reacts in any situation that occurs. More than anything else, in trying to help a patient, the nurse uses herself as a person; oftentimes she may be the first person her patient really gets to know during his illness.

The psychiatric nurse also functions as a medical nurse in many instances. She is responsible for dispensing the psychiatric drugs, knowing what results to expect from them, and observing the patients for any undesirable side effects. She also assists the psychiatrist in giving shock treatments and is responsible for the nursing care of the patient before and after the treatment.

In a case like that of Cary Fayton, who was completely unresponsive for two weeks, the nurse must assume all physical care of the patient. This includes keeping him clean, especially when he cannot control his bowels or bladder; exercising his inactive limbs; making sure he gets sufficient nourishment; and, in short, taking over for Cary all the daily activities he can no longer perform for himself. Thus, while utilizing her medical background the nurse also uses her psychiatric skills in observing Cary for any small indication that he is starting to respond.

The psychiatric nurse also has the job of teaching and supervising the nonprofessional staff. These include orderlies, nurses' aides, licensed vocational or practical nurses, and psychiatric technicians (staff members who have completed a special course or who have had at least a year's experience working with psychiatric patients). These staff members also work closely with the patients and depend on the nurse for directions and guidance. She has the opportunity to teach them skills in observing patients, reporting observations to the doctors, and using themselves as tools to help the patients get better.

When a patient is admitted to the hospital the doctor sets up goals he hopes to achieve. For example, with the patient Cary Fayton, the first goals were to care for Cary in his unresponsive state and, when he recovered from that state, to accept him as he was, not arguing with him while he believed he was King of the World.

At the same time as the doctor is setting up goals, the nurses decide what part they can play in helping the patient achieve these goals. With Cary, at first it was practicing good nursing care of an unconscious patient. Later they hoped to help Cary by letting him talk about his ideas and accepting him as he was. By following this plan, perhaps Cary could learn to accept himself. Each time the patient's condition changed, the nurses had to revise their nursing-care plan in order to help the patient effectively in accordance with the doctor's directives.

The psychiatric nurse's role is changing as she perfects old skills and acquires new ones. In many psychiatric hospitals nurses are wearing street clothes instead of uniforms. This change has been initiated in hopes of conveying to the patient the image of the nurse as a real person—someone he can talk with and trust—rather than a nurse whom he may see as an unapproachable authority figure. It has been found that treating patients in a group may be more successful than treating them individually. Thus, on some wards nurses are leading group-therapy sessions and are proving effective as group leaders with proper supervision from experienced group therapists.

At this time the main role of the nurse is working in the hospital. As psychiatry moves out into the community to help people *before* they have to come into a hospital, the nurse has a part to play there also. Just as a public-health nurse visits patients in their homes to prevent physical illness and hospitalization, the psychiatric nurse will be visiting patients to try to prevent mental illness and hospitalization. As we learn more about mental illness, the contributions of the psychiatric nurse become more and more varied.

C. Pastoral Counseling

by Muriel James, Ed.D.*

1

What is pastoral counseling?

Pastoral counseling is not a particular method of counseling like psychoanalysis. It is counseling performed by a pastor, minister or priest. Pastoral counseling is older than civilization. The prototype of the pastor was the medicine man who was priest, physician, and pastor. He fought evil spirits with magic and faith. He healed the sick and tried to protect his people from the impersonal forces of nature. Some of the first books on pastoral care, or "the cure of souls," were written during the fifth century when confession, acceptance, and forgiveness, mediated through priests, had become customary and were believed to have beneficial results.

Although the "cure of the souls" has always been a pastoral function, it is because of Anton Boisen's theological training and his own mental illness, that pastoral counseling took a new direction. It was in 1922, after having been institutionalized several times, that Boisen began studying at the Boston Psychopathic Hospital; later he worked at Worcester State Hospital. As a result of this, his psychosis and his training, Boisen began experimenting. In 1925 he brought theological students to work in the hospitals as ward attendants, so that they could get firsthand information and clinical training. Since then the relation of mental disorder and religious experience has had increasing attention.

2

What is the training for pastoral counselors?

A 1956 study of 690 Protestant clergymen by Samuel Blizzard shows that the parish clergyman of today is expected to be a

* Dr. James is Dean of the Laymen's School of Religion in Berkeley, California, and is a Special Member of the International Transactional Analysis Association.

specialist in each of his six central functions; he acts as administrator, organizer, pastor, preacher, priest and teacher. His role as pastor (which includes counseling) requires about one fourth of his time. For this reason, most institutions training clergymen now offer basic psychological courses. A rapidly increasing number of clergymen have done graduate work in psychotherapy. There is also a slowly increasing number of clergymen who are certified psychiatrists and clinical psychologists.

In 1963 the American Association of Pastoral Counselors was established. The association sets standards for training and practice. It provides certification for clergymen who are in specialized ministries of counseling, such as chaplaincies, and is the agency empowered to accredit pastoral counseling centers and training programs. Many theological schools draw on the Council for Clinical Training and the Institute of Pastoral Care to educate their students. Clinical training, including written reports, individual evaluation, and interdisciplinary supervision by adequately trained supervisors, are standard procedures.

3

Where do people go for counseling?

A nationwide interview survey by the United States Joint Commission on Mental Illness and Health, using the usual cross-section sample, showed the following statistics about the source used by people who sought professional help for a personal problem:

Source of Help

clergyman	42%
medical doctor	29%
psychiatrist or psychologist	18%

Sources of professional help used by people who had feelings of impending nervous breakdown were:

Source of Help

clergyman	3%
medical doctor	88%
psychiatrist or	
psychologist	4%

4

What happens in pastoral counseling?

Pastoral counselors do much the same as other counselors. They try to avoid the teaching or advising which may be necessary in some of their other functions. They also try to recognize their limitations and refer persons with serious emotional disturbances to psychiatrists. Their function is to work with emotional problems related to daily existence, not the disturbances that may lie in the depth of the psyche. Their aim is to help relatively normal people understand their inner conflicts, develop new insights and attitudes that will enable them to solve present difficulties, and make intelligent future decisions.

The pastoral counseling process may be long or short, may be healing or not, may occur in a group or in person-to-person counseling, and may or may not include religious concerns. As with any other form of therapy, it can be interrupted or finished, successful or unsuccessful, but if the pastor has adequate training and integrity of purpose, the negative possibilities are reduced.

D. Community Psychiatry

by W. Ray Poindexter, M.D.*

1

What is community psychiatry?

The way a community psychiatrist works and helps people differs from that of the office psychiatrist. A psychiatrist doing individual

* Dr. Poindexter is consultant to the Navy Supply Center, Oakland, California, and a Teaching Member of the International Transactional Analysis Association.

therapy spends a lot of time helping a few patients. A psychiatrist working in the community will, in a short period of time, help a lot of people—before they become patients. The prevention of psychiatric disorder, rather than the treatment of mental illness, is his goal. He helps the leaders in a community make decisions about how they will handle psychiatric problems in their locality. The Community Health Center Bill, passed by Congress in 1963, making Federal, state, and local funds available for buildings and therapists for mental-health centers, was the real beginning of community psychiatry.

Mental-health centers and clinics have psychiatrists who are M.D.'s, psychologists who have Ph.D.'s, and psychiatric social workers who are M.S.W.'s. Most clinics provide up to five psychiatric services—(1) out-patient psychotherapy; (2) in-patient hospitalization; (3) day-and-night treatment; (4) twenty-four-hour emergency treatment; (5) consultation and educational services (for people in administrative and helping professions).

2

What the five psychiatric services offer

1. *Out-patient psychotherapy is office psychiatry.* Now that people are becoming aware that emotional problems are mostly due to usnatisfactory human relationships, many are seeking psychiatric help earlier. With psychotherapy readily available at fees people are able to pay, the demand for help is increasing, and new ways of assisting patients are being tried. Various forms of short-term or emergency psychotherapy make hospitalization unnecessary in many cases where it was formerly used.

2. *In-patient hospitalization.* People with acute emotional problems receive immediate attention. Formerly, these patients were removed to larger state mental hospitals because there was no other place to go, but now they are often taken care of in local hospitals.

3. *Day-and-night treatment.* Working people can stay in the hospital half-time—all day or all evening—and go about their

business the rest of the time. It is found that often such part-time treatment is enough even for the more severely disturbed person.

4. *Twenty-four-hour emergency treatment.* This means that a clinical therapist is on duty at all hours, so that therapy can begin any time of the day or night. This emergency meeting may be followed by a regular out-patient clinic appointment; or, if necessary, immediate hospitalization will be offered.

This first-aid type of treatment relieves immediate suffering, but crises frequently become a way of life that is passed on by parents to their children. Parents, therefore, should have the first opportunity for psychiatric treatment if we are interested in preventive psychiatry. The next step is to provide psychiatric consultation and educational services for key people in the community. It is through these decision-makers in politics, industry, and education, that we can help prevent psychiatric problems.

5. *Consultation and educational services.* This helps people succeed before they fail—as parents, as teachers, as judges, and as police officers. Psychiatrists and other scientists studying human behavior (psychologists, sociologists, and anthropologists), ministers and educators, probation and correctional people, can all help here.

3

Why a community psychiatrist can be useful

A psychiatric patient frequently differs from other people only because he is interested in seeking help. Others may need it just as badly but avoid it for various reasons. This is often the case with company executives, school principals, judges, and family physicians, for example.

Because of patterns of thinking carried over from childhood, an executive may fail to delegate authority and to make decisions because he is too preoccupied with details. As a consequence, his subordinates have headaches, backaches, ulcers, and depressive reactions.

A school principal may be unable to stand spontaneity and may choose teachers with similar prejudices. Then the students suffer and may develop school phobias. A judge with a certain childhood training may be overly concerned with cleanliness and perfection, so that only orderly and exemplary behavior is tolerated in himself and others. Some family physicians need to become more aware of emotional problems in their patients and more ready to refer them to psychiatrists when indicated. These are some types of people who, being in positions of influence, can seriously interfere with the satisfactions of the rest of the community, and a community psychiatrist may be able to reach them.

Perhaps new kinds of professionals are needed for psychiatric education in the community—more like schoolteachers, perhaps, than like psychiatrists.

The writer's own experience of teaching transactional analysis to lay audiences is an example of this kind of "psychiatric schoolhouse." In 1962, ten business executives came to listen to a series of eight weekly one-hour lectures on this subject. This number has now grown to thirty-five senior employees, ranging from senior executives to first-line supervisors, who regularly attend these continuing management-training lectures. The lectures are also recorded on tape and synchronized with picture slides so that the entire work force of four thousand employees can learn about transactional analysis.

In 1964, a similar educational series of lectures was offered to a few patients at a community mental health clinic. Many of the patient-students reported that they were "better" following the lecture series. One mother said: "My daughter isn't failing in school now. I've taught her some of these ideas and we are better. I can help her because I understand myself better." A production worker told of reducing his drinking and gambling by 50 per cent and of turning in six work-improvement suggestions (none previously), and of receiving a promotion.

Today, one hundred people are attending these lectures each week. Many in the audience are relatives, friends, and neighbors of former student-patients. They have demonstrated that many human beings can use their intellects to improve their performances if someone provides them with an easily understandable scientific theory of what a human being is.

4
How can psychiatry help industry?

A psychiatrist who works with employees on the job must know how employees feel and how management thinks. With this knowledge, he can influence management decisions and improve the company's profits, the executives' health, and the welfare of all employees. Presently, however, there are only about fifteen full-time psychiatrists working in this field of preventive psychiatry, which is concerned with the working environment, especially the factories and organizations where the majority of people spend one third of their waking hours. The industrial psychiatrist helps management specialists produce goods or services through the more human and effective use of people, so that both the company and the employees profit. His main role is training (1) the personnel director to select employees who are likely to do good work, do it well along with others, and do it for a long time; (2) the supervisors to supervise with reasonable demands; (3) the managers to manage only when necessary; (4) the top executive to let the others do most of the work.

Such training reduces accidents and absenteeism, and raises production. Some of the psychiatrist's time is also spent in the company medical department assisting the doctors and nurses in evaluating employees who may have emotional problems. Meanwhile, he is available for consultation with all levels of employees. Department heads are frequently able to locate and find solutions to personnel as well as production problems after talking to him. Sometimes the problem lies in the manager's own ways of doing things, such as oversupervising. When this is the case, most executives who have sought help appreciate finding out why and feel better—if not immediately, then after a while. And so do their wives and children, although they may never know why daddy has changed and become less tense. This is the rewarding part of community psychiatry—being able to do so much for so many people, even beyond one's expectations.

Footnotes for Philosophers, Chapter Ten

C. Pastoral Counseling

For the origin of modern pastoral counseling, as a result of Anton T. Boisen's experience, see his book *The Exploration of the Inner World* (New York: Harper & Row, 1962).

D. Community psychiatry

For a review of community psychiatry in the United States, see:

Action for Mental Health; Final Report, Joint Commission on Mental Illness and Health. New York: Basic Books, 1961.

"Community Mental Health Centers Act" (Public Law 88–164), 1963.

Handbook of Community Psychiatry and Community Mental Health, Leopold Bellak, editor. New York: Grune & Stratton, 1964.

Mental Health Directory 1966, issued by the National Clearinghouse for Mental Health Information, is a reference guide to mental health programs and services throughout the United States. Price sixty cents. Superintendent of Documents, U.S. Government Printing Office, Washington, D.C. 20402.

For publications on Institutional Games, see:

"Employment of Former Mental Patients," by W. Ray Poindexter, in *Current Psychiatric Therapies,* edited by J. H. Masserman. New York: Grune & Stratton, 1964.

Games People Play by Eric Berne. New York: Grove Press, 1964.

Selected articles and abstracts in *Transactional Analysis Bulletin,* published quarterly since 1962. Bound volumes of back issues can be obtained from Transactional Pubs., P.O. Box 5747, Carmel, California, 93921.

For the idea of a "psychiatric schoolhouse," see:

"Needed: A Conceptual Breakthrough," by George W. Albee, Chairman, Department of Psychology, Western Reserve University, formerly Director, Task Force on Manpower, Joint Commission on Mental Illness and Health. (Unpublished manuscript, 1966.)

The most recent review of occupational mental health activity is available from the National Institute of Mental Health:

"Occupational Mental Health—Review of an Emerging Art," by Alan A. McLean, 1967.

The National Institute of Mental Health is encouraging the development of industrial mental health programs and issues *Occupational Mental Health Notes,* for scientists, professional workers, and executives in management and labor. Each issue contains abstracts of current literature and reports on recent developments in the field. Subscriptions to the *Notes* and computerized retrieval searches on particular areas of information (such as alcoholism, absenteeism, etc.) may be requested from National Clearinghouse for Mental Health Information, National Institute of Mental Health, 5454 Wisconsin Avenue, Chevy Chase, Maryland 20203.

11

DRUGS AND OTHER METHODS

1

The older drugs

Up to about thirty years ago, the only drugs available to help the psychiatrist treat his patients were sedatives, such as morphine, bromides, barbiturates, chloral hydrate, and paraldehyde. Most of these drowsed the patient or put him to sleep, and they did little or nothing to improve his condition when he was alert and awake. And as we have already seen, most of them have to be used cautiously, especially when they are given over a long period, because of the dangers of addiction or poisoning. In a sense, people who take such chemicals month after month are only half living.

From time to time, however, new drugs and new ways of using the old ones have been introduced into the treatment of neuroses and psychoses, usually with great enthusiasm and emphatic claims of their value. But the more experienced psychiatrists are just as careful as cancer specialists in judging the value of new treatments, and have preferred to wait five or ten years before committing themselves.

Two good examples of this have been the use of insulin in treating schizophrenia and the use of antabuse with alcoholics. At first it was claimed by some that both these drugs cured as high as 80 or 90 per cent of patients, but when they began to be used more widely it was found, unfortunately, that these claims could not be upheld. Insulin and antabuse have their modest places in psychiatry in the treatment of carefully selected cases under properly controlled conditions, but neither of them has completely solved the problems they were originally designed to remedy; they do not, for example, approach the efficacy which penicillin has in its proper field. The history of benzedrine in the treatment of depressions has followed a similar course, with the added difficulty that many people have abused this drug by self-medication and addiction. When they are fatigued, they reach for a pill instead of a pillow, which in the long run may have the same effect as whipping a tired horse.

Because there is so much room for improvement, psychiatrists have always been on the alert for new remedies, and since 1954 a whole new class of drugs has come into fashion. These are popularly called "tranquilizers," or more formally, "ataraxics" or "ataractics," from the ancient Greek *ataraktos,* a word used by Aristotle, for example, to mean "not disturbed by passion," the opposite of what Hippocrates, the father of medicine, called *tarache,* tumult. The first of these which came to public attention in this country was derived from Indian snakeroot, and was put on the market under the trade name of Serpasil. The story of snakeroot is one of the most interesting in the history of psychiatry.

2

Who discovered snakeroot?

For many centuries, physicians in India have employed, along with methods imported from Europe and later from America, native remedies derived from ancient writings. These ancient writings constitute the Hindu system of medical practice, called Ayur-Veda, under the symbol of Dhanvantari, the Hindu god of medicine. In 1948, when I visited the Government Mental Hospital at Kilpauk, just outside Madras, Dr. J. Dhairyam, the superintendent in charge of the 1,750 patients, described and demonstrated to me some of these mixed methods of treatment. Dr. Dhairyam received his medical degree at the local university and thus was familiar with both ancient and modern treatments for mental illnesses. He showed me on the one hand groups of patients doing carefully selected yoga exercises under the supervision of a yogi specially trained in psychiatric work; and on the other, patients who were receiving electric-shock therapy and the latest vitamin and glandular preparations.

He described some remarkable local drugs which he was using

systematically. These included Cobra venom, sea water obtained ten miles out in the Indian Ocean so that it would be pure, and ayurvedic herbs. He divided his patients into two groups: one group would receive some of these remedies, the other would not. In this way he studied the treatment of schizophrenia, manic-depressive psychoses, epilepsy, morphine addiction, and psychoses due to old age, high blood pressure, and kidney disease. He claimed that the patients who received the special treatments recovered more rapidly than the others, and stayed well longer. Furthermore, he claimed that twice as many patients were getting better since he introduced these methods than formerly, when psychiatrists trained in England and America had been in charge. These benefits were particularly evident, he stated, in manic-depressive psychoses and high blood pressure, where his favored remedy was an ayurvedic herb which he gave in doses of 30 grains, six times the weight of actual medicine contained in an ordinary aspirin tablet. By the use of this medication, he said, he had reduced the rate of recurrence in manic-depressive psychosis to about one fifth of what it was in America. He called this herb serpentine, and gave its scientific name as *Rauwolfia serpentina.*

When I published an account of this visit in a scientific journal a year later, I mentioned the use of "serpentine" in the treatment of manic-depressive psychoses. As far as I can ascertain, this was the first mention in an American scientific periodical of the specific use of *Rauwolfia serpentina* in psychiatry. But Dr. Dhairyam's claims were so surprising, and he had given me so much to think about, that I did not give any special attention to "serpentine" and was equally intrigued with his use of snake venoms, sea water, and yoga exercises. The psychiatric use of the drug did not begin in this country until 1954.

No one knows who discovered the tranquilizing effect of this herb, but for many years its use was confined to India. It was first noted in a scientific journal in 1931, after it had been used for centuries by ayurvedic physicians. Indian scientists took an active interest in it after that, but it was twenty years more before Western doctors gave it serious attention. Then they began to use it to treat high blood pressure, but they could not help noticing the unusual psychological effect it had on their patients. About this time a drug firm became interested in the snakelike roots, and succeeded in extracting a pure chemical, reserpine, which had a marked effect both on high blood pressure and on excitability. Various groups of doctors tried out the preparation, and in 1954 they held a meeting under the auspices of the New York Academy of Sciences. Their reports were so encouraging that the drug immediately came into general use.

Meanwhile, through one of those strange circumstances that so often occur in medicine, other drugs with similar properties were also being developed, so that two years later, in 1956, the market was flooded with a variety of preparations that claimed to have a tranquilizing effect, and it was said that psychiatry was entering on a new era. But snakeroot still remains the most interesting of these drugs because of the many legends which grew around it. For example, it was said in India that mongooses would chew it before fighting cobras.

3

The kinds of "tranquilizers"

Almost every drug firm has its own special brands of tranquilizers and similar medications, but the two most widely used and talked about are chlorpromazine and meprobamate, better known to the public under such trade names as Thorazine and Miltown. These differ from the old sedatives in that they affect a different layer of the nervous system. They are also supposed to be less likely to lead to addiction and safer to take. But there is no such thing as a safe drug. Even aspirin can be fatal in large doses, and it can have bad effects even in small doses. Therefore these new drugs should not be taken without medical supervision.

Actually, not all of these drugs should be called "tranquilizers." There are three large classes of such medications, and in order for the doctor to know which is which he has to call them by their chemical names rather than by the brand names which the drug manufacturers give them. The snakeroot drug reserpine was formerly popular in the treatment of psychoses, but it has now been largely replaced by a group of chemicals called the "phenothiazines." Thorazine is probably the most widely used drug of this type. It is said that at least fifty million people have taken phenothiazines in recent years. The phenothiazines are "mind clearers," and their purpose is to relieve the confusion which psychotics feel. There are many other mind clearers which have been used less widely, and some of them are still in experimental stages. The object is to find one which will not cause the unpleasant side effects, such as jaundice and muscular stiffness, sometimes seen with the phenothiazines.

The tranquilizers, which are used to treat anxiety and agitation, include meprobamates, such as Miltown, and diazepams, such as Valium, as well as the barbiturates. For the relief of depression, there are two main types of "happy pills" called the "MAO inhibitors," such as Nardil, and the "imipramines," such as Tofranil.

Another way of classifying these drugs is according to the way they are taken. Some tranquilizers can be "popped," that is, taken whenever the person feels anxious. The effects are rapid and they also wear off quickly. Others of these preparations, such as the MAO inhibitors, have to be taken regularly over a long period (two to six weeks), before the effects begin to take hold, and if they are merely "popped" at irregular intervals or whenever the person happens to feel bad, they will not work.

Some of these medications are so powerful that the doctor often prefers to split the prescription between two or three of them, adding to and subtracting from the effects of one by prescribing another along with it to get the best treatment response with the least possibility of side effects. For instance, instead of prescribing a large dose of a single mind clearer, he may prescribe smaller doses of two different ones, and also a third drug to prevent the stiff neck which often occurs when the phenothiazines are taken over a long period. On the other hand, he is careful not to prescribe certain of these drugs together because they are incompatible, and he is careful to inform his patients that they must not drink alcohol while taking any of these drugs. Thus it takes a great deal of medical skill and experience to decide which drug or combination of drugs is best in any given case.

The choice of a particular drug for the treatment of a particular psychiatric patient depends on the judgment, skill and experience of the psychiatrist. There is no way for a layman to decide which is the best drug for himself or a relative; nor can he prescribe the special blood tests and other examinations which may be advisable in order to detect side effects in their early stages so that they can be headed off.

Recently the use of lithium in controlling the ups and downs of manic-depressive psychosis has received considerable attention. The results so far appear to be good. While lithium may control the mood swings, it does not affect the underlying neurotic and psychotic disturbances. But it does make the patient's life smoother, takes a burden off his family, and makes it easier for the doctor to carry on psychotherapy.

Many of the things that have been said about sedatives apply also to these new drugs. Experienced psychotherapists do not feel that they are a substitute for treatment of the underlying problems. Diabetes can be controlled by insulin, and the pain of certain chronic diseases by drugs and glandular preparations, but it would be better if there were a cure for these conditions. It appears that neurotics and psychotics whose symptoms are controlled by pills, no matter how effective these may seem, are in the same precarious position as a diabetic whose condition is controlled by insulin. It is hard to tell when something may go wrong, with the passage of time, resulting in a complicated and sometimes difficult situation. Since psychotherapy is the recognized treatment for the conflicts underlying psychiatric symptoms, this treatment should be obtained if it is available, even if the actual day-to-day suffering can be effectively relieved by drugs.

4

What about "truth serum"?

Various drugs have been used at different times for the purpose of loosening people's emotional blocks and making them feel and talk more freely. Nowadays, as a result of war experience, two drugs are occasionally used by psychiatrists: in America, sodium amytal, often used orally as a sleeping powder, is usually employed; in England many psychiatrists prefer sodium pentothal. This latter drug is used in both countries as an anesthetic for short operations. In the treatment of neuroses, these drugs are injected into the blood until a state of drowsiness results and the patient is then questioned in his drowsy state. Since his repressions are weakened by the drug, he is supposed to be likely to say things under these conditions that he could not talk about or feel about without the injection.

Almost everything that has been said about hypnosis applies to the use of these drugs. The drugged condition is an "artificial" state like hypnosis, and so it is difficult for the patient to bring the things that happen into relationship with his waking personality. And again it has to be remembered that removing a symptom weakens the patient's defenses against inner turmoil, and while it may be temporarily satisfying to the patient and his family to have a symptom "cured" quickly and dramatically, in the long run it may do the patient more harm than good. Unless the doctor takes the time to give him some source of security to replace the symptom, he may substitute general unhappiness, sluggishness, and depression for inability to talk, or a psychosis for severe headaches.

The case of Moses Tock illustrates one of the dangers of drug treatment. Mr. Tock, the junior partner in the law firm of Savitar, Teazle, & Tock, began to suffer from blinding headaches. Dr. Treece, who knew Mr. Tock well, had been worried about him for some time. He suspected that he was paranoid. All medical tests were negative, so Dr. Treece allowed one of the interns at the hospital to try sodium amytal "narcoanalysis" as a way of curing the headaches. The treatment worked. For three days Mr. Tock was in fine shape. Then he began to complain of pains in his lower abdomen. After a while he began to hint that he had been poisoned. Two days later he said flatly that the pain was being caused by mental radio and that he knew just who was behind it all, namely, Mr. Savitar. A week later he had a paranoid psychosis in full flower. His headaches had been his last defense against a slowly developing and carefully hidden psychosis of two or three years' duration. Dr. Treece never forgot the lesson about sodium amytal; after that, he always made absolutely sure that he was not dealing with a psychotic before he allowed the drug to be injected.

Just as in the case of hypnosis, most psychiatrists feel that nothing can be accomplished with such injections that cannot be accomplished better by psychotherapy, with the help of tranquilizers and other medications where necessary. They maintain that the patient will rarely give any information about himself or show any feelings under either drugs or hypnosis that he will not reveal in the waking state with skillful handling. They also feel that if the patient is "ready" to get better, the result usually will be more lasting if "artificial" aids are not used. In the days before psychotherapy, for example, hypnosis was widely used in treating hysteria; in fact, Sigmund Freud used it for this purpose for some years, until he decided that better, deeper, and more lasting results could be obtained without it, and with a few exceptions, most psychotherapists in the last fifty years have agreed with him.

Carbon dioxide is familiar as the gas which forms the bubbles in soda pop. If this gas is breathed in heavy concentrations, it may throw the patient into a coma, and when he recovers he is often in a highly emotional state due to the release of pent-up tensions. Spectacular results have recently been claimed following ten, fifty, or a hundred such treatments, usually combined with psychotherapy. The majority of psychiatrists regard this treatment with some skepticism and, in any case, all the questions and cautions which apply to hypnosis and "truth serum" apply just as strongly here.

5

What about shock treatments?

Shock treatment is generally given in one of two forms. Some psychiatrists have experimented with other methods, but the recognized ones are electric shock and insulin shock.

There are two kinds of electric-shock treatment. In one, called electronarcosis, the patient is temporarily stunned. In the other he is thrown into a convulsion similar to an epileptic fit. These remedies are properly applied only in cases of severe psychosis, as an alternative to months or years in a mental hospital. Then they are used about three times a week for two to eight weeks or more. In extreme cases, however, some psychiatrists give as many as three electric-shock treatments a day over a period of several weeks—a procedure which most doctors would hesitate to encourage. Anesthetics or special medications are often used along with electric-shock treatment to make it easier on the patient.

Electric shock is given by means of a special medical machine which can be set for the proper dose. When the switch is pulled the machine delivers the amount of current it was set for, which might be, for example, 200 milliamperes at 110 volts flowing for half a second. The results claimed for this treatment in various psychoses differ in different clinics. Most authorities feel that it yields the best results in the long-lasting depressions of the change of life, the so-called "involutional melancholias," which before this form of treatment was introduced often required years of hospitalization.

No one knows how these treatments work. Many psychiatrists feel that it is advisable in each case to consider very carefully whether other methods, such as psychotherapy, cannot be used instead of shock treatment. Most of these doctors agree that there are certain cases where electric shock should *not* be used.

1. Very few doctors favor its use for neuroses, and fewer and fewer are using it for schizophrenia.

2. Many psychiatrists object to its use as an office treatment, since the patient may be temporarily confused after a certain number of shocks, making it inadvisable for him to be at liberty to wander outside of a hospital or sanitarium.

3. Conservative psychiatrists refuse to use it if there is any chance that the patient will get better without it. This applies especially if the patient has had a previous psychosis and has recovered by himself. It is a good policy to call in two outside psychiatrists before shock is given, to confirm the opinion that the patient will not get better without it, and it is best to include one psychoanalyst in the consultation.

4. Shock should never be used merely for the purpose of quieting the patient unless he is suicidal, homicidal, or is wearing himself out to a dangerous extent by overactivity; and even then it should be given only as a last resort, and in such cases a consultation with a psychoanalyst is also advisable.

While electric shock is most commonly used for cases of prolonged melancholia, insulin is chiefly used in schizophrenia, particularly in younger people. The same insulin is used which is used to treat diabetes. With diabetics, one of the doctor's main concerns is to avoid giving too much insulin, as an overdose will cause weakness, shakiness, and finally unconsciousness. With schizophrenics, such a state of insulin shock with unconsciousness is deliberately produced under the constant eye of doctors and nurses who do not leave the patient alone even for a moment. As the large dose of insulin (twenty to fifty times as much as a mild diabetic uses) begins to take effect, the patient gradually grows more and more drowsy, until he goes into a state from which he cannot be roused by ordinary methods.

After he has been in this state for an hour or two, he is given a large quantity of sugar by injection or otherwise, and then occurs an astonishing event: in a mere matter of seconds, the previously psychotic patient comes out of his profound coma to sit up and talk normally. Other substances can be used to bring him out of it more slowly. The long-term effectiveness of the treatment, many psychiatrists think, depends mainly upon the use made of this period just after waking up, when even very sick schizophrenics may be able to respond normally for an hour or two. This gives the doctor a chance to carry on psychotherapy which he could not do otherwise because the patient would not cooperate sufficiently. Insulin is thus properly used, conservative psychiatrists say, as a method of getting the patient into such a state that the doctor can conduct psychotherapy. Many psychiatrists, on the other hand, feel that the curative properties of insulin are due almost entirely to its chemical effect on the patient's brain, regardless of psychotherapy. It requires from thirty to fifty daily shocks to "cure" a schizophrenic in favorable cases.

Since the three types of shock treatment we have described are regarded by some merely as methods for making psychotherapy easier, the question comes up as to whether psychotherapy alone could not be used in psychoses, without first exposing the patient to shock therapy. The answer is that we are learning more and more about how to do that, particularly by means of group therapy. Unfortunately, this is available to only a small percentage of psychotics. There are not enough doctors who specialize in psychotherapy to take care of the hundreds of thousands of people in mental hospitals as well as the millions suffering from neuroses who could benefit from psychiatric treatment. Since a doctor can earn more with the same amount of training and skill in other specialties, the psychiatric profession loses a certain number of recruits.

It has been found that cutting the bundles of nerves in various parts of the brain seems to benefit some patients who have suffered from incurable agitation and melancholia for long periods. After such "psychosurgery," they may leave the hospital, perhaps for the first time in years, and start again to live more or less normal lives. Sometimes, however, they are *too* irresponsible and carefree after the operation and have to be watched constantly to keep them from getting into mischief, so that in some cases the cure seems to the relatives to be as bad as the disease. Fortunately this does not always occur. While the operation itself is not serious, its effects are permanent, since the nerves never grow together again. Occasionally unforeseen and serious complications arise, so that it is usually done only in the most serious and prolonged cases. This operation should not be undertaken unless at least two well-qualified psychiatrists who are not on the staff of the hospital have agreed that it is the best possible treatment, and only after every other form of treatment has definitely failed.

Nowadays this operation is seldom undertaken in up-to-date hospitals, because of the large selection of drugs presently available for the treatment of psychiatric disorders, and because the same results can often be obtained by a well-trained group therapist.

6

What are brain waves?

We have already noted that there are electric currents going up and down the nerve cords, and that these can be measured by a galvanometer, and that the brain itself also gives off pulses of electricity. These are so small that they are quite impossible to measure by ordinary methods; they have a power of about 20 millionths of a volt (ordinary house electricity is 110 volts). They can be detected, however, by carefully built amplifiers, and the waves can be recorded by means of special magnetic pens or thrown on the screen of a television tube. The shape and size of the waves give much information about the state of the brain, or *encephalon,* and these electric telegrams, or *electroencephalograms,* are of great value in detecting certain diseases of the nervous system.

The waves which come from different parts of the brain have different shapes. Usually eight to eighteen small discs of metal, about the size of a split aspirin tablet, are glued to the scalp in various places and connected to the amplifiers by thin wires. Then the receiver is turned on and the "broadcast" is recorded.

As a fascinating experiment, instead of making the magnets control a pen they can be connected to a loudspeaker so that the pulses make noises instead of ink lines. In this way the electric throbbing of the brain as it works can actually be heard.

The German, Italian, American, Russian, and English doctors who first discovered these brain waves found that they were changed by many things. They changed with age, and when the subject opened or closed his eyes. They changed when he tried to work arithmetic problems, or when he became excited or anxious. They changed when he fell asleep, but not when he was hypnotized (showing that this state is different from sleep).

The chief medical use of the *electroencephalograph* is in detecting epilepsy and brain tumors. Epileptic records show runs of smooth waves suddenly interrupted by bursts of powerful electrical discharges. Similar bursts occur in the families of epileptics in many cases, even in relatives who never had and may never have epilepsy, showing that the tendency to have fits is sometimes inherited, but that the emotions and other strains which actually cause fits may not affect everybody who has the tendency. This helps us to understand why epileptic fits may begin after a severe emotional shock or an auto accident in people who have not had them before but do have epileptic relatives.

Naturally it is necessary to know which part of the brain a tumor is growing in before an operation can be undertaken, and sometimes the electroencephalogram supplies the best clue. Since the tissue in the tumor is different from the tissue in the rest of the brain, it gives off a different kind of electric wave. By glueing electrodes to different parts of the scalp and "triangulating" as a surveyor would, the exact point of origin of the abnormal impulses can often be located, and this tells the surgeon just where to go in.

No one knows exactly which part of the brain the normal waves come from, except that they probably arise in the same parts that handle conscious, "thinking," or Ego, activity, since if these parts are removed from an animal a different kind of wave appears that seems to come from the "unconscious" or "feeling" parts of the brain. The fact that the usual waves come from the "conscious" parts of the brain enables us to understand why they change when the person is asleep or in an epileptic fit, since in such cases the "conscious" is no longer in its usual state.

7

What is an air encephalogram?

X-ray pictures are shadow pictures. X rays do not pass easily through bone, but they do pass easily through flesh. In an X-ray picture of an arm, the bones cast more of a shadow than the flesh and therefore show up more whitely. If a bone is broken, the X rays pass through the gap where the fracture is and make a flesh shadow where a bone shadow should be, so that the doctor knows that the bone is interrupted at that spot.

The brain is something like a coconut. It is a thick shell with watery fluid in the middle of it. Since X rays go through the fluid and the brain equally well, an X ray of the head does not tell much about the shape and size of the inside of the brain, nor how much space inside the skull is taken up by fluid and how much by brain tissue. If the brain shrinks, it leaves a fluid-filled space between the brain and the bone; if a tumor grows out of the brain into the fluid space, naturally some of the fluid has to be pushed out to make room for the tumor. None of this can be seen in an ordinary X-ray picture because the brain and the fluid cast the same amount of shadow.

Air, however, does not cast any shadow in an X-ray picture and therefore can be used to show the outline of the brain.

The fluid is drained out from the skull and replaced by air or some other gas. The shape and size of the brain can then be seen, because where the brain isn't the air is, and the X rays will pass through and make no shadow; where the brain is and the air isn't, the X rays will be stopped and make a shadow on the film. If the brain is shrinking, it will make a smaller shadow than usual, surrounded by a lot of air. If a tumor is growing into the hollow in the center of the brain, it will make a shadow corresponding to its own shape, because where the tumor is the air isn't. Abnormal cavities in the brain will show up similarly, as in the case of Philly Porenza mentioned in the first chapter. Such "diagrams" of the brain made by means of air are called air encephalograms.

The fluid is drained out by performing a spinal tap, such as we have previously described, except that instead of taking away only a few drops of the fluid that drips out, it is all taken away. The more fluid that is removed and replaced by air, the better the X-ray pictures may be. The procedure is likely to cause a headache, so some doctors use special methods in order to make the patient more comfortable afterward. For example, they may inject some other gas instead of air, or remove less fluid.

Sometimes the procedure does more than just make it possible to take good X rays. In certain cases of epilepsy which are due to scars and bands going between the brain and the skull, taking the fluid out and putting air in may loosen or detach the scars so that they no longer pull on the brain and irritate it, and then the fits may stop.

Footnotes for Philosophers, Chapter Eleven

2. *Rauwolfia*

An account of the mental hospital at Madras with mention of serpentine can be found in:

"Some Oriental Mental Hospitals," by Fric Berne. *American Journal of Psychiatry,* Vol. CVI (November 1949), pp. 376–83.

Dr. Dhairyam gives details in his report to the Surgeon-General, Government of Madras, March 3, 1948. His use of other ayurvedic herbs was published in 1954. Unfortunately, he gives only the Indian names.

"A New Method of Treatment," by J. Dhairyam. *Indian Journal of Neurology and Psychiatry,* Vol. V (1954), pp. 44–48.

The first known clinical report concerning Rauwolfia published outside of India was Vakil's:

"A Clinical Trial of Rauwolfia Serpentina in Essential Hypertension," by R. J. Vakil. *British Heart Journal,* Vol. II (October 1949), p. 350.

The first psychiatric report did not appear in the American literature until 1954. The detailed history of the development of interest in this drug can be found in:

The Rauwolfia Story. Summit, N.J.: Ciba Pharmaceutical Products, 1954.

The properties and effects of reserpine were thoroughly gone over at a conference held in 1955 and the collected papers can be found in *Annals of the New York Academy of Sciences,* Vol. LXI, Art. 1, pp. 1–280.

3. *New drugs*

For more on these, see *Psychiatric Drugs,* edited by P. Solomon (New York: Grune & Stratton, 1966). Sound appraisal of these drugs is still a matter for the professional pharmacologist. Extensive information on their effects can be found in *The Pharmacological Basis of Therapeutics,* edited by L. S. Goodman and A. Gilman, 3d edition (New York: The Macmillan Company, 1965). For a recent article on lithium, see "The Use of Lithium in the Affective Psychoses," by R. N. Wharton and R. R. Fieve. *American Journal of Psychiatry,* Vol. 123 (December, 1966), pp. 706–11.

Of the thousands of papers published on psychopharmacology, one of the most interesting concerns the "curing" of "psychotic" goldfish by D. L. Keller and W. W. Umbreit; it appeared in *Science,* Vol. 124 (August 31, 1956), p. 407.

The ratings of the pharmacological effects of these drugs should be considered in the light of Feldman's demonstration that different psychiatrists make surprisingly varying estimates of the efficacy of a new drug. "The Personal Element in Psychiatric Research," by P. E. Feldman. *American Journal of Psychiatry,* Vol. 113, pp. 52–54 (July, 1956).

4. *Narcoanalysis and narcosynthesis*

One of the earliest and most interesting books on this subject was written during World War II. See *Men Under Stress,* by Grinker and Spiegel. For further information consult *American Handbook of Psychiatry,* pp. 1572–78.

5 and 6. *Shock treatment, psychosurgery, and EEG*

For further information about these subjects, consult *American Handbook of Psychiatry.*

For an interesting example of a long-standing chronic brain syndrome successfully treated with group therapy and discharged from the hospital, see: "Chronic Brain Syndrome Treated with Transactional Analysis," by R. L. Goulding. *Transactional Analysis Bulletin,* Vol. 2 (July 1963), pp. 75–76.

7. *Radiology*

This is a very technical procedure. For further details, consult texts on neurosurgery and on roentgenology of the skull.

12

PRACTICAL QUESTIONS

1

How to choose a doctor

There are so many different professions dealing with the human mind that the average citizen has difficulty telling them apart. The men in these professions, on the other hand, do not like to be confused with one another. It is especially necessary to be able to distinguish the various branches if one is thinking of going to somebody for advice or treatment.

A *psychiatrist* originally meant a physician who specialized in diseases of the mind. Nowadays, a psychiatrist means a doctor who not only treats neuroses, psychoses, and emotional disturbances, but also tries to prevent them. He tries to help people improve their judgment and he often gives them advice based on his experience with other human beings concerning their feelings about themselves, the world around them, and about the people among whom they live. A psychiatrist is invariably an M.D. If he is not an M.D. he cannot be a psychiatrist any more than he can be a brain surgeon.

After he has finished medical school, the student psychiatrist goes through a regular internship, during which he may deliver babies, remove tonsils and appendices, and perform autopsies; or he may prefer an internship where he can concentrate on internal diseases, such as diabetes, heart disease, stomach ulcers, and glandular disorders.

When his internship is over, he goes to a special training hospital for further study, just as do his colleagues who want to become surgeons, heart specialists, and so on. After this training period is finished, he may go into private practice. If he desires to be recognized as a specialist by the medical profession, however, he must continue his specialized studies for at least five years after his internship is over. He is then qualified to take a stiff examination, oral, written, and practical, from a group of older, established specialists. When he has passed the examination, he becomes an American Board Diplomate. (This is different from a National Board Diplomate, which refers merely to his license to practice medicine.)

Thus the psychiatrist, after his internship, will study for five years more in order to become eligible to take the examinations of the American Board of Psychiatry and Neurology. If he passes the examinations to the satisfaction of his older colleagues, he is recognized as a competent psychiatrist by the medical profession. There are a few qualified psychiatrists who do not elect to take the examinations, but the only way a layman can be sure that a psychiatrist knows his business, unless he is recommended by another trusted physician, is to ascertain that he is a Diplomate of the American Board of Psychiatry and Neurology. There is no law against any doctor calling himself a psychiatrist, but the best way to convince the medical profession is either to be preparing for, or to have taken, the board examinations.

A *neurologist,* too, must be an M.D. While a psychiatrist specializes in helping people improve their judgment and emotional stability, a neurologist specializes in diseases of the brain, spinal cord, and nerve cords. Many psychiatrists are also competent neurologists, and vice versa. There is some connection between the two fields, as is suggested by the name of the examining board, and a doctor may be certified by this board as qualified in either or both of these specialties. Sometimes a man who practices both is called a neuropsychiatrist.

Some psychiatrists, however, feel that there is more connection between the mind and the endocrine glands than there is between the mind and the brain, at least as far as practical medical treatment is concerned, so that they would rather concentrate on endocrinology than on neurology as a sideline.

A *psychoanalyst,* as we have said already, is a psychiatrist who specializes in the form of treatment known as psychoanalysis. In order to become a psychoanalyst, the psychiatrist must take additional special training after he has had some years of psychiatric training. He goes to a recognized Psychoanalytic Institute and studies under a group of experienced analysts. Every analyst must be analyzed himself before he is recognized by the profession. Thus, he may have a total of six or eight years of training after his internship before he is considered ready to practice psychoanalysis.

There is a small group of psychoanalysts, many of them very skillful, who are exceptions to this rule. These are called "lay analysts." They do not have medical degrees. They were carefully chosen for their intelligence, sincerity, integrity, education, emotional stability, and understanding of human nature before they were admitted to the Psychoanalytic Institutes for training. Most of the lay analysts belong to another period, since Psychoanalytic Institutes in America no longer train people to be analysts unless they have medical degrees. Of course, many social workers, nurses, psychologists, teachers, lawyers, ministers, and others who have to handle human problems study at these Institutes in order to gain an increased understanding of human nature, and they are encouraged to do so, but such "laymen" are not recognized by the profession as qualified actually to psychoanalyze other people.

Many years ago the British Medical Association made an investigation concerning the use of the term *psychoanalyst,* and announced their official conclusion as follows:

> There is in the medical and general public the tendency to use the term "psychoanalysis" in a very loose and wide sense. This term can legitimately be applied only to the method evolved by Freud and to the theories derived from the use of this method. A psychoanalyst is therefore a person who uses Freud's technique, and anyone who does not use this technique should not, whatever other method he may employ, be called a psychoanalyst. In accordance with this definition and for the purpose of avoiding confusion, the term "psychoanalyst" is properly reserved for members of the International Psycho-Analytical Association. . . .

Medical and nonmedical therapists who follow the theories of Jung or Horney are also required to undertake prolonged and rigorous training in those schools of thought before they are fully qualified to practice those types of analysis. Transactional analysis is still too young to have training standards which come up to those of psychoanalysis, but as the use of this approach spreads, the requirements for becoming a clinical member of the International Transactional Analysis Association are becoming more strict.

A *psychologist* is a nonmedical student of the human mind. Where a psychiatrist has a medical degree, a psychologist has an M.A. or a Ph.D. degree. There are a few psychiatrists with M.D. degrees who are also qualified psychologists, having a Ph.D. degree in addition. The science of psychology is divided into numerous branches. After a psychologist has graduated from college, he selects a special field of study for his M.A. or Ph.D. degree. A psychometrist is a psychologist who specializes in measuring the powers of the mind. Psychometrists are specially trained to administer tests such as intelligence tests, vocational tests, and inkblot tests. The physiological psychologists are interested in the connection between the mind and the various organs serving it, such as the brain, the eye, and the ear. Social psychologists are interested in what happens between people, both in large groups, such as communities, and in small groups.

Psychologists who do psychotherapy are called clinical psychologists. A few clinical psychologists in the past were admitted to Psychoanalytic Institutes and became qualified psychoanalysts, but this is no longer possible in this country, at least as far as the American Psychoanalytic Association is concerned. Because of this, psychologists have formed their own psychoanalytic associations, and are trying to bring their standards up to those of the American Psychoanalytic Association.

Psychologists who are properly trained to do psychotherapy are so labeled in the Directory of the American Psychological Association. In addition, in many states a Bureau of Professional Standards makes rules for psychologists who wish to practice psychotherapy. Those who cannot meet the standards are not allowed to call themselves psychotherapists. In other states, however, psychologists are not certified, and anyone who wishes may hang out a neon sign reading "Psychologist," "Psychoanalyst," or "Marriage Counselor." This is dangerous to those who seek help, since their condition may be aggravated by quacks, and they may be swindled out of so much money that they are unable to afford the sound treatment from a properly trained person which is what they really require.

Anyone who wishes psychotherapy or psychiatric advice should be sure to go to a qualified person. Some well-trained social workers, psychiatric nurses, sociologists and clergymen practice psychotherapy or counseling. In many states it is illegal for them to do more than give counseling advice, unless they are working under the supervision of a qualified psychiatrist. In most cases, a person who needs treatment rather than advice should only go to someone in those professions if the therapist is working under the supervision of a well-trained psychiatrist.

There are several ways to check the standing of anyone who claims to be or is called a psychiatrist, clinical psychologist, psychotherapist or psychoanalyst.

The Directory of the American Medical Association, which is available in most public libraries, contains the name of each licensed physician in the United States and Canada, together with his medical school and his specialty, if any, and also notes whether he is a diplomate of his specialty board.

The yearly List of Fellows and Members of the American Psychiatric Association contains the names of all physicians who belong to this association, which includes nearly all the doctors in the country with psychiatric training, and states whether or not they are diplomates of the American Board of Psychiatry and Neurology. The Association has on file the professional qualifications of every member, at the office of the Executive Secretary, 1700 Eighteenth Street N.W., Washington, D.C. 20009. The American Psychiatric Association also publishes every few years a biographical directory of all its members, which gives full information about their background and professional training. There are now 15,000 members of the American Psychiatric Association.

The Directory of Medical Specialists contains the names of all diplomates of all the American specialty boards, including surgeons, obstetricians, psychiatrists, et cetera. Every psychiatrist who has passed the examinations of the American Board of Psychiatry and Neurology is listed there, and also the various professional societies to which he belongs. A listing in this directory is a guarantee of training and competence. Those who are not listed there may or may not be competent. Some older psychiatrists have not taken the Board examinations, so that their names do not appear in this directory.

Nearly all qualified psychoanalysts in this country are members of the American Psychoanalytic Association.

In most large cities there is also a group of younger apprentice analysts who are not members of the national Association but are connected with the local Psychoanalytic Institute, which is recognized by the Association. Membership in the American Psychoanalytic Association is a guarantee of competence in this field. Those who are not members are reliable if they are connected with the local Institute. If anyone calling himself or herself a "psychoanalyst" does not belong to either the local Institute or the national Association, he or she has either broken away from the orthodox analysts, or else has not had orthodox psychoanalytic training.

According to the Directory of the American Psychoanalytic Association, there are now 1,200 fully trained psychoanalysts in this country, distributed among twenty-six local psychoanalytic societies, with twenty approved training institutes. Most of these psychoanalysts are collected in the larger cities, and a few states have none at all. The local Psychoanalytic Institute or Society, if there is one, will be found listed in the telephone book. The qualifications of anyone who calls himself or herself a psychoanalyst can be checked at the headquarters of the American Psychoanalytic Association, 1 East 57th Street, New York, N.Y. 10022.

The qualifications of clinical psychologists can be checked in the Directory of the American Psychological Association. If this is not available, an inquiry can be forwarded to the headquarters of the American Psychological Association, 1333 Sixteenth Street N.W., Washington, D.C. 20036. There are now about 25,000 members in this Association.

If none of the Directories mentioned above is to be found in the local library, the County Medical Society, the State Medical Society, or the American Medical Association (535 N. Dearborn Street, Chicago, Illinois 60610) may be consulted.

The yellow pages of the telephone book must be used carefully in trying to locate a psychiatrist or psychoanalyst. Many well-qualified men in the field deliberately keep their names out of the sections headed "Psychiatrist" or "Psychoanalyst" in some cities, so as not to be confused with the unqualified people, many of them outright quacks, who claim to belong to these branches and so list themselves in the telephone directory. Genuine psychiatrists will be found listed, along with other physicians and surgeons, in the "Physicians & Surgeons, M.D." section of the yellow pages, and clinical psychologists are listed under "Psychologists." In some cities the listing in the telephone book also indicates whether or not a psychologist is licensed by the state to practice clinical psychology. In states where there is no Bureau of Professional Standards for psychologists, it is very difficult to know whether a psychologist listed in the telephone book has had proper training. This is best determined by checking with the American Psychological Association, unless a certain practitioner is recommended by a reliable professional man.

Any psychotherapist who has a neon sign outside his office is undoubtedly *not* qualified. Genuine specialists in any branch of medicine, surgery or psychotherapy are highly ethical and do not believe in advertising.

With these hints, anyone who feels in need of skilled help in handling personality or emotional problems should be able to locate a competent, well-trained specialist. If one is fortunate enough to have a family physician who is sincerely interested in finding proper psychiatric help and guidance for those of his patients who need it, his assistance, of course, is important. In many towns there are also recognized psychiatric and mental-health clinics, and veterans hospitals, to which the individual can go for psychiatric help and advice. Any such clinic will be glad to give the names of some private psychiatrists to anyone who feels the need of more intensive treatment than a clinic is able to give. The local "Physicians' & Surgeons' Information Bureau," which can usually be found listed as such in the telephone directory, will also be glad to refer inquirers to a psychiatrist if there is one in the community.

In large cities where many qualified men can easily be found it matters little which individual doctor is chosen, training and qualifications being equal. It is generally unwise for someone seeking psychiatric treatment to go shopping around from one doctor to another. If such treatment is described or recommended, he should make a clear-cut decision and act upon it promptly. Once he (or she) is in the hands of a qualified psychotherapist, it is usually better to let his (or her) attitude toward, or criticism of, the therapist become a problem of the treatment, rather than an excuse for delay or for revoking the decision. If, however, the person feels a genuine antipathy toward the first therapist he visits, he may be warranted in trying another one. Also, if the treatment has gone on for more than two years and the patient feels he is not making progress, he is justified in asking for a consultation with one of the senior psychiatrists in the community to evaluate the situation. All ethical medical practitioners are willing to have consultations with well-qualified colleagues if there is any doubt as to the efficacy of any treatment. And the patient should not feel disloyal or guilty if, after giving the treatment a long and conscientious trial, he feels dissatisfied and wants another expert opinion.

2

Can mental illnesses be cured?

More and more psychoses and neuroses are being cured as new methods of treatment are devised. All over the world thousands of psychiatrists and chemists are working on this problem. Every year there is a little progress here and a little progress there, and some years there is a breakthrough of major importance.

There are two ways in which a person with psychiatric symptoms can improve. One is called "making progress," and the other is called a cure. Making progress means that a patient gradually improves up to a certain point and may stay that way, or under unfavorable circumstances may slide back. A cure means that the person gets completely well and stays that way. This does not mean that a completely well person will be free of all anxieties. He still has to live in the world, earn a living, get along with his spouse, and raise his children. And, like anyone else, he runs into two kinds of difficulties: first, the world is competitive and does not always make things easy; and secondly, other people have minds of their own and are not always considerate of those around them. Teen-agers, for example, even in the best-regulated families, often do things which distress their parents. The cure of a psychiatric condition does not change the outside world or eliminate the spontaneous activities of other people. It only frees the person so that he can use all his faculties to deal with whatever life confronts him with, without any crippling symptoms such as phobias, psychosis, or addiction to alcohol.

The first thing to remember is that a large percentage of psychiatric disorders get better without any psychiatric treatment. Some of them get better by themselves, and some can be handled by a good family doctor. The psychiatric drugs used nowadays can bring about the relief of almost any psychiatric symptom, and some of the most severe disorders, such as the suicidal depressions of later life, can be relieved (usually only temporarily) by shock treatment. With the help of drugs the patient can be prepared for psychotherapy, which, as far as we know now, is the only way to bring about an actual cure. Of the various forms of psychotherapy, psychoanalysis, transactional analysis, group therapy, and behavior therapy seem to give the best results. Formal psychoanalysis, which involves visits several times a week to a qualified psychoanalyst, is probably the best treatment for hysteria, obsessions, compulsions and phobias. Phobias which cannot be cured by psychoanalysis may sometimes be cured by behavior therapy. For all other conditions, group therapy is probably the best form of treatment. Psychoanalytic group therapy gives good results, and the indications are that transactional-analysis group treatment is equally good or better. Most patients, however, will make progress with almost any kind of psychotherapy with a properly trained therapist.

It is difficult to give figures to prove any of this. In the first place, to be of any value the figures should extend over a five-to-ten-year period, and it is very difficult to track down a large number of patients five or ten years after they have finished their treatment. Secondly, it is difficult to know what questions to ask to determine whether a patient is cured or has stayed cured. Good results are difficult to evaluate, while bad results are easier to check. For example, if the patient has committed suicide or gone back to the state hospital, that would certainly be called a bad result. But if the patient has got a divorce, who is to say whether this means an improvement because he freed himself from a marriage which was spoiling his life, or a symptom because he was unable to adjust to family life? Evaluating good results is usually an individual matter. Formerly, this had to be decided between the patient and the therapist. Nowadays, with so many patients going into group therapy, the opinion of the other members of the group is valuable in deciding whether a patient is getting worse, standing still, making progress, or actually being cured. In any case, as the years go by, more and more patients are making progress, and more and more patients are being cured of even the most serious psychiatric disorders. The final answer to the question "Can psychiatric patients be cured?" is "Yes, they can! Don't despair, and never say die!"

Footnotes for Philosophers, Chapter Twelve

1. *Choosing a doctor*

For an interesting study of what can go wrong in this respect, see: *Where Do People Take Their Troubles?* by Lee R. Steiner. Boston: Houghton, Mifflin, 1945.

Persons interested in obtaining psychoanalytic treatment might benefit from reading *Practical and Theoretical Aspects of Psychoanalysis,* by Lawrence S. Kubie. The discussion concerning the proper definition of "psychoanalysis" according to the findings of the British Medical Association is quoted by Kubie from the *British Medical Journal* for June 29, 1929.

For a general discussion of the doctor-patient relationship, see *The Doctor-Patient Relationship,* by Kevin Browne and Paul Freeling (London: E. & S. Livingstone, 1967).

For a discussion of the relationship between psychiatrists and psychologists in psychotherapy see: "The Physician and the Clinical Psychologist: Comparison of Their Education and Their Interrelationship," by H. A. Dickel, *Journal of the American Medical Association,* Vol. 195 (January 31, 1966), pp. 365–70.

For a countrywide list of places to go for advice about psychiatric treatment, see *Encyclopedia of Mental Health,* Vol. 6 (New York: Franklin Watts, 1963), pp. 2079–85. This includes national and state agencies, as well as suggestions for local sources, which may be found in the telephone directory.

2. *Results*

The results of all forms of treatment in psychiatry have always been difficult to evaluate. This difficulty is particularly prominent nowadays because almost every patient receives more than one mode of treatment— for example, various combinations of drugs, shock, and psychotherapy. Even "pure" psychotherapists, such as psychoanalysts and behavior therapists, find it difficult to obtain a statistically adequate series of cases uncontaminated by drug therapy. But almost all experienced clinicians would agree that the results have improved steadily during the last thirty years. Certainly the mental-hospital population has decreased.

The following figures will give some idea of what is happening. In 1955, the year psychotropic drugs first began to be widely used, there were more than 550,000 people in public mental hospitals in this country. In 1967, this had fallen to 426,000. The prevalence of mental illness is indicated in some figures given by Mike Gorman, executive director of the National Committee Against Mental Illness. He estimates that in 1965, 19,000,000 people needed psychiatric treatment, and 3,921,000 actually received treatment. Of these, 807,000 were cared for during the year in state and county mental hospitals. (Quoted from *Medical World News*, August 4, 1967, and *Mental Health Statistics*, National Institute of Mental Health, January 1968.

In 1952, the American Psychoanalytic Association started a study of the results of treatment by psychoanalysis and psychotherapy. In the October, 1967 issue of the *Journal of the American Psychoanalytic Association* (D. A. Hamburg et al., Vol. 15, pp. 841–861) it was reported that only half the patients "completed treatment." Of those who did, 97% were judged by their therapists to be improved in "total functioning," and 96% of these patients said they "felt benefited." What happened to those who completed treatment without feeling benefited is not stated. The results were about equal for psychoanalysis and for psychotherapy done by psychoanalysts. On the other hand, "symptom cure" is reported for only 27% of these patients. Since it is noted that this 15-year attempt to study about 10,000 patients treated by 800 psychoanalysts was not very effectively planned or carried out, these figures are thought-provoking, but not necessarily reliable.

APPENDIX

BEYOND SCIENCE

In 1922, Freud stirred up great interest among his disciples by publishing an article called "Dreams and Telepathy." Mental telepathy is now considered a legitimate subject for investigation by many psychiatrists and psychologists. Freud was interested also in certain aspects of fortunetelling.

It is not an original idea, therefore, to include a section on these and allied subjects, which are sometimes covered by the term *parapsychology,* in a book on psychiatry and psychoanalysis. Fortunetelling, intuition, and what is now known as *extrasensory perception,* are all manifestations of the human mind in action. These matters are of such general interest, and force themselves so regularly upon the attention of those who practice psychiatry and especially psychoanalysis, that it seems warranted to discuss them here.

There is no known way to acquire or train parapsychological faculties. Each observer is a law unto himself and can work only under conditions which are suitable for his individual self and which he himself is usually unable to define exactly. The present attitude of psychiatrists toward parapsychological experiences is based on the following considerations:

1. Nearly all psychiatrists rely extensively on intuition in their daily work and find that it rarely fails them (or the patient).
2. Many psychoanalysts have published observations indicating their belief in the existence of telepathic phenomena.
3. If the subject is mentioned, almost everyone except certain types of personalities can and does relate personal parapsychological experiences. Many of these experiences can be explained in other ways, but because there are other possible explanations does not necessarily mean that the "other" explanation is nearer the truth than the parapsychological one.

1
What about fortunetellers?

In this section we shall deal with graphology and palmistry, and mention some other methods of "fortunetelling" in passing.

A person's handwriting can be judged in two ways: first, by scientific methods, that is, by studying the characteristics of a large number of scripts and relating them to the characteristics of the writers, so that standards of comparison are set up and can be used for classifying people. This is known as *scientific graphology.* There are many books on this subject, some of them written by reputable psychologists. This method of study is preferred by strict scientists. Some people, however, feel that they can better form an opinion about what an individual writer is likely to do in various practical situations by using the second way of judging handwriting, which is known as *intuitive graphology.*

In practicing intuitive graphology, the graphologist puts himself into a state of deliberate concentration, and retraces in his thoughts or with his finger the exact movements made by the writer in forming one or more letters. If he is fortunate enough to possess the proper intuition, he will then sense things about the writer's emotional state which are not revealed by the known facts or the material in the script, and some of which may be repressed and therefore not known even to the writer himself. From this apparently meager information, an experienced psychiatrist or psychologist may form a good idea of the writer's personality structure and his probable emotional tensions of the moment which will guide his actions in the near future.

One of the biggest problems in graphology is to discover which personality characteristics should be expected to show up in handwriting. In other words, it is as difficult to know which question to ask as it is to find the answer. But the fine movements of handwriting are an expression of the individual's whole personality, and it is reasonable to suppose that some meaning can be found in them if we only know exactly what kind of meaning to look for.

Palmists, phrenologists, and other fortunetellers who study physical structure probably notice unconsciously the position and movements of the facial and other muscles in making their judgments of people. Consciously, however, they believe that their judgments are based on permanent bodily characteristics, such as the bumps on the skull or the lines on the palm of the hand. Since the bumps on the skull have nothing to do with the personality, we need not consider phrenology any further.

As for reading palms by lines, it is not scientifically sound to think that an anatomical line on a person's hand tells anything about his past or future. Successful palm prophets consciously or unconsciously base their statements on other factors, perhaps including mental telepathy and clairvoyance, if such things exist. An obvious source of information is the shape of the hand. Undoubtedly many palmists classify people accordingly with some success, and they may have an inkling or actual knowledge of the differences between endomorphs, mesomorphs, and ectomorphs. This information is not difficult to exploit. It is natural to suppose that the young ectomorph is likely to be "preoccupied with love troubles," and that the mature endomorph is more likely to "hear some good news at a banquet." By using such guides, the palmist can increase the percentage of correct hits.

A person's palm may also reveal his occupation and the palmist may use this knowledge in a subtle way with or without realizing it. The much-callused hand of a laborer immediately suggests money troubles, while the smooth hand of a playboy suggests sexual complications. In the first case the palmist might say: "The money will come soon, don't worry." If by chance it does in even one case, her name will be made among the laborer's friends, no matter how many other times she has missed. In the second event she might prophesy: "A blonde artiste will soon come into your life and give you much happiness; later she will cause trouble!" If the playboy gets around the following week to taking out a dancing girl from the Chimera Club, something he had been planning to do for a long time anyway, and if he later has to make a financial settlement with her, the palmist's future is assured.

With female clients, the case is even simpler. If a toil-worn housewife wearing a crucifix comes in with "diaper hands," the palmist need not hesitate to say: "You will have another baby within the year." If the client is a hard-faced, highly manicured bar girl in a mink coat, the palmist might build her reputation by predicting: "A rich man will soon give you a lot of money." If we reverse these prophecies, we can see how obvious and simple they are. It would be unsound to tell the laborer's worn-out wife that a rich man was going to set her up on Park Avenue, and equally poor judgment to tell a girl of the night who was obviously out for all she could get that she was going to have another baby within the year.

While a debutante who happens to be named Celeste is apt to have a different career from a proletarian girl who happens to be named Mabel, this is not because of the numerology of the names. Similarly, some people may possibly be affected by the moon and the barometric pressure, but it should be a matter of indifference to any sensible person, unless he is interested in the science of astronomy, as to whether it is Mars or Mercury which is having a conjunction with Venus at any particular moment. We must attribute lucky hits on the part of numerologists and astrologers either to chance, to vague language, or to the types of observations mentioned previously. The same applies to the readers of tea leaves, birds' entrails, and so on.

We have only hinted at the use of intuition, which is probably an important factor in all these cases. The question of mental telepathy and clairvoyance also has to be considered seriously when fortunetellers hit regularly in questions involving numbers, such as dates, money, ages, and family size. As for foretelling the future, Balzac probably put it best when he said: "Predicting the future is like seeing a man in fireman's clothes and predicting he will chase fires."

For people who give public demonstrations of mind reading or fortunetelling on the stage or on television, there are a large number of tricks available, some of them amazingly ingenious. In any mind-reading act, the moment the victim is asked to write anything down, no matter how innocent the writing paper looks, he may assume that he is going to be made the victim of legerdemain. Even without writing, there are astonishingly effective methods of "reading minds" by trickery. Apparatus and systems for the most mystifying "mind-reading" acts can be purchased at any magic supply house.

2

What is intuition?

The matters related in the following sections will have to be accepted for what they are worth as true accounts of personal experiences. Similar occurrences have been demonstrated to fellow psychiatrists and before groups of doctors, and of course the patients and others involved can verify what happened, but there is no way of demonstrating the veracity of these events to the individual reader.

Intuition is the acquiring of knowledge through sensory contact with the object, without the intuiter being able to explain to himself or to others exactly how he came to his conclusions. In other words, intuition means that we can know something without knowing how we know it.

Intuition is a fragile and personal thing, and its study has been discouraged by those who cling strictly to scientific principles and refuse to admit that such a faculty exists unless its effects can be produced and reproduced at will. Unfortunately, at present intuition can be exercised only at such times and under such circumstances as the intuiter himself feels are correct. He is either "on the beam" or he isn't, and until someone can discover how to control intuition so that it can be brought into play at will and investigated under proper laboratory conditions, we shall have to accept people's word for what happened, just as we did during the "anecdotal" stage of animal psychology, in the days of the good and learned Reverend J. G. Wood.

Now let us study some examples of intuition from the writer's experience.

When on night duty in various hospitals, I used to gather social pleasure and bits of knowledge by passing the time with the patients in the wards whenever opportunity offered. One evening I walked into the office of a ward in a large hospital and found one of the patients sitting on the desk. Knowing that he should not have been there, he got up to leave, but since I felt that I was in an intuitive mood, I invited him to stay. We had never seen each other before and did not know each other's names. The incident took place in a part of the hospital far from the psychiatric section where I worked during the day, on a ward which was completely strange to me.

Before the man had a chance to say anything, I asked him to be seated again, and inquired:

"Does Philadelphia mean anything to you?"

"Yes," he replied. "I was brought up there."

"Well," I said, "but you left home when you were fifteen."

"That is correct," he replied, beginning to wonder what was going on.

"If you will permit me to say so," I continued, "I believe your mother disappointed you."

"Oh, no, doctor. I love my mother very much."

"Nevertheless, I think she disappointed you. Where is she now?"

"She's at home. She's not well."

"How long has she been ill?"

"Most of her life. I've been taking care of her since I was a young fellow."

"What's her trouble?"

"She's always been nervous. A semi-invalid."

"Then in that sense she disappointed you, don't you think? She had to take emotional support from you rather than give it to you, from your earliest years."

"Yes, doctor, that's correct, all right."

At this point another man entered the office, and was invited to sit down. He sat on the floor with his back against the wall and said nothing, but he listened with great interest.

"You give me the impression that your father was ineffective from the time you were about nine," I continued with the first man.

"He was a drunkard. I believe about the time I was nine or ten, he began to drink more heavily."

This conversation took more time than its description does, since it was punctuated by frequent groping silences on my part. The second man now requested that I tell him something about himself.

"Well," I replied, "I think your father was very strict with you. You had to help him on the farm. You never went fishing or hunting with him. You had to go on your own, with a bunch of rather tough fellows."

"That's right."

"He began to scare you badly when you were about seven."

"Well, my mother died when I was six, if that had anything to do with it."

"Were you pretty close to her?"

"I was."

"So her death left you more or less at the mercy of your tough father?"

"I guess it did."

"You make your wife angry."

"I guess I did. We're divorced."

"She was about sixteen and a half when you married her."

"That's right."

"And you were about nineteen and a half when you married her."

"That's right."

"Is it right within six months?"

He stopped to figure for a moment and then replied:

"They're both right within two months."

There was another long silence, but by this time I could feel the intuitive feeling slipping away so I said:

"Well, fellows, that's as far as I can go."

"Doctor," said the second man, "could you guess my age?"

"I don't think I'm in the groove for guessing ages tonight."

"Well, try, Doc!"

"I don't think I'll get this, but I'll try. You were twenty-four in September."

"I was thirty in October."

These two cases are selected out of a large number, mainly because these men later consented to appear at the regular weekly meeting of the staff doctors of the hospital, where they bore witness to the authenticity of the observations. (At this meeting I was attempting to demonstrate how the early emotional adventures of the individual leave their marks not only on his later personality but also on his muscular set, particularly in the face, and these two men seemed ideal for such an occasion.)

Most of these observations were the results of "intuition,"

specifically, what doctors call "clinical intuition." Just as the old family doctor could diagnose typhoid fever "by the smell" because of his vast experience with this disease, so nowadays the observant psychiatrist learns to judge many things about his patients "by intuition." Since he is continually seeing patients and inquiring about their ages, marital status, home life, parents' characters, and so on, it is to be expected that after some years he should acquire the ability to make pretty shrewd guesses on sight.

Such shrewdness is not confined to psychiatrists, nor to the medical profession. Any professional becomes pretty "intuitive" about his own business. Professional age-guessers and weight-guessers at fairs and carnivals make their living through such intuition, which they cultivate by practice and experience. The average person can judge ages and weights fairly accurately, yet perhaps no one could put into words exactly how he makes such judgments. Not even portrait painters, who are accustomed to copying intuitively the very visual clues from which such information is derived, can explain how they tell the difference between a man of twenty-three and one of twenty-six.

It is important to realize, then, that we can know something without being able to put into words exactly how we know it; but we can know it surely, nevertheless. This was clearly shown in the first case above, where I knew that the man's mother had "disappointed" him. So sure was I of this knowledge that when he denied it I insisted upon my judgment, and it finally turned out to be correct. On the other hand, the gross error I made in guessing the second man's age, after I had guessed all the "more difficult" things accurately, but after my intuition had worn itself out, shows that without intuition to aid him, even an experienced observer can be easily led astray.

These impressions are not ruled by the laws of chance. It is not a question of being right part of the time through coincidence. When one has "that feeling," one rarely makes a mistake. When one doesn't have the feeling, one's guesses do follow the laws of chance. Guessing the age when fifteen men left home and being right in two or three cases would be one thing; guessing different things about fifteen men and being right almost a hundred per cent of the time is another. That is why it is so difficult to study these things properly. They cannot be done by request. The feeling of being "on the beam" comes only at certain times, and then it is gone.

3
How does intuition work?

To understand intuition, we have only to rid ourselves of the belief that in order to know something we have to be able to put into words what we know and how we know it. This belief is the result of an overdevelopment of the modern scientific outlook, which has taken us in some ways too far in the direction of *testing* reality, and away from nature and the world of natural happenings. By chaining the Child in us, we have imprisoned much that could be useful and beneficial. Those with enough control should be able to allow intuitive faculties to develop without endangering their necessary contact with reality. As Freud says, "All this is highly speculative and full of unsolved problems, but there is no need to be alarmed by it." Intuition is simply induction without words. When we are able to put into words what we intuit and how we came to our conclusions, we have verbalized induction, which is commonly called Science.

An admirable opportunity for studying the intuitive process at work was offered in interviewing 25,000 men for the United States Government at the rate of two hundred to five hundred per day. Under such pressure, the individual "psychiatric examinations" were a matter of seconds rather than of minutes. With such a strict time limit, one's judgments had to be based more on intuition than on examination. In order to study the problem, two stock questions were first devised. An attempt was then made to predict by intuition what each man's answer to these questions would be. The intuitions were recorded, and then the questions were asked. In a surprisingly large percentage of cases (over 90 per cent), the intuitions were found to be correct. The two questions were: "Are you nervous?" and "Have you ever been to a psychiatrist?" After much study, the grounds for making the predictions in each case could be put into words, so that eventually, instead of using intuition to predict the answers, they could be predicted by applying certain rules which could be written down.

After confirming these rules in several thousand cases, another study was undertaken. An attempt was made to guess each man's occupation before he spoke, simply by watching him come into the room and sit down. The men were all clothed alike in a maroon bathrobe and cloth slippers. Again it was found that the guesses, or intuitions, were surprisingly accurate. On one occasion, the occupations of twenty-six successive men were guessed correctly by this method, ranging through farmer, bookkeeper, mechanic, professional gambler, salesman, warehouseman, and truck driver.* Once more the grounds for making the prediction in each case were studied until some of them could be put into words, so that eventually, for at least two occupational groups, instead of using intuition to predict the answers, they could be predicted in a large percentage of cases by applying certain rules which could be written down.

After the rules upon which the predictions were based were discovered, an interesting observation came to light. The conscious intention in the second experiment was to diagnose occupations. It was found, however, that it was not occupations which were being diagnosed at all, but ways of handling new situations! It was found in the two occupational groups that were most clearly understood, that it just happened that those men who handled the examination situation in one way (passive waiting) were nearly all farmers, while those who handled it in another way (alert curiosity) were nearly all mechanics. Thus it turned out that intuition did not diagnose occupations, but emotional attitudes, even though the conscious intention was to diagnose the former.

This was an important discovery. It meant that since intuitions are not known through words, the Ego doesn't really know what it is that is known. All the Ego can do for the intuiter and those around him is to try to put a very subtle feeling into words as best it can, and it often merely comes close to the truth rather than actually hitting it. Secondly (really another aspect of the above),

---

* In this situation there was no fatigue, such as occurred in the hospital, because the "examinations" were the writer's sole occupation during this period and he arrived fresh each morning, whereas the hospital scene took place after a hard day's work with heavy responsibilities. It is also easier to see a lot of people in a given time than to spend it with one person, since in the former case there is no personal involvement such as develops in a longer interview.

intuition cannot be asked any specific question but can only be guided in one or another general direction; it presents us with an impression and then we have to look for the answer in the material which it puts at our disposal.

It was further found that with each new rule that was written down, the accuracy of guessing by conscious observation went up, but was always less than the intuitive accuracy. It thus seemed evident that the feeling of "things arranging themselves without conscious control" which had been observed during intuition had to do with a large number of factors which were being noticed and arranged without being put into words, by something below the conscious level. Since all of these factors could not be put into words, the intuitive accuracy was always greater than the accuracy obtained by applying consciously those rules which could be written down.

Thus a psychological definition of intuition can be stated. Intuition is subconscious knowledge without words, based on subconscious observations without words, and under the right circumstances it is more reliable and accurate than conscious knowledge based on conscious observation.

As we have seen in the last section and in this section, intuition deals with at least two different aspects of the personality. The first is the early childhood emotional relationships between the individual and those around him, such as his parents and relatives, and the adult representatives of those relationships: emotional attitudes toward various people who are important to the individual. These are based on ungratified Id tensions. The second is the individual's way of experiencing and handling new situations. This, though based on Id tensions, actually relates to the attitude of the Ego, and its reaction to reality. We can say roughly that we may have intuitions about Id tensions, and about Ego attitudes.

Careful study during the experiments led to the tentative belief that intuitions about Id tensions are mostly formed by watching the mouth of the subject, while intuitions about Ego attitudes mainly come from observing the eyes. Thus we may tentatively venture to say that in a certain sense the muscles about the eyes serve chiefly to express Ego attitudes, while the muscles about the mouth serve chiefly to express Id tensions. In the classical anal erotic, such as we have pictured in Mr. Krone, this idea is strikingly illustrated. In the cold eyes of such a person we read his consciously suspicious approach to the world and its new situations, while in his tight-cornered mouth we read his constipation, his stubbornness, his stinginess, his orderliness, and his cruelty, the classical symptoms derived directly (as his suspiciousness is indirectly) from his anal interests.

It is worth noting that much intuitive knowledge may depend upon the sense of smell. The odor of a person's breath and sweat can change with his emotional attitude. Some people are more aware of smells than others, and the distance over which smells can influence emotions is incredible; certain moths can detect sexual odors a mile away. The fact that we are not aware of a smell does not mean that it is not affecting our emotional attitude. Smells can change dreams without being perceived as smells.

Further study of intuition from the point of view of transactional analysis indicates that this faculty belongs to the Child ego state. If the Child is left free of influences from the Adult and Parent ego states, intuition is at its best. The moment the Adult comes in with conscious reasoning, or the Parent with its prejudices and preconceived ideas, intuition is impaired as the Child retreats before these superior forces. Intuition also fails if the Child is corrupted by an offer of rewards or a threat of punishment. In other words, this is a fragile faculty which can be easily disturbed or distorted by external pressures, which is one reason it is not forthcoming on demand.

4

What is extrasensory perception?

Many people are familiar with the extrasensory perception or "ESP" cards, which are now sold for use as a parlor game. This is a pack of twenty-five cards with five different designs on their faces, so that the pack consists of five circles, five squares, five stars, five crosses, and five "wavy lines." The game is to try to guess which design is on a card without looking. It seems evident that by the laws of chance, since there are five possible guesses, one guess in five should be correct.

The reason this game is of scientific interest is that in the Duke University laboratory of Dr. J. B. Rhine, who designed these cards, many people were able to guess correctly, in thousands of trials, an average of more than one time out of five. Dr. Rhine felt that these good guessers must become aware of what the next card should be by some method other than the use of their senses; he therefore chose the name of "extrasensory perception" for this ability to guess correctly more often than was expected by the laws of chance.

Dr. Rhine designed the cards for the purpose of studying mental telepathy and clairvoyance. If an assistant looks at a card and thinks about it hard, as though he were trying to telegraph what it is to the guesser, that is called mental telepathy. The guesser may be sitting behind a screen in the same room or he may be in another room many miles away; but, in any case great care is taken to prevent him from seeing the card.

If the guesser tries to guess which card is coming up next, a card which no one has seen and no one can be thinking about, this is called clairvoyance. In both cases, by the laws of chance as we know them today, over many thousands of trials, an average of one guess in five should be correct.

In the course of years, with millions of trials by different subjects, Dr. Rhine found out many interesting things. The most important was that certain people nearly always got a high percentage of correct guesses, while others hardly ever did. It seemed as though some people were regularly more telepathic or clairvoyant than others. Secondly, if the high guessers got tired, or if they were given sedative drugs to dull their minds, their percentage of correct guesses went down until it averaged just about the expected one out of five; while if they were given coffee or some other stimulant, their accuracy improved.

The results seemed to show that certain people have clairvoyant or mental telepathic abilities, and this naturally caused a sensation in scientific circles. His work was immediately criticized from many quarters. First, his mathematics was questioned. It was said that in the way he did the experiments, chance alone could account for the high results. Since the Institute of Mathematical Statistics formally declared in 1937 that his mathematics was correct and approved of the way he applied the laws of chance, this kind of criticism is rarely heard any more. It can still be said, however, that our ideas of the laws of chance have only been worked out on paper. It may even be that Dr. Rhine's results are the true laws of chance for that situation, since no one had ever tested those laws before by trying them out as many times as he has done.

Secondly, the quality of his cards was criticized. With a little practice they can be read from the back by sight and from the front by touching them without seeing them, and this disposes of some of his experiments. There are other experiments with good results, however, where there was no chance for the subject to see or touch the cards at all, especially those carried on over the telephone or with the subject in another room, sometimes many miles away.

Thirdly, the conscious and unconscious sincerity of the experimenters was questioned. It was felt that they might have been fooling themselves, deliberately or unconsciously. Many of the experiments can be questioned on these grounds, but not all by any means.

Fourthly, the experiments do not work for others as regularly as they do at Duke University. The British Society for Psychic Research, which tried to be open-minded about Dr. Rhine's ideas, but criticized his methods, was unable to find any subjects who showed convincing evidence of telepathy or clairvoyance when tested by this method.

Taking all his experiences and all the criticism into account, it is difficult to avoid the conclusion that either this is a method for demonstrating extrasensory perception, or else the laws of chance are different from what we think they are. Many interested people believe, however, that mathematics is not the best way to study this problem; that telepathy and clairvoyance exist, but should be studied by other methods. The most interesting problem, of course, if one accepts the belief that people can perceive extrasensorially, is *how* they do it, and it seems unlikely that mathematics could ever answer this question.

Dr. Rhine has also worked on another problem which will be of interest to a good many people—namely, can the thrower influence the dice? So far, his answer seems to be yes. People who just roll without caring don't seem to roll their point as often as people who roll with "plenty of schmaltz on the bones." By using a mechanical roller, Dr. Rhine eliminates any chance of "educating" the dice. This problem is not so difficult to study in everyday life as the problems of clairvoyance and telepathy. In every group of dice players there is always someone who makes his point with surprising regularity, and someone else who hardly ever makes it.

5

How does extrasensory perception work?

We can communicate clearly with ourselves and with others only by using words, but we can know things without using words. Ordinary knowledge is based on sense impressions which we can describe in words. We know that the girl is wearing a red coat because we see that the coat is red. Intuition is based on more subtle sense impressions which we cannot describe in words. We know that the girl has a red coat in her trunk because we "can tell" that she is "the kind of a girl who likes red coats." What seems to be clairvoyance or mental telepathy is based on something else. We suddenly suspect, for no known reason, that the girl's older sister has two red coats.

Clairvoyantlike and mental-telepathy-like happenings are most strikingly brought to our attention when they deal with numbers. When we become aware in the case of a complete stranger of the correct number of teeth which she has, or the correct street in New York where she is going on a visit, we are practically forced to conclude that such knowledge is arrived at by some method other than the use of the senses.

It is almost safe to assume that we have three ways of getting knowledge of our surroundings; that these are not sharply separated, but blend subtly into each other; and that each probably makes a contribution in sizing up any situation. First is ordinary knowledge, gained by the Adult ego state from practical experience; second is intuitive knowledge, developed in early years to ensure survival, and remaining as a function of the Child ego state; third is extrasensorylike perception, gained by unknown means of communication.

We do not know how extrasensory perception works, if it exists. Psychoanalysts have written a good deal about mental telepathy.

This generally takes the form of "extrasensory perceptions" which have to be interpreted by psychoanalytic methods before the thing which was perceived becomes apparent. This is evidence that extrasensory perception may be a function of the deeper layers of the mind.

Footnotes for Philosophers, Appendix

1. *Fortunetelling*

The "intuitive" approach to graphology is reminiscent of the Stanislavski method of dramatic training and of the James-Lange theory of the emotions. The validity of such intuitive methods of judgment can be adequately controlled by using as material the Bender Gestalt test instead of handwriting, subsequently verifying the conclusions by clinical studies. Careful work on graphology has been done by Roman.

Handwriting: A Key to Personality, by Klara G. Roman. New York: Pantheon Books, 1952.

With ten to sixty minutes of coaching, depending upon which method of trickery is used, a person of average intelligence can become a "mindreader," and call off playing cards, street addresses, and the numbers on dollar bills which he has never seen, either from the same room, or over the long-distance telephone.

2. and 3. *Intuition*

For a review of the literature on this subject see:

Toward a Contemporary Psychology of Intuition, by M. R. Westcott. New York: Holt, Rinehart and Winston, 1968.

An interesting discussion of the properties of smell can be found in: *Aromatics and the Soul*, by Dan McKenzie. New York: Paul B. Hoeber, 1923.

For further details concerning the matters mentioned in these sections, see my series of papers on the subject.

"The Nature of Intuition," by E. Berne. *Psychiatric Quarterly*, Vol. 23 (1949), pp. 203–26; "Concerning the Nature of Diagnosis," *International Record of Medicine*, Vol. 165 (1952), pp. 283–92; "Concerning the Nature of Communication," *Psychiatric Quarterly*, Vol. 27 (1953), pp. 185–98; "Intuition IV: Primal Images and Primal Judgment," *Ibid.*, Vol. 29 (1955), pp. 634–58; "Intuition V: The Ego Image," *Ibid.*, Vol. 31 (1957), pp. 611–27; and "Intuition VI: The Psychodynamics of Intuition," *Ibid.*, Vol. 36 (1962), pp. 294–300.

Compare "Acting In: Postural Attitudes Observed During Analysis," by M. A. Zeligs. *Journal of the American Psychoanalytic Association*, Vol. 5 (1957), pp. 685–706.

4. *ESP*

For details of Dr. Rhine's work, see:

Parapsychology, by J. B. Rhine and J. G. Pratt. Springfield, Ill.: C. C. Thomas, 1962.

Continuing work in this field is reported in a special journal, *The Journal of Parapsychology,* published by the Duke University Press at Durham, N.C.

The most interesting discussion on the subject in recent years, by eminently qualified believers and skeptics, such as Soal, Rhine, and Bridgman, can be found in a series of communications in the January 6, 1956 issue of *Science,* the official publication of the American Association for the Advancement of Science, with bibliographical references for those who wish to go into the matter further. Bridgman's comments on probability are similar to the viewpoint taken here.

5. *The nature of ESP*

One of the basic papers on the psychoanalytic approach to the problem of telepathy is found in Freud's *Complete Introductory Lectures on Psychoanalysis,* Chapter XXX, "Dreams and Occultism." Other articles in English can be found in various psychoanalytic journals, especially the easily available *Psychoanalytic Quarterly,* but these are difficult to evaluate, since many of the perceptions were not appreciated directly, but had to be dug out of the material by technical psychoanalytic interpretations, which in some ways obscures their validity.

For a survey of the whole field of matters "beyond science," with careful though skeptical discussion, see:

Illusions and Delusions of the Supernatural and the Occult, by D. H. Rawcliffe. New York: Dover Publications, 1959.

There has been a recent surge of interest here and in Russia, in telling colors by feel. For an interesting discussion of this, see:

"Dermo-optical Perception: A Peek Down the Nose," by M. Gardner, *Science* 151:654–57 (February 11, 1966).

WORD LIST

The definitions below give the meanings of the words as they are used in this book. In most cases these are the same as the meanings generally understood by psychiatrists, but a few words have been given broader meanings than the generally accepted ones, and others are defined from an unusual point of view, though much the same happenings are referred to as in the conventional definitions. The list is intended as an aid to the reader, and not as a psychiatric dictionary. Words which are used only in a single section of the book, therefore, are for the most part not included, as their explanation can be located by referring to the index.

For those with a more comprehensive interest in the psychiatric vocabulary, there is a *Psychiatric Dictionary,* by L. E. Hinsie and R. J. Campbell, 3rd ed. (New York: Oxford University Press, 1960) and a *Dictionary of Psychoanalysis,* by N. Fodor and F. Gaynor (New York: Philosophical Library, 1950).

A

ACTIVE Taking the initiative.

ADRENAL GLAND A small piece of tissue adhering to the kidney on each side. One section of the gland manufactures a chemical which helps prepare the body for extraordinary feats in time of emergency, as in the face of danger or frustration. Another section of the gland, the cortex, manufactures chemicals which affect a variety of other bodily functions, especially those concerned with fighting diseases. It is the former with which we are mainly concerned here.

ADULT (referring to an ego state) A state of mind which is interested in objectively gathering information and making estimates about external reality and bodily and mental processes.

AGGRESSION An attempt to inflict damage upon an object.

AGGRESSIVENESS The intensity with which the individual expresses his constructive and destructive impulses in his behavior.

AIM The specific act which reduces emotional tension.

AMBIVALENCE The existence side by side in the same individual of two apparently "opposite" feelings toward the same object, such as simultaneous love and hate of the husband or wife. Both feelings may be either conscious or unconscious, or one of the pair may be conscious and the other unconscious.

ANAL   Referring to the rectum, anus, and feces. Anal pleasure, or "anal erotism," may be seen in children and psychotics quite undisguised, and in neurotics and "anal characters" in disguised form, as in the pleasures of being stingy or messy.

ANXIETY   The feeling which arises when a conscious or unconscious tension is stirred up and seeks a method of relief.

AUTONOMIC NERVOUS SYSTEM   The part of the nervous system which "automatically" controls the organs and functions which cannot be controlled by the will. It supplies nerves to the heart, lungs, stomach, blood vessels, skin, etc. It consists of two parts: the sympathetic nervous system, which is the one chiefly stimulated by the adrenal glands and which prepares the individual for emergency action; and the parasympathetic, which prepares him chiefly for the pleasures of life, such as defecation and sexual intercourse.

B

BARBITURATES   A class of drugs used as sleeping powders. The most widely known are phenobarbital, Sodium Amytal, Nembutal, and Seconal.

C

CASTRATION COMPLEX   The system of ideas and feelings, conscious and unconscious, frank and disguised, and their effects as shown in behavior which results from the childlike idea that females once had a penis and lost it, and that males may lose theirs if they do not behave properly. The

castration complex shows itself chiefly as "penis envy" in women, and as "castration fear" in men.

CEREBROTONIC   An individual who is interested mostly in thinking rather than in action or sociability. The lanky, serious-minded college professor is often a good example. Ectomorphs are usually cerebrotonic.

CHARACTER   The ways each individual develops to handle his energy. Some can store energy and some cannot. Some express it directly, others filter it through a variety of deeply rooted, early acquired psychological attitudes. Each individual has his own way of dealing with his energy problems.

CHILD (referring to an ego state)   A state of mind which reproduces the thoughts, feelings, and reactions which the person had when he was actually an infant or a very young child (under six).

CLAIRVOYANCE   The ability to predict what is going to happen without any observation of the situation.

CLITORIS   A little penislike organ which is found in women just above the urinary opening.

COMPLEX   A system of ideas and feelings, conscious and unconscious, which influences behavior as strongly as many "intelligently thought-out" decisions. Example: castration complex.

COMPULSION   An inner urge which cannot be controlled by the will even when its uselessness or harmfulness is realized. It usually involves doing the same thing over and over, such as washing the hands four times, again and again, throughout the day.

CONSTITUTION   The qualities and make-up, both physical and mental, that the individual is born with. Large bones and musical talent are constitutional.

D

DEATH INSTINCT   A tension which has as its aim separation, injury, destruction, or killing. The energy of the death instinct is called mortido, which may be directed inwardly or outwardly.

DEPRESSION   Sadness. A "depression" is an illness characterized by sadness and loss of energy, appetites, and interest in life. When severe it may be called "melancholia." Its manifestations are mainly due to inwardly directed mortido.

DISPLACEMENT   The use of an aim or object other than the one really required or wished for, in order to relieve a tension partly or temporarily. Sarcasm may be an aim displacement for killing, and loving a horse may be an object displacement for loving a man.

E

ECTOMORPH   An individual who develops lengthwise rather than in thickness or breadth, with emphasis on the tissues which come from the outside layer of the egg, namely, the brain and skin. The lanky, long-faced college professor is an example. Ectomorphs tend to be cerebrotonic.

EGO   That part of the mind which is in contact with the outside world on one hand and with the Id and Superego on the other. It attempts to keep thoughts, judgments, interpretations, and behavior practical and efficient in accordance with the Reality Principle. Here we have used the word somewhat inexactly as almost synonymous with the conscious part of the mind.

EGO IDEAL   The ideal image which the individual has of what he would like to be like, and which he tries to live up to. It is the Ego Ideal which leads men to imitate their fathers, Robin Hood, Sigmund Freud, Jesse James, or Jesus.

EGO STATE   A well-organized set of feelings, thoughts, and reactions related to a corresponding well-organized set of behavior patterns. There are three types of ego states: Parent, Adult, and Child.

ENDOCRINE GLANDS   Small pieces of tissue found in various parts of the body, including among others the adrenal, thyroid, and sex glands, which manufacture special chemicals that percolate into the blood and affect the way the body and mind work.

ENDOMORPH   An individual who develops in thickness rather than in length or breadth, with emphasis on the tissues which come from the inside layer of the egg, especially the digestive organs. A stocky, paunchy, thick-necked conventioneer is a good example. Endomorphs tend to be viscerotonic.

EXTRAVERT   One whose Id instincts are directed outward.

F

FREE ASSOCIATION Reporting every thought and feeling which comes to mind during the psychoanalytic sessions, when the mind is kept free of all censoring, control, or sorting of thoughts.

FRUSTRATION Inability to relieve a tension because of difficulties in outside reality or a conflict within the mind. A convict is frustrated by reality and a prude is frustrated by his own conflicts.

FUNCTION The way things work. A functional illness or change means a change in the way the body works without enough detectable structural change to account for the amount of disorder. Many stomach disorders, such as excessive belching, and heart disorders, such as pounding, are of this variety.

G

GAME A set of transactions between two or more people whose goal is not what it appears to be (the con), which appeals to weaknesses in both parties (the gimmick), and which ends in each party collecting a good or bad feeling (the payoff).

GENITAL The final stage of personality development wherein the individual gets his greatest satisfaction from making other people happy because *he* likes *them* (and not in order to make *them* like *him,* or to square his conscience, or because of what they give him). In the genital stage, pleasure is shared, and the individual uses the sexual organs, rather than the mouth or the lower digestive tract, to obtain the most direct and intense satisfactions.

GRATIFICATION Any thought or act which relieves tension and anxiety and brings the human energy system closer to energy balance.

H

HEREDITY The process by which qualities come from the parents so that their possibilities are present in the egg from the moment it is fertilized.

HORMONES The chemicals manufactured by the endocrine glands, which affect the functions of the body and the mind.

HYPOCHONDRIASIS A form of self-love which manifests itself as paying undue attention to bodily sensations and attracting the attention of others by continually referring to one's inward organs.

HYSTERIA An illness wherein an emotional tension is partly relieved by a physical symptom which has some connection with the expression of the emotion. A man with an unconscious impulse to strike his father may suddenly find his right arm paralyzed for no reason that he knows of or that physical examination can reveal. The people who are especially likely to get such illnesses are overemotional, dramatic, changeable, and unreliable in their behavior, and are called "hysterical characters." Such people are particularly subject to the sudden outbursts of emotional expression which are popularly called "hysterics."

I

ID   The reservoir of psychic energy, derived from the raw life and death instincts. The Id works according to the pleasure principle. Its energy is libido and mortido, each with its own specific aims and objects.

IMAGE   The idea which the individual has of himself and the things around him, and according to which he feels, thinks and acts. An image consists of a representation, or picture, and an emotional charge, or feeling, about the picture. A man in love is a man under the strong influence of a highly charged image which even if it is far different from the reality as other people see it, nevertheless guides his feelings, ideas, and behavior.

INFERIORITY COMPLEX   A system of thoughts and feelings which results in the individual continually comparing himself unfavorably with other people, even when the facts do not warrant such discouraging comparisons.

INTROVERT   One whose Id instincts are directed inward.

INTUITION   Knowledge based on observations which cannot be put into words.

L

LIBIDO   (libee'doe) The energy tensions which are relieved by construction, creation, and bringing closer together. The energy of the life instinct. Its greatest satisfaction is obtained in the adult by a sexual orgasm, and its "purpose" seems to be the preservation of the race.

LSD   "Dextrorotatory lysergic acid diethylamide." The "laevorotatory isomer" of the same substance is inactive. LSD resembles substances derived from ergot, a parasite of the rye plant, which caused epidemics called "St. Anthony's Fire" in the Middle Ages. Devotees of LSD believe it to be psychedelic, or "mind broadening." Taken in very small quantities, it causes a temporary toxic psychosis called a "trip."

M

MAO INHIBITORS   Monoamine oxidase inhibitors, a class of drugs used to relieve depressions. "Happy pills."

MASOCHISM   An effort to satisfy inwardly directed mortido at the same time as libido is being satisfied. Masochistic women often choose drunkards for husbands because they know from experience or by intuition that a drunkard will be cruel to them both mentally and physically.

MESOMORPH   An individual whose chief development is in breadth rather than in length or thickness, with emphasis on the tissues which come from the middle layer of the egg, such as the muscles and connective tissue. Li'l Abner and athletic lifeguards are good examples. Mesomorphs tend to be somatotonic.

MORTIDO   (mortee'doe) The energy tensions which are relieved by destruction, injuring, elimination, and separation. The energy of the death instinct. Its greatest satisfaction is obtained in the adult by murder or suicide, and its "purpose" seems to be the preservation of the individual.

N

NARCISSISM Inwardly directed libido.

NEURASTHENIA An old term for a form of self-love manifested by unwillingness to expend effort, by multiple physical complaints, by undue worrying, and by lack of pleasure in normal relationships. Nowadays such conditions are usually classified as either anxiety neuroses or neurotic depressions.

NEUROLOGIST A physician who specializes in diseases of the nerve cords, spinal cord, and brain.

NEUROSIS A condition characterized by excessive use of energy for unproductive purposes so that personality development is hindered or stopped. A man who spends most of his time worrying about his health, counting his money, plotting revenge, or washing his hands, can hope for little personality development.

NEUROTIC ACTIVITY The use of energy for unproductive purposes, which may be part of a neurosis and hinder development, or may partly relieve bothersome tensions and thus help to leave the individual free to concentrate on other things. Smoking is a good example of the latter.

NREM SLEEP "Non-rapid-eye-movement" sleep. Quiet sleep during which the eyeballs are still and dreaming seldom occurs.

O

OBJECT That person or thing which may be used to relieve tension.

The object of libido may be a rare postage stamp or a woman, and the object of mortido may be a harmless person or an enemy. Many people have mainly themselves as libido and mortido objects.

OBSESSION An idea, feeling, or impulse which keeps intruding into consciousness and which cannot be suppressed by will, even though the individual realizes that it is unreasonable or harmful. Jealousy of a faithful wife or husband may become an obsession.

OEDIPUS COMPLEX The feeling of a child that he would like to gratify his libido by being closer to one parent and his mortido by eliminating the other. These feelings often persist into adult life in disguised form.

ORAL Those tendencies of behavior and feeling which first arise during the nursing period and often persist into adult life in frank or disguised form.

P

PARENT (referring to an ego state) A state of mind which is borrowed from and reproduces the thoughts, feelings, and behavior of one of the person's actual parents.

PHENOTHIAZINE A class of drugs used to relieve mental confusion. "Mind clearers."

PHOBIA Exaggerated fear of a specific object or situation.

PHYSIS The growth force of nature, which makes organisms evolve into higher forms, embryos develop into adults, sick people get better, and healthy people strive to attain their ideals. Possibly it is only one aspect of inwardly directed libido, but it may be a more basic force than libido itself.

PLEASURE PRINCIPLE The tendency of tensions to seek immediate and complete relief without regard to the consequences. The Id is guided by the pleasure principle, and therefore has to be curbed by the Ego in accordance with the Reality Principle.

POT The American form of cannabis, or marijuana, a vulgar relative of the real thing, which is Indian hemp and its resin hashish. Pot is smoked in cigarettes called "joints" to obtain a mild toxic psychosis, or "trip."

PSYCHE (sykee) The human mind, conscious and unconscious, including its ideals and aspirations.

PSYCHIATRIST A physician who specializes in helping, advising, and treating those who suffer from emotional difficulties, faulty relationships, or more obvious difficulties in interpreting their feelings and surroundings correctly. A qualified psychiatrist is *always* an M.D.

PSYCHOANALYSIS A system of studying, changing, and thinking about human behavior developed by Sigmund Freud. It deals mainly with the psychology of the Id and the way the Ego handles the Id tensions. As a method of treatment, it usually requires almost daily sessions of one hour for several years, since the Id is difficult to domesticate.

PSYCHOANALYST A physician with psychiatric training who spe-cializes in treating his patients by psychoanalysis. There are also some qualified psychoanalysts who are not physicians. The most highly trained psychoanalysts are connected with psychoanalytic societies affiliated with the International Psycho-Analytical Association.

PSYCHOLOGIST One who studies the mind. As usually used, the term refers to one who studies behavior and mental processes in special situations. Qualified psychologists have M.A. or Ph.D. degrees. A few have medical degrees in addition. Recognized psychologists are usually members of the American Psychological Association.

PSYCHOLOGY The study of the mind, usually referring to behavior and mental processes in special situations. Psychiatry is concerned with the prevention and treatment of emotional and mental disorders. Psychoanalysis studies chiefly the psychology of the unconscious mind.

PSYCHONEUROSIS Used here as exactly synonymous with neurosis.

PSYCHOPATH An individual who does not restrain himself from doing things which are harmful to others. The term is also used to refer to any individual whose personality structure is not well balanced.

PSYCHOSIS A mental illness resulting in the unconscious becoming conscious and taking over control of the individual. Since he then attempts to act in accordance with the pleasure principle instead of the Reality Principle, he can no longer get along in society. Psychosis is the medical word roughly corresponding to the legal term *insanity*.

PSYCHOSOMATIC This word is used by some in an attempt to emphasize the idea that emotions can contribute to diseases of the body, and that diseases of the body can affect the emotions.

PSYCHOTHERAPY Treatment of illness through a professional relationship with the therapist as a person rather than by means of medication or surgery.

R

REALITY The way things actually are. That is, the possibilities for interrelationship at any given moment of all the energy systems in the universe. A clear understanding of reality would enable the individual to predict the results of various ways of behaving in any situation.

REALITY PRINCIPLE The guiding principle which leads the individual to attempt to judge beforehand the consequences of various courses of action, instead of acting immediately in accordance with the Id tensions of the moment. The Ego has to curb the Id in accordance with the Reality Principle.

RELATIONSHIP The connection between two or more people, ideas, feelings, or things.

REM SLEEP "Rapid-eye-movement" sleep. Disturbed sleep during which the eyeballs move rapidly, and during which dreaming occurs.

REPRESENTATION The shape or form of a mental image, conscious or unconscious, without regard to the kind or amount of feeling it is charged with.

REPRESSION Pushing something into the unconscious, or keeping something from becoming conscious. Repression keeps the individual from being in a continual state of confusion by preventing him from becoming aware of many things, though what is forgotten or unknown still remains an active force in the unconscious part of the mind.

S

SADISM An attempt to satisfy outwardly directed mortido at the same time as libido is being satisfied. Drunken women make good mates for sadistic men because they often encourage men to be cruel to them physically and mentally.

SCHIZOPHRENIA (skitsofree′neeya) A mental illness characterized by a change in the person's behavior and emotional responses which surprises the people around him. He responds to what goes on in his head, even to imaginary voices, regardless of the realities which confront him.

SCRIPT A life plan which is formed in early childhood and which goes through various "rewrites" as the person grows up, with the plot and the ending remaining essentially unchanged.

SOMATOTONIC An individual who is interested in expressing himself mainly through muscular action. Li'l Abner, Superman, and athletic lifeguards are good examples. Mesomorphs are usually somatotonic.

STRUCTURE The way things are made and what they are made of.

SUBLIMATION Aim displacement or object displacement (or both) of libido or mortido, with partial relief of tension through socially acceptable, creative, or useful activity. A hammering sculptor attacks and destroys as he constructs and creates, thus relieving both mortido and libido, with a result which is valuable to society.

SUPEREGO The images charged with inwardly directed mortido which guide and restrain the free expression of the Id impulses, and even overrule the judgments of the Ego. Any conscious or unconscious thought, feeling, or action which is out of accord with the Superego gives rise to a tension which, if it becomes conscious, is usually felt as guilt. The term as used here includes the conscious conscience, the unconscious Superego, and the Ego Ideal.

T

TELEPATHY Receiving knowledge from another individual without communication through any medium known to us at present.

TENSION A state of energy imbalance. All processes in nature are based on the principle of restoring energy balance and reducing tension.

TRANQUILIZER A drug used to allay anxiety.

TRANSACTION A stimulus from one person and a related response from another person.

TRANSACTIONAL ANALYSIS A system for studying, thinking about, predicting, and changing human behavior by analyzing the individual's transactions with the people around him into their component ego states.

TRANSFERENCE The emotional relationship which develops between any two or more people, especially between an adviser and his client or a doctor and his patient, when it is based on emotional attitudes left over from childhood which are transferred to the current situation.

TRIP A temporary toxic psychosis deliberately brought about by taking drugs or other substances for kicks.

U

UNCONSCIOUS Mental processes which the individual is not aware of. "The Unconscious" is a part of the mind where repressed images and their charges are stored and whence they continue to influence the individual's behavior.

V

VISCEROTONIC An individual who is chiefly interested in absorbing energy. He likes to absorb food, air, and affection. The stocky, sociable delegate is a good example. Endomorphs are usually viscerotonic.

W

WISH An urge which tends to guide the individual toward definite aims and objects which will relieve his tensions. Only living organisms can wish.

NAME INDEX

(Subject Index starts on page 375)

SUBJECT INDEX